Colin Wilson was one of the most prolific, versatile and popular writers of the past 50 years. He was born in Leicester in 1931, and left school at sixteen. After he had spent years working in a wool warehouse, a laboratory, a plastics factory and a coffee bar, his first book, *The Outsider*, was published in 1956. It received outstanding critical acclaim and was an immediate bestseller. He wrote many books on philosophy, the occult, crime and sexual deviance, plus a host of successful novels that won him an international reputation. His work has been translated into Spanish, French, Swedish, Dutch, Japanese, German, Italian, Portuguese, Danish, Norwegian, Finnish and Hebrew. Colin Wilson died in December 2013.

Colin Stanley was born in Topsham, Devon, UK in 1952 and educated at Exmouth School. Beginning in 1970, he worked for Devon Library Services, studying for two years in London, before moving, with his wife Gail, to Nottingham where he worked for the University of Nottingham until July 2005. He is Colin Wilson's bibliographer, Managing Editor of Paupers' Press and has worked part-time for the Universities of Oxford and Nottingham Trent, spending the rest at the cinema and theatre, listening to music, writing, editing, reading and watching cricket. He is the author of two experimental novels and several books and booklets about Colin Wilson and his work including students' guides to his 'Outsider Cycle', 'Occult Trilogy', 'Existential Criticism' and, most recently, *An Evolutionary Leap: Colin Wilson on Psychology*. He edited *Around the Outsider* a festschrift for Wilson's 80th birthday and wrote a Foreword to the 2015 Watkins edition of *The Occult*. He is also the editor of Colin Wilson Studies, a series of books and extended essays written by Wilson scholars worldwide, and convener of the 2016 and 2018 International Colin Wilson Conferences at the University of Nottingham. His collection of the author's work forms the basis of a Wilson archive at the University which now includes many of his manuscripts, letters, journals, etc. He now resides with Gail by the River Trent, close to Trent Bridge cricket ground.

Also by Colin Wilson
published by Watkins

Super Consciousness
The Occult
Beyond the Occult
Mysteries
The Supernatural

The Ultimate

Colin Wilson

EDITED BY COLIN STANLEY

WATKINS
Sharing Wisdom Since 1893

This edition first published in the UK and USA in 2019 by
Watkins, an imprint of Watkins Media Limited

Unit 11, Shepperton House
89-93 Shepperton Road
London N1 3DF

This is an updated and expanded edition of *The Essential Colin Wilson*, published in 1985
by Harrap Limited

enquiries@watkinspublishing.com

1 3 5 7 9 10 8 6 4 2

Typeset by Integra Software Services Pvt. Ltd, Pondicherry

Printed and bound in the United Kingdom by TJ International Ltd

A CIP record for this book is available from the British Library

ISBN: 978-1-78678-253-3

www.watkinspublishing.com

CONTENTS

CONTENTS

The Estate of Colin Wilson is grateful to the Orion Publishing Group and Tarcher (an imprint of the Penguin Publishing Group) for permission to reprint from *The Outsider* and to Aristeia Press for permission to reprint from *Religion and the Rebel*.

EDITOR'S PREFACE

Colin Stanley

Selected, edited, and with an introduction and postscript by the author himself, *The Essential Colin Wilson* was published in the U.K. by Harrap Limited in 1985 and Celestial Arts in the U.S. a year later. A paperback edition appeared in the U.K., in 1987, published by Grafton.

It is true that writers can be notoriously bad when it comes to looking at their own work objectively but Wilson was certainly the exception in this case and he succeeded in compiling an important collection for anyone approaching his work for the first time. At the age of just 54, it was his 74th published book and, in the 28 years prior to his death in 2013, he produced another 100 titles providing plenty of material for an update.

To this end I have asked four experts on Colin Wilson's work: Nicolas Tredell, Geoff Ward, Gary Lachman and Vaughan Rapatahana, to recommend a post-1985 essay/book extract which they consider important. To these I have added a choice of my own.

Because this new edition completes the original, it has been decided to update the title to *The Ultimate Colin Wilson*.

It is my hope that Colin Wilson would not have been displeased.

INTRODUCTION (1985)

As I look back over fifty-odd books, whose subjects range from mysticism to criminology, I can see that a single thread runs through all my work: the question of how man can achieve these curious moments of inner freedom, the sensation of sheer delight that G. K. Chesterton called 'absurd good news'.

Yeats described the sensation in a short poem:

My fiftieth year had come and gone,
I sat, a solitary man,
In a crowded London shop,
An open book and empty cup
On the marble table-top.

While on the shop and street I gazed
My body of a sudden blazed;
And twenty minutes more or less
It seemed, so great my happiness,
That I was blessed and could bless.

Such sensations seem to occur when we relax below some threshold of tension that normally traps us in a more superficial consciousness. There is a sensation of freedom, of peace and serenity. In such moments we also feel that our energies are more-than-adequate to meet any challenge — in sharp contrast to normal consciousness, which always seems to be 'in a hurry', and in which we have a vaguely uncomfortable sense that our energies are never quite adequate.

The feeling of absurd good news is often contradicted by its opposite — what might be called 'absurd bad news' — a feeling that we are helpless victims of forces far stronger than we are. In these moods, it seems that all our 'values' are illusions created by the body. There is a scene in *A Farewell to Arms* where the hero is being prepared for an operation by a nurse with whom he is in love. He asks her if she will be on duty that night after the operation. She says:

'I probably will. But you won't want me.'
'Yes, 1 will.'
'No, you won't. You've never been operated on. You don't know how you'll be.'
'I'll be all right.'

After the operation, he admits:

'I was sick, and Catherine was right. It did not make any difference who was on night-duty.'

When he looks at her before the operation, he can see that she is beautiful and desirable; ergo, he will want to make love to her after the operation. He acknowledges that he may feel sick, but he is certain that he will simply overrule his sickness. In the event, it overrules him. The underlying suggestion is that our values, like our desires, are merely physical sensations.

The same thing is suggested even more chillingly in Flecker's *Hassan*. After the two lovers have been tortured to death — because the girl has refused to give herself to the Caliph — their ghosts meet by the fountain in the Caliph's garden. The fountain ghost tells her: 'As long as you remember what you have suffered, you will stay near the house where your blood was shed.' She replies: 'We will remember that ten thousand years.' The ghost tells her: 'You have forgotten you are a spirit. The memories of the dead are thinner than their dreams.' And when the wind from eternity blows, she calls to her lover: 'Speak to me, speak to me, Rafi', and his ghost answers: 'Rafi — Rafi — who was Rafi?' Here Flecker sounds a note of pessimism that goes beyond the tragedy of their deaths: the suggestion that they have died for a delusion, and that all men die for delusions ....

For me, the problem first presented itself at Christmas-time as a child. That marvellous feeling of richness and excitement made it obvious that life is not difficult and boring and repetitive. Then came the new year and return to school, and it was like waking up from a pleasant dream in an icy bedroom. The glow of Christmas seemed an illusion. Yet the moment the moods of happiness and freedom came back — on a day-trip to the seaside or picking blackberries on an autumn afternoon — it was quite plain they were not some kind of delusion or wishful thinking. It was again self-evident that the world was a far bigger and more exciting place than we normally give it credit for.

Now this raised an interesting question. When you have learned to solve some puzzling problem — like how to remove a bicycle tyre or extract a square root — the solution stays in your head permanently; you do not forget it the next day. Yet in the case of this question — whether the 'absurd good news' is a delusion or reality — the 'solution' seemed to evaporate into thin air the next day, so it was impossible even to remember what I had felt so happy about.

I was in my early teens when I discovered that I was not the first person to brood on this problem. It had been encountered by whole generations of writers and artists of the nineteenth century — a movement we call Romanticism. The Romantics were always experiencing these strange moods of delight and relaxation in which they seemed to see the answer to all the problems of existence. And the next day the insight had vanished, leaving them miserable and fretful. This seemed to explain the high rate of suicide and early deaths from tuberculosis among the Romantics.

Here, I could see, the problem had taken a slightly different form. The Romantics suspected that the truth about the world is ordinariness and triviality: that human beings are basically selfish, short-sighted, narrow-minded little animals, and that all these attempts to convince ourselves that we can reach for the stars are a game of make-believe, like children playing at kings and queens. As human beings grow up, they learn to look more dignified and purposeful, but inside every one of us there is still a child whose basic interests are food, amusement and creature-comforts. And when we feel tired and discouraged, the child seems to take over again.

My first book, *The Outsider*, was about this problem: men who experienced moments of intense ecstasy and affirmation, then found themselves dragged down by the 'triviality of everydayness' (Heidegger's phrase) and the misery of unfulfilment. To such men as Van Gogh, Nietzsche, Nijinsky, Dostoevsky, the problem presented itself in terms of Carlyle's 'Everlasting Yes' versus 'Everlasting No'. Paintings like Van Gogh's *Starry Night* express ultimate faith in the power of life over death; all the same, he committed suicide, leaving a note saying 'Misery will never end'. Yet in the last pages of that book, it became clear that mystics like William Blake and Sri Ramakrishna had come altogether to arriving at a satisfactory solution to the problem. This is why my second book *Religion and the Rebel* — which is really merely the second part of *The Outsider* — dealt mainly with saints and mystics and religious visionaries.

There was, in fact, a period in my teens when I felt that my own answer might lie in this direction: entering a monastery or travelling to India to study 'the perennial philosophy' at its source. The problem, I felt, amounted to finding something to *do*, a way of living that would be a direct expression of this urge to explore visionary states of awareness.

Every way of living that I explored — from working as a farm labourer to washing dishes in a restaurant — seemed to lead away from my objective, or at best, run parallel to it. It was a frustrating feeling, like trying to approach a mountain which is perfectly visible and finding that no road seems to get you any closer.

After writing *Religion and the Rebel* this frustration seemed to disappear — I presume because, now I was able to devote my life to writing, I had found a way of living that led straight towards my objective. This certainty increased when, in 1963, I received a letter from the American psychologist Abraham Maslow, who told me about his own discovery that all healthy people seemed to have 'peak experiences' — my 'moments of affirmation'. Maslow believed that it was impossible to induce peak experiences at will, but I felt he was mistaken: for example, Graham Greene had done precisely that by playing Russian roulette with a loaded revolver. In due course I was to write a biography of Maslow, the first chapter of which is included in this book.

I continued to explore the problem in the remaining four books of the 'Outsider cycle', investigating the role of the imagination in *The Strength to Dream*, and of sexual ecstasy in *Origins of the Sexual Impulse. Beyond the Outsider*, the sixth volume of the series, was my most comprehensive attempt to date to summarize the problem. From the beginning, I had been aware that the problem can only be fully understood in terms of history — the evolution of man in the past ten thousand years or so. It was essential that I should spread my net as wide as possible. Yet as far as reaching an audience was concerned, this attempt was often self-defeating; I could see why hostile critics thought my books were merely summaries of cultural history. Yet I felt there were times when, by this method, I succeeded in going straight to the heart of the matter; the chapter called 'The Strange Story of Modem Philosophy' is a good example.

I had been on two lecture tours of America in the early 1960s, and the need to repeat my ideas over and over again had the effect of enabling me to see new perspectives. I made yet one more attempt to summarize all I had done so far in a small volume called *Introduction to the New Existentialism* (reprinted in 1980 as *The New Existentialism*). I argued that the philosophy we call existentialism is actually 'Romanticism Mark Two'.

The Romantics felt that the human spirit is engaged in a hopeless battle with a hostile world, and that the end is bound to be defeat and despair. The existentialists — Heidegger, Jaspers, Sartre, Camus — started from the same position, but arrived at a slightly less gloomy conclusion: man is free, he has a certain power of choice, even if life is totally meaningless. Hemingway summarized it in the phrase 'A man can be destroyed but not defeated', My own feeling was that I had no wish to be either defeated or destroyed: there had to be another answer. Hence my attempt to create a more optimistic form of existentialism — a kind of 'Romanticism Mark Three'. This, I would say, is still a fairly good summary of my basic aim. The present book includes the central chapter of *The New Existentialism*.

At this point I found myself exploring the problem in a new direction. I was asked by an American publisher to write a book about 'the occult'. Ever since childhood I had been interested in the paranormal, and had explored it in books like *Rasputin and the Fall of the Romanovs* and *Man Without a Shadow*. But I had never felt that it had any bearing on this question of 'absurd good news'. Now I began a systematic study of 'psychic powers' and I saw I had been mistaken. In the past ten thousand years or so, man has deliberately narrowed his consciousness in an effort to achieve the efficiency necessary to survive. One of the powers he has suppressed is the faculty we call 'second sight', and the example of Peter Hurkos — who regained the power when he fell off a ladder and smashed his skull — struck me as specially significant. In narrowing his faculties, man has also suppressed those states of 'cosmic consciousness', heightened awareness, experienced by mystics like Boehme and Blake. These faculties can, to some extent, be regained by means of drugs such as mescalin and LSD: but they merely put back the clock of human evolution to an earlier stage. It was clear to me that we can regain these powers by another method: by the deliberate intensification of consciousness by intellectual and spiritual disciplines. Many people have achieved accidental glimpses of such states — Proust, for example, experienced such a state when he tasted a cake dipped in herb tea. This heightened power of perception I called 'Faculty X', and the concept is explored in the first chapter of *The Occult*, included herein.

Many readers of the earlier books must have felt that this preoccupation with 'the occult' was a change of direction. I knew differently: that it was a breakthrough into a new field of exploration. There is a direct connection between psychic powers, mystical awareness and the control over heightened states of awareness achieved by Gurdjieff. I made this connection clear in the introductory chapter of *Mysteries*, before launching into a more general study of 'cosmic forces' and man's ability to 'tune in' to them.

I was writing the last section of *Mysteries* when I came upon *The Origin of Consciousness in the Breakdown of the Bicameral Mind* by Julian Jaynes, and for the first time grasped the full significance of split-brain research. I had always been aware that one of the basic problems of consciousness is that man has two selves inside his head and that, as I put it in 'The Strange Story of Modem Philosophy', 'the left side of the mind doesn't know what the right side is doing'. But I had not realized that my intuition was so literally true — that we literally have another 'self' living in the right hemisphere of the brain, and that the person I call 'me' lives in the left hemisphere. There was no space in *Mysteries* to explore this insight to the full; yet I could see that it provided the unifying principle I had always been looking for. The existence of the two halves of the brain explained poetic inspiration and 'psychic powers'. I explored the implications of split-brain physiology for the first time in a little book called *Frankenstein's Castle*, written for a friend, Robin Campbell, who was just launching his own publishing firm. Not long after this I encountered in Finland a man who seemed to have achieved a remarkable breakthrough in learning to make active use of his right brain; the result was *Access to Inner Worlds, The Story of Brad Absetz*. In both these books I feel that I have come close to a definitive solution of the problem I first propounded in *The Outsider*. Lack of space decided me against printing all but a brief extract from *Frankenstein's Castle* in the present volume, but their basic ideas are summarized in the piece on 'The Laurel and Hardy Theory of Consciousness', as well as in the Schumacher Lecture 'Peak Experience'.

The Outsider was a by-product of my first novel, *Ritual in the Dark*. Ever since then I have continued to write fiction as well as non-fiction. At the age of fourteen I was impressed by Shaw's assertion that the artists of the future would have to be artist-philosophers. In many cases there is a specific link between my novels and works of non-fiction — as between *Ritual in the Dark* and *The Outsider*, or *Man Without a Shadow* and *Origins of the Sexual Impulse*. I have written novels for two reasons: because I enjoy writing them and because I feel that there are certain things that can be expressed in a novel that cannot be expressed in non-fiction. But the connection remains close; the germ of two novels — *The Mind Parasites* and *The Black Room* — can be found in *The New Existentialism*, while the preoccupation with brain physiology in *The Philosopher's Stone* anticipates my discovery of split-brain research by ten years. I would have liked to include many more extracts from the novels in this book; but it was a question of choosing between fiction and non-fiction, and the non-fiction undoubtedly expresses my main ideas with greater economy. (After all, economy is not the main concern of the novelist; an 'economical' version of *War and Peace* would be a bore, while Somerset Maugham's attempt to cut *The Brothers Karamazov* to economic proportions was a disaster.) But I am glad to reprint central sections of *The Black Room* and *The Mind Parasites*, while I have always had a sneaking fondness for the Uncle Sam section of *The World of Violence*, which expresses the essentially self-destructive nature of romanticism.

All this left very little space for one section of my output to which I attach considerable importance — the studies in criminology. I have always seen crime as one of the more interesting forms of romantic revolt, rather lower on the scale than Uncle Sam's determination to have nothing more to do with the world, yet allied to it in spirit. In many cases it can be seen as a crude attempt to achieve a kind of mystical self-fulfilment; looking at the corpse of a girl he had just strangled and raped, Reginald Christie commented: 'Once again I experienced that quiet, peaceful thrill. I had no regrets.'

The criminal is significant because he shows us what is wrong with all of us. His approach to the problems of existence is so crude and simplistic that the stupidest person has no difficulty seeing why it doesn't work. The criminal lacks subtlety; he lacks complexity; he lacks insight. But then, so do we all. Moreover, if we ask ourselves what went wrong with the lives of so many men of genius, we can see that the answer lies in that same 'criminal' tendency: a certain spoilt-ness, a certain childishness, a failure to control negative emotions. Dante's bitterness betrays a tendency to self-pity. Shakespeare's pessimism hints at a manic-depressive streak. His friend Ben Jonson was a braggart with more than a touch of paranoia. Balzac was a spendthrift and a show-off. Dostoevsky was a compulsive gambler. Proust was a sadist who enjoyed torturing rats. H. G. Wells was an incorrigible seducer. In their classic work, *The Criminal Personality*, Yochelson and Samenow describe the criminal as fundamentally weak, lazy, vain, self-pitying and capable of almost endless self-deception. There are very few human beings who do not answer to that description. Criminality is mankind's 'original sin'. Fortunately, man's astonishing creativity is its 'redemption'. *A Criminal History of Mankind* is my most comprehensive attempt to explore this insight. It is an attempt to demonstrate that both criminality and creativity can only be understood as a part of man's total evolutionary pattern.

The book that follows is, in the last analysis, my own attempt to understand this pattern.

THE OUTSIDER, TWENTY YEARS ON

Written for the Pan paperback edition of
The Outsider in 1976

Christmas Day, 1954, was an icy, grey day, and I spent it in my room in Brockley, South London. I recall that I had tinned tomatoes and fried bacon for Christmas dinner. I was alone in London; my girl-friend had gone back to her family for the holiday, and I didn't have the money to return to my home town, Leicester. Besides, relations with my family were rather strained; my father felt I'd wasted my opportunities to settle down in a good office job, and prophesied that I'd come to a bad end.

For the past year I'd been living in London, and trying to write a novel called *Ritual in the Dark*, about a murderer based on Jack the Ripper. To save money during the summer, I'd slept out on Hampstead Heath in a waterproof sleeping bag, and spent my days writing in the Reading Room of the British Museum. It was there that I'd met the novelist Angus Wilson, a kindly and generous man who had offered to look at my novel and — if he liked it — recommend it to his own publisher. I'd finished typing out the first part of the book a few weeks before; he had promised to read it over Christmas. Now I felt at a loose end. So I sat on my bed, with an eiderdown over my feet, and wrote in my journal. It struck me that I was in the position of so many of my favourite characters in fiction: Dostoevsky's Raskolnikov, Rilke's Malte Laurids Brigge, the young writer in Hamsun's *Hunger*: alone in my room, feeling totally cut off from the rest of society. It was not a position I relished; I'd always been strongly attached to my home and family (I'm a typical Cancer), and missed being with them at

Christmas. Yet an inner compulsion had forced me into this position of isolation. I began writing about it in my journal, trying to pin it down. And then, quite suddenly, I saw that I had the makings of a book. I turned to the back of my journal and wrote at the head of the page: 'Notes for a book "The Outsider in Literature".' (I have it in front of me now as I write.) On the next two pages, I worked out a fairly complete outline of the book as it eventually came to be written. I fell asleep that night with a feeling of deep inner satisfaction; it seemed one of the most satisfying Christmas Days I'd ever spent.

Two days later, as soon as the British Museum re-opened, I cycled there at nine o'clock in the morning, determined to start writing immediately. On the way there, I recalled a novel I had once read about, in which a man had spent his days peering through a hole in the wall of his hotel room, at the life that comes and goes next door. It was, I recollected, the first major success of Henri Barbusse, the novelist who had later become world famous for *Le Feu*, the novel of the First World War. When I arrived at the Museum, I found the book in the catalogue. I spent the next few hours reading it from cover to cover. Then I wrote down a quotation from it at the head of a sheet of paper: 'In the air, on top of a tram, a girl is sitting. Her dress, lifted a little, blows out. But a block in the traffic separates us....' During the remainder of that afternoon, I wrote the opening four pages of *The Outsider*.

It now strikes me as interesting that I chose this opening, with the man hoping to see up a girl's skirt, and being frustrated by passing traffic. For although I say very little about sex in the book, it was undoubtedly one of the major forces behind its conception. I understood precisely what Barbusse's hero means when he describes going to bed with a prostitute, then going through the banal ritual of copulation, and feeling as if he has fallen from a height. This had been one of the central obsessions of my teens: the fact that a glimpse up a woman's skirt can make her seem infinitely desirable, worth pursuing to the ends of the earth; *yet the act of sex cannot provide full satisfaction of this desire*. When he actually gets the girl into bed, all the perspectives have changed....

This had been the main theme of my novel *Ritual in the Dark*. Like Barbusse's hero, my own Gerard Sorme finds himself continually surrounded by objects of sexual stimulation; the advertisements showing girls in their underwear on the London underground cause violent frustration, 'like a match tossed against a petrol-soaked rag'. And in the course of the novel he seduces a middle-aged Jehovah's Witness (partly for the piquancy of overcoming her religious scruples) and her teenage niece; yet the basic sexual desire remains unsatisfied. One scene in the book had particularly deep meaning for me. Sorme had spent the afternoon in bed with Caroline — the niece — and made love to her six or seven times. He feels physically satiated, as if the sexual delusion has finally lost its hold over him. Then he goes out to the doorstep — it is a basement room — to collect the milk, and catches a glimpse up a girl's skirt as she walks past the railings. Instantly, he feels the stirrings of an erection....

I was not concerned simply with the intensity of male sexual desire — although I felt that it is far more powerful than most men are willing to admit. It was this element of 'un-achievableness'. It reminded me of the feeling I used to get as a child if I was on a day-trip to the seaside, and the coach went over a river or past a lake: a curious, deep *longing* for the water that would certainly not be satisfied by drinking it or swimming in it. In the same way, C. S. Lewis has spoken of how he used to be convulsed with desire by the *idea of autumn* — the brown leaves and the smell of smoke from garden bonfires, and that strange wet smell about the grass.... Sorme has the same suspicion about sex: that it is ultimately unattainable: that what happens in bed is a kind of confidence trick. For this reason, he experiences a certain abstract sympathy with his new acquaintance, Austin Nunne, when he begins to suspect that Nunne is the East End sex murderer. It seems to him that this *could* be a valid way to achieve the essence of sex: to grab a girl in the moment she arouses violent desire and rip off her clothes. Oddly enough, it never strikes him that this is unlikely to be Nunne's motive; he knows Nunne to be a homosexual, yet his own sexual obsession blinds him to its implications.

The theme is repeated in the first pages of *The Outsider*. Barbusse's hero watches a girl undressing in the next room; but when he tries to re-create the scene in imagination, it is only a poor carbon copy. 'These words are all dead. They leave untouched...the intensity of what was.' Again, he is present at the dining table when someone describes the sex murder of a little girl. Everyone at the table is morbidly interested — even a young mother with her child; but they all try to pretend to be indifferent. The irony, of course, is that Barbusse cannot speak his meanings clearly. If, in fact, he watched a girl undressing in the next room, he would probably masturbate; as it is, he tries to convince the reader that it was an experience of spiritual beauty. For all his talk about truth, the narrator cannot be honest.

In *Ritual in the Dark*, this inability to grasp the essence of sexuality becomes the symbol of our inability to grasp the essence of anything important — of autumn, of water.... This, it seemed to me, is the basic difference between human beings. Some are perfectly satisfied with what they have; they eat, drink, impregnate their wives and take life as it comes.

Others can never forget that they are being cheated; that life tempts them to struggle by offering them the essence of sex, of beauty, of success; and that she always seems to pay in counterfeit money. In the novel, Nunne — the purely physical type — pursues his will o' the wisp with a despairing ruthlessness. The painter, Oliver Glasp, is obsessed by a ten-year-old female model, but horrified at the idea of any physical lovemaking; he sublimates his desire in decadent romantic pictures. Sorme, the intellectual outsider, also pursues his desires with a touch of ruthlessness, but a fundamentally kindly nature makes him incapable of causing pain....

Sometime shortly before that Christmas of 1954, I was walking along the Thames Embankment with my closest — and oldest — friend, Bill Hopkins, explaining to him the ideas of the novel. I explained that Sorme is an intellectual outsider; he has discipline of the intellect, but not of the body or emotions. Glasp, like Van Gogh, is the emotional outsider; he has discipline of the emotions, but not of the body or the intellect. Nunne, like the dancer Nijinsky, is a physical outsider; he has discipline of the body, but not of the emotions or the intellect. All three are 'lopsided'. And all three are capable of becoming insane. I went on to point out that Dostoevsky had used the same categories in the three Karamazov brothers. This, I believe, was the actual seed of *The Outsider*. In due course, the chapter contrasting the three types of outsider ('The Attempt to Gain Control') became the core of the book.

When it came to the actual writing, there was a certain amount of material that had to be scrapped. I had, for example, intended to write a chapter about the Faust figure, from Marlowe to Mann's Dr Faustus — Mann's feeling about the un-attainableness of the ideal was obviously close to my own. There was a chapter on criminal outsiders that was abandoned after a few pages — the fragment was later reprinted in *An Encyclopedia of Murder*. And there was an interesting outline of a chapter on 'the weak outsider' — characters like Oblomov, the great Gatsby, Hamlet, the poets of the 1890s like Dowson and Johnson and Verlaine.... I was particularly fascinated by Gatsby because the essence he craved was the essence of 'success'. I was convinced that this, like all the other essences, is a fraud. Yet my romanticism found this hard to accept....

A year and a half after writing the first page of *The Outsider*, I had a chance to find out for myself. I had written most of the book by the middle of 1955. (The most difficult parts, I found, were the links between the various sections; it cost me two weeks' hard work to write the link between Wells and Sartre in the first chapter; it finally came in a flash of inspiration as I was hitch-hiking on the back of a lorry near Oxford.) I tried sending a few pages, together with an outline, to the publisher Victor Gollancz. To my surprise, he replied almost immediately, saying that he liked the outline and would like to see the rest. At this time, I was working during the evenings in a coffee bar in the Haymarket, so that I could spend my days writing in the British Museum. In the autumn I sent him the completed manuscript and he accepted it. That winter, I gave up work for a few weeks — for the first time since I'd left school at 16 — and lived on the £75 advance that Gollancz gave me. Somehow, I had no doubt that the book would be a success. I think I had too little doubt about the importance of what I had to say to feel misgivings. Gollancz, understandably, had no such confidence; he finally decided to take the risk of printing five thousand copies.

Publication day was set for Monday, 28th May 1956. Even before this, I was beginning to smell the breath of fame, and finding it exciting. Edith Sitwell, the poetess who had 'discovered' Dylan Thomas, had read the book in proof, and told Gollancz she thought I was going to be 'a truly great writer'. A journalist on one of the London evening newspapers asked to interview me; I spent an evening at his flat talking into his tape recorder — which struck me as a fabulous device — and listening to a record of the latest hit show, *My Fair Lady*. Gollancz told me he had been promised a review in the *Evening News* on the Saturday before publication. My girlfriend, Joy, was spending the weekend with me — I was now living in a room in Notting Hill Gate — and we bought the paper as soon as it appeared; but there seemed to be no review. I went to bed that night oddly depressed — my bicycle had been stolen a few hours before, and it seemed a bad omen. The next morning, we woke up early and rushed to the corner of Westbourne Grove to buy the two 'posh' Sunday papers. Both of them had devoted their lead review to *The Outsider*, and both were full of praise. When we got back to my room, someone told us that there *had* been a review in the previous evening's newspaper; we looked again, and found a headline: 'He's a major writer — and he's only 24'.

Before that day was out, I had no doubt that I was famous, whatever that meant. I had no telephone — naturally — but our neighbours in the basement had one, and it began to ring at about nine o'clock that morning — my editor ringing me up to congratulate me, and to ask my permission to give the telephone number to the press. Within a couple of hours I had agreed to be interviewed by half a dozen newspapers, and to appear on radio and television. Moreover, a playwright named John Osborne had achieved success on the same day; his play *Look Back in Anger* had been produced at the Royal Court a few days earlier, and reviews by Kenneth Tynan and Harold Hobson launched him to fame as the first

'Angry Young Man'. (The actual phrase was invented by J. B. Priestley, who wrote an article about the two of us under that title in *The New Statesman* the following week.) In fact, Osborne and I had only one thing in common — that both of us had been turned into 'outsiders' by our working-class backgrounds, and the suspicion that we would spend the rest of our lives stuck in dreary obscurity. But the fact that we appeared on the literary scene at the same time somehow doubled the furore.

It was a strange experience. On the 26th of May 1956, I had been totally unknown. I had never doubted my own abilities, but I was quite prepared to believe that 'the world' would decline to recognize them. The 'famous' seemed to be a small and very exclusive club, and the chances of getting into it were about equal to those of winning the football pools. And then, suddenly, on the 27th, I had apparently been elected without opposition, and the pundits of the Sunday newspapers were assuring the public that I was at least as important as Sartre and Camus, a real British home-grown existentialist. And when the press got hold of the story about sleeping on Hampstead Heath, I became notorious as well as famous....

The enormous publicity was partly due to the fact that I was one of a group, a 'new group', not just of writers, but of all kinds of personalities who were always worth a paragraph in a gossip column. It included Elvis Presley and Marilyn Monroe and Brigitte Bardot and Arthur Miller and Sandy Wilson and Pietro Annigoni (who had painted the Queen) and Francis Bacon and Stirling Moss and Mort Sahl, and a couple of dozen more assorted celebrities who somehow seemed typical of the mid-fifties. And it included a large-ish crop of young writers — Amis, Wain, Iris Murdoch, Brendan Behan, Francoise Sagan, Michael Hastings (who was eighteen), Jane Gaskell (who was fourteen) and even a nine-year-old French poetess called Minou Drouet. I have a feeling that the newspapers had an unconscious urge to manufacture an 'epoch' — like the 1890s or 1920s. And, for better or worse, I was in the middle of it, cast as the 'boy genius'. Somehow, Osborne and I were supposed to prove that England was full of brilliantly talented young men who couldn't make any headway in the System, and were being forced to go it alone. We were supposed to be the representative voices of this vast army of outsiders and angry young men who were rising up to overthrow the establishment.

Oddly enough, it was not particularly interesting or exciting to be involved in all this ferment. To begin with, the newspaper publicity was on such a moronic level (as it is more or less bound to be) that it seemed a travesty of what we were trying to do as individuals. It invited derision — and, of course, received it. I was delighted to know that I would never have to return to a factory or office. But otherwise, fame seemed to have no great advantages. It didn't bring any startling new freedom. I ate good food and drank wine, but since food and drink had never interested me much, this was unimportant. I wasn't fond of travel. If I hadn't been settled with Joy, the greatest bonus would probably have been the sexual possibilities; but since I had no intention of getting rid of her, I had to put that temptation behind me. I admit that this was my keenest regret.

What the newspapers really wanted from this new generation was scandal. Early in 1957, I inadvertently provided it, when Joy's parents turned up at the room we now shared in Notting Hill Gate, determined to drag her away from this life of sin; her father had even brought a horsewhip. Joy and I were giving supper to a villainous old queer named Gerald Hamilton, the original of Christopher Isherwood's Mr Norris. As Joy's family tried to drag her off down the stairs, Gerald rushed to the nearest telephone and rang every gossip columnist he knew (and his acquaintance was wide). Ten minutes after I'd persuaded her family to leave (with some help from the police), the reporters and photographers started to arrive on the doorstep. After seeing the first ones, we sneaked out of the back door, spent the night with a friend, and then fled to Devon, to take refuge with the writer Negley Farson. The press caught up with us there after a few days, and then pursued us across to Wales and Ireland. The story occupied the front pages and gossip columns for about two weeks, until we returned to London. Victor Gollancz told me that my reputation as a serious writer was ruined, and that if I didn't get out of London, I'd never write another book. The man who lived in the room below us offered to rent us a cottage near Mevagissey, in Cornwall. We took Gollancz's advice, moved from London and have been here ever since.

On the whole, Gollancz was right. The silly publicity made it impossible for Britain's intellectual establishment to take me seriously, and they showed their displeasure when my next book appeared. I had, it seemed, achieved 'recognition', and then lost it just as suddenly. I never had any great difficulty in finding publishers — my notoriety at least had that advantage — but the critics made sure that I had no more best sellers. Books like *Religion and the Rebel*, *The Age of Defeat* and *The Strength to Dream* were received with the kind of review that began: 'More pretentious rubbish from this intellectually confused and thoroughly overrated young man....' *Ritual in the Dark* achieved a certain success when it finally appeared in 1960, but critics who had decided that I was a flash in the pan had no intention of reconsidering me as a novelist. *The Outsider* had made me about £20,000 in its first year — a considerable sum in 1956. Subsequent books seldom made more than £1,000. We were never poverty stricken, but invariably overdrawn at the bank. In the 1960s, I made several lecture tours of America to try and stabilize my finances. I usually returned to England with just enough money to pay all the outstanding bills, and start again from square one....

I suppose this particular story has a kind of happy ending. When *The Outsider* appeared, T. S. Eliot told me that I had achieved recognition the wrong way; it was fatal to become known to too many people at once. The right way was to gradually achieve an audience of regular readers, and slowly expand from there, if at all. As the 1960s drew to a close, I realized that this was what was happening. Second-hand shops told me that certain people were obsessive collectors of my books, and would pay fairly high prices for them. In *The New Statesman*, there was an advertisement asking for members for a Colin Wilson Society (apparently the founders were under the impression that I was dead). They succeeded in continuing for a couple of years (a remarkable feat, since they all regarded themselves as outsiders) during which time they met twice a week to study my books. I was becoming a 'cult figure' — but still having considerable difficulty making a decent living. In 1967, an American publisher commissioned me to write a book on 'the occult'. I had always enjoyed reading about such subjects, without taking them very seriously. The book, when finished, was a thousand pages long (in typescript) and I had now ceased to take the subject lightly. In fact, it was clear that my investigation into the mysteries of consciousness led straight into the heart of the 'paranormal'. Unfortunately, the English publisher who had also commissioned the book did not share my excitement; he gasped at the size of the manuscript, and asked me to take it elsewhere. Fortunately, a more enterprising publisher — Hodder & Stoughton — accepted it, and actually asked me to expand it. My editor, Robin Denniston, told me that he thought it was about time for a 'Colin Wilson revival'; he even decided to issue a pamphlet about me as advance publicity. I shook my head and thought: 'Poor devils, they'll lose their money'.

To my amazement, they proved to be right. The reviews had a serious and respectful tone that I hadn't heard since *The Outsider*. With a kind of dazed incredulity, I realized that I'd finally become an 'establishment' figure. I was no longer the 'boy genius' who'd proved to be a pretentious fraud. As if conveying the blessing of England's literary establishment, Cyril Connolly and Philip Toynbee — the two critics who had launched *The Outsider* on that bewildering Sunday fifteen years earlier, and then damned my subsequent books — produced lengthy and thoughtful reviews of *The Occult*, full of the kind of praise that can be extracted and used in advertisements. Apparently all was forgiven. In fact, publication week of *The Occult* was rather like that of *The Outsider*, but more dignified: interviews, appearances on television, requests for articles and book reviews. What was rather more important was that the book sold as well as *The Outsider*; and since it cost five times as much, royalties were correspondingly high — even enough to compensate for inflation. If *The Occult* didn't actually make me rich — few non-fiction books ever sell that well — it at least managed to give me a delightful sensation of not being permanently broke and overdrawn at the bank. It has also supported me during the six years I have taken to write a sequel, *Mysteries*, whose last chapter I have broken off to write this introduction....

And how do I feel about *The Outsider* in retrospect? In order to answer that question I settled down the other day to re-read it — and found it impossible to gain a sense of perspective. It still produces in me the same feeling of excitement and impatience that I experienced as I sketched the outline plan on that Christmas Day of 1954. Why impatience? Because it aroused some enormous anticipation. At the same time, I mistook this for anticipation of success (for somehow, I never had the slightest doubt that it would be a success). Now I recognize it for what it was: the realization that I had at last settled down to the serious business of living: that after the long-drawn-out and messy years of childhood, and the teenage agonies of self-consciousness, I had at last ceased to waste my time; I was starting to do what I had always intended to do. There was a feeling like leaving harbour. It made no difference that the critics later tried to take back what they'd said about the book. They couldn't take back the passport they'd given me.

THE COUNTRY
OF THE BLIND

From *The Outsider*, 1956

At first sight, the Outsider is a social problem. He is the hole-in-corner man.

> In the air, on top of a tram, a girl is sitting. Her dress, lifted a little, blows out. But a block in the traffic separates us. The tramcar glides away, fading like a nightmare.
>
> Moving in both directions, the street is full of dresses which sway, offering themselves airily, the skirts lifting; dresses that lift and yet do not lift.
>
> In the tall and narrow shop mirror I see myself approaching, rather pale and heavy-eyed. It is not a woman I want — it is *all* women, and I seek for them in those around me, one by one....

This passage, from Henri Barbusse's novel *L'Enfer*, pinpoints certain aspects of the Outsider. His hero walks down a Paris street, and the desires that stir in him separate him sharply from other people. And the need he feels for a woman is not entirely animal either, for he goes on:

> Defeated, I followed my impulse casually. I followed a woman who had been watching me from her corner. Then we walked side by side. We said a few words; she took me home with her.... Then I went through the banal scene. It passed like a sudden hurtling- down.

Again, I am on the pavement, and I am not at peace as I had hoped. An immense confusion bewilders me. It is as if I could not see things as they were. *I see too deep and too much.*

Throughout the book, this hero remains unnamed. He is the anonymous Man Outside.

He comes to Paris from the country; he finds a position in a bank; he takes a room in a 'family hotel'. Left alone in his room, he meditates: He has 'no genius, no mission to fulfil, no remarkable feelings to bestow. I have nothing and I deserve nothing. Yet in spite of it, I desire some sort of recompense.' Religion...he doesn't care for it. 'As to philosophic discussions, they seem to me altogether meaningless. *Nothing can be tested, nothing verified.* Truth — what do they mean by it?' His thoughts range vaguely from a past love affair and its physical pleasures, to death: 'Death, that is the most important of all ideas.' Then back to his living problems: 'I must make money.' He notices a light high up on his wall; it is coming from the next room. He stands on the bed and looks through the spy-hole:

I look, I see.... The next room offers itself to me in its nakedness.

The action of the novel begins. Daily, he stands on the bed and stares at the life that comes and goes in the next room. For the space of a month he watches it, standing apart and, symbolically, above. His first vicarious adventure is to watch a woman who has taken the room for the night; he excites himself to hysteria watching her undress. These pages of the book have the kind of deliberate sensationalism that its descendants in post-war France were so consistently to be accused of (so that Guido Ruggiero could write: 'Existentialism treats life in the manner of a thriller').

But the point is to come. The next day he tries to recreate the scene in imagination, but it evades him, just as his attempt to recreate the sexual pleasures with his mistress had evaded him:

I let myself be drawn into inventing details to recapture the intensity of the experience. 'She put herself into the most inviting positions.'
No, no, that is not true.
These words are all dead. They leave untouched, *powerless to affect it, the intensity of what was.*

At the end of *L'Enfer*, its nameless hero is introduced to a novelist who is entertaining the company with an account of a novel he is writing. A coincidence…it is about a man who pierces a hole in his wall and spies on all that happens in the next room. The writer recounts all of the book he has written; his listeners admire it: Bravo! Tremendous success! But the Outsider listens gloomily. 'I, who had penetrated into the very heart of mankind and returned, could see nothing human in this pantomimic caricature. It was so superficial that it was false.' The novelist expounds: 'Man stripped of his externals …that is what I wish to show. Others stand for imagination… I stand for truth.' The Outsider feels that what he has seen *is* truth.

Admittedly, for us, reading the novel half a century after it was written, there is not so much to choose between the novelist's truth and the hero's. The 'dramas' enacted in the next room remind us sometimes of Sardou, sometimes of Dostoevsky when he is more concerned to expound an idea than to give it body in people and events. Yet Barbusse is sincere, and this ideal, to 'stand for truth', is the one discernible current that flows through all twentieth-century literature.

Barbusse's Outsider has all of the characteristics of the type. Is he an Outsider because he's frustrated and neurotic? Or is he neurotic because of some deeper instinct that pushes him into solitude? He is preoccupied with sex, with crime, with disease. Early in the novel he recounts the after-dinner conversation of a barrister; he is speaking of the trial of a man who has raped and strangled a little girl. All other conversation stops, and the Outsider observes his neighbours closely as they listen to the revolting details:

> A young mother, with her daughter at her side, has half got up to leave, but cannot drag herself away….
>
> And the men; one of them, simple, placid, I heard distinctly panting. Another, with the neutral appearance of a bourgeois, talks commonplaces with difficulty to his young neighbour. But he looks at her as if he would pierce deeply into her, and deeper yet. His piercing glance is stronger than himself, and he is ashamed of it….

The Outsider's case against society is very clear. All men and women have these dangerous, unnameable impulses, yet they keep up a pretence, to themselves, to others; their respectability, their philosophy, their religion, are all attempts to gloss over, to make look civilized and rational something that is savage, unorganized, irrational. He is an Outsider because he stands for Truth.

That is his case. But it is weakened by his obvious abnormality, his introversion. It looks, in fact, like an attempt at self-justification by a man who knows himself to be degenerate, diseased, self-divided. There is certainly self-division. The man who watches a woman undressing has the red eyes of an ape; yet the man who sees two young lovers, really alone for the first time, who brings out all the pathos, the tenderness and uncertainty when he tells about it, is no brute; he is very much human. And the ape and the man exist in one body; and when the ape's desires are about to be fulfilled, he disappears and is succeeded by the man, who is disgusted with the ape's appetites.

This is the problem of the Outsider. We shall encounter it under many different forms in the course of this book: on a metaphysical level, with Sartre and Camus (where it is called Existentialism), on a religious level, with Boehme and Kierkegaard; even on a criminal level, with Dostoevsky's Stavrogin (who also raped a small girl and was responsible for her death). The problem remains essentially the same; it is merely a question of discounting more or less as irrelevant.

Barbusse has suggested that it is the fact that his hero *sees deeper* that makes him an Outsider; at the same time, he states that he has 'no special genius, no message to bestow', etc., and from his history during the remainder of the book, we have no reason to doubt his word. Indubitably, the hero *is* mediocre; he can't write for toffee, and the whole book is full of clichés. It is necessary to emphasize this in order to rid ourselves of the temptation to identify the Outsider with the artist, and so to oversimplify the question: disease or insight? Many great artists have none of the characteristics of the Outsider. Shakespeare, Dante, Keats were all apparently normal and socially well-adjusted, lacking anything that could be pitched on as disease or nervous disability. Keats, who always makes a very clear and romantic distinction between the poet and the ordinary man, seems to have had no shades of inferiority complexes or sexual neuroses lurking in the background of his mind; no D. H. Lawrence-ish sense of social-level, no James Joycian need to assert his intellectual superiority; above all, no sympathy whatever with the attitude of Villiers De Lisle Adam's Axel (so much admired by Yeats): 'As for living, our servants can do that for us.' If any man intended to do his own living for himself, it was Keats. And he is undoubtedly the rule rather than the exception among great poets. The Outsider may be an artist, but the artist is not necessarily an Outsider.

What can be said to characterize the Outsider is a sense of strangeness, of unreality. Even Keats could write, in a letter to Browne just before he died: 'I feel as if I had died already and am now living a posthumous existence.' This is the sense of unreality, that can strike out of a perfectly clear sky. Good health and strong nerves can make it unlikely; but that may be only because the man in good health is thinking about other things and doesn't look in the direction where the uncertainty lies. And once a man has seen it, the world can never afterwards be quite the same straightforward place. Barbusse has shown us that the Outsider is a man who cannot live in the comfortable, insulated world of the bourgeois, accepting what he sees and touches as reality. 'He sees too deep and too much', and what he sees is essentially *chaos*. For the bourgeois, the world is fundamentally an orderly place, with a disturbing element of the irrational, the terrifying, which his preoccupation with the present usually permits him to ignore. For the Outsider, the world is not rational, not orderly. When he asserts his sense of anarchy in the face of the bourgeois' complacent acceptance, it is not simply the need to cock a snook at respectability that provokes him; it is a distressing sense *that truth must be told at all costs*, otherwise there can be no hope for an ultimate restoration of order. Even if there seems no room for hope, truth must be told. (The example we are turning to now is a curious instance of this.) The Outsider is a man who has awakened to chaos. He may have no reason to believe that chaos is positive, the germ of life (in the Kabbala, chaos — *tohu bohu* — is simply a state in which order is latent; the egg is the 'chaos' of the bird); in spite of this, truth must be told, chaos must be faced.

The last published work of H. G. Wells gives us an insight into such an awakening. *Mind at the End of Its Tether* seems to have been written to record some revelation:

> The writer finds very considerable reason for believing that within a period to be estimated by weeks and months rather than by aeons, there has been a fundamental change in the conditions under which life — and not simply human life but all self-conscious existence — has been going on since its beginning. If his thinking has been sound... the end of everything we call life is close at hand and cannot be evaded. He is telling you the conclusions to which reality has driven his own mind, and he thinks you may be interested enough to consider them, but he is not attempting to impose them on you.

This last sentence is noteworthy for its curious logic. Wells's conviction that life is at an end is, as he says, a 'stupendous proposition'. If it is true, then it negates the whole pamphlet; obviously, since it negates all life and its phenomena. Vaguely aware of the contradiction, Wells explains that he is writing 'under the urgency of a scientific training that obliged him to clarify the world and his ideas to the limits of his capacity'.

> His renascent intelligence finds itself confronted with strange, convincing realities so overwhelming that, were he indeed one of those logical, consistent people we incline to claim we are, he would think day and night in a passion of concentration, dismay and mental

struggle upon the ultimate disaster that confronts our species. We are nothing of the sort. We live with reference to past experience, not to future events, however inevitable.

In commenting on an earlier book called *The Conquest of Time*, Wells comments: 'Such conquest as that book admits is done by time rather than man.'

> Time like an ever rolling stream bears all its sons away
> They fly forgotten as a dream dies at the opening day.

This is the authentic Shakespearian pessimism, straight out of *Macbeth* or *Timon*. It is a surprising note from the man who had spent his life preaching the credo: If you don't like your life you can change it: the optimist of *Men Like Gods* and *A Modern Utopia*. Wells declares that, if the reader will follow him closely, he will give the reason for this change of outlook:

> The reality glares coldly and harshly upon any of those who can wrench their minds free...to face the unsparing question that has overwhelmed the writer. They discover that a frightful queerness has come into life.... The habitual interest of the writer is his critical anticipation. Of everything he asks: To what will this lead? And it was natural for him to assume that there was a limit set to change, that new things and events would appear, but that they would appear consistently, preserving the natural sequence of life. So that in the present vast confusion of our world, there was always the assumption of an ultimate restoration of rationality.... It was merely the fascinating question of what forms the new rational phase would assume, what over-man, Erewhon or what not would break through the transitory clouds and turmoil. To this the writer set his mind.
>
> He did his utmost to pursue that upward spiral...towards their convergence in a new phase in the story of life, and the more he weighed the realities before him, the less he was able to detect any convergence whatever. Changes had ceased to be systematic, and the further he estimated the course they seemed to be taking, the greater the divergence. Hitherto, events had been held together by a certain logical consistency, as the heavenly bodies have been held together by gravitation. Now it is as if that cord had vanished, and everything was

driving anyhow to anywhere at a steadily increasing velocity.... The pattern of things to come faded away.*

In the pages that follow, these ideas are enlarged on and repeated, without showing us how they were arrived at. 'A harsh queerness is coming into things', and a paragraph later: 'We pass into the harsh glare of hitherto incredible novelty.... The more strenuous the analysis, the more inescapable the sense of mental defeat.' 'The cinema sheet stares us in the face. That sheet is the actual fabric of our being. Our loves, our hates, our wars and battles, are no more than phantasmagoria dancing on that fabric, themselves as insubstantial as a dream.'

There are obviously immense differences between the attitudes of Wells and Barbusse's hero, but they have in common the Outsider's fundamental attitude: non-acceptance of life, of human life lived by human beings in a human society. Both would say: Such a life is a dream; it is not real. Wells goes further than Barbusse in the direction of complete negation. He ends his first chapter with the words: 'There is no way out or round or through.' There can be no doubt that as far as Wells is concerned, he certainly sees 'too deep and too much'. Such knowledge is an impasse, the dead end of Eliot's Gerontion: 'After such knowledge, what forgiveness?'

Wells had promised to give his reasons for arriving at such a stupendous proposition. In the remainder of the pamphlet (nineteen pages) he does nothing of the sort; he repeats his assertion. 'Our doomed formicary', 'harsh implacable hostility to our universe', 'no pattern of any kind'. He talks vaguely of Einstein's paradox of the speed of light, of the 'radium clock' (a method geologists use to date the earth). He even contradicts his original statement that *all* life is at an end; it is only the species *Homo sapiens* that is played out. 'The stars in their courses have turned against him and he has to give place to some other animal better adapted to face the fate that closes in on mankind.' In the final pages of the pamphlet, his trump of the last judgement has changed into the question: Can civilization be saved?

---

*Readers of Professor Whitehead will probably feel that Wells is a bad example of Whitehead's old enemy, 'the bifurcation of nature' — i.e. that as a man of science, he has gone to extremes of dividing nature into 'things as they are' (i.e. the things science is concerned with) and things as they are perceived by human beings (i.e. the things art and music are concerned with), and that Wells's feeling that mind and nature have ceased to run parallel is only an extreme consequence of his attitude. Certainly Whitehead's 'philosophy of organism' is concerned with making the same demands for a wholeness of conception of mind and nature that I am concerned with in this book; a parallel of the thought of Professor Whitehead with that of T. E. Hulme would probably shed a great deal of light on the problems of contemporary humanism.

But my own temperament makes it unavoidable for me to doubt that there will not be that small minority who will see life out to its inevitable end.

All the same, the pamphlet must be considered the most pessimistic single utterance in modern literature, together with T. S. Eliot's 'Hollow Men'. And Eliot's despair was essentially religious; we should be tempted to assume that Wells's despair is religious too, if it were not for his insistence that he is speaking of a scientific fact, an objective reality.

It is not surprising that the work received scant attention from Wells's contemporaries: to make its conclusions credible it would need the formidable dialectical apparatus of Schopenhauer's *Welt als Wille und Vorstellung* or Spengler's *Decline of the West*. I have heard it described by a writer-contemporary of Wells as 'an outburst of peevishness at a world that refused to accept him as its Messiah'. Certainly, if we accept it on the level on which he wrote it — acquiescing to every sentence — we feel the stirring of problems that seem to return into themselves. Why did he write it if he can hold out no hope of salvation? If the conclusions he has reached negate his own past life, and the possible futures of all the human race, where do we go from there? Wells's thesis is that we have never been going anywhere — we have been carried along by our delusions, believing that any movement is better than none. Whereas the truth is that the reverse, *no movement*, is the final answer, the answer to the question: What will men *do* when they see things as they are?

It is a long way from Mr Polly's discovery (If you don't like your life you can change it) to: There is no way out or round or through. Barbusse has gone half-way, with his: Truth, what do they mean by it?, which has as a corollary: Change, what difference does it make? Wells has gone the whole distance, and landed us on the doorstep of the Existentialist problem: Must thought negate life?

Before we pass on to this new aspect of the Outsider's problem, there is a further point of comparison between Barbusse and Wells that deserves comment. Barbusse's hero is an Outsider when we meet him; probably he was always an Outsider. Wells was very definitely an Insider most of his life. Tirelessly he performed his duty to society, gave it good advice upon how to better itself. He was the scientific spirit incarnate: reviewing the history of the life and drawing conclusions, reviewing economics and social history, political and religious history; a descendant of the French Encyclopedists who never ceased to compile and summarize. From him: Truth, what do they mean by it? Would have elicited a compendious review of all the ideas of truth in the history of the seven civilizations. There is something so shocking in such a man's becoming an Outsider that we feel inclined to look for physical causes for the change: Wells was a sick, a tired man, when he wrote *Mind at the End of Its Tether*. May we not accept this as the whole cause and moving force behind the pamphlet?

Unfortunately, no. Wells declared his conclusions to be objective; if that is so, then to say he was sick when he wrote them down means no more than to say he was wearing a dressing-gown and slippers. It is our business to judge whether the world can be seen in such a way that Wells's conclusions are inevitable; if so, to decide whether such a way of looking at things is truer, more valid, more objective, than our usual way of seeing. Even if we decide in advance that the answer is No, there may be much to learn from the exercise of changing our viewpoint.

***

The Outsider's claim amounts to the same thing as Wells's hero's in *The Country of the Blind*: that he is the one man able to see. To the objection that he is unhealthy and neurotic, he replies: 'In the country of the blind, the one-eyed man is king.' His case, in fact, is that he is the one man who knows he is sick in a civilization that doesn't know it is sick. Certain Outsiders we shall consider later would go even further and declare that it is human nature that is sick, and the Outsider is the man who faces that unpleasant fact. These need not concern us yet; for the moment we have a *negative position* which the Outsider declares to be the essence of the world as he sees it. 'Truth, what do they mean by it.' 'There is no way out, or round, or through.' And it is to this we must turn our attention.

When Barbusse made his hero ask the first question, he was almost certainly unaware that he was paraphrasing the central problem of a Danish philosopher who had died in 1855 in Copenhagen. Søren Kierkegaard had also decided that philosophic discussion was altogether meaningless, and his reason was Wells's reason: Reality negates it. Or, as Kierkegaard put it, existence negates it. Kierkegaard's attack was directed in particular against the German metaphysician Hegel, who had (rather like Wells) been trying to 'justify the ways of God to man' by talking about the goal of history and man's place in space and time. Kierkegaard was a deeply religious soul for whom all this was unutterably shallow. He declared: Put me in a system and you negate me — I am not just a mathematical symbol — I *am*.

Now obviously, such a denial that logic and scientific analysis can lead to truth has curious consequences. Our science is built on the assumption that a statement like 'All bodies fall at thirty-two feet per second in the earth's gravitational field' has a definite meaning. But if you deny the ultimate validity of logic, it becomes nonsensical. And if you don't deny logic, it is difficult, thinking along these lines, to pull up short of Wells and John Stuart Mill. That is why Kierkegaard phrases it: Is an Existentialist System possible; or, to put it in another way, Can one live a philosophy without negating either the life or the philosophy? Kierkegaard's conclusion was No, but one can live a religion without negating life or religion. We need not pause here over the reasoning that led him to this conclusion (readers interested enough can consult the *Unscientific Postscript*). What is worth noticing at this point is that his affirmation of Christian values did not prevent him from violently attacking the Christian Church on the grounds that it had solved the problem of living its religion by cutting off its arms and legs to make it fit life. It is also an amusing point that the other great Existentialist philosopher of the nineteenth century, Frederick Nietzsche, attacked the Christian Church on the opposite grounds of its having solved the problem by chopping down life to fit the Christian religion. Now, both Kierkegaard and Nietzsche were trained thinkers, and both took a certain pride in stating that they were Outsiders. It follows that we should find in their works a skilled defence of the Outsider and his position. And this in fact is what we do find.

Nietzsche and Kierkegaard evolved a philosophy that started from the Outsider; nowadays, we use Kierkegaard's phrase in speaking of it, and call it Existentialism. When, in the nineteen-twenties, Kierkegaard was re-published in German, he was taken up by the professors, who discarded his religious conclusions, and used his methods of analysis to construct the so-called *Existenzphilosophie*. In doing so, they removed the emphasis from the Outsider and threw it back again on to Hegelian metaphysics. Later, in France, Existentialism was popularized by the work of Jean-Paul Sartre and Albert Camus, who once more restored emphasis to the Outsider, and finally arrived at their own conclusions upon the question of how to live a philosophy: Sartre in his 'doctrine of commitment' (which we shall touch upon later) and Camus with the belief: Remain an Outsider. We must examine each of these in turn.

***

In his early novel, *La Nausée*, Sartre skilfully synthesizes all the points we have already considered in connection with Wells and Barbusse: the unreality, the rejection of people and civilized standards, and, finally, the 'cinema sheet' of naked existence, with 'no way out or round or through'.

La Nausée purports to be the journal of an historian named Roquentin: not a full-fledged scientific historian like Wells, but a literary historian who is engaged in unearthing the life of a shifty diplomat-politician named Rollebon. Roquentin lives alone in a Hotel in Le Havre. His life would be a quiet record of research, conversations in the library, sexual intercourse with the café *patronne*: 'I live alone, entirely alone; I never speak to anyone, never; I receive nothing, I give nothing....'

But a series of revelations disturb him. He stands on the beach and picks up a flat stone to skim on the sea, and suddenly...'I saw something which disgusted me; I no longer know whether it was the stone or the sea.' He drops the stone and walks off.

Roquentin's journal is an attempt to objectify what is happening to him. He searches his memory, examines his past. There was something that happened in Indo-China; a colleague had asked him to join an archaeological mission to Bengal; he was about to accept —

...when suddenly I woke up from a six-year slumber.... I couldn't understand why I was in Indo-China. What was I doing there? Why was I talking to these people? Why was I dressed so oddly?....Before me, posed with a sort of indolence, was a voluminous, insipid idea. I did not see clearly what it was, but it sickened me so much I couldn't look at it.

Certainly something is happening. There is his ordinary life, with its assumptions of meaning, purpose, usefulness. And there are these revelations, or, rather, these attacks of nausea, that knock the bottom out of his ordinary life. The reason is not far to seek. He is too acute and honest an observer. Like Wells, he asks of everything: to what will this lead? He never ceases to notice things. Of the café *patron*, he comments: 'When his place empties, his head empties too.' The lives of these people are contingent on events. If things stopped happening to them, they would stop being. Worse still are the *salauds* whose pictures he can look at in the town's art gallery, these eminent public men, so sure of themselves, so sure that life is theirs and their existence is necessary to it. And Roquentin's criticism is turning back on himself; he too has accepted meanings where he now recognizes there were none. He too is dependent on events.

In a crowded café, he is afraid to look at a glass of beer. 'But I can't explain what I see. To anyone. There: I am quietly slipping into the water's depths, towards fear.'

A few days later, again, he describes in detail the circumstances of an attack of the nausea. This time it is the braces of the café *patron* that become the focus of the sickness. Now we observe that the nausea seems to emphasize the sordidness of Roquentin's surroundings. (Sartre has gone further than any previous writer in emphasizing 'darkness and dirt'; neither Joyce nor Dostoevsky give the same sensation of the mind being trapped in physical filth.) Roquentin is overwhelmed by it, a spiritual counterpart of violent physical retching.

> ...the nausea is not *inside* me; I feel it *out there*, in the wall, in the suspenders; everywhere around me. It makes itself one, with the café; I am the one who is within it.

Like Wells, Roquentin insists on the objective nature of the revelation.

Somebody puts on a record; it is the voice of a Negro woman singing *Some of These Days*. The nausea disappears as he listens:

> When the voice was heard in the silence I felt my body harden and the nausea vanish; suddenly it was almost unbearable to become so hard, so brilliant.... I am *in* the music. Globes of fire turn in the mirrors, encircled by rings of smoke.

There is no need to analyse this experience; it is the old, familiar aesthetic experience; art giving order and logic to chaos.

> I am touched; I feel my body at rest like a precision machine. I have had real adventures. I can recapture no detail, but I perceive the rigorous succession of events. I have crossed seas, left cities behind me, followed the course of rivers or plunged into forests, always making my way towards other cities. I have had women; I have fought with men, and never was I able to turn back any more than a record can be reversed.

Works of art cannot affect him. Art is thought, and thought only gives the world an appearance of order to anyone weak enough to be convinced by its show. Only something as instinctively rhythmic as the blues can give him a sense of order that doesn't seem false. But even that may be only a temporary refuge; deeper nervous exhaustion would cause the collapse of the sense of order, even in *Some of These Days*.

In the Journal, we watch the breaking-down of all Roquentin's values. Exhaustion limits him more and more to the present, the here-now. The work of memory, which gives events sequence and coherence, is failing, leaving him more and more dependent for meaning on what he can see and touch. It is Hume's scepticism becoming instinctive, all-destroying. All he can see and touch is unrecognizable, unaided by memory; like a photograph of a familiar object taken from an unfamiliar angle. He looks at a seat, and fails to recognize it: 'I murmur: It's a seat, but the word stays on my lips. It refuses to go and put itself on the thing.... Things are divorced from their names. They are there, grotesque, stubborn, huge, and it seems ridiculous to call them seats, or to say anything at all about them. I am in the midst of things — nameless things.'

In the park, the full nature of the revelation comes to him as he stares at the roots of a chestnut tree:

I couldn't remember it was a root any more. The words had vanished, and with them, the significance of things, their methods of use, and the feeble points of reference men have traced on their surface. I was sitting... before this knotty mass, entirely beastly, which frightened me.... It left me breathless. Never, until these last few days, had I understood the meaning of existence. I was like the others.... I said with them: The ocean *is* green, that white speck up there *is* a seagull, but I didn't feel that it existed.... And then suddenly existence had unveiled itself. It had lost the look of an abstract category; it was the very paste of things; this root was kneaded into existence.... These objects, they inconvenienced me; I would have liked them to exist less imposingly, more dryly, in a more abstract way....

He has reached the rock bottom of self-contempt; even things negate him. We are all familiar enough with his experience in the face of other human beings; a personality or a conviction can impose itself in spite of resistance; even the city itself, the confusion of traffic and human beings in Regent Street, can overwhelm a weak personality and make it feel insignificant. Roquentin feels insignificant before things. Without the meaning his Will would normally impose on it, his existence is absurd. Causality — Hume's bugbear — has collapsed; consequently *there are no adventures*. The biography of Rollebon would have been another venture of 'bad faith', for it would have imposed a *necessity* on Rollebon's life that was not really there; the events didn't really cohere and follow one another like a story; only blindness to the fact of raw, naked existence could ever produce the illusion that they did.

What then? Is there no causality, no possible meaning? Sartre summarizes life: '*L'homme est un passion inutile*.' There is no choice, in Roquentin's reckoning; there is only being useless and knowing it and being useless and not knowing it.

Yet Roquentin had had his glimpse of meaning and order; in *Some of These Days*. There was meaning, causation, one note following inevitably on another. Roquentin wonders: why shouldn't he create something like that; something rhythmic, purposive — a novel, perhaps, that men could read later and feel: There was an attempt to bring order into chaos? He will leave Le Havre and the life of Rollebon; there must be another way of living that is not futile. The Journal comes to an end on this note.

***

Roquentin lives like Barbusse's hero; his room is almost the limit of his consciousness. But he has gone further and deeper than the hole-in-the-wall man. His attitude has reached the dead-end of Wells; 'Man is a useless passion': that could be taken as a summary of *Mind at the End of Its Tether*. Complete denial, as in Eliot's 'Hollow Men': We are the hollow men, we are the *salauds*. Roquentin is in the position of the hero of *The Country of the Blind*. He alone is aware of the truth, and if all men were aware of it, there would be an end of life. In the country of the blind, the one-eyed man is king. But his kingship is kingship over nothing. It brings no powers and privileges, only loss of faith and exhaustion of the power to act. Its world is a world without values.

This is the position that Barbusse's Outsider has brought us to. It was already explicit in that desire that stirred as he saw the swaying dresses of the women; for what he wanted was not sexual intercourse, but some indefinable freedom, of which the women, with their veiled and hidden nakedness, are a symbol. Sexual desire was there, but not alone; aggravated, blown-up like a balloon, by a resentment that stirred in revolt against the bewilderment of hurrying Paris with its well-dressed women. 'Yet in spite of this I desire some compensation.' In spite of the civilization that has impressed his insignificance on him until he is certain that 'he has nothing and he deserves nothing', in spite of this he feels a right to…to what? Freedom? It is a misused word. We examine *L'Enfer* in vain for a definition of it. Sartre and Wells have decided that man is never free; he is simply too stupid to recognize this. Then to what precisely is it that the Outsider has an inalienable right?

The question must take us into a new field: of Outsiders who have had some insight into the nature of freedom.

AN AUTOBIOGRAPHICAL INTRODUCTION

From *Religion and the Rebel,* 1957

The Outsider was an incomplete book. It was intended to document and order a subject which, for personal reasons, I find particularly absorbing: the subject of mental strain and near-insanity.

Over many years the obsessional figure whom I have called the Outsider became for me the heroic figure of our time. My vision of our civilization was a vision of cheapness and futility, the degrading of all intellectual standards. In contrast to this, the Outsider seemed to be the man who, for any reason at all, felt himself lonely in the crowd of the second-rate. As I conceived him, he could be a maniac carrying a knife in a black bag, taking pride in appearing harmless and normal to other people; he could be a saint or a visionary, caring for nothing but one moment in which he seemed to understand the world, and see into the heart of nature and of God.

The more I considered the Outsider, the more I felt him to be a symptom of our time and age. Essentially, he seemed to be a rebel; and what he was in rebellion against was the *lack of spiritual tension* in a materially prosperous civilization. The first nine books of Saint Augustine's *Confessions* are an Outsider document, and Saint Augustine lived in a disintegrating Roman society. It did not seem a bold step to conclude that the Outsider is a symptom of a civilization's decline; Outsiders appear like pimples on a dying civilization. An individual tends to be what his environment makes him. If a civilization is spiritually sick, the individual suffers from the same sickness. If he is healthy enough to put up a fight, he becomes an Outsider.

The study of the spiritually sick individual belongs to psychology, but to consider him in relation to a sick civilization is to enter the realm of history. That is why this book must attempt to pursue two courses at once, probing deeper into the Outsider himself, while at the same time moving towards the historical problem of the decline of civilizations. One way leads inward, towards mysticism; the other outward, towards politics. Unfortunately, I have almost no turn for practical politics, so the emphasis in this book is on religion and philosophy. Where the road disappears into the thickets of political theory, I leave it, and hope that someone less averse to politics than I am will press on where I have shirked the problem.

Various critics have objected — with some justification — that the term 'Outsider' is loose; that a word which can be applied to Boehme as well as Nijinsky, to Fox and Gurdjieff as well as Lawrence, Van Gogh and Sartre, is almost meaningless. But my use of the term 'Outsider' is deliberately vague. The ultimate question that, for me, lies behind the Outsider is: How can man extend his range of consciousness? I believe that human beings experience a range of mental states which is as narrow as the middle three notes of a piano keyboard. I believe that the possible range of mental states is as wide as the whole piano keyboard, and that man's sole aim and business is to extend his range from the usual three or four notes to the whole keyboard. The men I dealt with in *The Outsider* had one thing in common: an instinctive knowledge that their range *could* be extended, and a nagging dissatisfaction with the range of their everyday experience.

This, I must admit, is the urge that underlies all my thinking and writing. I state it here so that there shall be no doubt in any reader's mind about the central preoccupation of my book.

The publication of *The Outsider* brought me some interesting insights. It received more attention than I or my publisher had expected, and, quite suddenly, I became involved in all kinds of activities. For many months after it was published, I had almost no time alone, caught up as I was in a round of interviews by reporters, lectures, broadcasts, reading and answering letters, invitations to dinner and so on. The result was exactly what I had been afraid of: I found myself losing the preoccupations that had led me to write *The Outsider*. Strangers who claimed to be Outsiders wrote me long letters explaining their symptoms and asking for advice, until I began to suspect parody. In this whirl, I discovered that I ceased to be aware of the states of consciousness that lie beyond my ordinary two or three notes. In my own terminology, I had started to become an Insider.

I record this because it is of central importance to the theme of this book. Most men I know live like this as a matter of course: working, travelling, eating and drinking and talking. The range of everyday activity in a modern civilization builds a wall around the ordinary state of consciousness and makes it almost impossible to see beyond it. The conditions under which we live do this to us. It is what happens in a civilization that always makes a noise like a dynamo, and gives no leisure for peace and contemplation. Men begin to lose that intuition of 'unknown modes of being', that sense of purpose, that makes them more than highly efficient pigs. This is the horror the Outsider revolts against.

Some years ago, in Winchester Cathedral, I came across a pamphlet by Mr T. S. Eliot; it was an address which Mr Eliot had delivered in the Cathedral, and it had the unpromising title: 'On the Use of Cathedrals in England.' For three quarters of the pamphlet, Mr Eliot talks like a studious country parson about the relation of the cathedral to the parish churches. And then, towards the end, he speaks of the position of the dean and chapter, and his pamphlet suddenly becomes an impassioned plea for leisure in a modern civilization. He attacks the view that the dean and chapter should be general runabouts, preaching sermons all over the parish, and emphasizes that good theological thinking requires quiet and contemplation. He adduces his own example to strengthen his point: he has always worked as a publisher to give himself the necessary leisure for writing, and any permanent value which his work may possess (he modestly claims) is due to the fact that he wrote only what he wanted to write, under no compulsion to please anyone but himself.

I remember being excited by this at the time. T. E. Lawrence had made the same point in *The Seven Pillars*: '...of these two poles, leisure and subsistence, we should shun subsistence...and cling close to leisure.... Some men there might be, uncreative, whose leisure is barren; but the activity of these would have been material only.... Mankind has been no gainer by its drudges.'

For my own part, I found that I preferred working as a navvy or washing dishes to life in an office; for although I had no more than the normal reluctance to face hard work, I had a very real fear of that deadening of the nerves and sensibilities that comes of boredom and submitting to one's own self-contempt. I was sticking down envelopes with a damp brush one afternoon, when a young man who seemed to enjoy being a civil servant commented: 'Soul-destroying, isn't it?' A commonplace phrase, but I had never heard it before, and I repeated it like a revelation. Not soul-destroying, but life-destroying; the stagnating life-force gives off smells like standing water, and the whole being is poisoned. Desmond — that was his name — always looked well-groomed and efficient, and I never saw him lose his temper. My own predisposition to boredom and irritable wretchedness inclined me to divide the world into two classes: people who disliked themselves, and people who didn't. And the former disliked the latter even more than they disliked themselves.

Such experiences were the groundwork of all my analyses, my starting point; and all my thought aimed at discovering some solution that would enable the people who disliked themselves to find reasons — or methods — of overcoming self-contempt, without numbing themselves into complacency. I called the people who disliked themselves Outsiders. Boredom, I knew, meant not having enough to do with one's life energies. The answer to it, quite simply, lies in extending the range of the consciousness: setting emotions circulating, and setting the intellect working, until new areas of consciousness are brought to life in the way that the blood starts flowing again through a leg which has gone numb.

That was just the starting point. It is not enough to have leisure; leisure is only a negative concept, the wide, clear space where one can build decent houses after knocking down slums. The next problem is to begin to build. I found it tiresome to work for an employer in a factory or laundry, and envied those men who can make a living by doing the things they enjoy. But closer acquaintance with such men — writers, artists, journalists — has usually proved to me that they have knocked down one slum only to build another — slightly more to their own taste, but still a slum. From the point of view of spiritual health, I do not think there is much to choose between the workman who has worked in the same factory for forty years and is spiritually warped and stunted in consequence, and the novelist who writes the same kind of novels for forty years and has a house on the Riviera.

It is unnatural to work for forty years in the same factory, but no more unnatural than it is to be born. Nature is dead; every act of will is unnatural, against nature. The more one has to fight against, the more alive one can be. That was why, for me, the problem of living resolved itself into the question of choosing obstacles to stimulate my will. Instantly, I came to recognize that our civilization is flowing in the opposite direction; all our culture and science is directed towards enabling us to exercise as little will as possible. Everything is made easy; and if, after a week of office routine and travelling on buses, we still feel the need to work off excess energy, we can always enjoy ourselves playing all those games involving artificial obstacles, where the will is applied to beating another team of cricketers or footballers, or simply to wrestling with the imaginary Sphinx who sets the newspaper crossword puzzles. We have also invented a form of thought that fits in with this abdication of the will. We call it abstract philosophy. It is essentially the product of Western civilization.

There was an element of disguised autobiography in *The Outsider*; obviously, since I spent most of the book calling on other men to bear witness to my own beliefs. Underlying the whole argument there was the belief that real philosophy should be the result of applying the analytical faculty — the mathematical faculty — to the stuff of one's own experience. Too much experience flows over us like water through a channel: it means nothing to us; we are unchanged by it, unconscious of it. For years before I wrote *The Outsider* I had kept a journal in which I had been mainly concerned with applying mathematical analysis to my own experience, and making a note when I read something that showed the same preoccupation. There was a slow, deliberate accumulation of material that I was able to transfer almost unchanged into the book. That material was chosen — naturally — to exclude myself.

But it is time now, before launching into further analysis of other writers, to explain my own relation to my data. What I wish to give is as full an account as possible of how the problems of the Outsider came to preoccupy me. Philosophy is nothing if it is not an attempt to take one's own experience apart under a microscope.

When I was eleven years old, my grandfather gave me a tattered and coverless science-fiction magazine. (This was in the second year of the war, and I had never seen such a thing before.) It was here that I discovered a name of which I had never heard: Albert Einstein. It was difficult to determine, from the references in the stories, precisely what Professor Einstein had done, but every writer in the magazine mentioned him at least once, and the Letters to the Editor were sprinkled with his name.

The stories themselves excited me more than anything I had ever read. They were mostly about Experiments that got Out of Hand. There was one about a scientist who made a speck of grey protoplasmic matter, which was somehow thrown into the sea and grew larger as it ate up the fishes, until finally it developed a habit of engulfing passenger liners or depopulating small islands. There was another about a scientist who made an Atomic Fire that was inextinguishable, and went on burning until it threatened to burn up the whole world.

I had never read anything like it. Compared to boys' papers and comics, it was erudite and intellectual. And one had a feeling of far more serious issues at stake than in stories about football games and ragging in the Lower Fourth. ('Yarroo, you rotter! I'll tell old Quelchy!') There was talk about

positrons and cyclotrons and the theory of probability. Not to mention
Professor Einstein.

I found Einstein's own little volume, *Relativity, the Special and General
Theory*, and conscientiously plugged away at it, skipping the mathematics
and wondering what the devil he meant by 'orientation'. But Sir James
Jeans was easier; his explanation of the Michelson-Morley experiment
simplified everything. From then on I thought I understood relativity. I
enjoyed a certain amount of consideration among the boys at school as a
consequence of tangling up the physics master on obscure questions about
the speed of light in a moving co-ordinate system. They nicknamed me
'Professor', and relied on me to waste as much of our physics lectures as
possible by objecting that Newton was out of date and discredited. But
secretly I admired Newton, for I imagined him as occupying a place in
the hierarchy — Archimedes, Galileo, Newton, Planck, Einstein — which
would one day include myself.

But my curiosity was not confined to purely scientific questions. Sir
James Jeans begins *The Mysterious Universe* with a passage that might have
been a sermon on Pascal's text: 'The eternal silence of these infinite spaces
terrifies me.' This, and other passages of speculation, produced a sense of
mystery that was so intolerable to me that I once wrote a twenty-page letter
to Sir Arthur Eddington, asking him if he could please explain to me what
the universe was all about. When I asked the local librarian where I could
find his address, she told me that he had died earlier in the year. I was
not wholly disappointed, since I had come to the conclusion that he was
unlikely to know the answer anyway. This was in 1944.

I see now that it was Jeans and Eddington who were responsible for
my sudden mental awakening at the age of twelve; at the time, I thought
of Einstein as 'the master'. I believed that Einstein had taught me the
impossibility of making a final judgement on anything. I tried to explain to
school friends that space was infinite and yet bounded; and it seemed to me
that the possibilities of human life were also infinite and yet bounded: that
within its framework of endless repetition, anything could be done. It was to
be another five years before I read *Zarathustra* and discovered that Nietzsche
also recognized Eternal Recurrence as the foundation of an essentially
optimistic philosophy.

But this notion was of secondary importance compared to that of the
Will to Power. This is so central to my way of thinking that I should perhaps
explain at some length how my ideas on the subject originated.

In some popular textbook of psychology, I had read summaries of the
systems of Freud, Jung and Adler. Freud's insistence on childhood influences

and the sexual urges seemed even then to be nonsense; Jung's theory of types struck me as equally irrelevant. But Adler's idea of the Power Instinct came to me as a revelation; it seemed to tie together all my observations of human beings, to add the final touch to the edifice that Einstein had begun. A great deal of a child's time is spent in being treated unfairly and wondering about the rights and wrongs of the case; also in observing that, although all adults seem to him to be equally self-possessed and balanced in judgement, yet there are some who are badly spoken of by others, or labelled as shifty, dishonest or stupid by one's parents. It is all very confusing. It leads the child to realize that he cannot leave the business of making judgements entirely to the adult world. And when such a child tries to form his own judgements, the real confusion begins. In most issues between adults, there seems very little to choose. It is less a matter of rights and wrongs than of individuals with their own will to self-assertion. So my summary of the situation went like this: 'right' and 'wrong' are relative terms; they have no final meaning; the reality behind human conflicts is only a will to self-assertion. Nobody is right; nobody is wrong; but *everyone* wants to be thought right.

Adler's use of the term 'inferiority complex' supplied me with my fundamental idea. I decided that the desire of every human being is to appear in as good a light as possible to himself. And since the opinions of other people affect the way we see ourselves, we seek to preserve our complacency by winning their respect or friendship. Of course, there is another way: to cut oneself off completely from the opinion of other people and build a wall around one's own self-esteem. The lunatic who believes he is Napoleon or Christ has done this — so I felt. The difference between the lunatic and the sane person is only that the sane person prefers to get other people to co-operate in maintaining his delusions.

There came a day when I took up a pen and settled down to writing a long essay about these ideas. I began it in a new school notebook that had written inside the cover 'Colin Wilson, Form 2C', and underneath it, in block capitals printed in red ink: 'These notes are based on the relativity theory of Albert Einstein, and the system of Individual Psychology of Alfred Adler.'

The writing of that essay was an unforgettable experience. Years later, when I read in *The Varieties of Religious Experience* of Jouffroy's feelings of terror while analysing his own unbelief,* I remembered that night in 1944 when I wrote my 'Essay on Superiority' at a single sitting. It seemed that I had penetrated deeper into unbelief than any other human being; that by

---

*Vide *The Outsider* (Gollancz, 1956), pp. 123—4.

questioning too deeply, I had cut myself off from the rest of the human race. My brother came to bed in the same room while I wrote. Towards three o'clock in the morning, I turned off the light and climbed into bed beside him, feeling at the same time an awful fear that God would strike me dead in the night. I felt that I had destroyed in myself a certain necessary basis of illusion that makes life bearable for human beings. I had done this in the name of 'truth'; and now I felt no elation, only a sort of fatigue of the brain that would not let me sleep. Truth, it seemed, had no power of intensifying life; only of destroying the illusions that make life tolerable.

I still remember my surprise when I woke up in the morning and found I was still alive. God either didn't care, or didn't exist.

This was the beginning of a long period in which the key word, for me, was 'futility'. During this period, I felt that 'futility' was the final comment on human life. It was the worst and most depressing period of my life. It was not a case of my ideas depressing me; there was a social maladjustment for which the ideas provided the excuse. At thirteen I should have had friends — especially girl-friends. Instead, I spent three years in my bedroom, reading and writing. The sexual desires I knew at the time were mere physical urges; there was no need or desire for friendly human intercourse. My admiration went to a certain ideal of cold brutality of intellect; while I wondered with despair where the motivation for such an attitude could lie, if not in the realms of delusion and self-assertion that I despised. When I read some sage or philosopher proclaiming that human beings are hopelessly deluded, I wondered what reason he had for saying so, other than a deluded wish to be admired for his cynicism. Human life seemed a vicious circle; the desire for life a delusion. I asked myself: Who made the delusion? And decided that, whatever inscrutable aim inspired the Great Delusion-Maker, it presupposed human futility and vanity. I was not even certain that the Great Delusion-Maker himself might not be inspired by delusions.

Added to this was the exhaustion of reading and thinking too much; also, of course, the sexual unfulfilment. Shaw comments in one of the later prefaces that most young men need sex several years before it is socially convenient for them to have it. This, I think, is especially true nowadays, and the consequence is a residue of sexual hunger that may take years of libertinism to assuage. At all events, I believe that sex played as important a part as my eschatological doubts in making me wretched in my early teens.

I wrote as an antidote to misery or boredom. I became ashamed of the 'Superiority' essay, and wrote further essays in which I sought a more technical terminology. The central theme was always the same: that men are machines driven by emotions, that the 'desire for truth' is always some less creditable urge disguised by the emotions; that 'truth' would be as useless to human beings as bookcases are to cows. I find the two little notebooks of 'Subjective Essays' filled with speculations on the nature of human impulses, and can see now that these speculations were an attempt to track down the element of free will in man. In the essay on Fanaticism, I state that the fanatic is the luckiest of all living beings, for he is driven by the most intense delusions. Somewhere — in Wells's *Outline of History*, I think — I have seen those huge Egyptian statues of Amenhotep III that are called the Colossi of Memnon; and in them I saw my symbol of the real philosopher, the man who could say that his reason was not prejudiced by emotion; huge, eyeless, immobile. Only in the dead, I felt, was there no emotional prejudice; consequently, only the dead may be called sane. And somewhere in the essays, I acknowledge that free will may exist, but in such a small degree as to be hardly knowable. I found myself confronted by an urge to analyse my way to truth that concluded in a recognition that truth is of no use for survival.

I had other pursuits that kept me from complete abdication of will. From the age of eleven, physics and chemistry had been my major interests, and by the age of twelve I had made the spare room into a laboratory in which I spent most of my weekends and evenings; the pocket money I earned from a paper round was spent on chemicals. Then, in the August holiday of 1944, I conceived the idea of writing a book which would summarize, in formula and laws, all my knowledge of chemistry and physics. The scheme fascinated me so much that I soon made it more ambitious, and decided to write chapters on Astronomy, Geology, Psychology, Aeronautics, Philosophy and Mathematics. I had bought, at some church bazaar, six volumes of a self-educator with 'courses' on all these subjects. With the help of this and books from the local library, I began my attempt to summarize all the scientific knowledge of humanity. I wrote it in notebooks that held about fifteen thousand words each, and had filled six of these before it was time to go back to school. It was my first book, and I worked on it continuously and systematically — the best possible training for a writer.

In those years of the 'Subjective Essays,' the greatest impact on my mind was Bernard Shaw. I had seen Gabriel Pascal's film of *Caesar and Cleopatra* without being particularly impressed; it reminded me too much of Shakespeare, whom I had always found unreadable. But during the first week of the BBC's Third Programme, I switched on the radio one evening to hear Mr Esmé Percy's voice declaiming:

Friends and fellow brigands. I have a proposal to make to this meeting. We have now spent three evenings in discussing the question Have Anarchists or Social-Democrats the most personal courage? We have gone into the principles of Anarchism and Social-Democracy at great length. The cause of Anarchy has been ably represented by our one Anarchist, who doesn't know what Anarchism means....

It was the beginning of the third act of *Man and Superman*. Even now, after more than ten years, I find it impossible to read this act without a curious feeling of awe. It was a totally new experience. I will not pretend that I was enthralled. I was not; I was partly bored, and could not follow a lot of it. But I was astounded that another man had actually thought and written about the problems that preoccupied me. Up till then, I had had a little private game with myself in which I examined everyone I met and tried to decide how close they were to seeing the world as I saw it; there was always an element of self-congratulation in the fact that I felt certain no one ever had. I was already beginning to enjoy that first terror of feeling myself completely alone. It had become a commonplace of my thinking that no man asked himself what life was about; or if he did, answered with arrant nonsense or wishful thinking. (I once asked my grandfather — during an argument about the existence of God — if he understood the purpose of life, and he told me solemnly that he did, and that he would explain it to me when I was fourteen. Nothing I could say would draw him out. Unfortunately, he died when I was eleven.) Now I heard Shaw speaking quite plainly about the purpose of life, and answering that it was a will to self-understanding. It sounded plausible. It seemed paradoxical enough. And the devil expressed my central obsession with the idea of futility and purposeless repetition:

> ...Where you now see reform, progress, fulfilment of upward tendency, continual ascent by Man on the stepping stones of his dead selves to higher things, you will see nothing but an infinite comedy of illusion. You will discover the profound truth of the saying of my friend Koheleth, that there is nothing new under the sun. Vanitas vanitatum....

And Don Juan interrupts impatiently:

> ...Clever dolt that you are, is a man no better than a worm, or a dog than a wolf, because he gets tired of everything? Shall he give up eating because he destroys his appetite in the act of gratifying it?

I went to bed that night with a sort of mental numbness. I felt that something of tremendous importance had happened to me, something which I could not yet fully grasp. During the night, I woke up and put out my hand to my brother; the bedclothes had slipped off him and he was as cold as tin. For a moment I believed him dead, and it seemed the natural and inevitable result of knowing too much and prying too deep. It was an immense relief when I covered him up and he grew warm again; and as much a surprise, in its way, as the morning I woke up and found I was still alive.

I listened to the repeat of the play the following evening, all six hours of it, and borrowed it from the local library and read it through the day after that. I think that no other forty-eight hours of my life has given me such a sense of a mental earthquake. Subsequently I read through all the plays (although not, at that time, the prefaces). The English master at school told me that an admiration for Shaw was something that often 'happens' in the teens, and disappears after five years or so. I find that, after twelve years, Shaw still seems to me the greatest figure in European literature since Dante.

Shaw was less of a mental tonic than might be expected. At that time, a sense of exhaustion and greyness seemed to wash around on the edge of my mind. I made a habit of wandering into churches and engaging the priest in arguments about the existence of God and the purpose of life. Sometimes, if the argument went on too long, I left the church feeling a little dizzy, and with an underlying certainty that stupidity and futility were the inescapable warp and weft of living. These periods of depression sometimes lasted for days. (One such priest, I remember, advised me to read nothing but newspapers for a year, telling me that I was suffering from mental indigestion from reading too much. I was delighted later when, in Fox's Journal, I read about the priest of Mancetter who advised him to take tobacco and sing psalms.*) I had passed beyond my period of militant atheism. The idea that there was no God no longer gave me a feeling of freedom. In my childhood I had been greatly given to praying mentally while I walked around; I was an incorrigible talker, and enjoyed keeping up a one-sided conversation when there was no one else to talk to, frequently apologizing to God when my attention was distracted and I lost the thread of the discussion. Now I would have been glad to pray — except for the gloomy certainty that it would be mere emotional dishonesty. I had begun

---

*The Outsider (Gollancz, 1956), Chap. 8, pp. 209—10.

to read T. S. Eliot's poetry at this time, stimulated by some remark of the French master about his obscurity. In the first few lines I read, I found the words:

> And I pray that I may forget
> These matters that with myself I too much discuss
> Too much explain

and

> Teach us to care and not to care
> Teach us to sit still.

Immediately I felt I knew what he was talking about. After that, I tended to repeat 'Ash Wednesday' as a form of mental prayer. It furnished a sort of antidote to depression and exhaustion that Shaw could not provide.

When I was sixteen, I left school, having passed my School Certificate. I had wanted to take some job where I could study for a B.Sc. (My chief ambition was still to be a scientist.) Unfortunately I needed five credits to be exempt from matriculation; I only had four, and had to take the maths exam again. In the meantime, I took a job in a warehouse; it involved weighing crates of wool when they came into the warehouse, keeping a number of girls and machines supplied with hanks of wool, and 'weighing out' the wool when it had been wound on to spools. I was not particularly miserable, but the hours were longer than any I had known before — from eight till six, with a break for lunch — and the work was heavier. After a while, the job began to bore me, and I tried various remedies to counteract my growing detestation for it. I read a great deal of poetry, because I found it relaxed me and refreshed me; I planned short stories and a long play while I worked, and wrote them in the evenings. After two months, I passed my maths exam with the necessary credit, and left the warehouse without regrets. I hated hard work.

In comparison, my job as a laboratory assistant at my old school seemed like a holiday. But I now found that I had lost all interest in science. I had written three acts of an immensely long play, designed as a sequel to Shaw's *Man and Superman*, and was convinced that I could make a living as a writer. I had my first short story published at about this time — it was in a factory magazine printed in Yorkshire. An uncle who worked in Durham had submitted the story for me, and the editor had written saying he thought I had talent, and would be glad to receive further contributions.

The magazine collapsed about a month later, but by then I had conceived and begun to write another half-dozen short stories and some one-act plays. I wrote a long dialogue, set in the Temple at Jerusalem, between Jesus (aged sixteen) and a member of the Sanhedrin, putting my own arguments into Jesus's mouth, and the views of the priests with whom I had talked into the old man's. (I left this lengthy play on a bus shortly after I had finished it and never recovered it.)

I was causing an increasing dissatisfaction among the science masters at school. I spent most of my 'study time' in the library, writing plays and short stories, and most of my physics and maths lectures reading *The Pickwick Papers* under the desk. It is a sign of the patience and amiability of the headmaster that no one called me to account until the yearly exams made it impossible to ignore my complete loss of interest in science. Even then, I was exhorted to mend my ways, and told that I could stay on conditionally. I explained that I wanted to be a writer. They sympathetically paid me two months' wages and sacked me.

It would be untrue if I gave the impression that my term as a laboratory assistant was a period of peace and relaxation. I found too much leisure more of a nuisance than too little, and suffered agonies of boredom. I had a standing feud with one of the masters, who was adept at inflicting petty indignities and irritated me intensely. I frequently took days off, alleging illness, and spent them cycling out to Warwick or Matlock or Nottingham to work off my surplus energies. The periods of depression came more frequently and lasted longer. I had begun to keep a journal, inspired by some BBC programme about Marie Bashkirtseff. Now I filled page after page every evening with expressions of my boredom and frustration, analyses of the books I had read (I had begun to read Ibsen, Pirandello and Joyce; I hated *Ulysses*) and diatribes against the people I disliked. Once, when an English master had been scathing about an essay I had written denouncing the concept of Shakespearian tragedy, I covered twenty pages of the journal before my indignation had subsided enough to allow me to sleep. I wrote the journal with the idea of ultimate publication, as I had no doubt that every word I had ever written would one day be of interest to students. I filled ten large-sized notebooks in just over a year, and then one day destroyed them all in a fit of disgust. I also had innumerable short stories and plays rejected by publishers, and finally stopped sending them out, finding that the remote possibility that they might be accepted scarcely justified the depression which I underwent each time they were returned. The underlying feeling of futility was still my major problem. My one-act plays were comedies, and most of the short stories owed their style to *The*

Pickwick Papers, and I disliked myself for writing such stuff. Occasional attempts to write like Poe made me feel worse. I wrote with a sense of obsession, hating the medium. I also knew most of T. S. Eliot's poetry by heart now, but it had no notable influence on my style.

The worst insight came during the long Easter holiday of 1948. I had been reading far too much — out of boredom — and spent a whole day reading Janko Lavrin's little book on Russian literature. It is not very cheerful reading, with its descriptions of the stories of Chekhov, Saltykov's *Golovlyov Family*, Goncharov's *Oblomov*. I went into the kitchen to switch on the stove to make tea, and had a blackout. It was a strange sensation. I stood there, fully conscious, clutching the stove to keep upright, and yet conscious of nothing but blackness. There was an electric sensation in my brain, so that I could readily have believed that I had been given an electric shock. It was as if something were flowing through me, and I had an insight of what lay on the other side of consciousness. It looked like an eternity of pain. When my vision cleared, I switched on the kettle and went into the other room. I could not be certain what I had seen, but I was afraid of it. It seemed as if I were the bed of a river, and the current was all pain. I thought I had seen the final truth *that life does not lead to anything*; it is *an escape from something*, and the 'something' is a horror that lies on the other side of consciousness. I could understand what Kurtz had seen in *Heart of Darkness*. All the metaphysical doubts of years seemed to gather to a point, in one realization: What *use* is such truth? Later in the day, I went out cycling; there seemed to be a supreme irony in every manifestation of life that I saw. Eliot's lines from 'The Waste Land' ran in my head:

> On Margate sands.
> I can connect
> Nothing with nothing.
> The broken fingernails of dirty hands...

Later, I wrote about it in my journal, with a sense that the futility had now come its full circle; for until then, writing in my journal had been the one action that did not seem futile; now I was recording my certainty of the futility of *everything*. And yet I recorded it with a compulsive sense that everything should be told.

I think I recognized how far the source of these periods of exhaustion was physical. It seemed a further reason for nihilistic unbelief. All things depended upon mere physical energy. Therefore, there was no will. I had seen the word 'nihilism' somewhere, and asked the English master at school what it meant. 'Belief in nothing,' he told me, and at once I thought I had found a name for my own state of mind. It was not just *lack* of belief in *anything* — it was active *belief in Nothing*. I cannot now understand the significance that that word 'Nothing' carried for me then. I remember, though, how I discovered the *Tao Te Ching* in a compilation called *The Bible of the World*, and read:

> There is a thing inherent and natural,
> Which existed before heaven and earth.
> Motionless and fathomless,
> It stands alone and never changes;
> It pervades everywhere and never becomes exhausted.
> It may be regarded as the Mother of the Universe
> I do not know its name.
> If I am forced to give it a name,
> I call it Tao, and I name it Supreme.
> Supreme means going on;
> Going on means going far;
> Going far means returning.

Therefore Tao is supreme; heaven is supreme; earth is supreme; and man is also supreme. There are in the universe four things supreme, and man is one of them.

I was certain that 'Tao' was my positive principle of Nothingness. The line 'Going far means returning' I took to mean a recognition that all thought chases its own tail: *vanitas vanitatum*. As to the last section, with its 'Man is supreme', my already Swiftian views on the stupidity and futility of human beings led me to decide that 'Man' was a mistranslation for 'I'; that, in fact, Lao-tse was merely expressing his inability to escape complete solipsism. I could not (and still do not) accept the view that Taoism is a humanism.

My solipsism I had arrived at by reading of Berkeley and Hume in some textbook of philosophy. I remember explaining to a group of friends in the playground at school why a bar of chocolate existed only in their own minds. Berkeley, added to Einstein and Eliot's 'Hollow Men', made a vertiginous mixture.

Then, quite suddenly, my 'nihilism' received a check. A day came when I seriously contemplated suicide. It was during the long, hot summer of 1947, when I was working as a laboratory assistant. I arrived home one evening in a state of nervous exhaustion, and tried to 'write away' my tension in my journal. I found writing simply an aid to reflection, a crutch for my thoughts. And after about an hour of writing, I found my resistance slowly returning. I thought clearly: This must cease immediately; *I will not go on living like this*. I was all too familiar with these revivals of strength that was sucked away again the next day. Then I saw the answer: Kill myself.

It cheered me immensely. I cycled to my evening classes with a feeling of having at last learned to master my destiny. I arrived late, and listened to the professor's sarcasms without interest. It was our evening for analytical chemistry practice. A glass tray contained a mixture of powders which we had to separate. I took some in my watch glass, sniffed it, tested it in a bunsen flame, and then went into the other room to the reagent shelves. Glass bottles contained cobalt chloride, silver nitrate, potassium iodide and various acids. In the middle there was a bottle of hydrocyanic acid. As I took it down, my mind made a leap, and for an instant I was living in the future, with a burning in my throat and in the pit of my stomach. In that moment, I was suddenly supremely aware that what I wanted was not less life, but more. The sensation of drinking the acid was so clear that it was almost as if it had actually taken place. I stood there for a second with the bottle in my hand, but the experience was so vivid that it seemed to last for hours. Then, as someone stood beside me, I put it back, vaguely, as if I had taken it by mistake, and reached down for the methyl red. In one second, I had seen something that I have striven to see all my life since.

My insight that evening did not last for long, perhaps because I was too anxious to cling to it. I remember the feeling of having been suddenly awakened to the possibilities of my own will power, and the dreamlike quality of the rest of the evening. And when I got home, I did not try to write about it. For the first time, I had a sense of something too real to write about. Later, when I came to analyse the experience in my journal, I recognized it as one of many such experiences which I had had, differing only in degree. I did not discover Hermann Hesse until six years later; I am certain that if I had, *Steppenwolf* would have become the bible of my teens. Hesse recognizes these fluctuations of insight as being the very stuff of the artist's life. At any time in my adolescence, asked what is the final goal of life, I would have replied without hesitation: Insight. Later deliberations have made me less certain.

My year as a civil servant was the dreariest I had yet known. In my journal, I wrote that the chief qualification for a tax collector is an ability to simulate work. I hated pretending to file Schedule A forms that did not need filing. I envied Shaw when I read in Hesketh Pearson's biography that he had been so efficient as an office boy that his employers had refused to accept his resignation. I was frankly incompetent and outspoken about my dislike of the job. I took half a dozen books to the office every day and read them when I had finished filing. In slack periods I slipped out to the local library and stayed there for hours at a time. I was an appallingly bad office boy. The head of the office was a pleasant, middle-aged Londoner; when he had nothing to do he asked me into his office, and 'talked philosophy' — which meant that he told me long, rambling stories about his life to illustrate his own incorrigibly optimistic point of view. Whenever I had to be reprimanded for some oversight or piece of incompetence — which was pretty frequently — he delegated the job to his second-in-command (a good-tempered Scot, who also took a lenient view of my inefficiency). After six months in the Inland Revenue office, I took the examination for establishment in the Civil Service. I can still remember my despair when I received the letter congratulating me on having passed. I celebrated my establishment by writing a long story about the end of the world; I produced it in a single eight-hour sitting one Saturday afternoon. No one ever liked the story, and I destroyed it later. It was distinctly indebted to Wells's *The Star*.

The only occurrence of importance in my year as a civil servant was my definite abandonment of Dickens as a master of style. One day, in a state of boredom and disgust, I began a story in the 'stream of consciousness' style and found that it expressed my emotions so well that from then on I experimented with it continually.

I had always detested the idea of National Service, but my period in the RAF came as a relief. The first eight weeks of square-bashing were so hectic that I had no time to think, and my mental faculties enjoyed the vacation. This was followed by a tedious month spent in a Birmingham training camp, where I had little to do except learn to be a Clerk, General Duties. I had not chosen it myself — the clerking job — and I resented it. Finally, I was posted to a station near Nottingham, and given a little office all to myself, where I was as bored as I had been in the tax office. One day, in a state of wild irritation, I was thoroughly rude to the adjutant, who, instead of sending for the guard, asked me sympathetically why I disliked office work so much. He hoped to get me transferred to some medical unit where I might exercise my incompetence among malingerers who were hoping to escape parades. He had been unlucky in having had a series of inefficient clerks whose oversights had brought unending complaints from G.H.Q., and hoped to exchange me for better or worse. Somehow, he overshot his mark, and a month later I found myself on my way home with my discharge papers. The whole story is unprintable. I left the RAF with a delighted recognition that one's salvation can lie in proceeding to extremes of indiscretion and ignoring the possible consequences. It was the first time I had had a chance of putting Mr Polly's advice into practice, and it had worked.

The sheer joy of walking out of the RAF gave me a great sense of emotional release. I determined that I would never go back into an office. I sent in my resignation to the Civil Service, and received a long letter pointing out the gravity of what I was doing, and asking me to reconsider it. I stayed at home for a month until my discharge pay ran out, and then left home with a haversack and hitchhiked north. I had intended to find work, but found myself so reluctant to begin that I delayed until the last of my money was spent. Then I hitchhiked home again. In my fortnight's wanderings I had approached a dozen or so theatres with the idea of training to act in repertory. Luckily, no one had any time for me. At home I worked for a fortnight on a building site, and then set out again, this time travelling southward. I wanted to spend a night at Stonehenge — for no particular reason — and then head for Southampton, where I hoped I might be able to get a boat to India. Two RAF policemen saw me emerging from a haystack wearing a grubby RAF uniform (without shoulder flashes) and arrested me. I explained that I was not a deserter, but I had no discharge papers and they didn't believe me. I was sent home again.

I took a number of jobs in quick succession. I worked on a fairground, selling tickets for a gambling machine. I met a girl with whom I carried on an affair for the rest of the year. It was my first sexual experience, and it contributed to the tremendously optimistic state of mind that I experienced all that year. I took a building job that involved wheeling a thousand barrow loads of concrete a day up an inclined plank and along a trench to a half-finished building. After a week I handed in my notice and took a job in some government scheme for training farm labourers. For the rest of that summer, I worked on various farms in Leicestershire, learning to milk cows — electrically and by hand — make hay, shovel cow dung into barrows, harness and unharness horses, and dislike the English countryside intensely. Luckily, my dislike did not survive my period as a farm hand.

I had ceased to read Eliot; I even gave away all his works, alleging that he was 'morbid' and 'anti-life'. Instead, I carried Synge around with me, and read Herrick, Rabelais, Boccaccio, Blake — and, of course, Shaw. I preferred Joyce's Buck Mulligan to Stephen Dedalus. My interest in comparative religion also developed, and I read Buddhist and Hindu texts for the first time. My first reading of the *Bhagavad-Gita* was so important to me that I had my copy bound in leather and carried it around with me wherever I went. The idea of entering a monastery also became increasingly attractive. Not necessarily a Christian monastery — I did not count myself a Christian, in the sense of believing in redemption by Christ. Rather, the monastery symbolized serenity and time for meditation. Yeats's 'storm-beaten old watch-tower' would have done as well. My most acute problem, I felt, was to discover a means of escaping work, escaping the complications of having to find food and drink and a change of clothes. I started instruction in Catholicism, feeling that to become a Catholic would be the first step toward a monastery. But what I read of the strenuous life in monasteries discouraged me. My final disqualification, of course, was my failure to see any need for Christ. The need for God I could understand, and the need for a religion; I could even sympathize with devotees like Suso or St Francis, who wove fantasies around the cross, the nails and all the other traditional symbols. But ultimately I could not accept the need for redemption by a Saviour. To pin down the idea of salvation to one point in space and time seemed a naïve kind of anthropomorphism, like portraying Lao-tse's Unchanging with a beard and white hair.

The solution seemed simpler. As an adolescent, I had been puzzled and made wretched by a feeling that sudden moods of vision and insight — what Wordsworth calls 'the glory and the freshness of a dream'— could not be retained or recalled at will. The Buddhist and Hindu scriptures prescribed simple disciplines for retaining them. It was a short step from there to deciding that most men lead such dull and second-rate lives because the concept of a spiritual and intellectual discipline is so foreign to them. Even the men who talk about the need for discipline never practise it; at any rate, this was what I felt at the time.

By the time I had been back in civilian life for six months, I had begun to see my personal problems more clearly. Previously, my chief enemy had been boredom. I thought I had found an answer when I left the RAF. Hitchhiking into London from Wendover one day, lines from Rupert Brooke running in my head:

Thank God, that's done! And I'll take the road,
Quit of my youth and you,
The Roman road to Wendover
By Tring and Lilley Hoo,
As a free man may do...

it had suddenly seemed that the answer was to keep on the move: never to stay anywhere long enough to get bored.* I felt that nothing counted except

---

*After writing this, I was interested to find a passage in Nietzsche's *Morgenröte* that expresses precisely the same attitude: 'I will rather emigrate and try to become master of fresh countries and, above all, of myself, changing my abode as often as any danger of slavery threatens me; not avoid adventure and war, and be prepared for death if the worst happens — but no more of this indecent serfdom, this irritation, malice and rebelliousness.'

to achieve the intensity of a visionary, and that the only way to do this was to care more about it than anything else; to be willing to sacrifice everything to the ideal.

It did not work out. Wandering entailed too much 'thought for the morrow'; it made life a perpetual anxiety. In its way, it was as bad as being drained of one's vitality in an office job. I wanted to be allowed to meditate and write; but wandering gave me no time or freedom to meditate, while working at a 'regular job' destroyed the inclination. The alternatives were equally poisonous. By the end of the summer, I had come to realize that the intolerable problem of subsistence was still unsolved. Of only one thing I was certain: it was no use staying at home and hoping. My will had to be constantly stimulated by new challenges.

In September 1950 I decided to go to France. It was not that I wanted to write in a garret on the Left Bank, or seek Murger's *vie de bohème* off the rue du Bac. My desire to write had almost died out, and I felt that intellect was a disease keeping me away from life. I was not sure what I hoped to find in France, but any movement was better than sitting still in Leicester. I set off to hitchhike to Dover, working for a week near Canterbury picking hops, and then for a fortnight near Dover, picking potatoes. During this second job, the farmer allowed me to sleep in an old cottage that he used for storing the potatoes; I slept in an upstairs room, settling myself in the corner of the floor that looked soundest. Most of the floorboards were missing in the rest of the room; I always installed myself before dark, and then refrained from moving in case I fell through into the cellar. At the end of the fortnight, I crossed to France.

Altogether, the two months I spent there confirmed my feeling that a life without security is dreary and demoralizing. In Paris I lived for a time in the 'Akademia' of Raymond Duncan, brother of the dancer Isadora. He was a naïvely egotistic old American who printed his own Whitmanesque poems on a printing press that only had capital letters and issued a weekly newspaper called *New-Paris-York*, written entirely by himself in bad French. His long grey hair was fastened by a band around his forehead and he wore a toga and sandals. He preached a philosophy which he called 'actionalism', which was a blend of Rousseauism and the commonsense practical beliefs of a self-made man who had once been a millionaire. He supported himself — like some mediaeval craftsman — by making things with his hands, and taught his 'disciples' (of whom I was enrolled as one) to do the same. He preached that a poet would be a better poet for being able to mend a lavatory cistern or dig a trench with a pick. For a few weeks I helped him to print his newspaper, and in exchange was given three vegetarian meals a day and a couch to sleep on (I had my own blankets). But he soon found me out — that the three meals a day meant more to me than the lectures which he delivered twice a week to selected audiences. He gave me a stiff dressing down, in which he told me that I was an adventurer and an impostor, and gave me twenty-four hours to find new lodgings. I was not resentful; it was true that my own approach had nothing in common with the diluted Platonism that he preached. When I had first come to the 'Akademia' I had hoped to interest Duncan in my own attitude; but it was useless. He was good-natured and easy-going, but old; too old to be interested in me; too old even to talk to me for more than a few minutes at a time. So, after a while, his hospitality began to weigh on my conscience, and the summary dismissal brought an element of relief.

I left for Strasbourg, where I had a pen friend with whom I had corresponded since I was fourteen. But my luck was no better there. Since I had last seen him, he had joined the Communist Party. In England, three years before, he had struck me as a fool. In three years, his Marxism had become an impregnable armour, and my own religious attitude had developed correspondingly. At first there was some talk of my staying in Strasbourg and working for his father —a rag merchant — but as our discussions became more heated and less friendly, this idea was dropped. Within a fortnight we could barely tolerate one another. One day, after a particularly sharp clash of our views, I went to the British consulate and borrowed enough money to return to England. Late the next day, I was back in Leicester. It was a few weeks before Christmas.

My three months' wandering, considered in retrospect, had given me a pleasant sensation of liberty, but I realized that none of my problems had been solved, and that I would never discover freedom by becoming a tramp. During the previous summer, when I had worked on farms, I had thought of certain poems of Synge, or certain pages in Hemingway — the El Sordo episode, for instance — and had been possessed by an imaginative vision of freedom — a feeling that I could escape the prison of my own personality in the impersonality of other places, in the 'otherness' of the world. It was a romantic vision — it owed something to those last pages of *Ulysses*, where Mrs Bloom suddenly becomes the earth spinning around the sun, and speaks of the 'flowers on her breast' crushed by her lovers. And it was hardly to be realized by crossing to France without money. But at least I had learnt that freedom could be discovered in retrospect, by 'recollecting in tranquillity' the episodes which had seemed so uninspiring at the time — such as reading the *Phaedo* while sitting at the roadside near Vitry-le-François, waiting for a lift. For a few weeks, I felt like a visitor in Leicester, and the place no longer oppressed me.

But not for long. I needed a job, and my father gave me a long lecture about wasting my time on manual labour; in his eyes, my resignation from the Civil Service was the most foolish act of my life. In deference to him, I again took an office job — this time in a large engineering works in Leicester. The pay was miserable, and after a few days, I began to hate the job as I have always hated work. Being in Leicester, working in a regular job, made me feel aimless, and robbed me of my sense of purpose. I have no doubt that I would have drifted back into my affair with the girl I had known previously, but while I was abroad she had thrown me over, and I was disgusted to find how much it hurt. However, I began to flirt with the works nurse, a slim, shy girl, ten years my senior, and I felt pleased at the way in which I appeared to have mastered my emotions.

The job followed the familiar pattern. The first few days there — the days I dreaded most — passed unexpectedly easily. Everything was new, and the office staff were pleasant. Part of my job involved walking around the works — they covered an enormous area — and delivering invoices to various departments. I liked to watch the red-hot metal being pounded by the steam hammer, or see long bars of it being cut into chunks. I especially liked watching it after dusk, when the great doors of the shop stood open, and the red glow made the half-naked men seem beautiful. In the shop where the white-hot metal was poured into moulds, it was necessary to stand near the doors, in case the splashes burnt holes in my clothes. At the time, I was reading a great deal of Blake — I had only discovered him six months before, through reading Joyce Cary's *The Horse's Mouth* — and the atmosphere of the Prophetic Books was well suited to that of the engineering works, for they were also full of talk of molten metal and hammers ringing on iron. I carried a copy of Blake with me all the time, and repeated it to myself as I walked around the works:

For every Space larger than a red Globule of Man's blood
Is visionary, and is created by the Hammer of Los:
And every Space smaller than a Globule of Man's blood opens
Into Eternity of which this vegetable Earth is but a shadow.

It snowed a lot that December. Some evenings, walking around the works, picking my way over girders covered with powdered snow, moving towards the white glow that came from the welding shops, the world would suddenly seem altogether good, no longer alien, and my feeling of self-contempt would vanish.

All the same, I began to hate the job. As soon as I grew used to it, I began to work automatically. I fought hard against this process. I would spend the evening reading poetry, or writing, and would determine that with sufficient mental effort I could stop myself from growing bored and indifferent at work the next day. But the moment I stepped through the office door in the morning, the familiar smell and appearance would switch on the automatic pilot which controlled my actions. The longer I stayed in the job the more impossible it became. Moments of insight became less frequent than ever. Repetition makes one into a machine, and all responses become automatic. But the important part of man — the creative part — is the part that is spontaneous. To escape the feeling of being a machine — to try to jar my being out of its automatic responses — I tried all kinds of exercise: getting up an hour earlier in the morning, and going for long runs in running shorts and tennis shoes; sleeping on the floor rather than in bed; sitting up in my bedroom half the night, cross-legged, trying to concentrate until I had broken the feeling of being merely another 'social animal'; staying out until three o'clock in the morning and running all the way home. But the longer I stayed in the job, the harder it became to escape the intolerable sense of being what society wished to make me, merely another human being in the human anthill.

Yet this problem of automatism is the problem of life itself. In childhood we respond freshly to everything, and nothing is automatic, but as we get older, life becomes more complex, and a part of our activities has to be handed over to the 'automatic pilot'. At first, new experiences stimulate us; after a while, no experience is new; it is intercepted by the automatic pilot. I am convinced that people die because they cease to want to live; what purpose is there in living when nothing challenges or stimulates us any longer, when everything is done by the automatic pilot? In my early teens, I had a terrible suspicion that wisdom meant becoming old and losing the desire to live; that the only way to live for a long time was to be so foolish that all sorts of trivial issues continued to excite one into old age, as an imbecile is excited by a child's playthings. It was not until I was eighteen, and read the *Bhagavad Gita*, that this suspicion finally loosened its hold on me, and I recognized that the visionary disciplines himself to see the world always as if he had only just seen it for the first time.

At all events, the office job beat me. No amount of discipline could prevent me from feeling abysmally depressed within a minute of entering the office. Even my affair with the nurse did not compensate for it; nor did the novel that I had begun to write, situated in Strasbourg and heavily indebted to Hemingway, nor the play inspired by Granville-Barker's *The*

Secret Life, nor the half-dozen other literary projects I had started work on at this time. I stuck the job until shortly after Christmas and then gave in my notice. I visited the Leicester Corporation offices and got myself another navvying job, which involved travelling miles to work every morning, and then working knee-deep in mud, digging trenches. I had hoped the hardship would stimulate me, but within a day or two I disliked navvying as much as I had disliked the office. It was free time that I wanted. One day I suddenly conceived the idea of asking the Leicester Corporation whether they would object if I worked for only three days a week. It seemed a brilliant idea to me; it would have meant foregoing pocket money, but the amount of free time I should create for myself would more than compensate. At first, the Corporation agreed; then they changed their minds, pointing out that the other men would object. In fury and disgust, I gave the job up and took another in a chemical factory.

I had got into the habit of reciting poetry as I worked. I liked the poetry of Synge, and that poem of Gogarty's that begins:

I will live in Ringsend
With a red-headed whore....

It expressed my new anti-intellectual attitude. I liked also to repeat the war poems of Wilfred Owen, especially 'Exposure' and 'Futility'. The active physical torment in the poems was a relief to my feeling of being stifled in trivialities. For the same reason, I looked at the painting of Van Gogh and read all I could find on his life, and read Nijinsky's *Diary* continually. The concept of the Outsider first began to form in my mind, and I started to use the word in my journals. I had to concentrate on the idea of torment and horror to obtain release from my sense of futility and pettiness.

But soon fresh complications were to alter my life completely. It now becomes impossible to tell the story fully, for it ceases to be my story alone, and becomes that of myself and my wife — I married in the June of that year. My marriage to the nurse — brought no answer to the problems; in fact, only intensified them, since I was now forced to support a wife — and later a son — as well as myself. There would be no point in telling of this marriage in detail. For eighteen months I worked in factories in London, and we moved from home to home with dismal regularity. The new feeling of security, of having a wife and a home, stimulated me to write, and I spent all my free time writing a novel about two Outsiders, one based on Nietzsche, and the other on Jack the Ripper. At the end of eighteen months, we separated 'temporarily' while I looked for another home for us; but the separation lengthened, while I spent more time writing my novel and a play than looking for rooms. I was working at this time as a porter in a hospital in Fulham. Finally, I got sick of the portering job — which involved, mostly, wheeling live patients to the wards and dead ones to the mortuary — and went to Paris again. But the problem of working for a living was not solved until the following year, when I had returned to London. In a few months I went through a series of jobs rapidly — a laundry, two office jobs (both firms sacked me), a plastic factory and a Lyons Corner House. Then, one day, the idea came to me that I was earning far more money than I strictly needed to keep alive. I earned £5 or £6 a week. Of this, 30s. was spent in rent, 12 or so on food, and the rest was sent to my wife, or spent on books and bus fares. I reasoned that of these, food is the only absolute necessity. One can buy a tent for 30s., and provide a roof over one's head. And a bicycle can make bus fares unnecessary. The tent idea excited me. It seemed a perfect solution — for summer, at all events. So I gave up my rooms (or rather, my landlady threw me out after a disagreement) and bought a tent. I did not give up work immediately: I was making a great deal of money by working overtime in a plastic factory in Whetstone. But I saved rent by setting up my tent at nights on a golf links opposite the factory. After a while, I realized that to put up a tent and take it down every day was an unnecessary labour. A waterproof sleeping bag would serve as well. So I bought one, together with an eiderdown sleeping bag, an immense army frame rucksack for my belongings, and a bicycle with a carrier on the back. In a few weeks, I had saved enough money to leave work with a certainty of not having to return for a few months provided my expenditure did not exceed £2 a week. I moved my quarters from the golf links to Hampstead Heath, and cycled down to the British Museum every day, to work from nine till five. I was making a determined effort to reduce some of the immense manuscript of my Jack the Ripper novel to publishable form. Mr Angus Wilson, who at that time was an official in the Reading Room, noticed me writing furiously, and offered to read the manuscript when it was completed, and, if he liked it, to submit it to his publisher.

But sleeping out was a nerve-racking business. I did not dare to go onto the Heath until after midnight; there were too many young lovers about. The police patrolled the Heath, but they stuck to the paths and only occasionally flashed a powerful torch around. I sometimes slept till ten (the Heath is a surprisingly quiet place on weekday mornings), and was often wakened by someone's dog sniffing at my face, or voices in the distance. Usually, I had breakfast at a busman's café at the bottom of Haverstock Hill: they did a remarkably cheap slice of bread and dripping and an enormous mug of tea for 2½d. The day in the Museum usually went by too quickly; but the evenings were the difficult time. After eight o'clock all the libraries were closed; there was nowhere where one could spend a few hours in warmth and quiet until midnight. A girl whom I had met in Leicester the previous Christmas was also in London at the time. She kept all my books for me, and sometimes entertained me in the evening; but it was too much to expect her to have to put up with me every evening. Her help and sympathy were invaluable; but all the same, I always felt exhausted and ill at ease as I cycled around London with my sleeping bags rolled up on the back; it was a strange sensation, having nowhere to go, nowhere to retire to at nights, nowhere to spend the evening reading. Besides, the girl's landladies objected if I turned up too often; they left her little notes telling her not to let me use the bathroom, and that I had to be out by ten o'clock.

Occasionally during that summer I ran out of cash. Then I had to take a job for a few weeks: one in Lyons, one in a dairy at Chiswick. I continued writing the book well into the autumn. In early November the weather became so bad that I was finally driven indoors. I took a room at New Cross, and another job in Lyons. At this time I was seeing a great deal of another young writer, Stuart Holroyd, whom I had met the previous year. He talked vaguely of writing a critical book, and advised me to do the same; but I was too busy at the time, trying to finish the first part of my novel (it was to be in three short parts). I had heard a rumour that Angus Wilson intended leaving the Museum, and I wanted to be able to hand him the typewritten manuscript before he left. At Christmas that year I worked at the post office in St-Martin's-le-Grand, sorting Christmas mail; by doing overtime, I made enough money to buy a secondhand typewriter. Over Christmas, alone in London, I finally completed the first part of the novel, and immediately settled down to typing it. A week later, lack of money made it necessary to find another job. There were long queues in the labour exchange, and only a few unskilled labouring jobs available. I accepted the first one they offered me — as I usually do — and the next day started to work in a laundry in Deptford. The job was so peculiarly detestable, and the conditions so appalling, that I overcame my usual laziness and cycled into London every day, trying to find evening work in a coffee bar. The laundry became completely intolerable to me when one day my journal was stolen out of my pocket. It had contained the entries of over a year past, and its loss enraged me. But the day after this happened, I found a job in a newly opened coffee bar in the Haymarket; I was the washer-up.

Compared with the laundry, conditions there were delightful. The kitchen was new and shiny and chromium-plated, and the food was unlimited and very good. I worked every evening from five-thirty till midnight, and had the day free to write. I finished typing the first part of the novel in a burst of energy, and handed it to Angus Wilson on the day he left the Museum. And then, suddenly, I felt a little lost. For many years, the novel had occupied my thoughts. Suddenly, it had gone out of my hands. If Angus found it bad, I would begin all over again. In the meantime, there was no point in going on with it. I began to wonder what I should do to occupy my days in the Reading Room.

It was at this point that Stuart Holroyd showed me the opening chapters of his *Emergence from Chaos*. Suddenly, I made a decision. I too would write a critical book — a credo. I would dash it off quickly, and then get back to the novel. In half an hour, one morning, I sketched out the plan of a book, to be called *The Outsider in Literature*. It would be a study in various types of 'obsessed men'. I immediately jotted down a list of the type of men who would interest me. Some immediately came to mind: Van Gogh, T. E. Lawrence, George Fox, Boehme, Joyce, Nijinsky. (I had written a long essay on Nijinsky several years before, which I had sent to Madame Nijinsky. She had replied kindly to a preliminary letter of mine, but never acknowledged the essay.) There were obviously many different types of Outsider. Some were men of action, some were the very reverse. So there would be a chapter on Oblomov and Hamlet and Hesse's Steppenwolf and the Great Gatsby. These would be classified together as 'weak Outsiders'. Then there would be a chapter on Goethe's Faust, Mann's Doctor Faustus, and Dostoevsky's Ivan Karamazov, from whom Mann drew in his own scene between Leverkühn and the Devil. A great deal of the book would also be devoted to religious figures: Boehme, Law, Fox, Newman, Luther, Wycliffe — all rebels against their time. The Outsider shades off one way into the weakling — the Hamlet — and the other way into the Rebel. Then there were the French Existentialists, and Heidegger and Jaspers — and of course, Kierkegaard — and these pointed to a tie-up with Nietzsche, while the study of pessimism would link up with Schopenhauer and Spengler. As I jotted down names, and pushed them around to try to find some logical order for them all, I realized with growing despair that there was no order that would embrace *all of them* — or at least, if there were, the book would be so vast that it would involve ten years' work. There was no point in being overwhelmed by it and trying to see it as a whole before I began it. I had been doing that with the novel for years, and here, with over half a million words written, had only a hundred pages in their final form. I decided to begin the book that afternoon in the Museum. On my way down there, I remembered a volume which I had read about years before in the Everyman edition of

Le Feu — Barbusse's *L'Enfer*. That would make a perfect starting point: the man who looks at life through a hole in his wall. In the Museum, I got the book and settled down to read it. In two hours I had finished it. It was within half an hour of closing time. Hastily, I looked up a striking sentence which I had noticed and copied it on to a sheet of paper: 'In the air, on top of a tram, a girl is sitting….' I copied on hastily until the bell rang for closing time. The next morning, I wrote on to the end of my analysis of Barbusse, and without hesitation, plunged into H. G. Wells's *Mind at the End of Its Tether* (of which I had had a copy since I was sixteen).

Once I actually started, I wrote quickly. I had written as far as the Lawrence chapter before I stopped for breath. I then reread my manuscript, and decided that it began too abruptly and proceeded too fast. I wrote an introduction, which began by quoting T. E. Hulme's prophecy of the decay of humanism, and stating that this book was to be an attack on humanism and an attempt to base the religious attitude on reasonable foundations. Hulme had promised to write a defence of his religious attitude, but had been killed in the war. I stated my intention of attempting to write the book that Hulme had never written; my method would not be philosophical, but psychological; not an attempt to prove the existence of God, but a search for meaning in human life.

At about this time I was offered a daytime job that involved no more than sitting at a desk and answering a telephone if it rang. It seldom rang more than twice a day; and I sat there for four hours a day, writing furiously and being paid 3s. an hour for writing. In this early stage, the book was called *The Pain Threshold*. One day, I installed my typewriter in the office and typed the three chapters that I had written. When I had typed the Introduction (which did not appear in the published version) I sent it to a publisher. To my delight, he replied within twenty-four hours, expressing interest. I sent him the three chapters as soon as they were typed. This time, he took longer but finally wrote to say that he would definitely publish the book. I was delighted, but it was no time to give way to the pleasure of having been 'accepted'. I suspected that I could not finish the book as well as I had begun it, and that the publisher would change his mind when he read it as a whole. Now I had started typing the book, I became too lazy to write it first and type later, and began to use a typewriter all the time. Three months later it was finished. The advance which I received enabled me, for the first time in my life, to give up work and do nothing but write.

By this time Angus Wilson had returned the novel, with the comment: 'I like it. Go on and finish it.' But I found creative work appallingly difficult after the easy writing of the critical book. The writing of *The Pain Threshold* had not made the novel any easier; every section seemed to need a dozen rewrites. I struggled on slowly, and managed to finish it in six months. But having finished it, I could hardly bear to reread it, and decided to start from the beginning again. *The Pain Threshold* was due out in a month, and I had tentatively suggested calling it *The Outsider* (tentatively, because I knew of two other books with the same title — Camus's and Richard Wright's). Reading the proofs of *The Outsider* had made me terribly dissatisfied with it: I hadn't managed to put in half as many things as I wanted, or to pursue half as many lines of thought. It needed, I realized, the same care and patience as the novel. Besides, I had begun to read Arnold Toynbee's *Study of History* and a great deal more of Whitehead, and I saw that the argument could be developed much further.

The success of the book winded me, and made me more certain than ever that it should have been twice as long and far more carefully planned. I had believed passionately in the book, and had never doubted its importance as I wrote it. But it was intended as essentially a preliminary step towards a far bigger statement. After the delight of the first good reviews, and the knowledge that new impressions were being called for, I became aware of what had happened to the book itself. I was congratulated by critics on having started a craze, on inventing a new parlour game to replace Nancy Mitford's 'U and Non-U,' called 'Outsider or Insider?' The whirl and publicity went on for months, and soon I realized that I had become a stranger to my own book. The people in it, who for years had seemed to live with me, had suddenly become alien; a painting by Van Gogh no longer moved me; Nijinsky's *Diary* stayed on my shelf unread. It was interesting to hear people discussing me — as when a child falls into a doze at a party, and hears the grownups talking about him — but only because it was like seeing myself in distorting mirrors. Besides, after a while, people began attacking the book, and declaring that it had all been a mistake, and that I was not a 'promising young writer' after all.

No doubt they were right. Although I have always used writing as a medium to clarify my thoughts, I have never thought of myself as primarily a writer. Writing is an instrument of my main purpose, and that purpose is my own business and no one else's. I am convinced, like my 'Outsider,' that all men who have ever lived have been failures. As a child, I thought of every adult I met: *I* shan't waste life like that. This problem is the impetus that drives my living, and my writing is merely one discipline for solving it. The answer seems to lie in achieving a certain state of mind called 'vision'; and above all other things I prefer to study the evidence that men have left of their moments of vision: Nietzsche's glimpse on the hilltop, Van Gogh's Green Cornfield, Pascal's *Memorial*, Boehme's 'pewter dish', the moment of great insight in which the purpose of all life is seen. Ultimately, this is the only thing worth achieving. Yeats called life 'a vast preparation for something that never happens', and yet one minute of such vision could turn all preparation into achievement.

These visions and the men who saw them occupy all my time and attention. To facilitate my own study of them, I wrote about them more or less consecutively in *The Outsider* (as I have been writing about them haphazardly for years in my journals). For myself, *The Outsider* and the present book are a sort of extension of my journals, a part of my working notes. I am grateful that their publication has made me enough money to allow me to continue to work on for a few more years; but their publication was not an essential part of my purpose. I am not necessarily a writer. The moment writing ceases to be a convenient discipline for subduing my stupidity and laziness, I shall give it up and turn to some more practical form. I wish this to be understood because I find that being regarded as a 'promising young writer', or attacked as a charlatan or a woolly-minded freak, tends to destroy my certainty of purpose. The prospect of spending my life trying to make myself worthy of a few pages in *The Cambridge History of English Literature* seems to me a particularly dreary kind of treadmill. I see now that I must try to escape the subtle falsifications of my aims that the success of *The Outsider* caused. I must retrace my steps to the period before it was published, and begin working again from there. In those days, I had a plan for drafting a vast critical credo that should define the area of my interest, to be followed by a series of novels and plays in which the Outsider idea would be explored in all its existentialist implications. But the idea of writing books merely because I am now known as a 'writer' is repellent to me. Temperamentally, my sympathy is still with Novalis and Jean Paul and other deniers of the daylight, and to know that anything is expected and demanded of me is enough to make me detest it.

PERSONAL NOTES
ON MASLOW

From *New Pathways in Psychology, 1972*

Some time in 1963, I received a letter from an American professor of psychology, Abraham H. Maslow, enclosing some of his papers. He said he had read my book *The Stature of Man*,* and liked my idea that much of the gloom and defeat of twentieth-century literature is due to what I called 'the fallacy of insignificance'. Maslow said this resembled an idea of his own, which he called 'the Jonah complex'. One day, he had asked his students: 'Which of you expects to achieve greatness in your chosen field?' The class looked at him blankly. After a long silence, Maslow said: 'If not you — who then?' And they began to see his point. This is the fallacy of insignificance, the certainty that you are unlucky and unimportant, the Jonah complex.

The papers he enclosed looked highly technical; their titles contained words like 'metamotivation', 'eupsychian', 'synergy'. I glanced at them and pushed them aside. Some months later I came across them again: this time, my eye was caught by the term 'peak experience' in one of the titles, and I started to read. It was immediately clear that I'd stumbled upon something important. Maslow explained that, some time in the late thirties, he had been struck by the thought that modern psychology is based on the study of sick people. But since there are more healthy people around than sick people, how can this psychology give a fair idea of the workings of the human mind? It struck him that it might be worthwhile to devote some time to the study of *healthy* people.

'When I started to explore the psychology of health, I picked out the finest, healthiest people, the best specimens of mankind I could find, and

*In England entitled *The Age of Defeat* (1959).

54

studied them to see what they were like. They were very different, in some ways startlingly different from the average....'

'I learned many lessons from these people. But one in particular is our concern now. I found that these individuals tended to report having had something like mystic experiences, moments of great awe, moments of the most intense happiness, or even rapture, ecstasy or bliss....'

'These moments were of pure, positive happiness, when all doubts, all fears, all inhibitions, all tensions, all weaknesses, were left behind. Now self-consciousness was lost. All separateness and distance from the world disappeared as they felt one with the world, fused with it, really belonging to it, instead of being outside, looking in. (One subject said, for instance, "I felt like a member of a family, not like an orphan.")'

'Perhaps most important of all, however, was the report in these experiences of the feeling that they had really seen the ultimate truth, the essence of things, the secret of life, as if veils had been pulled aside. Alan Watts has described this feeling as "This is it!" as if you had finally got there, as if ordinary life was a striving and a straining to get some place and this was the arrival, this was Being There!... Everyone knows how it feels to want something and not know what. These mystic experiences feel like the ultimate satisfaction of vague, unsatisfied yearnings....'

'But here I had already learned something new. The little that I had ever read about mystic experiences tied them in with religion, with visions of the supernatural. And, like most scientists, I had sniffed at them in disbelief and considered it all nonsense, maybe hallucinations, maybe hysteria — almost surely pathological.'

'But the people telling me...about these experiences were not such people — they were the healthiest people!... And I may add that it taught me something about the limitations of the small...orthodox scientist who won't recognize as knowledge, or as reality, any information that doesn't fit into the already existent science.'*

These experiences are not 'religious' in the ordinary sense. They are *natural*, and can be studied naturally. They are not 'ineffable' in the sense of incommunicable by language. Maslow also came to believe that they are far commoner than one might expect, that many people tend to suppress them, to ignore them, and certain people seem actually afraid of them, as if they were somehow feminine, illogical, dangerous. 'One sees such attitudes

---

*I have used an extract from a paper, 'Lessons from the Peak Experience', read in 1961 at the Western Behavioural Sciences Institute, La Jolla, California. It has not yet been printed in book form.

more often in engineers, in mathematicians, in analytic philosophers, in book-keepers and accountants, and generally in obsessional people.'

The peak experience tends to be a kind of bubbling-over of sheer delight, a moment of pure happiness. 'For instance, a young mother scurrying around her kitchen and getting breakfast for her husband and young children. The sun was streaming in, the children, clean and nicely dressed, were chattering as they ate. The husband was casually playing with the children: but as she looked at them she was suddenly so overwhelmed with their beauty and her great love for them, and her feeling of good fortune, that she went into a peak experience....

'A young man working his way through medical school by drumming in a jazz band reported many years later, that in all his drumming he had three peaks when he suddenly felt like a great drummer and his performance was perfect.'

'A hostess after a dinner party where everything had gone perfectly and it had been a fine evening, said goodbye to her last guest, sat down in a chair, looked around at the mess, and went into a peak of great happiness and exhilaration.'

Maslow described another typical peak experience to me later, when I met him at his home in Waltham, Mass. A marine had been stationed in the Pacific and had not seen a woman for a couple of years. When he came back to the base camp, he saw a nurse, and it suddenly struck him with a kind of shock that women are different to men. The marine had told Maslow: 'We take them for granted, as if they were another kind of man. But they're quite different, with their soft curves and gentle natures....' He was suddenly flooded with the peak experience.

Observe that in most peak experiences (Maslow abbreviates it to P.E.'s, and I shall follow him), the person becomes suddenly aware of something that he had known about previously, but been inclined to take for granted, to discount. And this matter had always been one of my own central preoccupations. My *Religion and the Rebel* (1957) had been largely a study in the experiences of mystics, and in its autobiographical preface, I had written about a boring office job: 'As soon as I grew used to it, I began to work automatically. I fought hard against this process. I would spend the evening reading poetry, or writing, and would determine that, with sufficient mental effort, I could stop myself from growing bored and indifferent at work the next day. But the moment I stepped through the office door in the morning, the familiar smell and appearance would switch on the automatic pilot which controlled my actions....' I was clearly aware that the problem was *automatism*. And in a paper I later wrote for a symposium of existential psychology,* I elaborated this theory of the automatic pilot, speaking of it as 'the robot'. I wrote: 'I am writing this on an electric typewriter.' When I learned to type, I had to do it painfully and with much nervous wear and tear. But at a certain stage, a miracle occurred, and this complicated operation was 'learned' by a useful robot whom I conceal in my subconscious mind. Now I only have to think about what I want to say: my robot secretary does the typing. He is really very useful. He also drives the car for me, speaks French (not very well), and occasionally gives lectures in American universities.

'He has one enormous disadvantage. If I discover a new symphony that moves me deeply, or a poem or a painting, this bloody robot promptly insists on getting in on the act. And when I listen to the symphony for the third time, *he* begins to anticipate every note. He begins to listen to it automatically, and I lose all the pleasure. He is most annoying when I am tired, because then he tends to take over most of my functions without even asking me. I have even caught him making love to my wife.'

'My dog doesn't have this trouble. Admittedly, he can't learn languages or how to type, but if I take him for a walk on the cliffs, he obviously experiences every time just as if it is the first. I can tell this by the ecstatic way he bounds about. Descartes was all wrong about animals. It isn't the animals who are robots; it's us.'

Heaven lies about us in our infancy, as Wordsworth pointed out, because the robot hasn't yet taken over. So a child experiences delightful things as more delightful, and horrid things as more horrid. Time goes slower, and mechanical tasks drag, because there is no robot to take over. When I asked my daughter if she meant to be a writer when she grew up, she said with horror that she got fed up before she'd written half a page of school-work, and couldn't even imagine the tedium of writing a whole book.

The robot is necessary. Without him, the wear and tear of everyday life would exhaust us within minutes. But he also acts as a filter that cuts out the freshness, the newness, of everyday life. If we are to remain psychologically healthy, we must have streams of 'newness' flowing into the mind — what J. B. Priestley calls 'delight' or 'magic'. In developing the robot, we have solved one enormous problem — and created another. But there is, after all, no reason why we should not solve that too: modify the robot until he admits the necessary amount of 'newness', while still taking over the menial tasks.

Now I was much struck by Maslow's comment on the possibility of creating peak experiences at will. Because his feeling was that it cannot be done.

*'Existential Psychology: A Novelist's Approach', in *Challenges of Humanistic Psychology* edited by J. F. T. Bugental (McGraw Hill, 1967).

'No! Or almost entirely no! In general, we are "Surprised by Joy", to use the title of C. S. Lewis's book on just this question. Peaks come unexpectedly.... You can't count on them. And hunting them is like hunting happiness. It's best not done directly. It comes as a by-product, an epiphenomenon, for instance, of doing a fine job at a worthy task you can identify with.'

It seemed to me that this is only partly true. I will try to explain this briefly.

Novelists have to be psychologists. I think of myself as belonging to the school known as the phenomenological movement. The philosopher Edmund Husserl noted that all psychological acts are 'intentional'. Note what happens when you are about to tickle a child. The child begins to squirm and laugh before your hands have actually reached him. On the other hand, why doesn't it tickle when you tickle yourself? Obviously, because you know it's you. The tickling is not something *physical* that happens when your hands encounter flesh and make tickling motions. It seems to be 99 per cent psychological. When the child screams with laughter, *he is tickling himself*, just as he might frighten himself by imagining ghosts in the dark. The paradoxical truth is that when someone tickles you, you tickle yourself. And when you tickle yourself, you don't tickle yourself, which is why it doesn't tickle.

Being tickled is a 'mental act', an 'intention'. So are all perceptions. I look at something, as I might fire a gun at it. If I glance at my watch while I am in conversation, I see the time, yet I don't *notice* what time it is. As well as merely 'seeing' I have to make a mental act of *grasping*.

Now the world is full of all kinds of things that I cannot afford to 'grasp' or notice. If I am absorbed in a book, I 'grasp' its content; my mind explores it as though my thoughts were fine, thin tentacles reaching every corner of the book. But when I put the book back on the shelf, it is standing among dozens of other books, which I have also explored at some time in the past. As I look at all these books, I cannot simultaneously grasp all of them. From being intimate friends, they have become mere nodding acquaintances. Perhaps one or two, of which I am very fond, mean more to me than the others. But of necessity, it has to be very few.

Consider Maslow's young mother getting the breakfast. She loves her husband and children, but all the same, she is directing her 'beam of interest' at making the coffee, buttering the toast, watching the eggs in the frying pan. She is treating her husband and children as if they were a row of books on a shelf. Still, her energies are high; she is looking forward to an interesting day. Then something triggers a new level of response. Perhaps it is the beam of sunlight streaming through the window, which seems to shake her arm and say: 'Look isn't it all wonderful?' She suddenly looks *at* her husband and children as she would look at the clock to find out the time. She becomes self-conscious of the situation, using her beam of interest to 'scan' it, instead of to watch the coffee. And having put twice as much energy into her 'scanning', she experiences 'newness'.

The mental act of looking at her family, and thinking: 'I am lucky', is like an athlete gathering himself for a long jump, concentrating his energies.

What happens if somebody returns a book that he borrowed from me a long time ago? I look at the book with a kind of delight, as though it were a returned prodigal: perhaps I open it and read a chapter. Yet if the book had stayed on my shelf for six months I might not even have bothered to glance at it. The return of the book has made me focus my beam of interest, like an athlete gathering for a leap.

When something occupies my full attention, it is very *real* to me. When I have put the book back on the shelf, I have un-real-ized it, to some extent. I have pushed it back to a more abstract level of reality. But I have the power to real-ize it again. Consider the mental act I make when I feel glad to see the book again. I 'reach out' my invisible mental tentacles to it, as I might reach out my hand to a friend I am delighted to see, and I *focus* my beam of interest on it with a kind of intensity — the kind of intentness with which a sapper de-fuses an unexploded bomb.

We do this 'real-izing' and 'un-real-izing' all the time — so automatically that we fail to notice that we are doing it. It is not just 'happening'. Like the athlete gathering himself to leap, it is the deliberate compression of mental muscles.

All this suggests that Maslow is mistaken to believe that peak experiences have to 'come' without being sought. A little phenomenological analysis, like the kind we have conducted above, reveals that the P.E. has a structure that can be duplicated. It is the culmination of a series of mental acts, each of which can be clearly defined.

The first pre-condition is 'energy', because the P.E. is essentially an overflowing of energy. This does not mean ordinary physical energy; Maslow points out that sick people can have P.E's as easily as healthy ones, if the conditions are right. If you say to a child: 'I'll take you to the pantomime tonight if you'll tidy your bedroom', he immediately seethes with a bustling energy. The normally boring act of tidying a room is performed with enthusiasm. And this is because he — figuratively — 'takes a deep breath'. He is so determined that the tidying shall be satisfactory that he is prepared to devote attention to every square inch of the floor. And the 'mental act' that lies behind this is a certain concentration and 'summoning of energy', like calling 'All hands on deck'. If I am asked to do a job that bores me, I summon only a small quantity of energy, and if the job is complicated, I skimp it. If I am determined to do it thoroughly, I place the whole of my interior army and navy 'on call'. It is this state — of vigilance, alertness, *preparedness* — that is the basis of the peak experience.

Healthy people — like Maslow's housewife — are people with a high level of 'preparedness'. This can be expressed in a simple image. My 'surplus energy' is stored in my subconscious mind, in the realm of the robot: this is like money that has been invested in stocks and shares. Nearer the surface of everyday consciousness, there are 'surplus energy tanks', energy which is ready-for-use, like money in my personal account at the bank. When I anticipate some emergency, or some delightful event (like a holiday) which I shall need energy to enjoy to the full, I transfer large quantities of 'ready energy' to these surface tanks, just as I might draw a large sum out of the bank before I go on holiday.

'Peakers' are people with large quantities of energy in the ready-energy tanks. Bored or miserable people are people who keep only small amounts of energy for immediate use.

But it must be borne in mind that both types of people have large amounts of energy available in their 'deep storage tanks' in the realm of the robot. It is merely a matter of transferring it to your 'current account'.

In a paper called 'The Need to Know and the Fear of Knowing', Maslow describes one of his crucial cases.

'Around 1938, a college girl patient presented herself complaining vaguely of insomnia, lack of appetite, disturbed menstruation, sexual frigidity, and a general malaise which soon turned into a complaint of boredom with life and an inability to enjoy anything. Life seemed meaningless to her. Her symptoms closely paralleled those described by Abraham Myerson in his book *When Life Loses Its Zest*.... As she went on talking, she seemed puzzled. She had graduated about a year ago and by a fantastic stroke of luck — this was the depression, remember — she immediately got a job. And what a job! Fifty dollars a week! She was taking care of her whole unemployed family with the money and was the envy of all her friends. But what was the job? She worked as a sub-personnel manager in a chewing-gum factory. And after some hours of talking, it became more and more clear that she felt she was wasting her life. She had been a brilliant student of psychology and was very happy and successful in college, but her family's financial situation made it impossible for her to go on into graduate studies. She was greatly drawn to intellectual work, not altogether consciously at first because she felt she *ought* to feel fortunate with her job and the money it brought her. Half-consciously then she saw a whole lifetime of greyness stretching out ahead of her. I suggested that she might be feeling profoundly frustrated and angry simply because she was not being her own very intelligent self, that she was not using her intelligence and her talent for psychology and that this might be a major reason for her boredom with life and her body's boredom with the normal pleasures of life. Any talent, any capacity, I thought, was also a motivation, a need, an impulse. With this she agreed, and I suggested that she could continue her graduate studies at night after her work. In brief, she was able to arrange this and it worked well. She became more alive, more happy and zestful, and most of her physical symptoms had disappeared at my last contact with her.'

It is significant that Maslow, although trained as a Freudian, did not try to get back into the subject's childhood and find out whether she experienced penis-envy of her brothers or a desire to murder her mother and marry her father. He followed his instinct — his feeling that creativeness and the desire for a *meaningful existence* are as important as any subconscious sexual drives.

Anyone who knows my own work will see why Maslow's approach appealed so much to me — and why mine, apparently, appealed to Maslow. My first book, *The Outsider*, written when I was 23, was about people like Maslow's girl patient—men driven by an obscure creative urge that made them dissatisfied with everyday life, and which in some cases — T. E. Lawrence, for example — caused them to behave in a manner that seemed masochistic. The book sprang from my own obsession with the problem of 'life failure'. Auden wrote:

Put the car away; when life fails
What's the good of going to Wales?

Eliot asks in *The Rock*: 'Where is the life we have lost in living?' And Shaw says of the Ancients in *Back to Methuselah*: 'Even at the moment of death, their life does not fail them.' Maslow's patient was suicidal because she felt she was losing her life in the process of living it. I had asked repeatedly in *The Outsider*: 'Why does life fail?' Maslow was replying, in effect: Because human beings have needs and cravings that go beyond the need for security, sex, territory. He states it clearly in the preface to the Japanese edition of *Eupsychian Management*, asserting that 'human nature has been sold short, that man has a higher nature which is just as "instinctoid" as his lower nature, and that this higher nature includes the need for meaningful work, for responsibility, for creativeness, for being fair and just, for doing what is worthwhile and for preferring to do it well'.

I must outline my own approach to this problem, as I explained it in subsequent correspondence with Maslow. *The Outsider* had developed from my interest in the romantics of the nineteenth century — Goethe, Schiller, Novalis, Wagner, Nietzsche, Van Gogh. What fascinated me was their *world rejection*. It was summed up by Villiers de l'Isle-Adam's hero Axel in the words 'Live? Our servants can do that for us.' Axel asserted that 'real life' is always a disappointment. The heroine, Sarah, has a long speech in which she speaks of all the marvellous places they might visit now they have found the treasure. Axel replies that the cold snows of Norway *sound* marvellous, but when you actually get there, it's just cold and wet. L. H. Myers had made the same point with fine precision in *The Near and the Far*, where the young Prince Jali stares at a splendid sunset over the desert, and reflects that there are two deserts: one that is a glory to the eye, and one that is a weariness to the feet. If you tried rushing towards that sunset, you would only get your shoes full of sand. It seems impossible to grasp 'the promise of the horizon'. And it was this feeling of despair about the near and the far — the feeling that they can never be reconciled — that led to so many early deaths among the romantics: suicide, insanity, tuberculosis. Obermann, in Senancour's novel of that name, says that the rain depresses him, yet when the sun comes out it strikes him as useless. *This* is life-failure.

But man's achievement is to have created a world of the mind, of the intellect and imagination, which is as real in its way as any actual country on the map. Sir Karl Popper, in one of his most important papers, calls it 'the third world'.* The first world is the objective world of things. The second world is my inner subjective world. But, says Popper, there is a third world, *the world of objective contents of thoughts*. If some catastrophe destroyed all the machines and tools on this earth, but not the libraries, a new generation would slowly rebuild civilization. If the libraries are all destroyed too, there could be no re-emergence of civilization, for all our carefully stored knowledge would have gone, and man would have to start regaining it from scratch. Teilhard de Chardin calls this 'third world' the *noösphere* — the world of mind. It includes the works of Newton, Einstein, Beethoven, Tolstoy, Plato; it is the most important part of our human heritage.

A cow inhabits the physical world. It has almost no mind, to speak of. Man also inhabits the physical world, and has to cope with its problems. But he has built civilization because *the physical world is not enough*. Nothing is so boring as to be stuck in the present. Primitive man loved stories for the same reason that young children do. Because they afforded

---

Epistemology without a Knowing Subject (Amsterdam, 1968).

an escape from the present, because they freed his memory and imagination from mere 'reality'. Einstein made the same point: '...one of the strongest motives that lead men to art and science is to escape from everyday life, with its painful crudity and hopeless dreariness.... A finely tempered nature longs to escape from personal life into the world of objective perception and thought; this desire may be compared to the townsman's irresistible longing to escape from his noisy, cramped surroundings into the silence of high mountains....'*

But my central point is this. Man is a very *young* creature: his remotest ancestors only date back two million years. (The shark has remained unchanged for 150,000,000 years.) And although he longs for this 'third world' as his natural home, he only catches brief glimpses of it. For it can only be 'focused' by a kind of mental eye. This morning, as I cleaned my teeth in the bathroom a fragment of Brahms drifted through my head and caused that sudden feeling of inner-warmth. The person labelled 'Colin Wilson' ceased to matter: it was almost as if I had floated out of my body and left him behind, as if the real 'I' had taken up a position somewhere midway between myself and Brahms. In the same way, when I am working well, I seem to lose my identity, 'identifying' instead with the ideas or people I am writing about. But very often, I cannot even begin to focus the 'third world'; the real world distracts me, and keeps my attention fixed on its banal 'actualities' like some idiot on a train who prevents you from reading by talking in a loud voice.

All the same, this 'third world' is a *place*; it is there all the time, like China or the moon; and it ought to be possible for me to go there at any time, leaving behind the boring person who is called by my name. It is fundamentally a world of pure *meaning*. It is true that my small personal world is also a world of meaning; but of trivial, personal meaning, distorted and one-sided, a worm's eye view of meaning.

It is man's evolutionary destiny to become a citizen of the third world, to explore it as he might now explore Switzerland on a holiday.

It is impossible to predict what will happen to human beings when that time comes: for this reason. Meaning stimulates the will, fills one with a desire to reach out to new horizons. When a man in love sees the girl approaching, his heart 'leaps'. When I hear a phrase of music that means something to me, my heart leaps. That 'leap' is vitality from my depths, leaping up to meet the 'meaning'. And the more 'meaning' I perceive, the more vitality rushes up to

*Einstein, *Ideas and Opinions* (London, 1956), p. 227.

meet it. As his access to the world of meaning increases, man's vitality will increase towards the superman level; that much seems clear.

Boredom cripples the will. Meaning stimulates it. The peak experience is a sudden surge of meaning. The question that arises now is: how can I *choose* meaning? If Maslow is correct, I can't. I must be 'surprised' by it. It is a by-product of effort.

At this point, I was able to point out to Maslow a possibility that he had overlooked, a concept I called 'the indifference threshold' or 'St Neot margin'. It is fundamentally a recognition *that crises or difficulties can often produce a sense of meaning when more pleasant stimuli have failed.* Sartre remarks that he had never felt so free as during the war when, as a member of the French Resistance, he was likely to be arrested and shot at any time. It seems a paradox: that danger can make you feel free when peace and serenity fail to arouse any response. It does this by forcing you to concentrate.

I stumbled on this concept in the following manner. In 1954, I was hitchhiking to Peterborough on a hot Saturday afternoon. I felt listless, bored and resentful: I didn't want to go to Peterborough — it was a kind of business trip — and I didn't particularly long to be back in London either. There was hardly any traffic on the road, but eventually I got a lift. Within ten minutes, there was an odd noise in the engine of the lorry. The driver said: 'I'm afraid something's gone wrong — I'll have to drop you off at the next garage.' I was too listless to care. I walked on, and eventually a second lorry stopped for me. Then occurred the absurd coincidence. After ten minutes or so, there was a knocking noise from *his* gearbox. When he said: 'It sounds as if something's wrong', I thought: 'Oh *no*!' and then caught myself thinking it, and thought: 'That's the first definite reaction I've experienced today.' We drove on slowly — he was anxious to get to Peterborough, *and by this time, so was I.* He found that if he dropped speed to just under twenty miles an hour, the knocking noise stopped; as soon as he exceeded it, it started again. We both listened intently for any resumption of the trouble. Finally, as we were passing through a town called St Neots, he said: 'Well, I think if we stay at this speed, we should make it.' And I felt a surge of delight. Then I thought:

'This is absurd. My situation hasn't *improved* since I got into the lorry — in fact, it has got worse, since he is now crawling along. All that has happened is that an inconvenience has been threatened, and then the threat withdrawn. And suddenly, my boredom and indifference have vanished.' I formulated then the notion that there is a borderland or threshold of the mind that can be stimulated by pain or inconvenience, but not pleasure.

(After all, the lorry originally stopping for me failed to arouse a response of gratitude.) I labelled it 'the indifference threshold' or — after the place I was travelling through at the time — the St Neot margin.

All that had happened, of course, was that the threat of a second breakdown had made me *concentrate my attention*. I spent a quarter of an hour listening intently to the engine. The threatened 'crisis' made me use my focusing-muscle, instead of allowing it to remain passive. Relaxing it — when he said we could probably make it — caused a rush of pleasure.

The same applies to Sartre. The constant danger of arrest kept him at a high level of *alertness*, of tension. Maslow's girl patient became so bored with her job in the chewing-gum factory that she allowed the focusing-muscle to go permanently flaccid.

If you allow the will to remain passive for long periods, it has the same effect as leaving your car in the garage for the winter. The batteries go flat. When the batteries go flat, 'life fails'.

These 'focusing muscles' must be used if we are to stay healthy, for they are the means by which the mind focuses on values, just as the eye muscles enable the eye to focus on distant objects. If we fail to use them for long periods, the result is a kind of mental short-sightedness, a gradual loss of the feeling of the reality of values, of meaning. This explains what happens if you watch television for too long, or read a very long book on a dull winter day until your eyes are aching. Your 'meaning focus' relaxes as your interest flags, and if you then go for a walk, everything seems oddly meaningless and dull. It just 'is', and it doesn't arouse any response.

The Greek poet Demetrios Capetanakis wrote in the early forties: '"Well," I thought when the war started, trying to hope for the best, "it will be horrible, but if it will be so horrible as to frighten and wake up the mind, it will be the salvation of many. Many are going to die, *but those who are going to survive will have a real life, with the mind awake*".... But I was mistaken.... The war is very frightening, but it is not frightening enough.'

The same thought struck me when I read the article Camus wrote for the resistance paper *Combat* when the Germans were being driven out of Paris.* It is called 'The Night of Truth' and is full of noble phrases. The skyline of Paris is blazing, he says, but these are the flames of freedom. 'Those who never despaired of themselves or of their country find their reward under this sky…the great virile brotherhood of recent years will never forsake us…

---

*Reprinted in *Resistance, Rebellion and Death*.

man's greatness...lies in his decision to be stronger than his condition', and so on. But Simone de Beauvoir's novel *The Mandarins* begins shortly after the liberation, and Camus is one of the characters. And they drift around the night spots of St Germain and drink too much and smoke too much and waste time on pointless adulteries. What had happened to the Night of Truth?

The answer is simple. Without the danger and injustice to keep the mind alert, they allowed a kind of inner-laziness to descend.

But didn't Camus *remember* their feelings about a completely different kind of future? The answer is: in the real sense of the word, no. Real memory brings a sense of meanings and values with it. False memory recalls the 'facts', but without their inner content of meaning. It must be squarely recognized that man suffers from a *very real form of amnesia*.

This is not a figure of speech but a reality. For the 'meaning' depends upon the mind's power of 'focusing'.

Must we, then, draw the pessimistic conclusion that mankind needs war and injustice to prevent him from lapsing into a condition of boredom, or at least, of preoccupation with trivialities?

The answer, fortunately, is no. 'Focusing' is a muscle, and it can be strengthened like any other muscle. Graham Greene, in an essay I have often quoted, describes how, in his teens, he sank into a condition of extreme boredom and depression, during which life became meaningless. He tried playing Russian roulette with his brother's revolver, inserting only one bullet, spinning the chambers, pointing it at his head and pulling the trigger. When there was just a click, he was overwhelmed by a feeling of delight, and a sense of the meaningfulness of life. The situation is fundamentally the same as in my 'St Neot martin' experience in the lorry, except that Greene's concentration was more intense, because the negative stimulus was greater. At a later stage, I discovered that a mild peak experience could easily be induced merely by concentrating hard on a pencil, then relaxing the attention, then concentrating again.... After doing this a dozen or so times, the attention becomes fatigued — if you are doing it with the right degree of concentration — and a few more efforts — deliberately ignoring the fatigue — trigger the peak experience. After all, concentration has the effect of summoning energy from your depths. It is the 'pumping' motion — of expanding and contracting the attention — that causes the peak experience.

Another interesting point arose when I was lecturing to Maslow's class at Brandeis University in early 1967. I was speaking about the peculiar power of the human imagination. I can imagine trapping my thumb in the door, and wince as if I had actually done it. I can go to see a film, and come out of the cinema feeling as if I have been on a long journey. Even so, it must be admitted that imagination only provides a dim carbon copy of the original experience. I may try to recall a particularly happy day, and even re-experience some of its pleasures; but compared to the original experience, it is like paste jewellery compared to the real thing. The hero of Barbusse's novel *Hell*, trying to recall the experience of watching a woman undress, admits: 'These words are all dead...they leave untouched, powerless to affect it, the intensity of what was.' Proust, tasting a madeleine dipped in tea, recalls with sudden intensity the reality of his childhood: but that is a fluke. He cannot do it by an ordinary act of imagination.

Yet the matter of sex appears to be an exception to this rule. A man can conjure up some imaginary scene with a girl undressing, and he responds physically as if there were a girl undressing in the room: his imagination can even carry him to the point of a sexual climax. In this one respect, man has completely surpassed the animals: here is a case where the mental 'act' needs no object....

At this point, Maslow interrupted me to point out that this is not quite true; monkeys often masturbate. I asked him if he had ever seen a monkey masturbating in total isolation, without the stimulus of a female monkey anywhere in the vicinity. He thought for a moment, then said he hadn't. Even if he had, it would not have basically affected my point. If monkeys can do problems for fun, perhaps they have more imagination than we give them credit for. But the interesting point is that in the matter of sex, man can achieve repeatedly what Proust achieved momentarily tasting the madeleine: a physical response *as if* to reality. Absurd as it sounds, masturbation is one of the highest faculties mankind has yet achieved. But its importance is in what it presages: that one day, the imagination will be able to achieve this result in *all* fields. If all perception is 'intentional', due to a 'reaching out', a 'focusing', on the part of the perceiver, then it ought to be possible to reconstruct any reality by making the necessary effort of focusing. We have only been kept from this recognition by the old, false theory of 'passive perception'.

Anyone who did chemistry at school will recall what happens if you mix sulphur and iron filings, and then heat them in a crucible. A small area of the sulphur melts and fuses with the iron. At that point, you can remove the flame of the bunsen burner; the reaction will continue of its own accord; the glow slowly spreads throughout the mixture until the whole crucible is red hot, and the end result is a chunk of iron sulphide. The same process goes on in the mind when we become deeply interested in anything. The warm glow produced by favourite poetry or music is often the beginning of this fusing process.

We are all familiar with the process of a wider glimpse of 'meaning' leading to the revitalizing of the will. This, in fact, is why people need holidays. As life drags on repetitively, they get tired; they stop making effort; it is the *will* that gets run down. The holiday 'reminds' them of wider meanings, reminds them that the universe is a vast spider's web of meaning, stretching infinitely in all directions. And quite suddenly they are enjoying *everything* more: eating, reading, walking, listening to music, having a beer before dinner. The 'meaning' sharpens the appetite for life — that is, the will to live.

It is our misfortune that we are not equally familiar with the reverse process: that a deliberate increase in willed concentration can *also* start the 'fusion' process working. This is, in fact, common sense. The deeper my sense of the 'meaningfulness' of the world, the fiercer and more persistent my will. And increased effort of will leads in turn to increased sense of meaning. It is a chain reaction. So is the reverse, when 'discouragement' leads me to stop willing, and the passivity leads to a narrowed sense of meaning, and the gradual loss of 'meaning' leads to further relaxation of the will. The result is a kind of 'down staircase' of apathy. On the other hand, any intense glimpse of meaning can cause a transfer to the 'up staircase'. This is most strikingly illustrated in an experiment that Maslow's colleague, Dr A. Hoffer, carried out with alcoholics.* Hoffer reasoned that alcoholics may be people of more-than-average intelligence and sensitivity. Because of this, they find that life is too much for them, and they drink because at first it produces peak experiences. But as often as not it doesn't; then they drink more to increase the stimulus, and become involved in guilt and depression. Hoffer tried giving these alcoholics mescalin — producing a far more powerful 'lift' than alcohol — and then deliberately induced peak experiences by means of music, poetry, painting — whatever used to produce P.E's before the subject became alcoholic. The startling result was that more than 50 per cent were cured. The peak experience is an explosion of *meaning*, and meaning arouses the will, which in turn reaches out towards further horizons of meaning. The alcoholic drinks because he wants peak experiences, but he is, in fact, running away from them as fast as he can go. Once his sense of direction had

---

*See Maslow's paper 'Fusions of Facts and Values' (1963). See also: 'The Psychedelic Experience — A New Concept in Psychotherapy' by J. N. Sherwood, M. J. Stolaroff and W. W. Harman, *Journal of Neuropsychiatry*, vol. 4, no. 2, Dec. 1962, and 'Personality Change Associated with Psychedelic (LSD) Therapy: A Preliminary Report' by Robert E. Mogar and Charles Savage, *Psychotherapy*, vol. l, no. 4, Autumn 1964.

been restored, he ceased to be alcoholic, recognizing that *peak experiences are in direct proportion to the intensity of the will.*

And what should be quite clear is that there is no theoretical limit to the 'chain reaction'. Why does a man get depressed? Because at a certain point, he feels that a certain difficulty is 'not worth the effort'. As he becomes more discouraged, molehills turn into mountains until, as William James says, life turns into one tissue of impossibilities, and the process called nervous breakdown begins. Having recognized that the cause of the trouble lies in the collapse of the will, there is no theoretical reason why the ex-alcoholic should come to a halt with the achievement of 'normality'.

There is, of course, a practical reason. The will needs a *purpose*. Why do we feel so cheerful when we are planning a holiday — looking at maps, working out what to pack? Because we have long-distance purpose. One can understand how Balzac must have felt when he first conceived the idea of creating the *Comédie humaine*, the excitement of working out a series of novels about military life, a series about provincial life, a series about the aristocracy…. 'Building castles in the air', this activity is called; but with a little effort, they actually get built. Man seems to need long-range purpose to get the best out of himself. And once the alcoholic has achieved 'normality' again, he may well say: 'All right, where do I go from here?'

If this were true, it would represent a kind of dead end. For undoubtedly, our civilization tends to deprive us of the kind of long-range purpose that our pioneer ancestors must have enjoyed. But it provides us with something else: the ability to live on the plane of the mind, the imagination.

And there is a still more important matter we have overlooked: the mind's capacity to *reach out* for meaning. This is perfectly illustrated by a story told in Romain Gary's novel *The Roots of Heaven*. In a German concentration camp during the war, the French prisoners are becoming increasingly demoralized: they are on a down-staircase. A man called Robert devises a way to arrest the decline. He suggests that they imagine an invisible girl in the billet. If one of them swears or farts, he must bow and apologise to the 'girl'; when they undress, they must hang up a blanket so she can't see them. Oddly enough, this absurd game works: they enter into the spirit of the thing, and morale suddenly rises. The Germans become suspicious of the men, and by eavesdropping they find out about the invisible girl. The Commandant fancies himself as a psychologist. He goes along to the billet with two guards, and tells the men: 'I know you have a girl here. That is forbidden. Tomorrow, I shall come here with these guards, and you will hand her over to me. She will be taken to the local brothel for German officers.' When he has gone, the men are dismayed; they know that if they 'hand her over', they won't be able to re-create her. The next day the Commandant appears with his two soldiers. Robert, as the spokesman, says: 'We have decided not to hand her over'. And the Commandant knows he is beaten: nothing he can do can force them to hand her over. Robert is arrested and placed in solitary confinement; they all think they have seen the last of him, but weeks later, he reappears, very thin and worn. He explains that he has found the way to resist solitary confinement — their game with the invisible girl has taught him that the imagination is the power to reach out to *other realities*, realities not physically present. He has kept himself from breakdown by imagining great herds of elephants trampling over endless plains....

The irony, in the novel, is that it is Robert who later becomes a hunter of elephants. But that is beside the point. The point is that the will *can* make an act of reaching towards meaning, towards 'other realities'.

In phenomenological terms, what actually happened 'when the prisoners began apologizing to the imaginary girl? First of all, they threw off their apathy and entered into a communal game. It was like a coach-load of football fans whiling away a tedious journey with community singing. But having raised their spirits by entering into the game, they also *reminded themselves* of circumstances in which they would normally be 'at their best'. Gorky's story *Twenty Six Men and a Girl* may be regarded as a parable about the same thing: the twenty-six overworked bakers keep up their spirits by idealizing the girl, treating her as a goddess.... And thereby reminding themselves of the response appropriate to a goddess.

And this leads naturally to a concept that has become the core of my own existential psychology: the Self-Image. A man could not climb a vertical cliff without cutting hand-holds in the rock. Similarly, I cannot achieve a state of 'intenser consciousness' merely by wanting to; at least, it is extremely difficult without training. We tend to climb towards higher states of self-awareness by means of a series of self-images. We create a certain imaginary image of the sort of person we would like to be, and then try to live up to the image. 'The great man is the play-actor of his ideals,' says Nietzsche.

One of the clearest expositions of the self-image idea can be found in a story called *The Looking Glass* by the Brazilian novelist Machado de Assis. A young man who has lived all his life in a small village in Brazil is called up for military service. In due course he becomes a lieutenant. When he returns home in his uniform he is the envy of the village; his mother calls him 'My Lieutenant'. One of his aunts is particularly delighted with him: she invites him to her remote farm, and insists on addressing him as 'Senhor Lieutenant'. Her brother-in-law and all the slaves follow suit. At first, the youth is embarrassed; he doesn't *feel* like a lieutenant. But gradually he gets used to the idea. 'The petting, the attention, the deference, produced a transformation in me....' He begins to feel like a lieutenant.

But one day, the aunt goes away to the bedside of a sick daughter, and takes the brother-in-law with her. The lieutenant is left alone with the slaves. And the next morning, they have all deserted, leaving him alone.

Suddenly, there is no one to feed his ego. He feels lost. In his room there is an enormous mirror, placed there by his aunt. One day he looks in the mirror — and his outline seems blurred and confused. The sense of unreality increases until he is afraid he is going insane. And then he has an inspiration. He takes his lieutenant's uniform from the wardrobe and puts it on. And immediately, his image in the mirror becomes solid and clear. His feeling of sanity and self-respect returns.

Every day thereafter, he puts on the uniform, and sits in front of the mirror. And he is able to stay sane through the remaining week before his aunt returns....*

Machado subtitles his story 'Rough draft of a new theory of the human soul'. And so it is, for a story written in 1882. His hero explains to his auditors that he believes man has two souls: one inside, looking out, the other outside, looking in. But this is crude psychology. He means that the subjective 'I' gains its sense of identity from actions and outward objects. But this implies that the 'inner me' remains unchanged. This in turn implies that the shy, nervous 'inner self' is the permanent sub-stratum of one's more confident layers of personality, and this is obviously untrue. Shyness is simply a disinclination to express oneself out of fear that it will turn out badly; confidence — such as he gained through the petting and admiration — is the ability to act decisively.

The key sentence is: 'The petting, the attention, the deference, produced a transformation in me.' For this type of transformation, I coined the word 'promotion'. It is, in effect, a promotion of the personality to a higher level. All poetic experience is a 'promotion' experience, since it raises the personality to a higher level. One has a sense of becoming a stronger, or more mature, or more competent, or more serious person.

If he had been a lieutenant for several years, being alone in the house would not have eroded his sense of identity. The trouble is that he is young, and that he is only just trying-on a new personality, the 'Senhor

---

* *The Psychiatrist and Other Stories,* translated by William L. Grossman and Helen Caldwell (University of California Press, 1963).

Lieutenant'. The image of himself in the looking glass provides the reinforcement he needs.

The resemblance between this story and Romain Gary's story of the prison camp need hardly be pointed out. In both cases, moral decline is arrested by *reminding oneself* of something that re-creates the self-image. The weakness of Machado's theory of two souls becomes clear when we consider that Robert keeps himself sane in solitary confinement by an effort of inner-strength, of imagination, not by evoking a more 'successful' level of his personality. The elephants are an image of freedom. The sensation of freedom is always accompanied by a feeling of *contraction* of one's inner-being. Such a contraction occurs when we concentrate intently upon anything. It also occurs in sexual excitement, and explains why the orgasm is perhaps the most fundamental — at least the most common — 'promotion' experience.

Donald Aldous, the technical editor of a well-known record magazine, told me a story that makes the role of the self-image even clearer. Before the war, the BBC hired a famous conductor to broadcast a series of concerts. They were to be relayed from the new sound-proof studios. The orchestra had never played there before, and the rehearsals lacked vitality. They explained that the studio was too dead: they could not hear the echo of their own playing. Donald Aldous was given the interesting job of arranging a system of loudspeakers around the walls that relayed the sound back to the orchestra a split second after they had played it, like an echo. As soon as they could 'hear themselves', the playing of the orchestra improved enormously.

What is at issue in all such cases is a certain inner-strength. Captain Shotover in *Heartbreak House* tells Ellie Dunne that as a young man, he 'sought danger, hardship, horror and death' — as captain of a whaler — 'that I might feel the life in me more intensely'. That is to say, he sought conditions that would keep him at a high level of tension and alertness, so as to develop the inner-muscle of concentration. And note that the function of this muscle is to produce a sense of inner-freedom. When it is feeble, I am easily bored, depressed, made to feel sorry for myself. I am a moral hypochondriac. When it has been strengthened by a long period of alertness and effort, I feel equal to most emergencies, and this is the same as to say that I feel inner-freedom.

The self-image notion is of immediate relevance to Maslovian psychology. And here we touch upon the very heart of the matter, the most important point of all

Let us consider the question: what is the mechanism by which a 'self-image' produces 'promotion'? The answer is: it provides me with a kind of artificial standard of objective values. It gives me a sense of external *meaning*. Why did the peak experience under mescalin cure the alcoholics? Because the peak experience is a flood of meaning, obviously pouring in from outside. As it pours in, you ask yourself the question: Why doesn't this happen all the time, if the meaning is always there? And the answer is obvious: because I allow the will to become passive, and the senses close up. If I want more meaning, then I must force my senses wide open by an increased effort of will. We might think of the senses as spring-loaded shutters that must be forced open, and which close again when you let them go.

It must be clearly understood that we live in a kind of room of subjective emotions and values. If I am not very careful, the shutters close, and I lose my objective standards. At this point, I may wildly exaggerate the importance of my emotions, my private ups and downs, and there is no feeling of objective reality to contradict me. A child beset by misery is more bewildered than an adult because he has nothing to measure it by; he doesn't know how serious it is. As soon as his mother kisses him and says, 'There, it doesn't really matter...', he relaxes. If I get myself 'into a state' about some trivial worry and then I hear that some old friend has died of cancer, I instantly 'snap out' of my black mood, for my emotions are cut down to their proper size by comparison with a more serious reality.

Moods and emotions are a kind of fever produced by lack of contact with reality. The shutters are closed, and the temperature in the rooms rises. It *can* rise to a degree where it becomes a serious fever, where the emotions have got so out-of-control that reality *cannot* break in. These are states of psychotic delusion — or perhaps merely of nervous overstrain. The characteristic of these states is exaggeration: every minor worry turns into a monstrous bogey. Inevitably, I cease to make efforts of will — for the will is at its healthiest when I have a firm sense of reality and of purpose. And we have seen what happens when the will becomes passive: the vital forces sink, and, at a certain point, physical health is affected. The 'existential psychologist' Viktor Frankl — of whom I shall speak at length later — remarked on 'how close is the connection between a man's state of mind — his courage and hope, or lack of them — and the state of immunity of his body', and tells a story that makes the point forcefully. Frankl was a Jew who spent most of the war in a German concentration camp:

'I once had a dramatic demonstration of the close link between the loss of faith in the future and this dangerous giving up. F—, my senior block warden, a fairly well-known composer and librettist, confided in me one day: "I would like to tell you something, Doctor. I have had a strange dream. A voice told me that I could wish for something, that I should only say what I wanted to know, and all my questions would be answered. What do you think I asked? That I would like to know when the war would be over for me. You know what I mean, Doctor — for me! I wanted to know when we, when our camp, would be liberated and our sufferings come to an end." '

' "And when did you have this dream?" I asked.'

' "In February, 1945", he answered. It was then the beginning of March.'

' "What did your dream voice answer?" '

'Furtively he whispered to me, "March thirtieth." '

'When F— told me about his dream, he was still full of hope and convinced that the voice of his dream would be right. But as the promised day drew nearer, the war news which reached our camp made it appear very unlikely that we would be free on the promised date. On March twenty-ninth, F— suddenly became very ill and ran a high temperature. On March thirtieth, the day his prophecy had told him that the war and suffering would be over for him, he became delirious and lost consciousness. On March thirty-first, he was dead. To all outward appearances he had died of typhus.'*

Frankl's composer friend was physically near the end of his resources; this is why the collapse of his will made such a difference. (Frankl also mentions the unprecedentedly high death rate in the camp between Christmas 1944 and New Year 1945, because so many prisoners had pinned their hopes on being home for Christmas.) It took a year of work in the chewing-gum factory to deplete Maslow's girl patient to the point where she ceased to menstruate. Normally healthy people possess a 'cushion' of energy to absorb shocks and disappointments, and this cushion is identical to the 'surplus energy tanks' of which we have spoken. It is maintained by will-power fired by the sense of meaning. We are only aware of this *direct* action of the will upon the body in physical extremes: for example, if I am feeling sick, I can disperse the sickness by 'snapping out' of my feeling of nausea and summoning subconscious forces of health. If we were more clearly aware of this connection between 'positive consciousness' and physical health,

---

*From *Death Camp to Existentialism* (Beacon Press, 1962). Later republished as *Man's Search for Meaning*, revised and enlarged. All quotations are from this later edition.

we would treat mental passivity as a form of illness. Another anecdote of Frankl's — from the same book — may be said to provide the foundation of an 'attitude psychology' closely related to Maslow's. The prisoners were transferred from Auschwitz to Dachau. The journey took two days and three nights, during which they were packed so tight that few could sit down, and half starved. At Dachau, they had to stand in line all night and throughout the next morning in freezing rain, as punishment because one man had fallen asleep and missed the roll call. Yet they were all immensely happy, laughing and making jokes: *because Dachau had no incinerator chimney.*

To summarize: man evolves through a sense of external meaning. When his sense of meaning is strong, he maintains a high level of will-drive and of general health. Without this sense of external meaning, he becomes the victim of subjective emotions, a kind of dream that tends to degenerate into nightmare. His uncontrolled fantasies and worries turn into an octopus that strangles him.

Man has evolved various ways of preventing this from happening. The most important is religion. This tells a man that certain objective standards are permanently true, and that his own nature is weak and sinful. The chief trouble with authoritarian religion is that it works best for intellectually-uncomplicated people, and fails to carry much conviction for the highly sophisticated and neurotic — who are the very ones who need it most.

In certain respects, art succeeds where religion fails. A great symphony or poem is an *active reminder* of the reality of meaning: it provides a stimulus like an electric shock, re-animating the will and the appetite for life. Its disadvantage is that we all assume that art is 'subjective' by nature, that it tells us about the emotions of the artist, not about the objective world. And so 'when life fails', the effectiveness of art diminishes.

Men of imagination have always tended to use the self-image method to prevent them from becoming victims of the octopus of subjectivity. It is essentially a method for pushing problems and disappointments to arm's length. Yeats has described how, when he was sure no one was looking, he used to walk about London with the peculiar strut of Henry Irving's Hamlet. In *Heartbreak House*, Hector whiles away an idle moment by pretending to fight a duel with an imaginary antagonist and then making love to an imaginary woman. But the self-image also plays a central role in all human creativity. The young artist, lacking certainty of his own identity, projects a mental image of himself that blurs into an image of the artist he most admires. Brahms's self-image is half- Beethoven; Yeats's is half- Shelley. And the ultimate value of their work — its inner-consistency and strength — depends upon how deeply they commit themselves to acting out the self-image.

According to Freud and Karl Marx, fantasy is an escape from reality and responsibility. According to Maslow, fantasy is the means by which a determined man masters reality.

'Reality' is the key word in existential psychology. It poses no philosophical problems. It means objective meaning, as opposed to subjective values. Eliot wrote: 'We each think of the key, each in his prison', implying that there is no escape from one's subjective prison. Blake knew better: he agreed that 'five windows light the caverned man', but added that through one of them, he can pass out whenever he wants to. That is to say that by an effort of reaching out to meaning, he can re-establish contact with reality. The situation could be compared to a child who becomes confused during a game of blind man's buff, but who has only to remove the bandage in order to re-orient himself to the room. And the most important point for psychotherapy is that he can do this by an *act of will*. Mental illness is a kind of amnesia, in which the patient has forgotten his own powers. The task of the therapist is to somehow renew the patient's contact with reality.

The first thing that will be observed about this 'third force psychology' I have outlined is that it is a great deal more optimistic than that of Freud, or even Jung. It implies that *all* human beings are closer to more intense states of consciousness than they realize. Somewhere in his autobiography, Stephen Spender remarks that everyone nowadays is neurotic, because it is inevitable at this stage in civilization. Maslow's feeling seems to be that neurosis is definitely abnormal, and that there is no reason why most people should not be capable of a high level of mental health and of peak experiences.

Among intelligent people, our cultural premises are certainly largely responsible for the prevailing pessimism. The Victorians went in for moral uplift and the belief in man's higher nature. Darwin and Freud changed all that. Darwin showed that we do not need the postulate of a creator to explain why man is superior to the ape. Freud denounced religion as a delusion based upon the child's fear of the father, and asserted that neurosis is due to the frustration of man's animal nature — specifically, his sex drives. After the First World War, despair and frustration became the keynote of literature; the optimists of the previous decade — Shaw, Wells, Chesterton — became almost un-mentionable. In science, philosophy, psychology, there was an increasing tendency to 'reductionism' — which Arthur Koestler has defined as the belief that all human activities can be explained in terms of the elementary responses of the lower animals, such as the psychologist's laboratory rat. This reductionism should not be construed as a materialistic jibe at idealism — although it often looks like that — but as *a desire to get things done*, accompanied by the fear that nothing will get done if too much is attempted. Maslow told me once that a respectable psychologist had leapt to his feet at a meeting of the American Psychological Association, and shouted at him — Maslow — 'You are an evil man. You want to destroy psychology.' The irony of the story is that by the time Maslow told it to me, he was president of the American Psychological Association! The old reductionist climate began to change in the early sixties. In Europe, the school of existential psychology was already well established. Sir Karl Popper — one of the original founders of the school of Logical Positivism — was arguing that science is not a plodding, logical, investigation of the universe, but that it proceeds by flashes of intuition, like poetry. Popper's most distinguished follower, Michael Polanyi, published in 1958 his revolutionary book *Personal Knowledge*, a carefully reasoned attack on the 'timetable or telephone directory conception of science' — i.e. the view that all future books on science could be written by an electronic brain, if it was big enough. Polanyi stated that what drives the scientist is *an increasing sense of contact with reality* — that is to say, precisely what drives the poet or the saint. In biology, the old rigid Darwinism began to relax; in 1965, Sir Alister Hardy, an orthodox Darwinian, and Professor of Zoology at Oxford, asserted in his Gifford Lectures that the genes might be influenced by telepathy, and that certain biological phenomena are only explainable on the assumption of some kind of 'group mind'. 'Reductionism' was breaking apart.

It was in 1968 that an American publisher suggested to me that I should write a book about Maslow. I asked him how he felt about the idea, and he approved — pointing out, at the same time, that another friend, Frank Goble, was also writing one. I decided to go ahead all the same, and Maslow patiently answered the questions I threw at him through 1969, although a heart attack had slowed him up considerably. At my suggestion, he made a pile of tapes, full of biographical and personal details, some for publication, some not. Meanwhile, I was reading my way steadily through a hundred or so papers he had sent me, dating back to the early thirties, when he was working on monkeys with Harry Harlow. But when I started writing the book, in Majorca, in the autumn of 1969, I realized that it was going to be more difficult than I had expected. I had intended to make it a straight account of Maslow's life and work, a short book that would stick to my subject. But, after all, Viktor Frankl was also part of the subject, and so were Erwin Straus, Medard Boss, William Glasser, Ronald Laing and many other existential psychologists. Worse still, it was hard to keep myself out of it, since Maslow's work had exerted so much influence on my own ideas, and since we had been engaged in a fragmentary dialogue for the past ten years.

In June, 1969, I told Maslow in a letter that it looked as if my book about him was going to be part of a larger book about the revolution in psychology, and asked more questions, which he answered on tape. A few days before this last batch of tapes arrived, I received a letter from his secretary telling me that he had died of a heart attack on 8 June 1970. Listening to his voice, it was hard to get used to the idea that he was dead.

I am still not certain whether this is the best way to write the book; but I can see no other. In this introduction I have tried to give a sketchy outline of the ideas that preoccupied Maslow — and myself — during the past ten years. In the first part of the book, I have tried to give a picture of the major trends in psychology from its beginnings in the nineteenth century, through the Freudian revolution, down to Maslow. Part Two deals exclusively with Maslow; it is the book I intended to write to begin with. Part Three discusses existential psychology in general, and attempts to state some general conclusions about the movement. Inevitably, this is the most personal part of the book, and may be regarded as a continuation of this introduction. The ultimate question is not one of psychology so much as of philosophy, or even religion. Viktor Frankl talks about 'the existential vacuum' writing: 'More and more patients are crowding our clinics and consulting rooms complaining of an inner emptiness, a sense of total and ultimate meaninglessness of their lives.' I coined the term 'nothingness neurosis' to describe this state. But in discussing it, I have tried to avoid generalizations, and to remain faithful to the phenomenological — the descriptive — method. That was always Maslow's own approach.

THE STRANGE STORY
OF MODERN PHILOSOPHY

From *Beyond the Outsider,* 1965. Updated as 'Philosophy':
Chapter 12 of *Super Consciousness,* 2009

This book has been constructed rather like one of the seminars I used to give
in the 1960s at the Esalen Institute at Big Sur, near San Francisco —
an attempt to draw in the readers with a practical sense of what can be
done through mental disciplines. But I usually insisted that we devote one
session to making a real intellectual effort to grasp this in terms of western
philosophy. Oddly enough, many students seemed to find this one of the
most rewarding sessions.

In my book *Beyond the Outsider* (1965) there is a chapter called
'The Strange Story of Modern Philosophy', and in what follows, I shall
recapitulate its arguments.

I begin by considering the 'world rejection' of Socrates, who tells his
followers that since the philosopher spends his life trying to separate his soul
from his body, his own death should be regarded as a consummation. This is
consistent with his questionable belief that only spirit is real, and matter is
somehow unimportant and unreal. The notion would persist throughout the
next 2,000 years, harmonizing comfortably with the Christian view that this
world is unimportant compared to the next. It may be needless to say that I
totally reject it.

Then came scientific thought, in the person of Galileo Galilei, who
introduced the spirit of experiment. He demonstrated that gravity makes all
bodies fall at the same speed, and 'invented' the telescope through which he

discovered the moons of Jupiter. From then on, human thought began to take a more purposeful direction. In 1642, the year Galileo died, Newton was born, and within forty years, science had advanced further than in the previous 2,000.

In philosophy, a similar leap forward had taken place while Galileo was still alive. René Descartes attempted to bring into philosophy the same kind of certainty that Galileo had brought to science. Galileo had explored the heavens with a telescope; Descartes decided to examine the human situation through a kind of magnifying glass. His aim was to ask what we can really know for certain.

His new method of achieving certainty was simplicity itself: *to doubt everything*. After seeing some toy robots driven by water in the park at Versailles, it struck him that human beings are almost entirely mechanical; we need stimuli to make us do something. Of course, men could not be made of clockwork, because they have souls. (Descartes was a good Catholic.) But animals could be, and probably are, machines.

How do I know I am not a machine? Because a machine has no self-awareness. On the other hand, I can think, 'therefore I am'. Such an assertion obviously leaves room for doubt. If some god could endow a washing machine with self-awareness, it would probably assume that it operates of its own free will, and might well say, 'I think, therefore I am.' It would clearly be mistaken.

The British philosopher John Locke — who was eighteen when Descartes died – recognized this. He did not actually argue that men are robots, but came very close to it when he said that we cannot know anything that does not come from our experience. There is nothing in the mind that was not first in the senses. When man is born, his mind is like a blank sheet of paper, a '*tabula rasa*'. Everything he then learns arises from things that happen to him. So what we call the mind — all our thoughts, responses, reactions — is a 'construct', like a house built of pieces of Lego.

Descartes had launched modern western philosophy with a dubious proposition, and now Locke continued it with an even more dubious one. This seems to be a typical characteristic of western philosophy: if someone makes a stupid howler, his successors try to justify it and carry the thing to even further lengths of absurdity, when common sense would suggest that they get their foundations right by going back to square one.

So it was perhaps inevitable that Bishop Berkeley should go a step further. If we can only know things through the mind, then why should we assume the outside world exists at all? Jam is not really sweet; it only produces a sensation of sweetness on the tongue. The sky is not really blue; it only produces a sense of blueness on the eyes. Perhaps objects only exist when we are looking at them, and when there is no one there to see them, they vanish. Or at least, they would if God was not there to see them.

This was obviously inviting some clever trouble-maker to suggest that, since there is no evidence that God exists, perhaps everything is an illusion? Which is more or less what the next 'great philosopher' did by carrying doubt even further. David Hume set out to reduce everything to materialism. The soul, which Descartes thought he had proved, is an illusion, because when I look inside myself, I do not become aware of 'the essential me', but merely of thoughts and sensations. So human beings are also made of Lego.

And when you look at things in this piecemeal way, they simply dissolve. Even cause and effect are seen to be an illusion, for 'every effect is a distinct event from its cause', and therefore 'cannot be discovered in the cause'. Perhaps God is pulling our legs when He makes a kettle boil on a fire; perhaps it is really supposed to freeze.

What Hume did was to sweep the world bare of all certainty, leaving philosophy looking like a landscape after the dropping of an H-bomb. In fact, his Scottish contemporary Thomas Reid had seen through the fallacy that underlies Hume's philosophy.

According to Hume, when we open our eyes in the morning, we do not see 'things' but 'ideas' (or 'impressions'). That object by the side of my bed is a clock, but if I had never seen or heard of a clock, I wouldn't know this. Before I can grasp what I am looking at I need to know what a clock is – and that is an idea. And the same goes for everything else — that door, window, chest of drawers.

Hume believed that ideas are simply faded impressions of sense. If he thought of Edinburgh Castle, what came into his head was something like a faded picture of Edinburgh Castle. So all we can really know is a faded universe of impressions inside our heads.

Now Reid was much influenced by his professor George Turnbull, who argued that our common-sense view of facts, such as that the external world exists, cannot be overturned by reasoning, and that philosophy should be based on our 'active power', the power of the will. So Reid could not accept that all our knowledge is based on mere ideas and impressions. I may believe this when I have spent the day writing and thinking, but that is because too much thinking makes things seem less real; but the moment I step outdoors and encounter the sun and the wind, I know better.

Now anyone who has read Aldous Huxley's book *The Doors of Perception* will recognize what he means. What startled Huxley after he had taken mescalin was the realization that everything is ten times as real as he thought. Millions of students in the 1960s experienced the same revelation when they took mescalin or LSD: that the world 'out there' is seething with pure existence. And if Hume had taken mescalin he would have recognized immediately that his belief that ideas are faded impressions of sense is simply untrue.

But Reid was not influential enough to counterbalance Locke, Berkeley and Hume and the doubts they had instilled, let alone Descartes.

The philosopher who tried to repair the damage was the Königsburg professor Immanuel Kant. And what he did was, in effect, to take a step backward to Bishop Berkeley, and make the mind the creator of reality.

He noticed the existence of what Husserl would later call 'intentionality' — that the mind makes sense of this chaotic world that surrounds us by imposing order on it. We divide things into categories — for example, everything I can see around me is either a liquid, a solid or a gas. We use clocks to impose order on the chaos of time, and measuring rods to impose it on space. We call things by words we have invented — that four-legged creature is a 'cat', and that one a 'dog'. You could say we invent space and time to make our world orderly enough to live in comfortably. It is as if we had invented a pair of spectacles that impose categories on the world.

Does that mean there is no 'true reality' behind all our categories? Yes, there *is* such an underlying reality, which Kant called the noumenon, to distinguish it from the world of mere 'phenomena' that surrounds us. *But since we can never remove the spectacles, we can never know this reality.*

The dramatist Heinrich von Kleist was so upset by Kant's bewildering variation on Bishop Berkeley that he committed suicide. At which point one of Kant's followers, a now almost forgotten thinker called Johann Gottlieb Fichte, called a halt to the madness — at least, he would have done if anyone had taken any notice of him. What Fichte said was: why bother about this 'noumenon'? If it is unknowable, we may as well forget it. In that case, man is left in a world created by his senses — just as Berkeley said. But if 'I' really created the universe, why do I not know that I did? There must be two 'me's', this everyday self who has no idea of what is going on, and another 'me' who is actually a kind of god who has created this world.

Descartes had sat in his armchair, or more likely lay in bed (he was notoriously lazy) and asked: 'What can I know for certain?' He answered: 'Two things are certain — my own existence and that world out there.' We call them the subjective and the objective worlds. Fichte said: 'No, there are three worlds — that world out there, and two "me's", the ordinary me and the me who is behind the scenes creating the world out there.'

The next question is: how could the ordinary 'me' begin to explore the extraordinary world created by the 'other me'? And this, of course, is the true task of phenomenology, to which we shall come in a moment.

Fichte made one more comment that is of immense importance: that the trouble with philosophy was that its attitude to the world is passive. But philosophy, he said (in *Addresses to the German Nation*), should regard itself as active, or at least as a prelude to action. This, of course, is very close to George Turnbull's common sense and his belief in the 'active power'.

Expressed in this way, this sounds unexciting — as if it is merely an earlier statement of Karl Marx's remark that the business of philosophy is not to understand the world but to change it. In fact, it was really a blinding flash of insight: that Kantian philosophy turned philosophers into armchair theorists, so that their whole attitude to knowledge was passive, when to really grasp reality it should be active.

As Buckminster Fuller once expressed it: 'I seem to be a verb.'

As to that other problem, that philosophical hare set running by Descartes, the solution seems to lie in Fichte's insight that we have 'two selves'. Descartes should have followed up his assertion 'I think therefore I am' with the question: 'Yes, but who am I?' He is failing to question his own identity, and this error will lead on to the errors of Locke, Berkeley, Hume, Kant, Hegel and the rest.

By the beginning of the 19th century, philosophy had fallen into a sad state. For the doubts planted by Locke, Berkeley and Hume had made the philosopher see himself as essentially passive — someone who sat in an armchair, asking what his reason could tell him about the world. Even as early as 1744, this attitude had led one French philosopher, Julien Offray de la Mettrie, to write a book called *Man the Machine*, suggesting that is all we really are.

We need not get too irritated by this, for la Mettrie's intention was not to convince us that life is meaningless, but to annoy the Church, which had exercised a stranglehold on freedom of thought for centuries. (He succeeded all too well, and after being dismissed from the army on the complaint of the chaplain, he was then forced to flee Leiden by angry theologians; fortunately Frederick the Great then offered him refuge in Prussia.) In most of Europe, Protestantism had taken hold, reducing the power of the Church to put heretics in jail, but in France, Italy and Spain, heretics could still be tried and imprisoned.

La Mettrie was followed by Etienne de Condillac and Pierre Cabanis. Condillac argued that our so-called mental life is merely a matter of physical sensations, and Cabanis, a doctor, that the brain secretes thoughts as the liver secretes bile. Just as the stomach and intestines receive food and digest it, so the brain receives impressions, digests them, and the result is thought.

Now Condillac and Cabanis were members of a group known as 'Les Philosophes', which might today be translated as 'the intellectuals'. A younger member of this group was an aristocrat called Maine de Biran, a soldier who retired to a castle in the Dordogne to devote his life to philosophy. Although he started off as a follower of Condillac, he gradually became more and more opposed to this idea that man is nothing more than a kind of penny-in-the-slot machine. His objection runs along these lines: when I am making a real effort, I have a clear feeling that it is I who am doing it, not a machine. I may feel mechanical when I'm doing something boring and automatic, but as soon as I exert my will, I become aware that I'm not a machine — that I possess an 'active power'.

This vital insight could have altered the course of French philosophy, but no one was interested in pursuing the notion that man possesses free will. Frenchmen at the end of the 18th century were so intoxicated at being able to give a two-finger salute to the Catholic Church — which had persecuted free thought for centuries — that they had no intention of conceding that man had an immortal soul. So no one paid the slightest attention to Maine de Biran's discovery that we have free will. The next major French philosopher, Auguste Comte, directed all his polemical powers at denouncing superstition (by which he meant religion), and declaring that man would never be free until he learned to live by logic and reason alone. He also regarded metaphysics — i.e. all attempts to deal with larger questions about man and the universe — as another form of superstition. Unfortunately, he was a poor advertisement for his religion of reason, for a disastrous marriage caused a nervous breakdown that drove him into an insane asylum, after which an unhappy love affair made him attempt suicide. In spite of this, his *Course of Positive Philosophy* had an enormous influence, and he even founded a 'Church of Humanity', which went on to become highly successful after his death.

In Germany, metaphysical philosophy showed that it still had plenty of life in it in the thought of G. F. Hegel, who also began as a sceptic and a rationalist, but then had some kind of revelation in which he saw the 'Idea' as the ultimate reality from which all other things derive, including Nature and Spirit.

Perhaps he was remembering St John's 'In the beginning was the Word.' This led him to a vision of history that has something in common with Toynbee's, in which all the miseries and torments of history nevertheless drive man 'upward and on', towards the expression of pure spirit. There was something very vital and positive about Hegel's philosophy that aroused immense enthusiasm in his contemporaries, and led to a revival of interest in metaphysics. At a time when the world was almost ready to surrender to French materialism, it was Hegel who brought a refreshing new impulse of Idealism. If it had not been for his tendency to write in incomprehensible abstractions, he would probably qualify as the most important philosopher since Plato.

The man who now seems to us to be one of the most original thinkers of the mid-19th century was totally unknown in his own time. Søren Kierkegaard, a brilliant but intensely neurotic Dane, might have been expected to regard Hegel as a fellow-spirit, since neither had the slightest inclination towards what the French called positivism. But studying Hegel at Copenhagen University put him off completely, since he felt this was all too abstract, and therefore had little to say to him as an individual. As a result, he developed an intense dislike of this philosopher who claimed to have answered every major question in the universe. It was Kierkegaard who first used the word existential (to mean the opposite of 'abstract') to explain his dislike of Hegel. When books like The *Concept of Angst* were rediscovered in the 1920s, they immediately found a large audience, because by that time everybody was suffering from it. Probably his best known statement is: 'Truth is subjectivity'.

Kierkegaard spent most of his short life (he died at the age of 42) in a state of depression, and collapsed on the day he went to withdraw the last of his money from the bank. In this sense he was typical of the Romantics who, ever since Rousseau, had been complaining that they found life too difficult and unrewarding to be worth the effort. And this is why Fichte's insight that there is a part of the mind that creates the world 'behind our backs' is so important. It suggested that if poets and philosophers knew enough about the hidden powers of that 'other self', they might find life less intolerable.

As to French philosophy, its mainstream remained as materialistic as ever. The man who was basically responsible for this was the father of scepticism, David Hume.

We have already noted Thomas Reid's attempt to demonstrate that Hume's philosophy was based on a fallacy: namely, that all our knowledge is based on ideas or impressions. But in the 20th century, a far more considerable thinker than Reid set out to refute Hume. His name was Alfred North Whitehead.

As we have seen, Hume argued that we have no true 'inner self'. He claimed that when he looked inside himself for 'the real David Hume', he only came across ideas and impressions, but nothing like a 'self'. And he concluded that all that can be found inside us is a 'stream of consciousness', a lot of scurrying thoughts whose only 'identity' is that they come one after another. This is the realization that comes, he says, when you look at your inner self through a magnifying glass.

In a little book called *Symbolism, Its Meaning and Effect*, Whitehead points out that this method of looking at something through a magnifying glass is a good way of missing its meaning. If, for example, you looked at a great painting through a magnifying glass, you would only see the texture of the paint. If you look at a newspaper photograph close up, you would only see disconnected dots. In both cases you are looking at individual trees and failing to see that they constitute a wood. In order to see the wood, we need to take a bird's-eye view, to stand back.

So we have two kinds of perception: bird's-eye and worm's-eye; far-off and close-up. Both only give half the picture.

Whitehead calls these two modes 'presentational immediacy' and 'causal efficacy'. The first is easy to understand — what is in front of your nose. The second is more difficult. The example Whitehead gives is the words 'United States'. You do not grasp these piecemeal: 'United — that means held together. States — yes, that means states like Florida and California. Oh yes, that means America.' You see the two words as one, Unitedstates, and register that as 'America'. Cause and effect blend into one.

Now Hume criticized causality by saying that every effect is quite distinct from its cause, and so is not 'necessarily' linked to it. Whitehead replies: When you grasp a 'meaning', cause and effect are not merely 'linked' — they are one.

We might say, then, that we have two 'modes of perception', which could be called 'immediacy perception' and 'meaning perception'. When you are very tired and depressed, your meaning perception becomes blurred. But this is an illusion, caused by tiredness. On the other hand, when you are drunk and feeling jolly, the world seems to be all meaning. Then it is your immediacy perception that becomes blurred; you cannot even get your key into the keyhole.

On the other hand, there are times — perhaps when you are feeling happy and excited on a spring morning — when the two modes of perception seem to blend together perfectly. You have a wonderful sense of meaning, yet your 'immediacy perception' is fully operational.

What happens then could be compared to the film *The Dam Busters*, in which the British planes had to drop bombs shaped like billiard balls that bounced along the Moener Lake and hit the dam at water level. The problem for the pilot was to know when he was at exactly the right height to drop them. The solution was to place two spotlights on the plane, one in the nose, one in the tail, whose two beams converged at exactly the right height. So when there was just one spot on the surface of the lake, he released the bombs.

According to Whitehead, our most brilliant moments of insight happen when the two beams — immediacy perception and meaning perception — converge.

This, then, is Whitehead's 'refutation of Hume', and it is a breakthrough in western philosophy because it provides new foundations. The question 'Do we have free will or are we robots?' becomes absurd. Instead, philosophy can get back to its proper business, which Bertrand Russell defined as 'understanding the universe'.

And what of that other question: of the 'me' behind the scenes, whose existence was recognized by Fichte?

This was the problem to which Edmund Husserl devoted his life. It has always seemed to me that Husserl is the greatest of modern thinkers.

When he was at university, in the 1880s, philosophy was still struggling to throw off the toils of Bishop Berkeley, and the notion that 'meaning' is something created by the mind. John Stuart Mill, for example, argued that the feeling of logical certainty is no more than that — a feeling — and that all logic can be therefore reduced to psychology. This notion is called 'psychologism', and in its broadest sense it holds that philosophy, logic — even mathematics —— can be explained in terms of psychology. This outraged Husserl, for it implied that all truth is 'relative', and Husserl could see that philosophy is never going to escape from muddle and confusion while it accepted such vagaries. So his starting point was the acceptance that logic deals with objective truth, not with relative ideas.

His first major work, *Logical Investigations*, was a sustained attack on psychologism, and an attempt to show that philosophy should be nothing less than a science.

This, of course, is what Descartes wanted to do when he asked the question: 'Of what can we be certain?' Husserl gave Descartes full credit for this, and even entitled one of his most important series of lectures 'Cartesian Meditations'. But, as we have seen, Descartes' problem was that he began with the wrong question: 'What can I know?', and failed to ask who was this 'I' who wanted to know.

Let me try putting this another way. In her book about 'female outsiders', *Alone, Alone*, Rosemary Dinnage discusses Bertrand Russell's affair with Lady Ottoline Morrell, and says:

> It is important to understand…that it was his underlying need to know whether anything could be established as true that shaped his whole mind… He himself felt that his search had made him into a 'logic machine', a 'spectator and not an actor', with a 'mind like a search light, very bright in one direction but dark everywhere else'.

What Russell had recognized was what Fichte had said a century earlier: that real philosophy demands an active attitude, rather than the passive one of the philosopher sitting in his armchair. To 'know' something merely with the mind is hardly to know it at all. Our whole being is somehow involved in true knowing. And when this happens, knowledge has a 'weight' that is not found in merely intellectual knowing.

Husserl's basic recognition is that *perception is intentional*; that when we 'see' something we fire our attention at it like an arrow. But if there is an 'intentional arrow', there must also be an archer who shoots it. In that case, Hume must have been wrong; there must be a 'real me' behind perception. And in trying to understand the way this 'real me' (transcendental ego) influences my perceptions and creates my life-world, Husserl saw himself as trying to 'unveil the secrets of the transcendental ego'.

This is also the essence of Husserl's revolution: that consciousness is intentional, that it is active, not passive. It is like a hand reaching out and grabbing things, not just a searchlight. And Russell's own career is a sad example of what happens when a thinker stays in the 'Cartesian' mode too long. Russell spent his whole life asking: 'What can we know for certain?' And the result is oddly disappointing, for he never found a satisfactory answer.

But if, like Rosemary Dinnage, we remove our attention from Russell the thinker to Russell the person, we become aware of the consequences of his 'passive' attitude to philosophy —— i.e. he totally failed to bring his interior philosopher and human being into line. As his second wife Dora put it to Rosemary Dinnage: 'Bertie could behave rottenly.' Until he was a very elderly gentleman he continued to pursue women, and to behave like an adolescent. As a person, he remained deeply unsatisfying to all the women he got involved with, and was dumped innumerable times. (I imagine his lifelong desire to screw any attractive female, from fifteen to fifty, was due to a gloomy conviction in adolescence that a person so ugly and preoccupied with ideas would remain love-starved, and by the time he learned different, the neurosis was too deep to be unrooted.)

But how could a person like Russell have benefited from Husserl's phenomenology? In fact, we may as well open the question out and ask, how could anyone?

Let me start by quoting the French phenomenologist Paul Ricoeur. He is talking about the 'reduction' or *epoché*, that method of 'standing back' and viewing things from a distance — rather like standing back from a large picture in an art gallery:

> By means of this reduction consciousness rids itself of a naiveté which it has beforehand, and which Husserl calls the natural attitude. This attitude consists in spontaneously believing that the world which is there is simply given. In correcting itself about this naiveté, consciousness discovers that it is in itself giving, sense-giving. The reduction does not exclude the presence of the world; it takes nothing back. It does not even suspend the primacy of intuition in every cognition. After the reduction, consciousness continues seeing, but without being absorbed in this seeing, without being lost in it. Rather, the very seeing itself is discovered as a doing [*opération*], as a producing [*oeuvre*] – once Husserl even says 'as a creating'. Husserl would be understood – and the one who thus understands him would be a phenomenologist – if the intentionality which culminates in seeing were recognised to be a creative vision.
>
> *Husserl: An Analysis of His Phenomenology*, 1987

But how?, the reader wants to ask. What is the trick of transforming ordinary perception into creative vision?

We can begin by noting that poets do it all the time, and so do great painters like Van Gogh. Read Shelley's 'Ode to the West Wind', and you can feel the 'phenomenological vision'. Or look at a great painting by Van Gogh or Vlaminck or Soutine. When I was working in a tax office in Rugby in my teens, I remember my boss saying with disgust that he thought Van Gogh simply distorted everything he painted. He was missing the point: that Van Gogh was saying, 'This is how I see things when I put on my creative spectacles.' Rupert Brooke said that on a spring morning he sometimes walked down a country road feeling almost sick with excitement.

Brooke realized that he could bring on this feeling by looking at things in a certain way. And what was really happening when he did this was that he had somehow become aware that he could see more, become aware of more, by looking at things as if they possessed hidden depths of meaning. For it is true. He was becoming conscious of the intentional element in perception, that his 'seeing' was in itself a creative act. We can suddenly begin to see what Ricoeur meant.

Here is another way of putting this point across. A normal young male feels spontaneous sexual excitement if he sees a girl taking off her clothes. He feels this is 'natural', like feeling hungry when you smell cooking. But supposing he is looking through an art book with reproductions of paintings, and he sees a picture of a model taking off her clothes. She is attractive, and he stares at the painting, and then — let us suppose — deliberately induces sexual excitement in himself. How does he do this? In that question lies the essence of phenomenology. You could say that he looks at the picture, and deliberately puts himself in the state of mind of a man about to climb into bed with her. He ceases to see the picture from 'the natural standpoint' ('this is just a picture') and endows it with a dimension of reality. And it can be seen that he is again 'putting on his creative spectacles'.

The mind can deliberately change the way it sees things. Brooke wrote a letter to a friend in 1910, in which he described how he could wander about a village wild with exhilaration:

> And it's not only beauty and beautiful things. In a flicker of sunlight on a blank wall, or a reach of muddy pavement, or smoke from an engine at night, there's a sudden significance and importance and inspiration that makes the breath stop with a gulp of certainty and happiness. It's not that the wall or the smoke seem important for anything or suddenly reveal any general statement, or are suddenly seen to be good or beautiful in themselves — only that for you they're perfect and unique. It's like being in love with a person... I suppose my occupation is being in love with the universe.

We can grasp what Ricoeur meant by 'the very seeing is discovered as a doing'. Brooke is so excited because he realizes he can make himself see things in a certain way, and respond to them — just as an adolescent is excited when he discovers that this body can produce a heady brew called sexual excitement. And this is the very essence of phenomenology: you might say that phenomenology is a prosaic way of developing the mystical faculty.

Husserl's theories galvanized philosophy. But unfortunately, his chief disciple, Heidegger, undid all his good work by placing the concept of 'Man' (*dasein*) at the centre of his philosophy, instead of the transcendental ego and its hidden secrets. Heidegger dragged philosophy back into the muddle and confusion of his predecessors. Sartre was much influenced by Husserl and Heidegger, but he began by declaring that there is no 'transcendental ego', no archer to fire the arrow of perception. 'Intentionality' is mechanical, like the tides being pulled by the moon. We live in a meaningless world, so although we are 'free', there is no 'way' that will lead us out of the morass. But, as I pointed out in *The Outsider*, it is as impossible to exercise freedom in a meaningless world as it is to jump while you are falling.

Sartre at least declared his belief in political commitment to revolution. His main successor, Michel Foucault, was bowled over by Beckett's *Waiting for Godot*, and decided that this would be his foundation – the view that life is so comically meaningless that all talk of 'commitment' is futile. According to Foucault, history is like the fashion industry; it changes periodically, but no one can say it progresses. Foucault used his immense erudition to demonstrate the way that one 'fashion' (he called them *epistemes*) replaces another in an endless meaningless progression which (unlike Hegel's notion of history) never gets anywhere. Another complication was that Foucault was a homosexual with powerful sado-masochistic leanings, so his works became a disguised polemic, arguing for a kind of Dionysian explosion of repressed impulses. He regarded the 'motor' of evolution as the Will to Power, but, like Schopenhauer, felt this was purposeless. So Foucault merely represents yet another swing of the pendulum in the opposite direction.

The same, I would suggest, is true of another influential modern philosopher whose despair was based upon guilt about his homosexuality: Ludwig Wittgenstein.

Born in Vienna in 1889, the youngest son of a wealthy iron-and-steel magnate, his original ambition was to become an engineer, like his father, which is why he went to England to study engineering at Manchester University. An increasing interest in the foundations of mathematics led him to Cambridge, where he studied under Bertrand Russell. But he was morbidly pessimistic by temperament and obsessed by the idea of suicide. (Three of his brothers killed themselves.) When he hastened to join the army at the outbreak of the First World War, it was (he admitted later) with the hope of being killed. Throughout the war he carried in his knapsack the manuscript of his first book, later to be called *Tractatus Logico-Philosophicus*.

This book, perhaps the most influential work in modern philosophy, sprang out of Wittgenstein's craving to establish some kind of basic philosophical certainty, like Descartes' 'I think, therefore I am'. He considered the result to be the definitive answer to all the problems of philosophy – not because he felt he had arrived at some ultimate truth about the meaning of life, but because he argued that philosophy has no business with such questions. Philosophy, he said, can only deal with what can be stated precisely in language. And language has certain sharply defined limitations. It is a picture of the real world just as the Mona Lisa is a portrait of a real person. And just as a piece of matter is made up of atoms, so our world is made up of 'atomic facts', which can be combined into more complex propositions. We might compare it to the pieces of a jigsaw puzzle with which we can build a picture. But that picture can only be of the real world that lies around us. There is no way of including God or universal meaning, as certain idealist philosophers would like to.

Wittgenstein is not denying the existence of ethical or religious truth, but he is saying that it cannot be expressed in language. This refreshingly down-to-earth view became the foundation of the philosophy known as Logical Positivism, which simply ruled out all forms of idealism as literally meaningless, like speaking of a square circle. But in the 1930s, he began to see that this view was too simplistic. Language is not simply a *picture* of reality. It is true that words are tools, but tools can be of many different kinds – hammers, drills, pincers, corkscrews… And someone who uses words to create a fairy story is using them in a completely different way to someone who is writing a computer repair manual. According to Wittgenstein, fairy stories and repair manuals are different language *games*, and philosophy is only one among many such games.

Although the method of Wittgenstein's 'Linguistic Analysis' is far more complex than that of Logical Positivism, the aims are virtually identical: to destabilize the foundations of much that has always been accepted as philosophy.

It should be clear that Wittgenstein's view of philosophy has little in common with the one being offered in this book. For Wittgenstein, the question asked by Kierkegaard: 'What am I doing in this world and what am I supposed to do now I am here?' would be quite meaningless, for there is no way we can go 'outside' the world in order to answer it. But there are thousands of human beings who feel that such questions cannot be dismissed as misunderstandings of language. To feel that they have meaning is to suggest a world of meanings and values which exists outside this reality that surrounds and entraps us.

It has been worth discussing Wittgenstein here because he epitomizes a certain view of reality that strikes me as demonstrably inadequate. Clearly a book like this one, which takes as its starting point William James's question of how human beings can learn to live at much higher levels of power, has little in common with a work that declares that all questions of philosophy can and should be expressed in 'common language'.

The real problem with such a view is that it sets out to impose limits on the world and its meaning. In that sense, Wittgenstein and Samuel Beckett are setting out from the same starting point — denial of any meaning that is beyond the narrow and commonplace. They are trapped in Heidegger's 'triviality of everydayness', and insist that this is part of the human condition, and that insofar as we want something more than that, we are suffering from delusions.

Jacques Derrida, Foucault's most influential successor, was another swing back towards Hume. Taking from the linguistic philosopher Ferdinand de Saussure the view that words have no innate 'meanings', but vary freely in different contexts, he applied this notion to philosophy, which he sees as a kind of spume on the surface of the sea of language. Derrida says there is no 'underlying reality' (he calls it 'presence') and of course, no 'real me' or self. So it is again back to Hume.

The truth is that there are only two pockets in the billiard table of philosophy: materialism and idealism, and no matter how 'original' a philosopher, he is bound to end in one or the other.

But the real problem here concerns philosophy itself. Philosophers have always aimed at some 'system' that explains everything. We have to grasp that this is a mirage because — as Kierkegaard said — it leaves me *and my free will* out of account.

In mathematics, Kurt Gödel caused a revolution by demonstrating something very similar. Until Gödel, mathematicians had tried to create mathematical systems (like geometry) that consist of a number of self-evident axioms, and a superstructure of 'truths' built on these. Gödel showed that this is impossible – that in any such system, there are always certain truths that cannot be proved *within* the system; they can only be proved within a larger system still, a meta-system. (For example, a classroom full of philosophy students could discuss the question: 'How important is love to human development?', but the students will have to leave the classroom and fall in love before they can really understand the question.) And within that meta-system there are again truths that cannot be proved — and so on ad infinitum.

So whenever you hear of some philosopher — like Hegel or Foucault (or Beckett, for that matter) — who claims to have created a system within which everything can be explained, you are entitled to shake your head and murmur, 'Gödel'.

This happens to be an appropriate ending to a chapter about the 'strange story of modern philosophy', which began with René Descartes and his attempt to place philosophy on a scientific basis by 'doubting everything', and which has ended by doubting practically everything out of existence. Clearly, it is time we began to look for our own meta-system.

EVERYDAY CONSCIOUSNESS IS A LIAR

From *Introduction to the New Existentialism,* 1966.

Let us be quite clear about the implications of all this, for they constitute a revolution in philosophy. 'Peak experiences' all seem to have the same 'content': that the chief mistake of human beings is to pay too much attention to everyday trivialities. We are strangely inefficient machines, utilizing only a fraction of our powers, and the reason for this is our short sightedness. Koestler's 'mystical' insight made him feel that even the threat of death was a triviality that should be ignored; 'So what.... Have you nothing more serious to worry about?' Greene's whisky priest: 'It seemed to him, at that moment, that it would have been quite easy to be a saint.' Death reveals to us that our lives have been one long miscalculation, based on triviality. Proust's Marcel, when he tastes the cake dipped in tea, says 'the vicissitudes of life had become indifferent to me, its disasters innocuous.... I had ceased now to feel mediocre, accidental, mortal.' In his diary, Nijinsky, on the point of insanity, wrote: 'I am God, I am God.'

What is revolutionary about the new existentialism is this: it asks whether there is not some logical method of investigating such insights and weighing their content against our 'everyday consciousness'. Nijinsky's statement 'I am God' was not the rambling of a sick mind; it was an insight of the same type as those of Koestler, William James and Proust; and we have agreed that these insights have a certain objective content. In that case, the question suggests itself: '*Was* he God?'

An empirical philosopher would reply: 'Clearly not. Next question....'
But this is an evasion — like Moore producing his watch to demonstrate
that time is not an illusion. A more reasonable objection would be: 'Is there
any logical method of investigating such a question?' To that we can answer:
Yes — through the phenomenological examination of consciousness. This
in turn implies the creation of a language and a set of concepts in terms of
which we can discuss it.

I think we should now be able to see clearly the fundamental issue
on which the 'new existentialism' differs from the older version. The old
existentialism emphasizes man's contingency. It says that since there is no
God, there are no 'transcendental values' either. Man is alone in an empty
universe; no act of his has any meaning outside itself — and its social
context. Existentialism has removed the universal backcloth against which
mediaeval man acted out his dreams, with a sense that everything he did
would be brought up on judgement day. In its place, says Sartre, there
is only the infinitude of space, which means that man's actions are of no
importance to anyone but himself.

Phenomenology replies: We grant you, for the sake of argument, that
all religious values are nonsense. But we cannot agree that man's everyday
sense of his 'self-evident contingency' represents the truth either. Everyday
consciousness is a liar, and most people have insights to this effect at least
once a week. If they concentrated upon this matter, they would get such
insights more frequently still. The question is simply how to give such
insights a philosophical status, and how to investigate them.

Once we see this clearly, it becomes astonishing that anyone bothers to
argue about it. Harley Granville Barker spoke of these insights as 'the secret
life' (in a play of that title), and points out that *all* men, no matter how
materialistic and trivial, draw their strength from 'the secret life'.

In other words, there *is* a standard of values 'external to human
consciousness', if we are talking about the everyday human consciousness
that most of us make the foundation of our values. In fact, both Sartre
and Heidegger recognize this in recognizing that man gains a sense of
'authenticity' in the face of death.

Such a recognition is only a beginning. Inauthenticity is to feel futile
contingent, without purpose. Authenticity is to be driven by a deep sense
of purpose. *Such a sense of purpose cannot exist unless we first make the
assumption that our sense of contingency is a liar, and that there is a standard of
values external to everyday human consciousness.*

In short, where both Sartre and Heidegger make a mistake is in supposing
that the flash of authenticity experienced under the threat of death is a more

or less 'mystical' sensation that cannot be carried over into ordinary human existence. It is not. It is a glimpse of a consciousness of purpose which, under certain circumstances, should be quite easily accessible to human beings. Once we have accepted James's idea that 'mystical consciousness' is only a change in the threshold of ordinary consciousness, the whole thing becomes more down-to-earth.

It might be mentioned, in passing, that this basic recognition differs in no fundamental respect from the metaphysics of the *Upanishads* or the *Bhagavad Gita*. The difference between the religious standpoint and the 'natural standpoint' is the difference between the 'external values system' of the new existentialism and the 'total contingency' of the old. (But I am speaking now of the metaphysics of religion, as distinguished from the element of dogma and the supernatural.)

This is the foundation. For biological reasons, we are 'blinkered', like horses in the traffic. The blinkers are a device for enabling us to concentrate on the present and its problems. A painter who is painting a large canvas has to work with his nose to the canvas; but periodically he stands back to see the effect of the whole. These over-all glimpses renew his sense of purpose.

Man's evolution depends upon a renewal of the sense of over-all purpose. For several centuries now, the direction of our culture has been a concentration upon the minute, the particular. In the field of science, this has produced our present high level of technological achievement. In the field of culture, we have less reason for self-congratulation, for the concentration upon the particular — to the exclusion of wider meanings — has led us into a *cul de sac*. Yeats described the result as 'fish gasping on the strand'— a minute realism that has lost all drive and purpose.

I have said that the next step consists in a phenomenological analysis of consciousness. We have no language to describe these important inner-states.

In the remainder of this book, I shall attempt to make a beginning upon a systematic phenomenology of consciousness. It should be possible to at least lay down the broad outlines of such a 'new science'.

Let us begin with a consideration of the word 'values'. What is a value? It is a kind of 'rate of exchange'. If I say that a certain object is not worth what the shopkeeper is asking for it, I mean that I am not willing to exchange money for it. If I say that a certain task is 'not worth the effort', I mean that I am not willing to exchange *vital energy* for the result it will obtain.

Everything that I experience causes a rise or fall in the immediate level of my vital energy. Eating when I am hungry, drinking when I am thirsty, causes a rise in the level of my vitality. A 'value' is that physical response of pleasure and vitality that I experience as I swallow food. So we might also say that *a value is a response*. This response determines what we consider 'worth doing'.

Religion and philosophy, of course, aim at absolute values. But we might also note that human beings in general aim at absolute values. Our life is an attempt to discard false values. A child enjoys cream cakes; but he discovers that too many of them make him sick; he therefore learns eventually not to over-indulge in cream cakes. The 'immediate' response to cream cakes is replaced by a more reasoned response that sees further.

But our value systems are not internally consistent; neither do they have to be. We adopt temporary systems of values according to the task in hand. A parent loves a child, but if the child needs correction, he places the love temporarily in abeyance and takes up the rod. He is actually practising what Husserl calls 'bracketing'. The same thing happens if I decide that I must finish a certain task in hand, even though there are other things I would prefer to do. I deliberately 'bracket out' my response (i.e. values) to the things I would prefer to do, and concentrate on the task that must be finished.

We are therefore capable of altering our immediate responses — and values — in favour of some more embracing value system. To some extent, therefore, every moment of our conscious lives depends upon the value systems we adopt.

Since the most ordinary act of living depends upon the handling of such complex 'values', it is obviously important that our over-all, basic values should be very clear indeed, to prevent confusion. But here we immediately encounter the great problem. A value is a response, an immediate warm flow of vitality and optimism. But since our consciousness is so limited, it is precisely our 'ultimate' values that are *not* responses. A saint like Ramakrishna may be able to establish immediate vital contact with his deepest values; but most of us have to work on in the dark.

All this talk about values makes the problem sound somewhat abstract, when it is anything but. It is purely practical. Our lives are enveloped in moods, in the ebb and flow of energy. The human beings we refer to as 'great' have seized the sense of purpose that comes with the moods of optimism, and tried to live by it. The problem is an absurd one. It is like the sequence in the Charlie Chaplin film where the tramp meets a man who is kind and generous to him when drunk, and rude and violent when sober. Which is the 'real' man? Or is the question unanswerable, as Pirandello seems to imply in various plays that deal with the same kind of subject? The question may sound 'meaningless' to an empiricist philosopher, but it is of vital importance to every human being who is more than half alive. Human beings experience life as a series of moods. (These 'moods' are actually intentional value-judgements.) Each 'mood' seems to offer them a different piece of advice on the question of how to live. In ages of faith, man possessed religious belief to act as a compass to steer him through his moods, but in an age of humanism, he is at the mercy of the 'moods'. Each mood seems to reveal the 'reality' of the world; in moods of extreme pessimism, life is a cheat, a swindler, and man's optimism is sheer gullibility; in moods of optimism, the pessimism seems to have been the outcome of feebleness and poor-spiritedness. Our usual state of mind is somewhere between the two; we plod on passively, avoiding great risks, hoping for the best. Obviously, we require an *objective* standard, so that we are no longer ships that change our course with every wind.

In saying this, I have stated the central aim of the 'new existentialism'. We immediately become aware of the complexity of the problem. A relativist would dismiss it by saying: How can you decide that the world is one thing or the other? But this is premature defeatism. One might say, in the case of Charlie Chaplin's drunk, that it is meaningless to ask which is his 'true' character: that drink simply reveals another aspect of his character. But any competent psychologist would set out to analyse the man's character in terms of basic impulses and their frustration, and would emerge eventually with an answer that would be somewhere near to the 'objective truth'. At least, it would be nearer than the defeatist idea that there's no such thing.

So when attempting to assess the degree of objective justification for the optimistic and pessimistic attitudes to human existence, we have to be prepared for a fairly complicated task. But once we pose the question of what constitutes human values, the problem ceases to look so formidable. We have taken a step as decisive as the realization that the sun is the fixed point in our planetary system. The shifting sands cease to shift. An apparently insoluble task suddenly begins to yield to our effort.

The new existentialism consists of a phenomenological examination of consciousness, with the emphasis upon the problem of what constitutes human values. And since moods of optimism and insight are less accessible than moods of depression and life-devaluation, the phenomenology of life-devaluation constitutes the most valuable field of study.

The analysis of language

Before I consider this problem in more detail, I must enlarge a point made in the previous chapter.

The analysis of consciousness is only half the task. The other half consists in the analysis of language. In this field, Wittgenstein was the great forerunner.

It was Wittgenstein who pointed out that we tend to treat language as a unity as if the language of Shakespeare, Hegel, Beatrix Potter and Freud all belonged somewhere on the same scale. Wittgenstein recognized that this apparent unity is actually a conglomerate of a number of different language systems (or 'games', as he preferred to call them), each with different sets of 'rules'. Different 'games' may have as little in common as football has with poker or cowboys and Indians. He used the simile of the cabin of a locomotive, full of different types of lever; some have to be pulled, others pushed, others wound in a circle, others worked back and forth...and so on. Words have just as many functions. Only in the simplest and most primitive language games does a word correspond simply to an object.

Wittgenstein's intention was apparently negative; he wished to show that most philosophy is a misunderstanding of language. But the deeper aim has much in common with Husserl's; he aimed at doing *foundation work* on which it would be possible to build a philosophy. In fact, his aim is obviously complementary to Husserl's; one was interested in a phenomenology of perception, the other of language.

It may be that, in terms of priorities, the phenomenology of language is more important than the phenomenology of perceptions and values. This would certainly be so if the 'new existentialism' aimed at being only a description of the 'human condition' in a general sense — for the scientist must begin by making sure that his measuring instruments are accurate. But since the 'new existentialism' concentrates upon a phenomenological account of perceptive-consciousness and value-consciousness, it has in-built safeguards in its active and permanent preoccupation with language.

Nevertheless, the point should be made here that a phenomenology of language is as vital to the development of a new existentialism as the phenomenology of values. The new existentialism is not all psychology.

Not the least important feature of the 'new existentialism' is that it is able to unite the two major traditions of twentieth century philosophy linguistic empiricism and phenomenological existentialism.

MAGIC — THE SCIENCE OF THE FUTURE

From *The Occult*, 1971

There is a passage in the Introduction to P. D. Ouspensky's *New Model of the Universe* that never fails to move and excite me:

It is the year 1906 or 1907. The editorial office of the Moscow daily paper *The Morning*. I have just received the foreign papers, and I have to write an article on the forthcoming Hague Conference. French, German, English, Italian papers. Phrases, phrases, sympathetic, critical, ironical, blatant, pompous, lying and, worst of all, utterly automatic, phrases which have been used a thousand times and will be used again on entirely different, perhaps contradictory, occasions. I have to make a survey of all these words and opinions, pretending to take them seriously, and then, just as seriously, to write something on my own account. But what can I say? It is all so tedious. Diplomats and all kinds of statesmen will gather together and talk, papers will approve or disapprove, sympathize or not sympathize. Then everything will be as it was, or even worse.

It is still early, I say to myself; perhaps something will come into my head later.

Pushing aside the papers, I open a drawer in my desk. The whole desk is crammed with books with strange titles, *The Occult World*, *Life after Death*, *Atlantis and Lemuria*, *Dogme et Rituel de la Haute Magie*, *Le Temple de Satan*, *The Sincere Narrations of a Pilgrim* and the like. These books and I have been inseparable for a whole month, and the world of the Hague Conference and leading articles becomes more and more vague and unreal to me.

I open one of the books at random, feeling that my article will not be written today. Well, it can go to the devil. Humanity will lose nothing if there is one article less on the Hague Conference....

When I first read this passage, my own circumstances gave it an added relevance. I was twenty years old, and I had been married for a year. My wife and our son were living in Earls Court, London, our fourth home in a year, and our half-insane landlady was the fourth — and worst — of a series. I was on the dole, and I found this almost as nervously wearing as the various factory jobs I had worked at since I was married. London seemed not merely alien, but somehow unreal. So I understood Ouspensky's feeling of nausea at the prospect of writing on the Hague Conference, and also that craving for *another world* of deeper meaning, represented by books on the occult. There is a passage in Louis-Ferdinand Céline that describes the world as rotten with lies, rotten to the point of collapse and disintegration. I had only to look at the advertisements in the London tube, or the headlines of the daily paper, to see that it was obviously true. Lies, stupidity, weakness and mediocrity — a civilization without ideals.

That was why I read Ouspensky, and all the other books on magic and mysticism that I could find in the local libraries: not only because they were an escape from the world of factories and neurotic landladies, but because they confirmed my intuition of another order of reality, *an intenser and more powerful form of consciousness* than the kind I seemed to share with eight million other Londoners.

But if, at that time, I had been asked whether I literally believed in magic, I would have answered No: that it was a poetic fiction, a symbol of the world that *ought* to exist, but didn't. In short, wishful thinking. In the first sentence of *Ritual Magic*, E. M. Butler writes: 'The fundamental aim of all magic is to impose the human will on nature, on man and the supersensual world in order to master them.' And if that was a fair definition of magic, then I agreed with John Symonds, the biographer of Aleister Crowley, who said, 'The only trouble with magic is that it doesn't work.' Magic, I felt, was no more than a first crude attempt at science, and it had now been superseded by science.

If I still accepted that view, I would not be writing this book. It now seems to me that the exact reverse is true. Magic was not the 'science' of the past. It is the science of the future. I believe that the human mind has reached a point in evolution where it is about to develop new powers — powers that would once have been considered magical. Indeed, it has always possessed greater powers than we now realize: of telepathy, premonition of danger, second sight, thaumaturgy (the power to heal); but these were part of its instinctive, animal inheritance. For the past thousand years or so, humankind has been busy developing another kind of power related to the intellect, and the result is Western civilization. His unconscious powers have not atrophied; but they have 'gone underground'. Now the wheel has come the full circle; intellect has reached certain limits, and it cannot advance beyond them until it recovers some of the lost powers. Anyone who has read modern philosophy will understand what I mean; it has become narrow, rigid, logical; and it attempts to make up for lack of broader intuitions with a microscopic attention to detail. It has cut itself off from its source.

And what is, in fact, the source of philosophy — or, for that matter, of any knowledge? It is fundamentally the need for power. You have only to watch the face of a baby who has just learned how to open a door by turning the handle, to understand what knowledge is *for*. In the twentieth century, power has become a suspect word, because it has become associated with the idea of power over other people. But that is its least important application. One of the fundamental myths of magic concerns the magician who seeks political power; he receives a number of warnings, and if he persists, he is destroyed. Political power strengthens the ego; magical power rises from the subconscious, from the non-personal urge. Ouspensky describes the beginning of his 'search for the miraculous':

> I am a schoolboy in the second or third 'class.' But instead of Zeifert's Latin grammar... I have before me Malinin and Bourenin's 'Physics.' I have borrowed this book from one of the older boys and am reading it greedily and enthusiastically, overcome now by rapture, now by terror, at the mysteries that are opening before me. All round me walls are crumbling, and horizons infinitely remote and incredibly beautiful stand revealed. It is as though threads, previously unknown and unsuspected, begin to reach out and bind things together. For the first time in my life, my world emerges from chaos. Everything becomes connected, forming an orderly and harmonious whole....

This kind of language may be off-putting ('horizons infinitely remote and incredibly beautiful'), but it is worth bearing in mind that Ouspensky was trained as a scientist, and he is trying to be strictly accurate. He means exactly that: the sudden sense of *meanings*, far bigger than oneself, that make all personal preoccupations seem trivial. Even Bertrand Russell, the founder of 'logical atomism', catches this feeling: 'I *must*, before I die, find some way to say the essential thing that is in me, that I have never said yet — a thing that is not love or hate or pity or scorn, but the very breath of life, fierce and coming from far away, bringing into human life the vastness and fearful passionless force of non-human things.'*

The power to be derived from this 'fearful passionless force' is only incidentally a power over things and people. It is basically power over oneself, contact with some 'source of power, meaning and purpose' in the subconscious mind.

The ability to become excited by 'infinitely remote horizons' is peculiar to human beings; no other animal possesses it. It is a kind of intellectual far-sightedness, that could be compared to a pair of binoculars. We have developed it over two million years of evolution. And at the same time, certain other faculties have fallen into disuse. For example, the 'homing instinct'. In *The Territorial Imperative*, Robert Ardrey devotes an interesting chapter (IV) to this phenomenon. A scientist named Johannes Schmidt made the discovery that every eel in the western world is born in the Sargasso Sea. In the autumn, the eels of Europe and eastern America make their way down the rivers and end in the Sargasso Sea, between the West Indies and the Azores. The following spring, the baby eels make their way to fresh water; two years later, when they are two inches long, the elvers make their way back home *alone*. Those with 115 vertebrae swim back to Europe; those with 107 vertebrae go west to America. The parents remain behind to die.

The green turtle of the Caribbean performs an equally spectacular feat, swimming 1,400 miles from Brazil to Ascension Island, in the mid-Atlantic, at breeding time. The tiny deer mouse of Wyoming, no bigger than the end of one's finger, can be transported a mile away from home — about a hundred miles in terms of human size — and unerringly find his way back to the fifty-yard patch that constitutes home. Homing pigeons return over hundreds of miles. It was once believed that this was the result of hard work by the human trainer, until someone discovered accidentally that baby pigeons return home just as unerringly without any training — and often make better time than the 'trained' adults!

In a few cases, science has been able to explain the homing instinct. Vitus B. Dröscher mentions some examples in *Mysterious Senses*. The black-cap bird navigates by means of the stars — as Dr Franz Sauer discovered by

---

*Letter to Constance Malleson, 1918, quoted in *My Philosophical Development* (Allen and Unwin), p. 261.

putting them in a planetarium. Salmon, strangely enough, navigate by a highly developed sense of smell. The eel probably does the same, although this does not explain how baby eels know their way back to rivers they have never seen. Bees and ants navigate by the sun. One scientist at Cambridge University suspects that pigeons navigate by taking an astronomical reading of their latitude and longitude by means of the sun and comparing it with the latitude and longitude of their home territory.

So perhaps there is no need to posit some mysterious 'sixth sense' by which animals find their way home. No doubt there are always 'natural' explanations. But in some cases, it is difficult to imagine what it could be. Scientists in Wilhelmshaven took cats, confined in a bag, on a long drive round the town. They were then released in the centre of a maze with twenty-four exits. Most cats made straight for the exit that lay in the direction of their home. A German zoologist, Hans Fromme, has discovered that the migratory instinct of robins is thrown into confusion when the robins are first placed in a steel strong room. The inference is that robins navigate by sensitivity to some electromagnetic vibration; the current hypothesis is that it originates in the Milky Way, but this is no more than a guess.

But even if this could be definitely proved, would it really constitute an 'explanation' of the homing instinct? We are dealing with degrees of sensitivity that are so far beyond our human perceptions that they are, to all intents and purposes, new senses. *Or rather, old senses.*

There must have been a time when human beings possessed a homing instinct of the same efficiency, for our primitive ancestors hunted their food in huge forests or featureless prairies. There is even more reason for supposing that man once possessed an unusually developed sense of impending danger, for our primate ancestors would otherwise have become extinct in the great droughts of the Pliocene era, more than five million years ago, when they were struggling for survival against creatures in every way more 'specialized' than they were. Man no longer has a great deal of use for the homing instinct or a highly developed premonition of danger. These faculties have fallen into disuse. But they have not vanished. There seems to be evidence that in circumstances where they are necessary, they become as efficient as ever. Anyone who has read the various books by Jim Corbett, author of *Man-eaters of Kumaon*, will recall a number of occasions when he was saved by his 'sixth sense'. One example will suffice. In *Jungle Lore*, Corbett describes how he was about to take a bath one evening when he noticed that his feet were covered with red dust. There was a place that lay on his route home where he might have walked through the dust; but he could think of no reason why he should have done so. Eventually he remembered the circumstances. He had walked over a culvert whose parapet was eighteen inches high. As he approached this, he had crossed the road to the other side, walking through the red dust at the side of the road. He crossed the culvert on the right-hand side, then re-crossed the road to the left again as he continued on his way home.

Corbett was baffled; he could not imagine why he had absent-mindedly crossed the road like this. The next day he retraced his footsteps. In the sandy bed of the culvert, on the left-hand side, he discovered the pug marks of a tiger that had been lying there. 'The tiger had no intention of killing me; but if at the moment of passing him I had stopped to listen to any jungle sound, or had coughed or sneezed or blown my nose, or had thrown my rifle from one shoulder to the other, there was a chance that the tiger would have got nervous and attacked me. My subconscious being was not prepared to take this risk and jungle sensitiveness came to my assistance and guided me away from the potential danger.'

How do we explain Corbett's jungle sensitiveness? As a 'sixth sense'? Or simply as some form of subconscious observation? I would argue that it makes no real difference. When Sherlock Holmes deduces that Watson has sent a telegram from the clay on his shoes and the ink stain on his finger, this is obviously what we mean by logical, scientific thinking. It is possible that Corbett's reasons for crossing the road were equally logical, although subconscious. An hour before he set out for home, he may have heard the tiger cough, and subconsciously registered the direction in which it was travelling. A few other small signs — the absence of birds near the culvert, a broken twig — and his subconscious mind was already reaching its conclusions in the best Holmes tradition. But if Corbett remained consciously unaware of all this, then we are dealing with a faculty that may be called a sixth sense, a subconscious faculty by comparison with which our powers of conscious observation are clumsy and inaccurate. We find this difficult to grasp because we use the conscious mind as an instrument of learning. Driving my car has become so natural to me that it might almost be called an instinct; but I had to learn to do it *consciously* first. But it would obviously be absurd to suppose that pigeons learned navigation by the sun in the same manner. There was no conscious process of learning; it was all done at the instinctive level.

We may be able to explain the pigeon's homing instinct in terms that Sherlock Holmes would understand; but it is important to realize that the subconscious mind works with a speed and accuracy beyond our conscious grasp, and that it may work upon data that are too subtle for our clumsy senses. How, for example, do we explain the power of water diviners? I have seen a man with a twig in his hand walking around the field in which our house is built, tracing the course of an underground spring, and distinguishing it clearly from a metal water pipe. (We later consulted the plans of the house and found that he was completely accurate about the water pipe.) He denied the suggestion that this was a 'supernormal' faculty, and insisted that he could teach anyone to divine water in less than an hour: 'Everyone possesses the faculty; it's merely a matter of training.' As far as I know, no scientist has even attempted to explain the power of water diviners, although they are accepted as a commonplace in any country district. And when they *are* finally understood, it will no doubt prove to be something as simple and startling as the salmon's sense of smell, or the robin's sensitivity to stellar radiation. There is no need to draw a sharp distinction between scientific 'commonsense' and powers that would once have been classified as 'magical'. In the animal kingdom, 'magical' powers are commonplace. Civilized man has forgotten about them because they are no longer necessary to his survival.

In fact, his survival depends upon 'forgetting' them. High development of the instinctive levels is incompatible with the kind of concentration upon detail needed by civilized man. An illustration can be found in the autobiography of the 'clairvoyant' Pieter van der Hurk, better known as Peter Hurkos.* In 1943 Hurkos was working as a house painter when he fell from the ladder and fractured his skull. When he woke up — in the Zuidwal Hospital in the Hague — he discovered that he now possessed the gift of second sight; he 'knew' things about his fellow patients without being told. This almost cost him his life. Shaking hands with a patient about to be discharged, he suddenly 'knew' that the man was a British agent, and that he would be assassinated by the Gestapo in two days' time. As a result of his prediction, Hurkos came close to being executed as a traitor by the Dutch underground; he was fortunately able to convince them that his clairvoyance was genuine.

The chief drawback of this unusual power was that he was no longer able to return to his old job as a painter; *he had lost the faculty of concentration.* 'I could not concentrate on anything in those days, for the moment I began to carry on an extended conversation with anyone, I would see visions of the various phases of his life and the lives of his family and friends.' His mind was like a radio set picking up too many stations. From the social point of view he was useless until he conceived the idea of using his peculiar powers on the stage.

*See *Psychic*, by Peter Hurkos (London, Barker, 1961).

Again, science has nothing to say about the powers of Peter Hurkos, or of his fellow Dutchman Gerard Croiset, although these powers have been tested in the laboratory and found to be genuine. Foretelling the future, or solving a murder case by handling a garment of the victim, is obviously a very different matter from Corbett's jungle sensitivity or the homing instinct. But it is worth bearing in mind that until the mid-1950s Schmidt's observations on eels — published as long ago as 1922 — were ignored by scientists because they failed to 'fit in'. Ardrey remarks that the Eel Story was classified with Hitler's Big Lie. That is, no one was willing to tackle the problem until science had reached a stage where it could no longer advance without taking it into account. No doubt the same thing will happen to the observations made on Hurkos by the Round Table Institute in Maine, and those on Croiset by the Parapsychology Institute of Utrecht University.

At this point it is necessary to say something of the course of evolution over the past million years or so. Some eleven million years ago, an ape called Ramapithecus seems to have developed the capacity to walk upright. He began to prefer the ground to the trees. And during the next nine million years, the tendency to walk upright became firmly established, and Ramapithecus turned into Australopithecus, our first 'human' ancestor. What difference did the upright posture make? First of all, it freed his hands, so that he could defend himself with a stone or a tree branch. Secondly, *it enlarged his horizon.*

As far as I know, no anthropologist has regarded this as significant — perhaps because there are many taller creatures than man. But the elephant and the giraffe have eyes in the side of their heads, so that their horizon is circular. The ape sees straight ahead; his vision is narrower but more concentrated. Could this be why the apes have evolved more than any other animal? Narrow vision makes for boredom; it also makes for increased mental activity, for curiosity. And when the inventiveness and curiosity were well developed, a certain branch of the apes learned to walk upright, so that his horizon was extended in another way. To see a long distance is to learn to think in terms of long distances, to calculate. Man's ability to walk upright and use his hands, and his natural capacity to see into the distance instead of looking at the ground, became weapons of survival. He developed intelligence because it was the only way to stay alive. And so, at the beginning of human evolution, man was forced to make a virtue of his ability to focus his attention upon minute particulars. No doubt he would have preferred to eat his dinner and then sleep in the sun, like the sabre-toothed tiger or the hippopotamus; but he was more defenceless than they were, and had to maintain constant vigilance.

In the course of time, this ability to 'focus' his attention and calculate became so natural that thinking became one of man's leisure activities. And it 'paid off' to an incredible extent. In a few thousand years, man evolved more than the great reptiles had evolved in several million. He created civilization, and in doing so, entered a new phase of self-awareness — the phase that human children now enter at the age of six or seven.

Self-consciousness brings heavy losses and enormous gains. The greatest loss is that instinctive 'naturalness' that small children and animals possess. But the vital gain is the sense of force, of power, of control. Man became the wilful animal, the most dangerous animal on the earth, never contented to live in peace for long, always invading the neighbouring country, burning the villages and raping the women. And this endless ego-drive has, in the past ten thousand years, separated him further and further from the apes in their dwindling forests and the swallows that fly south in the winter.

He is not entirely happy with this civilization that his peculiar powers have created. Its main trouble is that it takes so much looking after. Many men possess the animals' preference for the instinctive life of one-ness with nature; they dream about the pleasure of being a shepherd drowsing on a warm hillside, or an angler beside a stream. Oddly enough, such men have never been condemned as sluggards; they are respected as poets, and the soldiers and businessmen enjoy reading their daydreams when the day's work is over.

A poet is simply a man in whom the links with our animal past are still strong. He is aware that we contain a set of instinctive powers that are quite separate from the powers needed to win a battle or expand a business.

And he is instinctively aware of something far more important. Man has developed his conscious powers simply by wanting to develop them. He has travelled from the invention of the wheel to the exploration of space in a few quick strides. But he had also surpassed the animals in another respect: in the development of those 'other' powers. No animal is capable of the ecstasies of the mystics or the great poets. In his nature poetry, Wordsworth is 'at one' with nature in a quite different sense from the hippopotamus dozing in the mud. *Self-consciousness can be used for the development of man's instinctive powers*, as well as those of the intellect. The poet, the mystic and the 'magician' have this in common: the desire to develop their powers 'downward' rather than upward. In the *Symposium*, Socrates expresses the ideal aim: to do both at the same time — to use increased knowledge to reach out towards a state of instinctive unity with the universe. In the two and a half thousand years since then, civilization has been forced to devote its attention to more practical problems, while the artists and mystics have continued to protest that 'the world is too much with us', and that triumphant *Homo sapiens* is little more than a clever dwarf. If man is really to evolve, then he must develop *depth*, and power over his own depths.

And now, for the first time in the short history of our species, a large percentage of the human race *has* the leisure to forget the practical problems. And in America and Europe, there is a simultaneous upsurge of interest in 'mind-changing drugs' and in the 'occult'.

The psychedelic cult differs from the drug cults of the early twentieth century, or even the laudanum drinking of De Quincey and Coleridge, in being more positive in character. It is less a matter of the desire to escape from a 'botched civilization' than a definite desire to *get* somewhere, to 'plug in' to subconscious forces of whose existence we are instinctively certain. The same is true of the increased sexual permissiveness; it is not simply a matter of disintegrating morals, but the recognition that sexual excitement is a contact with the hidden powers of the unconscious. D. H. Lawrence describes Lady Chatterley's sensations after lovemaking: 'As she ran home in the twilight the world seemed a dream; the trees in the park seemed bulging and surging at anchor on a tide, and the heave of the slope to the house was alive.'

All Lawrence's work is concerned with the need for civilization to take a new direction, to concentrate upon the development of these 'other' powers instead of continuing to develop the intellect. It is not a matter of sinking into a kind of trance, a passive state of 'oneness with nature', like the cows Walt Whitman admired so much. The nature of which Lady Chatterley is aware as she runs home sounds more like those late canvases of Van Gogh in which everything is distorted by some inner force — by Russell's 'breath of life, fierce and coming from far away, bringing into human life the vastness and fearful passionless force of non-human things'.

In the same way, Ouspensky's preference for reading a book on magic instead of writing an article on the Hague Conference indicates something more positive than the poet's distaste for politics. At fourteen, Ouspensky is plunged into a state of ecstatic excitement by a book on physics, because it is a contact with the world of the impersonal. But science is a dead end for an imaginative youth; he doesn't want to end up injecting guinea pigs in Pavlov's laboratory. He has a feeling that all the *ways of life* offered by the modern world lead him in the opposite direction from the way he wants to go. In moments of depression he is inclined to wonder if this craving for distant horizons is not some odd illusion, 'the desire of the moth for the star'. But an instinct leads him to search persistently in books on magic and occultism; later, the same desire leads him to wander around in the

East, searching in monasteries for 'esoteric knowledge'. (It is ironical that he should have discovered what he was looking for when he returned to Moscow and met Gurdjieff.)

This sense of 'meanings' that are not apparent to ordinary consciousness is experienced by everyone at some time or another. One may ignore such hints for years, until some event brings them all into focus; or the 'focusing' may happen gradually and imperceptibly. Science declares that life began with the action of sunlight on carbon suspended in water, and that man has reached his present position by a process of natural selection. In that case, the laws of human existence are physical laws, and can be found in any textbook of science. But there occur moments of absurd certainty that seem to transcend the usual law of probability. Mark Bredin, a musician of my acquaintance, described how he came away from a rehearsal late at night and took a taxi home. He was very tired; there was little traffic about along the Bayswater Road. Suddenly, with total certainty, he knew that as they crossed Queensway, another taxi would shoot across the road and hit them. He was so certain that he was tempted to warn the driver, then decided that it would sound silly. A few seconds later, the other taxi rushed out of Queensway and hit them, as he had known it would. He attributes the flash of 'second sight' to extreme tiredness, when the conscious mind was relaxed and the subconscious could make itself heard.

We may reject the story as exaggeration, or explain it in terms of 'coincidence'. But the word 'coincidence' solves nothing. For again, everyone has noticed how often absurd coincidences occur. Some years ago, I made an attempt to keep notes of unlikely coincidences, and I find a typical example in my journal for January 1968. 'I was reading Hawkins's *Stonehenge Decoded*, the last section on the standing stones of Callanish, which Hawkins describes as a kind of Stone Age computer. I finished the book, and immediately picked up Bell's *Mathematics, Queen of the Sciences*. It opened at Chapter 6, and I found myself looking at a footnote on Stone Age mathematics. The chances against coming across it immediately after the piece on Callanish were probably a million to one. Again, last night I was reading an account of the Domenech murder case at Moher, in Galway, and noted that the victim had been at Mary Washington College in Fredericksburg, Virginia, where I had lectured recently. Ten minutes later I opened Wanda Orynski's abstracts of Hegel, and see that the introduction is by Kurt Leidecker of Mary Washington College....'

There is nothing very startling about these coincidences except the odds against them. I can add another one from the past week. An article in *The Criminologist* referred to a Nebraska murder case without mentioning the name of the murderer; I spent ten minutes searching through a pile of old *True Detective* magazines because I could recall that the man whose name I was trying to remember (Charles Starkweather) was featured on the cover of one of them. I took the magazine back to my armchair and finished the article in *The Criminologist*. It ended with a reference to a murderess named Nannie Doss, of whom I had never heard. I opened the *True Detective* magazine half an hour later, and discovered that the first article was on Nannie Doss. Oddly enough, as I looked at her photograph, and a caption mentioning the word 'Nannie', I experienced a sudden sense of total certainty that this was the woman I had been wondering about, although it took a few seconds longer to locate her surname in the text.

Similar coincidences are described in a remarkable book, *The Cathars and Reincarnation*, by Arthur Guirdham (which I shall discuss in detail later).* He describes how, one day in 1963, he began to discuss a village called Little Gaddesden, and tried to recall the name of a pub there. Later the same day, he took a book on the Pyrenees out of the public library, and on starting to read it at home, almost immediately came across the name of Little Gaddesden and the pub whose name he wanted to recall. The coincidence — one of several — occurred at the beginning of his strange involvement with a patient whose memories of a previous existence constitute one of the best-authenticated cases of reincarnation that I have come across.

To suggest that such matters are not entirely coincidence is not to suggest that 'hidden forces' were trying to draw my attention to Stone Age mathematics or Guirdham's to the name of a pub. Probably all that is at work is some 'vital sense' of the same order as the eel's homing instinct. The more the mind is absorbed, interested in a subject, the more frequently these useful coincidences seem to occur, as if the healthy mind has a kind of radar system. Distraction or depression will prevent the radar from working, or may prevent one paying attention until too late. The following is from a recent account of a murder case, written by the father of the victim:

It was a squally day of cold-front weather with alternations of bright sunshine and sudden rain or hailstorms. My wife and I were at the front of the house, in between the rain squalls, with two painters who were attempting to make some progress on the eaves and window frames. It was necessary to trim down a hedge outside one of the rooms.... At 4 p.m. my wife said: 'Where's Fiona?' Irrationally and unaccountably, we both felt an excess of acute anxiety and fear....'

*London, Neville Spearman, 1970.

Until the child was mentioned, both parents were preoccupied with other things, and the alarm signals of the unconscious were unobserved; then, with the question 'Where's Fiona?' they sound clearly, like a telephone that cannot be heard until the television is turned down. The child had been the victim of a sex killer.*

My own experience of 'premonitions' has not been extensive; in fact, I can call only one to mind. On 16 July 1964, an ordinary palmist at a fairground in Blackpool looked at my hand, and warned me that I would have an accident over the next month; she said it would probably be a car accident, and I would not be badly hurt. In mid-August 1964 I decided to take a guest out in a speedboat, although I had a strong premonition of danger. The sea proved far rougher than expected, and when I attempted to land on a rocky beach, a huge wave picked up the boat and dashed it on the rocks, completely wrecking it. No one was hurt, although we spent a bad half hour dragging the badly holed boat out of the heavy sea.

I have had two experiences of apparently telepathic response to another person. My first wife and I had been separated for some months in the summer of 1953, although there were still strong emotional links. One evening, in a café in central London, I suddenly felt sick, and had to rush out. I continued vomiting for several hours — in fact, until the early hours of the next morning. A doctor in the hospital where I was then working diagnosed the trouble as food poisoning, although I had eaten the same food as the other porters, and they were all well enough. I learned a few days later, however, that my wife *had* been suffering from food poisoning — from a bad tin of corned beef — at the time I was sick; her retching had begun and ended at exactly the same time as mine.

In 1965 1 had lectured at St Andrews University in Scotland, and was driving to Skye. I was feeling particularly cheerful when I set out because the weather was fine, and I was looking forward to stopping at a second-hand bookshop in Perth. But within half an hour of leaving St Andrews, I began to feel unaccountably depressed. Half an hour later, I asked my wife why she was subdued; she explained that she had had a toothache ever since we left St Andrews.

It was unfortunately a Saturday, too late to find a dentist in Scotland. On Sunday morning, the gum was now badly swollen. My own depression continued all day. In Kyle of Lochalsh, on Monday morning, we were told that a travelling dentist would arrive at a caravan sometime during the day; I left my wife waiting while I took my daughter for a walk round the town. Suddenly the feeling of oppression lifted. I said, 'Mummy's just had

*'Murder: A Father's Story,' by Michael Whitaker, *The Sunday Times* (29 March 1970).

her tooth out'. We arrived back in time to meet my wife coming out of the caravan, minus an impacted wisdom tooth.

When my children were babies, I quickly became aware of the existence of telepathic links. If I wanted my daughter to sleep through the night, I had to take care that I didn't lie awake thinking about her. If I did, she woke up. In the case of my son, I had to avoid even looking at him if he was asleep in his pram. When my wife asked me to see if he was still asleep, in the garden or porch, I would tiptoe to the window, glance out very quickly, then turn away. If I lingered, peering at him, he would stir and wake up. This happened so unvaryingly during his first year that I came to accept it as natural. After the first year, the telepathic links seemed to snap, or at least, to weaken. But when they began to learn to speak, I observed that this was again a delicate and intuitive business — not at all a matter of trial and error, of learning 'object words' and building them up into sentences, but something as complex as the faculty with which birds build nests.* And again there was a feeling — perhaps illusory — that the child could pick up and echo my own thoughts, or at least respond to them when attempting to express something.

But, among adults at least, thought-transference must be less usual than feeling-transference. And both of them seem to depend upon the right conditions, a certain stillness and sensitivity. On a still day you can sometimes hear the voices of people miles away.

In the above-mentioned experiences of telepathy — if that is what it was — the 'transference' was unconscious and automatic, like the crossing of telephone lines. This gives rise to the speculation whether hatred might be transmitted in the same unconscious manner. My own experience of this has been a doubtful one, and I mention it here only for the sake of completeness. I found myself thinking about it seriously when I read the following in Wilson Knight's book on John Cowper Powys: 'Those who have incurred his anger have so invariably suffered misfortune that he has, as it were, been forced into a life of almost neurotic benevolence.... Powys's early ambition to become a magician was no idle dream.'**

Before moving to Kensington in the autumn of 1952, my wife and I had lived in Wimbledon, in the house of an old man who suffered from asthma; my wife was his nurse. During the six months we lived in the house, he became increasingly querulous and difficult, until there was a perpetual atmosphere of tension like an impending thunderstorm. I am not given to nursing grudges, but the feeling of being steeped in pettiness, of being

---

*A closely similar view of child learning is held by Noam Chomsky, the linguistic philosopher.

** *The Saturnian Quest* (Methuen, 1964), p. 62.

prevented from concentrating on more important things, produced climaxes of loathing in which I wished him dead. In August we returned from a week's holiday to find that he had died of a heart attack.

It was when the situation repeated itself three months later that I found myself speculating idly whether thoughts can kill. The landlady was insanely suspicious, and violent scenes soon became a daily occurrence. Two months later, she visited a doctor, who diagnosed a cancer of the womb. She died shortly after we left the house. I now recalled the peculiar nature of those paroxysms of loathing. On certain occasions, the anger had increased to a pitch that in a paranoid individual would lead to an explosion of violence. But the explosion would be purely mental: a burst of rage and hatred, followed by relief, as if I had thrown a brick through a plate-glass window.

These mental explosions always had a peculiar feeling of authenticity, of reality. By this I mean they seemed somehow different from paroxysms of feeling induced by imagination. I cannot be more specific than this, but I suspect that most people have experienced the sensation.

In his *Autobiography*, Powys writes: 'The evidence of this — of my being able, I mean, and quite unconsciously too, to exercise some kind of "evil eye" on people who have injured me — has so piled up all my life that it has become a habit with me to pray to my gods anxiously and hurriedly for each new enemy.'*

The case of Powys is interesting because of the peculiar nature of his genius. Until he was in his mid-fifties, Powys spent much of his life lecturing in America, and three novels written in his early forties are interesting without being remarkable. Then, in his sixties, there appeared a series of immense novels — in bulk and in conception — beginning with *Wolf Solent* and *A Glastonbury Romance*. The most remarkable thing about these novels is their 'nature mysticism' and their incredible vitality; it is clear that he has tapped some subconscious spring, and the result is a creative outpouring that has something of the majesty of Niagara Falls. *A Glastonbury Romance* (1933) is probably unique in being the only novel written from a 'God's-eye' point of view. The simplest way of illustrating this is to quote its first paragraph:

At the striking of noon on a certain fifth of March there occurred within a causal radius of Brandon railway-station and yet beyond the deepest pools of emptiness between the uttermost stellar systems

---

*The Bodley Head, 1934, p. 480.

one of those infinitesimal ripples in the creative silence of the First Cause which always occur when an exceptional stir of heightened consciousness agitates any living organism in the astronomical universe. Something passed at that moment, a wave, a motion, a vibration, too tenuous to be called magnetic, too subliminal to be called spiritual, between the soul of a particular human being who was emerging from a third-class carriage of the twelve-nineteen train from London and the divine-diabolic soul of the First Cause of all life.

The abstractness of the language here gives a false impression of a book that is anything but abstract; but it also reveals Powys's desire to see his characters and events from some 'universal' point of view in which the algae in a stagnant pond and the grubs in a rotten tree are as important as the human characters.

One should note the presupposition of this first paragraph, which is present in all Powys's work: that there is a kind of 'psychic ether' that carries mental vibrations as the 'luminiferous ether' is supposed to carry light.

This I would define as the fundamental proposition of magic or occultism, and perhaps the only essential one. It will be taken for granted throughout this book.

What is so interesting about Powys is that he deliberately set out to cultivate 'multi-mindedness', to pass out of his own identity into that of people or even objects: 'I could feel myself in to the lonely identity of a pier-post, of a tree-stump, of a monolith in a stone-circle; and when I did this, I looked like this post, this stump, this stone' (*Autobiography*, p. 528).

It was an attempt to soothe his mind into a state of quiescent identity with the 'psychic ether', with the vast objective world that surrounds us. Everyone has had the experience of feeling sick, and then *thinking about something else* and feeling the sickness vanish. 'Objectivity' causes power to flow into the soul, a surge of strength, and contact with the vast, strange forces that surround us. In a famous passage in *The Prelude*, Wordsworth describes a midnight boating excursion when a huge peak made a deep impression on his mind, and how for days afterwards:

...my brain
Worked with a dim and undetermined sense
Of unknown modes of being; o'er my thoughts
There hung a darkness, call it solitude
Or blank desertion. No familiar shapes
Remained, no pleasant images of trees,
Of sea or sky, no colours of green fields;

But huge and mighty forms, that do not live
Like living men, moved slowly through the mind
By day, and were a trouble to my dreams. (Book l)

Wordsworth, like Powys, had acquired the ability to pass beyond his own personality and achieve direct contact with the 'psychic ether'. But as he grew older, he lost this ability to transcend his personality and the poetry loses its greatness. Powys never lost his power of summoning a strange ecstasy. In the *Autobiography* he describes how, lecturing on Strindberg in an almost empty theatre in San Francisco, there stirred within him:

…that formidable daimon which, as I have hinted to you before, *can* be reached somewhere in my nature, and which when it *is* reached has the Devil's own force.... I became aware, more vividly aware than I had ever been, that the secret of life consists in sharing the madness of God. By sharing the madness of God, I mean the power of rousing a peculiar exultation in yourself as you confront the Inanimate, an exultation which is really a cosmic eroticism.... (p. 531)

And again, in the Roman amphitheatre in Verona:

Alone in that Roman circle, under those clouds from which no drop of rain fell, the thaumaturgic element in my nature rose to such a pitch that I felt, as I have only done once or twice since, that I really *was* endowed with some sort of supernatural power.... I felt it again, only five years ago, when I visited Stonehenge.... The feeling that comes over me at such times is one of most formidable power... (p. 403)

There is reason to believe that Powys did not understand the mechanisms of this power. A strange story was related of Powys and his friend Theodore Dreiser:

Dreiser said that when he was living in New York, on West Fifty-seventh Street, John Cowper Powys came occasionally to dinner. At that time Powys was living in this country, in a little town about thirty miles up the Hudson, and he usually left Dreiser's place fairly early to catch a train to take him home. One evening, after a rather long after-dinner conversation, Powys looked at his watch and said hurriedly that he had no idea it was so late, and he would have to go at once or miss his train. Dreiser helped him on with his overcoat, and Powys, on his way to the door, said, 'I'll appear before you, right here, later this evening. You'll see me.'

'Are you going to turn yourself into a ghost, or have you a key to the door?' Dreiser laughed when he asked that question, for he did not believe for an instant that Powys meant to be taken seriously.

'I don't know,' said Powys. 'I may return as a spirit or in some other astral form.'

Dreiser said that there had been no discussion whatever during the evening, of spirits, ghosts or visions. The talk had been mainly about American publishers and their methods. He said that he gave no further thought to Powys's promise to reappear, but he sat up reading for about two hours, all alone. Then he looked up from his book and saw Powys standing in the doorway between the entrance hall and the living room. The apparition had Powys's features, his tall stature, loose tweed garments and general appearance, but a pale white glow shone from the figure. Dreiser rose at once, and strode towards the ghost, or whatever it was, saying, 'Well, you've kept your word, John. You're here. Come on in and tell me how you did it.' The apparition did not reply, and it vanished when Dreiser was within three feet of it.

As soon as he had recovered somewhat from his astonishment Dreiser picked up the telephone and called John Cowper Powys's house in the country. Powys came to the phone, and Dreiser recognized his voice. After he had heard the story of the apparition, Powys said, 'I told you I'd be there, and you oughtn't to be surprised.' Dreiser told me that he was never able to get any explanation from Powys, who refused to discuss the matter from any standpoint.*

Why should Powys refuse to discuss it from any standpoint? Because he had no idea of how he had done it and could not describe the process. It depended on the nature of the psychic link between himself and Dreiser: 'I used to be aware...of surging waves of magnetic attraction between Dreiser and myself...which seem super-chemical and due to the diffusion of some mysterious occult force....' The appearance was probably in Dreiser's own mind; another person in the room would not have seen it.

It may sound contradictory to say that Powys had no idea of how he had projected his 'apparition'; but it is not. For we are now concerned with the fundamental question of *conscious* control of the subconscious mind.

All my physical functions, from digestion to excretion, are controlled by my subconscious depths. If I am of a nervous disposition, I may find it

*W. E. Woodward, *The Gift of Life* (New York, Dutton, 1947). Quoted by Professor Wilson Knight in *The Saturnian Quest*, p. 128.

impossible to urinate in a public lavatory with other people standing near; no amount of conscious effort can destroy the inhibition; I need to relax and let my subconscious do the work. Stendhal suffered from an embarrassing sexual disorder which he called *le fiasco*. Whenever his sexual excitement reached the point at which he was prepared to make love, he would experience an embarrassing collapse of the ability to do so. No amount of conscious desire to oblige his disappointed partner could make any difference. If I try to remember a name I have forgotten, I again rely on my subconscious to 'throw it up', although in this case I may be able to dispense with its help: I may look up the name in my address book, or get at it by some trick of association of ideas.

There is no reason why a man should not learn the basic 'tricks' of telepathy, or even 'astral projection', as he might train his memory to greater efficiency or get rid of urinatory inhibition by auto-suggestion. He would still not be able to explain it, even to his closest friend.

Serious emotional upset can also stimulate the 'psychic faculties'. The case of the playwright Strindberg provides an interesting example. The break-up of his second marriage precipitated an emotional crisis in which he came close to insanity. He suffered delusions of persecution, all of which are described at length in his autobiographical volume *Inferno*. The result was an *unlooked-for* development of psychic powers that parallels the case of Peter Hurkos. In *Legends*,* he describes an involuntary astral projection:

> [In the autumn of 1895] I was passing through a dangerous illness in the French capital, when the longing to be in the bosom of my family overcame me to such a degree that I saw the inside of my house and for a moment forgot my surroundings, having lost the consciousness of where I was. I was really there behind the piano as I appeared, and the imagination of the old lady had nothing to do with the matter. But since she understood these kind of apparitions, and knew their significance, she saw in it a precursor of death, and wrote to ask if I were ill. (1912 edition, p. 86)

What is so interesting about this brief account is that Strindberg's power of astral projection was connected with the imagination. He clearly imagined the room in which his mother-in-law was sitting, playing the piano, and the intensity of his imaginative vision somehow 'projected' him into the real room. He had used the 'psychic ether' as he might have used a telephone or closed-circuit television.

*Published by Andrew Melrose.

In the same volume he describes an event that may have even deeper significance. In the early hours of the morning, in a period of emotional strain he was sitting in a wine shop, trying to persuade a young friend not to give up his military career for that of an artist.

> After arguments and endless appeals, I wished to call up in his memory a past event that might have influenced his resolve. He had forgotten the occurrence in question, and in order to stimulate his memory, I began to describe it to him: 'You remember that evening in the Augustiner tavern.' I continued to describe the table where we had eaten our meal, the position of the bar, the door through which people entered, the furniture, the pictures…. All of a sudden, I stopped. I had half lost consciousness without fainting, and still sat in my chair. I was in the Augustiner tavern, and had forgotten to whom I spoke, when I recommenced as follows: 'Wait a minute. I am now in the Augustiner tavern, but I know very well that I am in some other place. Don't say anything…I don't know you any more, yet I know that I do. Where am I? Don't say anything. This is interesting.' I made an effort to raise my eyes — I don't know if they were closed — and I saw a cloud, a background of indistinct colour, and from the ceiling descended something like a theatre curtain; it was the dividing wall with shelves and bottles.
> 'Oh yes!' I said, after feeling a pang pass through me. 'I am in F's wine shop.'
> The officer's face was distorted with alarm, and he wept.
> 'What is the matter?' I said to him.
> 'That was dreadful,' he answered. (pp. 92—93)

We may, of course, dismiss the whole thing as Strindberg's imagination, excited by emotional stress. On the other hand, this event is consistent with the theory of 'psychic faculties' that I have tried to outline, and has the ring of truth. (Strindberg is a remarkably honest man, in spite of his neuroses, as the reader discovers when it is possible to check his version of events against someone else's.) Again, he was exhausted — physically and emotionally. He was pushing himself to his limits as he exerted his powers of persuasion. And, as he remarks in the same book: 'In the great crises of life, when existence itself is threatened, the soul attains transcendent powers.'

One of the most interesting and consistent accounts of these powers is to be found in a book called *Psychic Self Defence* (1930), by 'Dion Fortune', a Freudian psychologist whose real name was Violet Firth. At the age of twenty (in 1911) she was working in a school, under a domineering principal, who took a dislike to her, and (so Violet Firth believed) directed a stream of psychic malevolence at her, using yogic and hypnotic techniques. The result was traumatic, a feeling of bewilderment and misery greater than would be caused by an actual physical attack. A need for self-analysis led her to study psychology (on which she wrote a number of books); later, she came to feel that even the theories of Freud and Jung fail to do justice to the complexity of the human mind, and became a student of occultism. (She had always possessed some degree of mediumistic powers.) She joined the Order of the Golden Dawn (a magical society that will be discussed in the second part of this book), and had further psychic clashes with Mrs Mathers, the wife of its founder. As a result of these alarming experiences, she came to believe that the human mind can repel the hostile psychic forces that emanate (often unconsciously) from malevolent people. Even more interesting is the implication that a healthy and optimistic mind repels ordinary misfortune, and that 'accident proneness' or general bad luck are the result of a psyche made vulnerable by defeat or stagnation.

And at this point, I must outline my own basic theory of these powers of the mind.

In Johnson's *Rasselas, Prince of Abyssinia*, there is a scene in which the hero looks at the peaceful pastoral scenery of the Happy Valley where he lives, and wonders why he cannot be happy like the sheep and cows. He reflects gloomily: 'I can discover within me no power of perception that is not glutted with its proper pleasure, yet I do not feel myself delighted. *Man has surely some latent sense for which this place affords no gratification*, or he has some desires distinct from sense which must be satisfied before he can be happy' (Chapter 2).

The italics are my own. The 'latent sense' is man's evolutionary appetite, the desire to make contact with reality. But that is not all. Who has not experienced this strange frustration that comes in moments of pleasure and fulfilment? As a child, I had this feeling about water. If my parents took me on a bus excursion, I used to crane out of the window every time we went over a bridge; something about large sheets of water excited a painful desire that I found incomprehensible. For if I actually approached the water, what could I *do* to satisfy this feeling? Drink it? Swim in it? So when I first read the passage from *Rasselas*, I understood immediately what Johnson meant by 'some latent sense...or desires *distinct from sense* which must be satisfied before he can be happy'.

I labelled this 'latent sense' Faculty X. And I came to see that Faculty X has something to do with 'reality'. In *Swann's Way* Proust describes how he tasted a madeleine dipped in tea, and was suddenly reminded of his childhood in Combray — reminded with such an intensity that for a moment he was actually there. 'An exquisite pleasure had invaded my senses.... And at once the vicissitudes of life had become indifferent to me, its disasters innocuous, its brevity illusory...I had now ceased to feel mediocre, accidental, mortal....'

Five minutes earlier, he could have said, 'Yes, I was a child in Combray,' and no doubt described it in detail; but the madeleine suddenly meant that he could say it *and mean it*. Chesterton says, 'We say thank you when someone passes us the salt, but we don't mean it. We say the earth is round, but we don't mean it, even though it's true.' We say something and mean it only when Faculty X is awake, that painful reaching-beyond-the-senses. Faculty X is the key to all poetic and mystical experience; when it awakens, life suddenly takes on a new, poignant quality. Faust is about to commit suicide in weariness and despair when he hears the Easter Bells; they bring back his childhood, and suddenly Faculty X is awake, and he knows that suicide is the ultimate laughable absurdity.

Faculty X is simply that latent power that human beings possess to *reach beyond the present*. After all, we know perfectly well that the past is as real as the present, and that New York and Singapore and Lhasa and Stepney Green are all as real as this place I happen to be in at the moment. *Yet my senses do not agree.* They assure me that this place, here and now, is far more real than any other place or any other time. Only in certain moments of great inner intensity do I know this to be a lie. Faculty X is a sense of reality, the reality of other places and other times, and it is the possession of it — fragmentary and uncertain though it is — that distinguishes man from all other animals.

But if the oppressive reality of this place and time is an illusion, so is my sense of being uniquely here, now. 'I am not here; neither am I elsewhere,' says Krishna in the *Bhagavad Gita*. So that if Faculty X can make Strindberg clearly aware of the reality of a place several hundreds of miles away, is it not conceivable that it might 'transport' him there in another sense?

It would be a mistake to think of Faculty X as an 'occult' faculty. It is not: it is the power to grasp reality, and it unites the two halves of man's mind, conscious and subconscious.

Think: what happens if a piece of music or a smell of woodsmoke suddenly reminds me of something that happened ten years ago? It is like touching the leg of a dead frog with an electric wire. My mind convulses and contracts, suddenly grasping the *reality* of that past time as though it were the present. The same thing happens to Marcel in Proust's novel *Swann's Way* when he tastes a madeleine dipped in tea — his past floods back as a reality. What happens is that our normally lazy and diffused consciousness *focuses*, as I might clench my fist. The tune or smell only provides the stimulus; my inner strength does the rest — *an inner strength of which I am normally unaware.*

A few years ago, psychologists performed a classic experiment with a cat. A wire was connected to the nerve between the cat's ear and its brain, and the other end of the wire was connected to a dial for measuring electrical impulses. When a loud noise sounded near the cat's ear, the needle of the dial swung over violently. Then a cage of mice was placed in front of the cat. It watched them intently. The same loud noise was sounded close to its ear. But the needle did not stir; the cat was so intent on the mice that it ignored the sound — and somehow it 'switched off' the physical impulse between the ear and the brain. *It chose to focus on something else.*

All living creatures have this power to 'focus' on something that interests them, and 'switch off' everything else. Someone accustomed to a modern city probably cuts out as much as 99 per cent of the stimuli that fall on the senses. We all know about this. But what we have not yet grasped is the extraordinary power we possess in being able to focus upon particular aspects of reality. This power *is* Faculty X, but at the moment, we hardly make use of it, unaware of its potentialities.

It is worth asking the question: What is consciousness *for*? When you are deeply asleep, you have no consciousness. When you are very tired, your consciousness is like a dim light that hardly illuminates anything. When you are wide awake and excited, consciousness seems to increase in sheer candle-power. Its purpose is to illuminate reality, to reach out into its recesses, and thus to enable us to act upon it and transform it. It is obvious that our basic aim should be to increase its candle-power. When it is low, reality becomes 'unreal'; as it becomes stronger, reality becomes 'realer': Faculty X.

One of the clearest examples of the working of Faculty X can be found in the tenth volume of Arnold Toynbee's *Study of History*, in which he explains how he came to write that work. He speaks of the sense of 'reality' that suddenly comes to historians:

'The writer of the present study had an authentic minor personal experience of the kind on 23 May 1912, as he sat musing on the summit of the citadel of Mistrà, with the sheer wall of Mount Taÿgetus bounding his horizon in the western quarter of the compass, towards which he was bound, and the open vale of Sparta stretching away in the opposite eastern quarter, from which he had made his way that morning....'

'The sensuous experience that activated his historical imagination was not a sound of liturgical chanting; it was the sight of the ruins among which he had wound his way upwards to the peak; and this spectacle had been appalling, for in this shattered fairy city Time had stood still since that spring of A.D. 1821 in which Mistrà had been laid desolate.... One April morning, out of the blue, the avalanche of wild highlanders from the Màni had overwhelmed her; her citizens had been forced to flee for their lives and had been despoiled and massacred as they fled; her deserted mansions had been sacked; and her ruins had been left desolate from that day to this....'

What struck Toynbee on this occasion was not simply the question of 'the cruel riddle of Mankind's crimes and follies', but the total *reality* of the scene conjured up by his imagination. He mentions half a dozen other experiences in which there was this same hallucinatory effect of reality. Reading how one of the proscribed leaders of the Italian Confederacy was refused help by his wife, and committed suicide in front of her eyes, he was 'transported, in a flash, across the gulf of time and space from Oxford in A.D. 1911 to Teanum in 80 B.C., to find himself in a back yard on a dark night witnessing a personal tragedy...'. He records similar experiences — all very brief — when reading Bernal Diaz describing the Spaniards' first sight of Tenochtitlan, Villehardouin describing his first sight of Constantinople during the Crusades, a Greek soldier describing how he tried to save a girl from rape. And finally, an experience in which the dividing line between Faculty X and mystical experience becomes blurred:

On each of the six occasions just recorded, the writer had been rapt into a momentary communion with the actors in a particular historic event through the effect upon his imagination of a sudden arresting view of the scene.... But there was another occasion on which he had been vouchsafed a larger and a stranger experience. In London in the southern section of the Buckingham Palace Road, walking southward along the pavement skirting the west wall of Victoria Station, the writer once, one afternoon not long after the date of the First World War...had found himself in communion, not just with this or that episode in History, but with all that had been, and was, and was to come. In that instant he was directly aware of the passage of History gently flowing through him in a mighty current, and of his own life welling like a wave in the flow of this vast tide. The experience lasted long enough for him to take visual note of the Edwardian red brick surface and white stone facings of the station wall gliding past on his left, and to wonder — half amazed and half amused — why this incongruously prosaic scene should have been the physical setting of a mental illumination. An instant later, the communion had ceased, and the dreamer was back again in the everyday cockney world which was his native social milieu…'*

These pages of Toynbee are among the clearest descriptions of the operation of Faculty X that exist, and they underline the point I have tried to make. When I am half asleep, my sense of reality is restricted to myself and my immediate surroundings. The more awake I am, the further it stretches. But what we call 'waking consciousness' is not usually a great deal better than sleep. We are still wrapped in a passive, sluggish day-dream. But this is not because there is some natural limit to consciousness, but only because we remain unaware that it can be stretched. We are like dogs who think they are on a chain when in fact they are free.

Faculty X is not a 'sixth sense', but an ordinary potentiality of consciousness. And it should be clear from what I have written above that it is the key not only to so-called occult experience, but to the whole future evolution of the human race.

*A Study of History (Oxford, 1954), vol. X, pp. 130—40.

THE LADDER OF SELVES

From *Mysteries*, 1978

At the time when I was still collecting materials for this book, I had a nasty but curiously fascinating experience: a series of attacks of 'panic anxiety' that brought me close to nervous breakdown. What surprised me most was that I was not depressed or worried at the time. I was working hard, and therefore under a certain amount of strain, but I seemed to be taking it all in my stride. For the past eighteen months I had been involved on the editorial board of a kind of encyclopedia of crime; but as every meeting ended in disagreement, it began to look as if the whole project would have to be abandoned. Then, at short notice, the publisher decided to go ahead. Suddenly, everything had to be completed in a few months; and I, as co-ordinator, was asked to produce around a hundred articles — 3,000 words each — at a rate of seven a week. I began to work at the typewriter for eight or nine hours every day and tried to unwind in the evenings with a bottle of wine and a pile of gramophone records.

One day, a couple of journalists came to interview me. In fact, they did most of the talking. They were young and enthusiastic, with a tendency to interrupt one another. When they left, at about two in the morning, my eyes were glazed with boredom, and I felt as if I'd been deafened with salvos of cannon fire. This, I later realized, was the trouble. When you become bored, you 'let go'; you sink into a kind of moral torpor, allowing your inner-pressure to leak away as if you were a punctured tyre. The next day they came back for another session with the tape recorder. When they left I felt too dull to do any work; instead I took the opportunity to perform a number of routine household chores.

That night, about 4 a.m., I woke up feeling unrested and lay there thinking about all the articles I still had to write, and the books I ought to be writing instead. Anxiety hormones began to trickle into my bloodstream, and my heartbeat accelerated. I actually considered going to my workroom and starting another article then realized that if I did *that*, I'd really be letting things get on top of me. Lying there, with nothing else to think about, I felt my energies churning, like a car being accelerated when the engine is in neutral. It was rather like feeling physically sick, except it was the emotions that were in revolt. When it was clear that I was not going to improve the situation by ignoring it, I tried making a frontal assault and suppressing the panic feeling by sheer will power. This proved to be a mistake. My face became hot, and I felt a dangerous tightness across the chest, while my heartbeat increased to a point that terrified me. I got up, went to the kitchen and poured myself a glass of orange juice. Then I sat down and tried to soothe myself as I might try to calm a frightened horse. Gradually, I got myself under control and went back to bed. As soon as I was in the dark, the process started again: rising panic, accelerating heartbeat, the feeling of being trapped. This time I got up and went into the sitting-room. I was inclined to wonder if I was having a heart attack. Quite clearly, *something* had gone wrong. The panic kept rising like vomit; the calm, sane part of me kept saying that it was absurd, some minor physical problem that would resolve itself within twenty-four hours. Like nausea, it came in waves, and between each wave there was a brief feeling of calm and relief.

The attack differed from nausea in that there was no point in giving way to it and making myself sick. This panic caused energy to disappear, like milk boiling over in a saucepan. There was a vicious-circle effect; the anxiety produced panic, the panic produced further anxiety, so the original fear was compounded by a fear *of* fear. In this state, it seemed that any move I made to counter the fear could be negated by more fear. In theory, the fear could overrule every attempt I made to overrule it. Like a forest fire, it has to be somehow contained before it destroyed large areas of my inner-being.

I *had* experienced something of the sort in my teens, but without this sense of physical danger. One day at school, a group of us had been discussing where space ended, and I was suddenly shocked to realize that the question seemed to be *unanswerable*. It felt like a betrayal. It suddenly struck me that a child's world is based on the feeling that 'Everything is OK'. Crises arise, apparently threatening your existence; then they're behind you, in the past, and you've survived. Or you wake up from a nightmare, and feel relieved to realize that the world is really a decent, stable sort of place. The universe *looks* baffling, but somebody, somewhere, knows all the answers.... Now it struck me that grown-ups are, in this respect, no better than children; they are surrounded by uncertainty and insecurity, but they go on living because that's all there is to do.

For years after that insight, I had been oppressed by a sense of some terrible, fundamental bad news, deeper than any social or human problem. It would come back with a sudden shock when life seemed secure and pleasant — for example, on a warm summer afternoon when I saw a ewe feeding her lambs, looking a picture of motherly solicitude, unaware that both she and her lambs were destined for someone's oven.

Now, as I sat in the armchair and tried to repress the panic, I realized that it was important not to start brooding on these fundamentals — our total ignorance, our lack of the smallest shred of certainty about who we are and why we are here. That way, I realized, lay insanity, a fall into a kind of mental Black Hole.

I suppose that what seemed most ironical was that I had always felt that I understood the cause of mental illness. A couple of years before I had written a book called *New Pathways in Psychology* in which I had argued that mental illness is basically caused by the collapse of the will. When you are making an effort, your will re-charges your vital powers as a car re-charges its battery when you drive it. If you cease to will, the battery goes flat, and life appears to be futile and absurd. To emerge from this state, all that is necessary is to maintain any kind of purposeful activity — even without much conviction — and the batteries will slowly become re-charged. That is what I had said. And now, struggling with the panic, all the certainty had vanished. Instead, I found myself thinking of my novel *The Mind Parasites*, in which I had suggested that there are creatures that live in the depths of our subconscious minds, draining our vitality like leeches. That seemed altogether closer to what I was now experiencing.

Finally, I felt sufficiently calm — and cold — to go back to bed. I lay there, staring at the grey square of the window to keep my mind from turning inward on itself; some automatic resistance seemed to have awakened in me, and I suspected that the daylight would make the whole thing seem as unimportant as a bad dream. In fact, I woke up feeling low and exhausted, and the 'bad-news' feeling persisted at the back of my mind as I worked. But the effort of writing another article made me feel better. In the evening I felt drained, and the fear began to return. I suspected myself of wanting to ignore something frightening and felt myself sinking into depression as into a swamp. I would make an effort, rouse myself to mental activity and suddenly feel better. Then something on television or in what

I was reading, would 'remind' me of the fear; there was a kind of inner jerk, like a car slipping out of gear, and the panic was back.

The articles still had to be written; in fact, a few days later, the editor rang me to ask if I could produce ten during the next week instead of the usual seven. An American backer was waving his chequebook and demanding speed. Since I had decided against the temptation to back out of the project, I stepped up my production to an article and a half a day. I was treating myself like a man with snake-bite, forcing myself to keep walking. Gradually, I was learning the tricks of this strange war against myself. It was rather like steering a glider. An unexpected flash of fear could send me into a nose dive; a mental effort could turn the nose upward again; sometimes this could happen a dozen times in an hour, until continued vigilance produced a feeling of inner-strength, even a kind of exhilaration. It was likely to be worst when I let myself get over-tired. Three months later, on a night-sleeper from London, I woke up with a shock, and the panic was so overpowering that I was afraid I might suffer cardiac arrest. At one point, I seriously considered getting off the train at the next stop and walking — no matter where. Then, in one of the periodic ebbs of panic, I forced myself to repeat a process I had taught myself in previous attacks: to reach inside myself to try to untie the mental knots. While I was doing this, it struck me that if I could soothe myself from panic into 'normality', then surely there was no reason why I shouldn't soothe myself *beyond* this point, into a still deeper state of calm. As I made the effort to relax more and more deeply, I felt the inner turmoil gradually subside, until the spasms ceased; then I pressed on, breathing deeply, inducing still greater relaxation. At the same time, I told myself that I was sick of being bullied by these stupid attacks, and that when I got home the next day I was going to do a perfectly normal day's work. My breathing became shallow and almost ceased. Suddenly, it was as if a boat had been lifted off a sandbank by the tide; I felt a kind of inner jerk and floated into a state of deep quiescence. When I thought about this later, it struck me that I had achieved a state that is one of the basic aims of yoga: Rilke's 'stillness like the heart of a rose'.

Slowly, I began to understand the basic mechanism of the attacks. They began with a fatigue that quickly turned into a general feeling of *mistrust* of life, a loss of our usual feeling that all is (more or less) well. Then the whole thing was compounded by the old problem of self-consciousness. If you think about itching, you begin to itch. If you brood on a feeling of sickness, you feel sicker. Consciousness directed back on itself produces the 'amplification effect' which is the basis of all neurosis (i.e. the harder a stutterer tries not to stutter, the worse he becomes). If I woke in the middle of the night and tried *not* to feel tense, my heartbeat would accelerate and the panic would begin. I had to develop the trick of turning my attention to some everyday problem, as if saying to myself, 'Ah yes, how interesting'. Once I had learned to do this, the attacks became easier to avert. It was a great comfort to me when a friend who had been through the same kind of thing told me that, even without treatment, the condition cures itself after eighteen months.

When I tried to think out the basic reasons for the panic, I had to acknowledge that my trouble was a certain 'childishness'. When a child is pushed beyond a certain limit of fatigue or tension, its will surrenders. Some instinctive sense of fair-play is outraged, and it declines to make any further effort. An adult may also feel like surrendering to a problem, but common sense and stubbornness force the will to further effort. As an obsessive worker, I am accustomed to drive myself hard. Experience has taught me that when I get over-tired, the quickest way to recovery is often to drive myself on until I get 'second wind'. But to do this effectively, you need the full support of your subconscious mind, your deep sense of inner-purpose and meaning. In this case, I was trying to push myself beyond my normal limits — by writing the equivalent of a full-length book every three weeks — and some childish element in my subconscious had gone on strike. It was sitting with folded arms and a sullen expression, declining to do its proper work of re-charging my vital batteries. And so, when I passed a certain point of fatigue, I would discover that there was no more energy to call on. It was like descending a ladder and discovering that the last half dozen rungs are missing. At which point I would force my conscious will to interfere; a thing it is reluctant to do, since the subconscious usually knows best. I had to tell myself that I was being bloody stupid; that in my younger days, I worked far harder as a navvy or machine operator than I have ever worked as a writer, and that writing for a living has made me lazy and spoilt.

The panic, then, was caused by a lower level of my being, an incompetent and childish 'me'. As long as I identified with this 'me', I was in danger. But the rising tension could always be countered by *waking myself up fully* and calling upon a more purposive 'me'. It was like a schoolmistress walking into a room full of squabbling children and clapping her hands. The chaos would subside instantly, to be succeeded by a sheepish silence. I came to label this 'the schoolmistress effect'.

I had always known that Gurdjieff was right when he said that we contain dozens of 'I's'. The aim of his method is to cause some of these 'I's' to fuse together, like fragments of broken glass subjected to intense heat. As it is, consciousness passes from one to the other of our 'I's' like the ball in a rugby game. Under these conditions, no continuity is possible, and we are at the mercy of every negative emotion.

The schoolmistress effect made me recognize a further fact about these multiple 'I's' — that they exist inside me not only on the 'rugby field', or horizontal plane but also at different *levels*, like a ladder. All forms of purposive activity evoke a higher 'I'. William James pointed out that a musician might play his instrument with a certain technical virtuosity for years and then one day enter so thoroughly into the spirit of the music that it is as if the music is playing *him*; he reaches a kind of effortless perfection. A higher and more efficient 'I' takes over. Gurdjieff's 'work' is based on the same recognition. His pupils were made to drive beyond their normal limits until the moments of 'effortless perfection' became everyday occurrences.

J. G. Bennett gives an interesting example in his autobiography *Witness*. He was staying at Gurdjieff's Fontainebleau Institute for the Harmonious Development of Man, and Gurdjieff himself was in charge of the 'exercises', based on Dervish dances. The aim of these exercises is to arouse man to a higher degree of alertness, to enable him to gain total control of his 'moving centre'; they involve an incredibly complicated series of movements — sometimes doing quite different things with the feet, the hands and the head. (To get an idea of the problem involved, try the old trick of rubbing your stomach in a circular motion with one hand and patting yourself on the head with the other.) Bennett was suffering from dysentery and feeling physically exhausted. One day, he found himself shaking with fever. 'Just as I was saying to myself: "I will stay in bed today," I felt my body rising. I dressed and went to work as usual, but this time with a queer sense of being held together by a superior Will that was not my own.' In spite of extreme exhaustion, he forced himself to join in a new and particularly difficult series of exercises. They were so complicated that the other students dropped out one by one; Bennett felt that Gurdjieff was willing him to go on, even if it killed him. And then: 'Suddenly, I was filled with an influx of an immense power. My body seemed to have turned into light. I could not feel its presence in the usual ways. There was no effort, no pain, no weariness, not even any sense of weight.'

The exercises were over, and the others went off for tea. Bennett went into the garden and began to dig.

> I felt the need to test the power that had entered me, and I began
> to dig in the fierce afternoon heat for more than an hour at a rate
> that I ordinarily could not sustain for two minutes. I felt no fatigue,

and no sense of effort. My weak, rebellious, suffering body had become strong and obedient. The diarrhoea had ceased and I no longer felt the gnawing abdominal pains that had been with me for days. Moreover, I experienced a clarity of thought that I had only known involuntarily and at rare moments, but which was now at my command. I returned in thought to the Grand Rue de Péra and discovered that I could be aware of the fifth dimension. The phrase 'in my mind's eye' took on a new meaning as I 'saw' the eternal pattern of each thing I looked at; the trees, the plants, the water flowing in the canal and even the space, and lastly my own body. I recognized the changing relationship between 'myself' and 'my pattern'. As my state of consciousness changed, 'I' and my 'pattern' grew closer together or separated and lost touch. Time and eternity were the conditions of our experience, and the Harmonious Development of Man, towards which Gurdjieff was leading us, was the secret of true freedom. I remember saying aloud: 'Now I see why God hides Himself from us.' But even now I cannot recall the intuition behind this exclamation.

This vision of the 'eternal pattern' behind trees and plants brings to mind Boehme's mystical experience when he walked in the field and saw 'the signature of all things', as if he could see the sap rising in the trees and plants. But Bennett went one stage farther still. He went for a walk in the forest and met Gurdjieff; Gurdjieff told him:

The real complete transformation of Being, that is indispensable for a man who wishes to fulfil the purpose of his existence, requires a very much greater concentration of Higher Emotional Energy than that which comes to him by nature. There are some people in the world, but they are very rare, who are connected to a Great Reservoir or Accumulator of this energy. This Reservoir has no limits. Those who can draw upon it can be a means of helping others. Suppose a man needs a hundred units of this energy for his own transformation, but he has only ten units and cannot make more for himself. He is helpless. But with the help of someone who can draw upon the Great Accumulator, he can borrow ninety more. Then his work can be effective.

Farther in the forest, Bennett recalled a lecture of Gurdjieff's leading disciple, Ouspensky.

He had spoken about the very narrow limits within which we can control our own functions and added: 'It is easy to verify that we have no control over our emotions. Some people imagine that they can be angry or pleased as they will, but anyone can verify that he cannot be astonished at will.' As I recalled these words I said to myself: 'I will be astonished.' Instantly, I was overwhelmed with amazement, not only at my own state, but at everything I looked at or thought of. Each tree was so uniquely itself that I felt I could walk in the forest forever and never cease from wonderment. Then the thought of 'fear' came to me. At once I was shaking with terror. Unnamed horrors were menacing me on every side. I thought of 'joy', and I felt that my heart would burst from rapture. The word 'love' came to me, and I was pervaded with such fine shades of tenderness and compassion that I saw that I had not the remotest idea of the depth and range of love. Love was everywhere and in everything. It was infinitely adaptable to every shade of need. After a time, it became too much for me; it seemed that if I plunged any more deeply into the mystery of love, I would cease to exist. I wanted to be free from this power to feel whatever I chose, and at once it left me.

Bennett's experience is a particularly striking example of what, in *The Occult*, I have called 'Faculty X'. When we say we know something to be true, we are lying. 'Ten people died last night in an air crash.' 'Yes, I know.' We *don't* know. The rescuers trying to free the bodies from the burning wreckage knew. For the rest of us, this knowledge is a poor carbon copy. And how can I claim to 'know' that Mozart wrote the Jupiter symphony? I cannot even grasp that Mozart really existed. If I walk into a room in Salzburg in which Mozart actually played, I might, if I were in the right mood, come a little closer to grasping that he actually lived. But I would still be a long way from 'knowing' it.

There are two ways in which I might 'know' that Mozart existed. I might sit in a room where he had played and deliberately induce a mood of deep calm, perhaps by some form of 'transcendental meditation'. *Then* I could grasp it, for I would have slowed my senses down, arrested their usual frantic forward rush. Or I might grasp it in a sudden flash of intuition, as I run my fingers over the keyboard he actually touched. To do this requires intense concentration; it is the mental equivalent of leaping a six-foot fence. And there is a third method, rather less satisfactory than those two, yet also less difficult. I might immerse myself in Mozart's music, read books about his life, study his letters. Art has the power of inducing a degree of

Faculty X. This is why human beings invented it. As we immerse ourselves in some composer's creative world, those inner 'leaks' that drain so much of our energy gradually close up, and our inner-pressure rises. We experience the 'magic carpet' effect, floating up above our own lives, seeing human existence as a panorama spread out below. The main problem with this kind of consciousness is that it makes it hard to come back to earth, and we find everyday reality futile and disgusting. Undiluted Faculty X has the reverse effect; it strengthens our power to cope with everyday reality by raising our inner-pressure.

Gurdjieff clearly possessed some curious ability to arouse hidden powers in other people. I have quoted elsewhere the episode in which Ouspensky describes how Gurdjieff began to communicate telepathically with him in Finland. There can be no doubt that Gurdjieff had achieved some degree of control over his Faculty X. Yet this control seems to have been only partial. This becomes plain from an anecdote in *Gurdjieff Remembered* by Fritz Peters, who knew Gurdjieff from boyhood. During the war, Peters was an American GI, and in 1945 he was experiencing severe strain and depression. In Paris, he called on Gurdjieff in a state verging on nervous breakdown. Gurdjieff persuaded him to lie down, but after a few minutes Peters went to look for Gurdjieff in the kitchen. Gurdjieff refused to give him aspirin but began to make coffee.

> He then walked across the small room to stand in front of the refrigerator and watch me. I could not take my eyes off him and realized that he looked incredibly weary — I have never seen anyone look so tired. I remember being slumped over the table, sipping at my coffee, when I began to feel a strange uprising of energy within myself — I stared at him, automatically straightened up, and it was as if a violent electric blue light emanated from him and entered into me. As this happened, I could feel the tiredness drain out of me, but at the same moment his body slumped and his face looked grey as if he was being drained of life. I looked at him, amazed, and when he saw me sitting erect, smiling and full of energy, he said quickly: 'You all right now — watch food on stove — I must go....'
>
> He was gone for perhaps fifteen minutes while I watched the food, feeling blank and amazed because I had never felt any better in my life. I was convinced then — and am now — that he knew how to transfer energy from himself to others; I was also convinced that it could only be done at great cost to himself.

It also became obvious within the next few minutes that he knew how to renew his own energy quickly, for I was equally amazed when he returned to the kitchen to see the change in him; he looked like a young man again, alert, smiling, sly and full of good spirits. He said that this was a very fortunate meeting, and that while I had forced him to make an almost impossible effort, it had been — as I had witnessed — a very good thing for both of us.

Gurdjieff's whole 'method' depends on forcing people to make unusual efforts, to release their 'vital reserves'. The effort of helping Peters apparently *reminded* Gurdjieff of something he had partly forgotten — how to call upon his own vital reserves. After his efforts to help Peters he looked exhausted: 'I have never seen anyone look so tired.' Being forced to help Peters awakened his own vital energies. So it would seem that Gurdjieff — in spite of the tremendous vitality that impressed everyone who met him — was not in permanent and habitual control of his own 'strange powers'.

It seems clear that, as Peters believed, Gurdjieff knew the secret of transmitting his energy directly to other people. Many 'healers' seem to possess this ability. There is a well authenticated story concerning the 'monk' Rasputin and the Tsarina's friend Anna Vyrubova. In January 1915, Anna Vyrubova was involved in a railway accident; her head was trapped under an iron girder and her legs badly crushed; in hospital, the doctor declared that there was no hope for her life. Rasputin heard of the accident twenty-four hours later — he was in disgrace at the time — and rushed to the hospital. Ignoring the Tsar and Tsarina, who were by the bedside, he went over to the unconscious woman and took her hands. 'Annushka, look at me.' Her eyes opened and she said: 'Grigory, thank God.' Rasputin held her hands and stared intently into her eyes, concentrating hard. When he turned to the Tsar and Tsarina, his face looked drained and exhausted. 'She will live, but she will always be a cripple.' As he left the room, he collapsed in a faint. But Anna Vyrubova's recovery began from this moment.

The question we have raised here is of central importance in the life of every human being: the question of how to gain access to our 'vital reserves'. The tensions of modern life mean that most of us suffer from a constriction in the pipeline that carries our vital energy supply. My experiences of panic attack made me aware that it can become a matter of life and death. The panic tends to feed on itself and I was like the driver of a car whose accelerator has jammed at top speed. In this condition I was aware of the frightening possibility of hypertension leading to 'exhaust status' and cardiac arrest. As I learned the basic tricks of controlling the attacks, I also gained a certain insight into the problem of vital reserves.

One of our highest human attributes is our power of concentration. But it involves a major disadvantage. When I concentrate on something, I *ignore* everything else in the universe. I lock myself into a kind of prison. If I stay in this prison too long, I begin to suffocate. This is what happens when we overwork or become obsessed by some trivial worry. We forget the universe that exists outside us until it becomes only a distant memory. Even when the task is finished, we often forget to re-establish contact and open the windows. The inner watchspring can get so overwound that we become permanently blind and deaf.

This is one of the worst habits we have developed in the course of our evolution. There is a parable of two Zen monks who encounter a girl waiting at a ford; one of them picks her up and carries her across the river, then sets her down on the farther bank. Ten miles farther on, the other monk bursts out: 'How could you do that? You know we're not allowed to touch women.' 'Put her down,' says his companion, 'You're still carrying her.' Most human beings carry a dozen invisible burdens.

The tendency is dangerous because our mental health depends on the 'meaning' that comes from the world around us. Meaning is something that walks in through the senses on a spring morning, or when you arrive at the seaside and hear the cry of the seagulls. All obsession cuts us off from meaning. My panic attacks began when I had overwound the watchspring and lost the trick of unwinding it. I was like a man slowly suffocating to death and, what is more, suffering because I was gripping my own windpipe.

It is important to realize that this throttling effect is quite automatic. It is the result of an aspect of the mind that I have called 'the robot', that unconscious servant who performs all the automatic tasks of everyday life. The 'robot' is now typing this page for me, while the 'real me' does the thinking. When I am feeling energetic and cheerful, the robot stays in the background, and I walk around with my senses wide awake. As I get tired, the robot takes over more and more of my functions, and the reality around me becomes less and less real. If I become nervously exhausted, the robot takes over completely and life becomes a permanent unreality. If, in this state, I am subjected to further pressures instead of being allowed to unwind, anxiety escalates into panic. It is the robot whose accelerator is jammed in the top-speed position.

I have always been fascinated by the way that shock or crisis can release us from the 'suffocation', bursting open the locked windows and often producing an almost mystical vision of meaning; my first book, *The*

Outsider, discussed many such cases. There was, for example, the experience of Nietzsche on a hill called Leutsch; he describes it in a letter to his friend von Gersdorff:

> Yesterday an oppressive storm hung over the sky and I hurried to the top of a nearby hill.... At the summit I found a hut, where a man was killing a kid, while his son watched him. The storm broke with tremendous force, gusting and hailing, and I had an indescribable sense of wellbeing and zest, and realized that we actually understand nature only when we must fly to her to escape our cares and afflictions.... Lightning and tempests are different worlds, free powers, without morality. Pure will, without the confusions of intellect — how happy, how free!

Even more significant is the experience of the modern Hindu saint Ramakrishna. He describes his first mystical ecstasy:

> I was suffering from excruciating pain because I had not been blessed with a vision of the Divine Mother... life did not seem worth living. Then my eyes fell on the sword that was kept in the Mother's temple. Determined to put an end to my life, I jumped up and seized it, when suddenly the Mother revealed herself to me.... The buildings...the temple and all vanished, leaving no trace; instead there was a limitless, infinite shining ocean of consciousness or spirit. As far as the eye could see, its billows were rushing at me from all sides.... I was panting for breath. I was caught in the billows and fell down senseless.

From this time onward, the mere name of the Divine Mother could send Ramakrishna into *samadhi*, a trance of ecstasy.

In both these cases, the release was preceded by a sense of oppression and narrowness, the 'overwound watchspring' effect. Their senses were closed, so that both were suffering from 'meaning starvation'. Human beings accept lack of meaning with stolid fatalism, as an animal accepts illness and pain. So the release comes like a thunderclap, like a sudden reprieve from death, bringing a sense of overwhelming joy and gratitude, and the recognition that meaning is always there. It is we who close our senses to it.

Once a man has experienced this revelation, he can never wholly forget it. He may still be subject to moods of fatigue and depression; but always, at the back of his mind, there is the memory of a paradoxical truth: *that men are far stronger than they suspect.* Their energies seem limited, their powers circumscribed, only because in some strange unconscious way, they set the limits themselves.

As my own energies became more constricted by the panic attacks, I had to learn to become conscious of these mechanisms. I was particularly intrigued by the 'schoolmistress effect'. The 'schoolmistress' seemed to be a higher level of my being, which became operative when I shook off my panic and forced myself into a state of vigilance and wakefulness. It reminded me of the experience of an academic friend who was subject to moods of depression and self-doubt. One summer holiday, he came to see us looking completely transformed; he had lost weight and radiated vitality. I asked him what had happened. He explained that his doctor had ordered him to lose weight and the thought had filled him with a sense of defeat. However, he tried eating less and walking to the university, and to his astonishment found it less difficult than he had expected. As the weight melted away his optimism increased; he began to feel that *all* problems could be solved with a little common sense and determination. He looked back on his earlier self with pitying condescension. A 'higher level' had taken control, and he felt it to be realer and truer than the old self.

Obviously, Ramakrishna's attempt at suicide had produced a more powerful version of the 'schoolmistress effect' and raised him to a higher level still. On the other hand, boredom and lack of purpose tend to produce the opposite effect: surrender to a conviction of weakness and general unworthiness. (As all sociologists know, this condition incubates crime.) If we revert to the image of a whole series of 'selves', arranged like the rungs of a ladder, we may say that consciousness can move up or down the ladder, identifying with different 'selves'.

But reflecting on this image, it struck me that the ladder is unusual in one respect: it is shaped like a triangle, so that the higher rungs are shorter than the lower ones. When I move up the ladder, I experience a sense of concentration and control. When I move down — through depression or fatigue — my being seems to become diffused, like a cloud, and I begin to feel at the mercy of the world around me. In this state, it seems obvious that 'I' am weak, selfish and incapable of doing anything worthwhile.

The interesting question, of course, is: what lies at the top of the ladder? Some ultimate 'me'? A mystic would say, God. Edmund Husserl talked about the 'transcendental ego', the being that presides over all consciousness, and defined philosophy as the attempt to uncover the secrets of the transcendental ego. Gurdjieff agreed, except that he doubted the value of philosophy. He insisted that the only way to explore the ladder is to climb it.

When I decided to write a sequel to *The Occult*, I considered restricting it to the question of human survival of death. But these insights introduced new complications into the project. To begin with, what precisely *is* it that dies? Biologically speaking, I am more like a city than an individual. I am full of colonies of bacteria called mitochondria, which are quite separate from 'me', yet are essential to my vital maintenance. Then, of course, my body is made up of billions of cells, all of which die off and are replaced every eight years, so that there is not now a single atom left of the person I was eight years ago. When a man is decapitated, every cell in his body goes on living as if nothing had happened — this is why the hair and nails continue to grow. Then what actually dies as the blade severs his neck? Clearly, some higher principle of organization, one or more of the 'higher selves'. But the higher selves do not die if a man falls into depression or takes to crime; they remain dormant or latent. Is there any logical reason to believe that they die with the death of the body?

This approach seemed to throw new light on all kinds of questions connected with the 'occult' or paranormal. For example, since I wrote *The Occult*, I have become fascinated by the subject of dowsing, particularly when I discovered that I could use a divining rod, and that it produced powerful reactions around ancient standing stones. But I have seen dowsers suspending their pendulums over a map and accurately locating hidden streams. They can even ask the pendulum questions — 'When was this stone circle erected?' — and get precise answers. The ancients knew about these effects, and assumed that the answers were given by spirits. It seems to me more logical to suppose that one of the 'higher selves' has access to the information and can transmit it through the pendulum, or the yarrow stalks, or the Tarot pack, or whatever method of divination is being used.

Then there is the curious mystery of 'multiple personality'. In *The Occult* I wrote briefly about Morton Prince's case of 'Miss Beauchamp', who was periodically 'possessed' by a totally different personality called Sally. In 1973, I worked on a series of BBC television programmes on the 'paranormal' and had a chance to study the case more closely, which in turn led me to re-examine the whole phenomenon of multiple personality. Dr Flora Schreiber's 'Sybil' exhibited no less than sixteen different personalities. The psychiatric view is that the personality becomes fragmented by shock, but that, like a broken mirror, each fragment retains a kind of identity. I found myself wondering whether that may not apply to all of us — that our everyday selves are a mere fragment of some ultimate personality towards which we are all striving. Professor Ian Stevenson, a parapsychologist of the University of Virginia, reported a case of reincarnation which has even stranger implications. A three-and-a-half-year-old Indian boy, Jasbir Lal Jat, apparently died of smallpox, but revived a few hours later with a totally new personality. The 'stranger' identified himself as a man from another village who had died after eating poisoned sweets, and his detailed knowledge of the man's life convinced his parents — and later Stevenson — that he was telling the truth. The strangest feature of the case was that the man had died at about the same time the child went into his 'death trance', suggesting the complete transfer of the personality from one body to another.

I was struck by the parallels between cases of multiple personality and those involving poltergeist activity. Another of the television programmes dealt with one of the best authenticated poltergeist cases on record, the 'Rosenheim spook'. The poltergeist played havoc with the electronic equipment in a lawyer's office; the culprit turned out to be a young clerk named Annemarie Schaberl. Yet Annemarie was clearly ignorant that she was the cause of the trouble. And this is so in the majority of poltergeist cases. (Professor Hans Bender, who investigated the Rosenheim poltergeist, emphasizes the importance of 'breaking it gently' to the children who are the unconscious cause of the disturbances, to avoid frightening them.) 'Miss Beauchamp's' alter-ego, Sally, was mischievous and given to practical jokes; it is easy to imagine a disembodied Sally behaving exactly like the Rosenheim poltergeist.

I was intrigued when the producer of the programmes, Anne Owen told me that she had been through a period when she could predict the future. Before a concert with a celebrated cellist, she had a premonition that he would break a string and asked the producer what they should do if this happened; he dismissed it as unlikely. But the string broke eight minutes before the end of the concert. (The cellist, hearing about her prediction, jumped to the conclusion that she had somehow made it happen, and refused to speak to her.) At a race meeting with her husband and some friends, she suddenly knew with certainty which horse would win the next race. Everyone rushed off and backed the horse, which won. But her husband had somehow mis-heard her and put the money on the wrong horse. Her conclusion was that such powers cannot be used for one's own profit. The number of famous psychics and 'occultists' who have died in poverty seems to bear out that judgment.

I found myself looking around for evidence that might link powers of prediction with my 'ladder of selves' theory. Dowsers have told me that the pendulum can answer questions about the future, and I have seen convincing evidence that this is true; but dowsers rely on the divining rod or pendulum, not upon some mystical illumination. Then I came across Alan Vaughan's book, *Patterns of Prophecy*, and found the example I was looking for. Vaughan describes how, in 1965, he bought an Ouija board to amuse a friend who was convalescing. When the radio announced the death of newspaper columnist Dorothy Kilgallen from a heart attack, they asked the board if this was correct; the board replied that she had died of poison. Ten days later, an inquest revealed this to be true.

One of the 'spirits' who made contact through the board identified herself as the wife of a Nantucket sea captain; she was called Nada. 'Then, both to my fascination and fear, "Nada" got inside of my head. I could hear her voice repeating the same phrases over and over again.' Asked about this, the board replied: 'Awful consequences — possession.'

In the presence of a friend who understood such matters, another spirit called 'Z' made Vaughan write out the message: 'Each of us has a spirit while living. Do not meddle with the spirits of the dead.'

> As I wrote out this message (writes Vaughan) I began to feel an energy rising up in my body and entering my brain. It pushed out both 'Nada' and 'Z'. My friends noted that my face, which had been white and pinched, suddenly flooded with colour. I felt a tremendous sense of elation and physical wellbeing. The energy grew stronger and seemed to extend beyond my body. My mind seemed to race in some extended dimension that knew no confines of time or space. For the first time, I began to sense what was going on in other people's minds, and, to my astonishment, I began to sense the future through some kind of extended awareness....

Vaughan's brief glimpse of 'extended powers' led him to embark on a programme of research into powers of 'prevision', whose results are described later in the book.

The phrase 'a tremendous sense of elation and wellbeing' brings to mind Nietzsche's 'indescribable sense of wellbeing and zest' and Bennett's 'influx of an immense power'. Here, then, we have a case in which the orgasmic upsurge of energy not only brings the typical sense of power and illumination, but also seems to trigger psychic faculties — telepathy and knowledge of the future.

This raises an interesting point. Most recorded instances of telepathy and prevision have taken place without the surge of heightened consciousness. The same goes for mediumship, thaumaturgy, second sight, telekinesis and the rest. So it would seem that if such powers depend upon our 'higher centres', then there are two ways of establishing contact: either clambering up the ladder, or through some form of short circuit that connects the higher self and the everyday self without the everyday self being aware of it. The first is Gurdjieff's way, the second Rasputin's.

Faculty X seems to be a combination of the two: a flash of extended awareness without the surge of energy. Proust's famous flash of 'remembrance of things past' occurred when he was tasting a cake dipped in tea and was suddenly made aware of the *reality* of his childhood. He writes: '...an exquisite pleasure had invaded my senses.... And at once, the vicissitudes of life had become indifferent to me, its disasters innocuous, its brevity illusory.... I had now ceased to feel mediocre, accidental, mortal.' William James, describing a similar experience, also says that it began when he was suddenly reminded of a past experience, and that this 'developed into something further...this in turn into something further still, and so on, until the process faded out, leaving me amazed at the sudden vision of increasing ranges of distant fact....' James makes it sound almost as if he had been snatched into the air, to a height where he could see reality spread out panoramically below him. Something similar happened to the historian Arnold Toynbee when he sat in the ruined citadel of Mistra and had a sudden vision of the reality of the day it was destroyed by barbarians; the experience produced a sense of history as a panorama, and led to the writing of *A Study of History*. Gibbon's *Decline and Fall* seems to owe its origin to the same kind of experience in the Capitol.

Perhaps the most interesting thing about these experiences is the sense of security, the feeling that 'all is well'. Which brings us back squarely to the central problem, not only of this book, but of human existence itself. A sense of security is essential to all conscious life. The happiest moments of childhood are filled with it; John Betjeman writes about a security that 'holds me as I drift to dreamland, safe inside my slumberwear'. Life gradually erodes this blissful security — but not the belief that security *is* achievable. This is why we work and scheme and buy houses on mortgage and furniture on hire-purchase; this is why we open savings accounts and accumulate possessions. And although we know about earthquakes and disasters and sudden death, the world around us still has a comforting air of permanence; if I fall asleep watching television, everything is still going on as usual when I wake up.

But then, if we are honest, we have to admit there is something wrong with this basic assumption. The child views the universe from the security of his mother's arms, and things look pleasantly reasonable. It may be puzzling, of course, but all puzzles can be solved. And puzzles are the grown-ups problem. Some people manage to pass their whole lives in this undisturbed state of mind. Others become aware that life is not as rosy as it looks. People die of disease or accident, or of old age after years of slow decay. Worse still, there seems to be something fundamentally queer about the universe. It contradicts our assumption that there are no questions without answers. The greatest questions are not only unanswered; they seem to be unanswerable. We cannot form even the *concept* of an answer to the question, 'When did the universe begin?' or 'Where does it end?' On earth, everything has a beginning and end; space and time seem to have neither. The same riddle confronts me when I think about myself. My birth certificate tells me I had a beginning; but the idea violates my sense of logic, so that I am naturally inclined to think of *something* before my birth: perhaps a disembodied existence in some kind of heaven, or a whole series of previous incarnations. I also know from observation that I shall die in due course. I *can* imagine simply 'fading out', because it happens to me every night in bed; yet again, my logic rejects the idea of extinction. It demands *some* kind of continuation.

How is it possible for people to go through life without seriously thinking of such questions? The answer is again disturbing. Because my thought is *tied down* to familiar things. As absurd as it sounds, the human mind does not seem to be really made for thinking. You realize this if you try to think about some fairly simple abstract problem, such as why a mirror reverses your left and right sides, but not your head and feet. The mind tries to grasp the problem, then skids, like a car on ice. It is as if some gravitational force pulled your mind back to the here-and-now as the ground pulls us back when we jump. You try to focus on big, universal problems, and a moment later find yourself wondering if you posted a letter. Philosophers who are aware of these problems are inclined to take the view that human life is brutal and meaningless. It is hard for a logical mind to disagree.

This explains why most intelligent people are suspicious of the idea of reincarnation, or of life after death. They see such ideas as another symptom of the human inability to face up to reality. We are hopelessly drugged by the biological sense of security — as sheep and cows are until they get to the slaughterhouse and smell blood. We like to soothe ourselves with the tacit assumption that things will always go on as they are now. And so most religions promise their followers an afterlife that bears all the signs of wishful thinking — from the Elysian Fields of the Greeks to the Happy Hunting Ground of the American Indians. Philosophers can see through the daydream, but they have no convincing alternative to suggest.

If we can drag our mind away from everyday trivialities and think honestly about these problems, we have to admit that the pessimists inspire no more confidence than the 'true believers'. Most of them use their pessimism as an excuse for not thinking. At first sight, this seems a reasonable attitude, since they believe that thinking only leads back to the conviction that life is meaningless. But then, some deep instinct tells us that when a man ceases thinking, he has thrown away his greatest advantage. There is an odd feeling of arrested development about most of the total pessimists, as if they had ceased to evolve as human beings.

Besides which, none of the pessimists — Schopenhauer, Andreyev, Artsybashev, Beckett, Sartre — has really come to grips with the central question about human existence. All right, I have no idea where I came from or where I am going to, and most of the meanings that I see around me are mere conventions. I am little more than a blinkered horse, plodding along patiently, doing more or less what I did yesterday and the day before, and I see all the human beings around me behaving in the same way. Yet there *does* seem to be a certain logic about human existence, particularly when I am gripped by a sense of purpose. When I experience a feeling of intensity, I catch a glimpse of meanings that seem far greater than the 'me' I know. But then, I get the feeling that the 'me' I know is some kind of temporary half-measure. On top of all this, I begin to believe that the pessimists are making a fundamental mistake about the rules of the game. 'Meaning' is revealed by a kind of inner-searchlight. (This is just another way of stating Husserl's insight: Perception is intentional.) The greater the intensity of the beam, the more meaning it reveals. So a man who stares at the world with a gloomy conviction of defeat is going to see as little meaning as he expects to see.

There *is* something absurd about human existence. You find yourself surrounded by apparently 'solid' meanings — which are all comfortingly trivial. But when you try to raise your eyes beyond them, all certainties dissolve. It is as disconcerting as walking through the front door of a magnificent building and finding that it is just a façade, with nothing behind it. The odd thing is that the façade seems solid enough. This world around us certainly looks consistent and logical. It is hard to believe it is part of a bad joke or a nightmare.

Which brings us back to this most fundamental of all questions. Is it possible that the ladder-of-selves theory is the key not only to 'psychic powers', but also to the basic question of human existence, the riddle that has always tormented philosophers and theologians and 'existentialist' thinkers? Mystics have declared that in flashes of revelation the answer to the mystery of the universe suddenly becomes obvious. And again and again, they have expressed the essence of this revelation in words like 'All is well' or 'Everything is good'. This is hard — in fact, impossible — to conceive. But that is not necessarily an ultimate objection. We cannot conceive infinity, yet Georg Cantor created a mathematics of infinity which has proved to be a valuable tool. We cannot conceive the notion that future events have somehow already taken place; yet cases of precognition seem to demonstrate that, in some baffling sense, this is true.

The ladder-of-selves theory certainly throws light on some other basic problems of human existence: for example, the problem of absurdity or meaninglessness. The world around us seethes with endless activity, and this normally strikes us as quite reasonable. But there are certain moments of fatigue or depression when this meaning seems to crack under us, like thin ice. Camus compares it to watching a man gesticulating in a telephone booth, but being unable to hear a word he is saying. We suddenly wonder if our whole relationship with the world is based on a misunderstanding. Man likes to think he has a symbiotic relation with the universe, but perhaps the universe has never heard of him? Sartre calls this same feeling 'nausea'; it comes if you stare at something until your sense of 'knowing' it dissolves, and it seems to become alien and strangely hostile. According to Sartre, this is because man has suddenly recognized the truth about his own nothingness. Simone de Beauvoir expressed it in a passage of *Pyrrhus et Cinéas*: 'I look at myself in vain in a mirror, tell myself my own story, I can never grasp myself as an entire object, I experience in myself the emptiness that is myself, I feel that I am not.'

According to the ladder-of-selves theory, this is precisely what one would expect in a state of low inner-pressure. But it is *not* an inescapable part of the human condition, still less a fundamental truth about the universe. In moments of intensity, of excitement, of creativity, I move up the 'ladder', and instantly become aware that the meaninglessness was an illusion. For I *can* 'tell myself my own story' and grasp it as a reality; I *can* look in a mirror and experience myself as an entire object. This is what is meant by Faculty X.

Another way of expressing the same conclusion would be to say that when my inner-pressure is low, consciousness is dominated by the robot, and life becomes unreal. The sense of the uniqueness of the present moment is lost, and you find it difficult to distinguish between something you have experienced and something you have only read about or dreamed. In this state, I become separated from my own life, as if by a glass wall; if I listen to music, it is the robot who hears it; if I eat, it is the robot who tastes the food. The higher I move up the 'ladder', the more I am able to experience my own life.

It is important to recognize that meaning can *draw* us up the ladder, and that when this happens, we feel revitalized and re-energized. Sex provides an obvious example: a state of boredom and fatigue can be instantly dissipated by a sudden sexual stimulus. The result is a kind of *invasion* of meaning that lifts us to a more concentrated and purposive state. A man who has discovered this simple trick — like Casanova — may spend his whole life repeating it. He believes it is the sex he is interested in; in fact, it is the 'intensity experience', the momentary glimpse of a less mediocre self. But since he fails to grasp the meaning-content of the insight, he continually falls back to a lower level.

On the other hand, when the meaning content *is* grasped the 'trick' can be used to tap vital energy reserves. This is clearly something Gurdjieff understood. Others — like Uri Geller and Matthew Manning — seem to be able to achieve contact with another form of energy that can be used for bending spoons or deflecting compass needles. The nature of this energy is still not understood, but of its existence there can be no doubt.

It seems too much to hope that any single theory could cover the whole field of the 'paranormal': In 1784, the Puységur brothers — disciples of the notorious Dr Mesmer — stumbled on the phenomenon of hypnotism when they were making 'magnetic passes' over a young shepherd, and he fell into a trance. Ever since then, hypnosis has been widely used in medical treatment; but still no one understands its nature. In 1848, mysterious rappings in the house of the Fox family in Hydesville, New York, led to a nationwide interest in the subject that became known as Spiritualism. The rappings always took place in the presence of the two daughters of the family — aged twelve and fourteen — and were probably some kind of poltergeist activity. But other 'mediums' went into trances and were apparently able to communicate with the spirits of the dead; they were usually taken over by a 'guide' from the other world. The Society for Psychical Research was set up to investigate the phenomena scientifically, and eminent investigators — like Professor Ernest Bozzano, Professor Charles Richet, F. W. H. Myers — attempted to construct theories that would serve as a foundation for 'psychic science'. None of them came even remotely near to succeeding. And this, on the whole, still remains true today.

But it is worth noting that many of the phenomena — from hypnotism to mediumship — seem to involve 'other levels' of the personality.

Of course, the notion of a ladder of selves is not even a theory. It is simply a convenient description of what happens when we feel 'more alive'. But since this sense of increased vitality and heightened awareness also involves a feeling of 'expanded powers', it may be worthwhile to see how far the 'ladder' hypothesis can be made to tie in with the known facts.

This raises another problem. In the past ten years or so, there has been such an 'information explosion' in the psychic field that it is difficult to know where to begin. Any comprehensive book on the paranormal is now expected to cover such subjects as plant telepathy, psychic surgery, transcendental meditation, bio-feedback, Kirlian photography, multiple personality and synchronicity, as well as such optional fringe topics as possession, UFOs, leys and the 'ancient religion'.

I have chosen an approach which has, for me, the virtue of straightforwardness. When he died in 1971, Tom Lethbridge was the author of nine books on 'occult' subjects, one of them still in typescript. His books cover an immense range; at one time or another he thought about all the major subjects that concern modern paranormal research.

When I wrote *The Occult*, I was familiar only with his early book *Witches: Investigating an Ancient Religion*. It was not until later that I discovered books like *Ghost and Divining Rod* and *ESP*, and experienced the excitement of encountering a first-rate intelligence that combined scepticism with imagination and a sense of humour. When I learned that he lived fairly close to me, in Devon, I wrote him a letter and sent him a copy of *The Occult*. His wife Mina replied, saying that he had died the previous year.

The more I read of Lethbridge, the more I became convinced that he is the only investigator of the twentieth century who has produced a comprehensive and convincing theory of the paranormal. Because this is scattered over nine books, it is still insufficiently known to the general reader. That is why I have devoted the first long section of this book to his work and ideas. It will serve the dual purpose of introducing him to readers who have not yet made his acquaintance and raising most of the topics that will be discussed in the rest of this book.

It will also enable me to pay a debt of gratitude to one of the most wide-ranging and original minds in modern parapsychology.

THE 'OTHER MODE'

From *Frankenstein's Castle*, 1980

As I approach the age of fifty — just twice the age at which my first book, *The Outsider*, appeared — I realize more clearly than ever that my life has been dominated by a single obsession: a search for what I call 'the other mode of consciousness'.

An example will clarify my meaning.

A musician friend once told me how he had returned home after a hard day's work feeling rather tired and depressed. He poured himself a whisky, and put a record on the gramophone — it was a suite of dances by Praetorius. As he drank the whisky, he began to relax. Suddenly, he says, he 'took off'. The music and the whisky entered into some kind of combination that produced a feeling of wild happiness, a rising tide of sheer exhilaration.

Why describe this as 'another mode' of consciousness, rather than simply as ordinary consciousness transformed by happiness? Because it can lead to experiences that seem completely beyond the range of 'normal' consciousness. A BBC producer friend told me how he had sat in an empty control room at the BBC and played himself a record of the Schubert Octet, which happened to be on the turntable. Suddenly, he said, he *became* Schubert. I was intrigued and tried to get him to be more precise. Did he have a kind of 'time slip' into Schubert's Vienna, so he knew what Schubert had eaten for lunch on the day he started composing? No, this was not what he meant. He tried to explain: that he had felt as if he was *composing* the music, so that he could understand why Schubert had written each bar as he had, and precisely what he might put into the next bar.... I saw that what he was describing was not a mystical or 'occult' experience, but simply an unusually deep sense of empathy. Sartre once said that to enjoy a book is to rewrite it; my friend had done the same for Schubert's Octet. We are bound to 'enter into' music if it is to be more than just a meaningless noise; but clearly, my friend had entered into it ten times as deeply as usual, like going down in a lift.

But then, perhaps it is a mistake to emphasize this element of empathy or sympathy. I had a similar experience when writing a book about Bernard Shaw. A friend had borrowed a book that I wanted to consult; and on this particular morning, he returned lt. So I sat down at my typewriter feeling pleased I had it back. It was a pleasant, warm day, with the sun streaming through on to my desk. I was writing the chapter about Shaw's marriage and 'breakthrough', after years of plodding around London's theatres and concert halls as a critic. No doubt I was 'identifying' with Shaw, imagining what it must have been like to feel that you have sailed out of a storm into a quiet harbour. But this was not what explained that sudden feeling of intense joy, as if my heart had turned into a balloon and was sailing up into the air. It was not just Shaw's life that was somehow passing through my mind; it was something bigger: a sense of the multiplicity of life itself. In a sense, I was back in Edwardian London; but it could just as easily have been Goethe's Weimar or Mozart's Salzburg.

In fact, this 'other mode' of consciousness is a state of perception rather than empathy — an awareness of a wider range of 'fact' — of the actuality of the world outside me. What has changed in such experiences is our perspective. I am used to seeing the world in what might be called 'visual perspective' — that is, with the objects closest to me looking realler and larger than the objects in the middle distance, which in turn look realler and larger than the objects on the horizon. In these experiences, we seem to sail up above this visual perspective, and the objects on the horizon are as real as my fingers and toes.

This is the experience that lay at the heart of *The Outsider*. The 'Romantic Outsiders' — Rousseau, Shelley, Hoffmann, Hölderlin, Berlioz, Wagner, Dostoevsky, Van Gogh, Nietzsche — were always experiencing flashes of the 'other mode' of consciousness, with its tantalizing hint of a new *kind* of perception, in which distant realities are as real as the present moment. But this created a new problem: intense dissatisfaction with the ordinary form of consciousness, with its emphasis on the immediate and the trivial. So the rate of death by suicide or tuberculosis was alarmingly high among writers and artists of the nineteenth century. Many of them seemed to feel that this was inevitable: that death and despair were the price you paid for these flashes of the 'other mode'. Even a relatively late-comer to the scene like Thomas Mann continued to think of the problem in terms of these bleak opposites: stupidity *and* health, or intensity *and* death.

I was inclined to question this equation. In many cases, the misery seemed self-inflicted. Eliot was right when he snapped: 'Shelley was a fool'. Shelley was a fool to fall in love with every pretty face that came by, a fool to believe England could be improved by violent revolution, a fool to give way to self-pity every time he got depressed and to feel that the situation could be improved by 'lying down like a weary child to weep away this life of care'. The same criticism applies to a large number of 'romantic outsiders'.

Still, even when full allowance was made for weakness and self-pity, there was another problem that could not be dismissed so easily. L. H. Myers had called it 'the near and the far' (in the novel of that title). The young Prince Jali gazes out over the desert in the light of the setting sun, and reflects that there are two deserts, 'one that was a glory for the eye, another than it was a weariness to trudge' — the near and the far. And the horizon, with all its promise, is always 'the far'. The near is trivial and boring. Huysmans had made the same point amusingly in *A Rebours*, where, after reading Dickens, the hero, Des Esseintes, has a sudden craving for London. While waiting for his train he goes to the English tavern near the Gare St Lazare, and eats roast beef and potatoes, and drinks pints of ale. Then it strikes him that he has, so to speak, tasted the essence of England, and that 'it would be madness to risk spoiling such unforgettable experiences with a clumsy change of locality'. So he takes a cab back home.

Yet Myers had also glimpsed an answer when he made Jali reflect: 'Yes, one day he would be vigorous enough in breath and stride to capture the promise of the horizon.' He may not have believed it himself, but it was still the correct answer: vitality. In 1960, my conviction was confirmed by the work of an American professor of psychology, Abraham Maslow. Maslow said he had got tired of studying sick people because they never talked about anything but their illness; so he decided to study healthy people instead. He soon made an interesting discovery: that healthy people frequently had 'peak experiences' — flashes of immense happiness. For example, a young mother was watching her husband and children eating breakfast when a beam of sunlight came through the window. It suddenly struck her how lucky she was, and she went into the peak experience — the 'other mode'. Maslow made another interesting discovery. When he talked to his students about peak experiences, they began recollecting peak experiences which they had had, but which they had often overlooked at the time. Moreover, as soon as they began thinking about and discussing peak experiences, *they began having them regularly.* In other words: the peak experience, the moment when the near and the far seem to come together, is a product of vitality and optimism. But it can also be amplified or repeated through *reflection*, by turning the full attention upon it instead of allowing it merely to 'happen'.

The case of the young mother reinforces the point. She was happy as she watched her husband and children eating, but it was an unreflective happiness. The beam of sunlight made her feel: 'I am happy', and instantly intensified it. It is as though we possessed a kind of mirror inside us, a mirror which has the power to turn 'things that happen' into *experience*. It seems that thought itself has a power for which it has never been given credit.

This was a major discovery. It meant that — contrary to the belief of the romantics — the 'other mode' *is* within our control. Shelley asked the 'spirit of beauty':

Why dost thou pass away and leave our state,
This dim vast vale of tears, vacant and desolate?

The answer, in Shelley's case, was clearly that he went around with the assumption that human existence is a 'dim vast vale of tears', and regarded the peak experiences as visitations of 'the awful shadow of some unseen power' — instead of recognizing that the unseen power lay within himself.

What we are speaking about is what Gottfried Benn called 'primal perception', that sudden sense of 'matchless clarity' that gives the world a 'new-minted' look. We find it in the sharp outlines of Japanese art, with its white mountain peaks and electric blue skies. T. E. Lawrence describes one in *Seven Pillars of Wisdom*:

We started out on one of those clear dawns that wake up the senses with the sun, while the intellect, tired after the thinking of the night, was yet abed. For an hour or two, on such a morning, the sounds, scents and colours of the world struck man individually and directly, not filtered through or made typical by thought: they seemed to exist sufficiently by themselves...

Lawrence has also put his finger on the reason that we experience 'primal perception' so infrequently: the filter of thought, of the mind's expectations. It could also be described as the robot, the mechanical part of us. Our 'robot' is invaluable; it takes over difficult tasks — like driving the car or talking a foreign language — and does them far more easily and efficiently than when we are doing them consciously. But it also 'gets used' to spring mornings and Mozart symphonies, destroying 'the glory and the freshness' that makes the child's world so interesting. The robot may be essential to human life; but he makes it hardly worth living.

The robot seems to be located in the brain. This is clear from the effects of psychedelic drugs like LSD and mescalin, which apparently achieve their effect by paralysing certain 'chemical messengers' in the brain. The result is certainly a form of 'primal perception' — as Aldous Huxley noted when he took mescalin; he quoted Blake's statement: 'If the doors of perception were cleansed, every thing would appear to man as it is, infinite.' So cleansing the 'doors of perception' is basically a matter of brain physiology.

In the mid-sixties I began reading books on the brain; one result was a novel called *The Philosopher's Stone*, in which I suggest that the secret of primal perception may lie in the pre-frontal cortex. But it was more than ten years later that I came upon a crucial piece of research that threw a new light on the whole question. The result was revelatory.

THE LAUREL AND HARDY THEORY OF CONSCIOUSNESS

From the magazine *Second Look* (October 1979)

A couple of months ago, I found myself involved in the re-writing of a film script about that legendary hero Flash Gordon. In one of the scenes, Flash's old friend and ally, Professor Zarkov, is being held prisoner by the secret police of Ming the Merciless, who proceed to brain-wash him with a machine that is intended to turn him into a loyal servant of Ming. But ten minutes further on in the movie, Zarkov has to reveal that the brain-washing was unsuccessful. The reason given by the previous script writer was unconvincing, not to say absurd. I decided on something that sounds at least more technically convincing. The human brain has two halves that are almost identical, and the question of why this should be so is still unsolved by the science of brain physiology. We have, it seems, two separate memory systems, and to some extent, each half of the brain stores the same information. If Ming's secret police happened to be unaware of this because the inhabitants of the planet Mongo have 'single' brains — then they might well leave one of Zarkov's memory systems intact....

Which left me with an interesting question, to which I have since devoted some thought. What would a single brained being be like? How would he differ from us? Why, in fact, *do* we have two brains?

Since I am not a brain physiologist, or even a scientist, any answers I have to suggest will be by way of pure speculation. Still, even mistaken theories can be useful. One of the most stimulating books I have read in recent years is *The Origin of Consciousness in the Breakdown of the Bicameral Mind*, by Julian Jaynes, in which he seriously suggests that our ancestors of a couple of thousand years B.C. lacked any kind of self-awareness — any sense of themselves as individual egos. I am certain that he is wrong; yet I've had more fun trying to work out why than in reading any number of more cautious and sober works of psychology. If my own suggestions can provide anything like the same stimulation, then the sufferings of Professor Zarkov will not have been in vain.

Let me begin by sketching the known facts. More than a century ago, the neurologist Hughlings Jackson noted that the left cerebral hemisphere seems to be concerned with expression — speech — while the right deals with recognition. The cerebral hemispheres — the top part of the brain — are the most specifically human part of us — our thinking apparatus. These hemispheres consist of two mirror-like halves, joined by a bridge called the commissure, the corpus callosum. But the purpose of this bridge is still obscure — Karl Lashley made the tongue-in-cheek suggestion that it was to stop the two halves of the brain from sagging. When the commissure is severed, as it sometimes is to prevent epileptic seizures, there is no obvious difference in the patient's behaviour. But in experiments with split-brain patients in Chicago in the early fifties, Roger Sperry and Michael Gazzaniga began to note some basic changes. Patients could not write meaningful sentences with the left hand — which is connected to the right side of the brain; neither could they read with the left eye. If the left eye (connected to the right brain) is shown an apple, and the right eye an orange, and the patient is asked what he has seen, he replies 'An orange'. Asked to write what he has seen with the left hand, he writes 'Apple'. But if he is not allowed to see what he has just written, but is asked to state it, he replies 'Orange'. If he is shown a picture of a nude woman — among a number of neutral images — he grins or giggles; asked why he is grinning, he replies 'I don't know'.

The 'I' who responds to questions clearly lives in the left half of the brain. The person who lives in the right hemisphere is by no means an idiot; he can, for example, make a more accurate sketch of a house — complete with perspective — than the left. (The left makes flat, two-dimensional representations.) But he is fundamentally silent. A person with left brain damage is unable to express himself verbally, but his pattern-recognition is unimpaired. A person with right brain damage sounds perfectly normal and intelligent: but he cannot copy even the simplest pattern — say, a four-pointed star.

More significant is an observation of what happens to the mathematical faculty in brain-damaged patients. They seem to be able to add and subtract as well as ever, but their ability to solve more interesting problems is reduced almost to nil. The left brain is analytical; but real problem solving requires an over-all grasp of the problem, which requires a creative approach.

Robert Ornstein, another investigator in this field, made a significant observation about ordinary (non split-brain) subjects. When they are engaged in doing boring calculations — adding up a grocery bill — the right brain shows alpha rhythms, as if it is asleep or idling.

Another interesting experiment showed the way in which the two hemispheres seem to react like two different people. If the left eye (connected to the right brain) is shown a series of flashing lights, either red or green, and the patient is asked to guess what colour he has just seen, the score ought to be precisely 50/50, since the left hemisphere has no idea of what its partner is seeing. In fact, it was far higher than that — and for an interesting reason. The patient would often make the wrong guess, then jump — as if someone had kicked him under the table — and change his guess. The 'silent' hemisphere had heard the wrong guess, and nudged him in the ribs.

These are the basic facts. And when I first came across the notion that our right and left hemispheres are separate personalities — in Ornstein's *Psychology of Consciousness* — they induced a state of considerable excitement. And I did what I always do — and what my more cautious friends (like Robert Temple) deplore: proceeded to extrapolate, and to spin interesting and totally unproven theories. Some of these I shall now proceed to outline.

My first thought was that this seems to offer a possible explanation of poltergeist activity. One of the oddest things about poltergeists (banging ghosts) — which, as we now know, are usually caused by emotionally disturbed adolescents — is that the person who is responsible for the disturbance is totally unaware of it. Hans Bender, one of the experts in this field of paranormal investigation, states in an article on poltergeists that the first rule is not to tell the child that he or she is causing it all. It scares hell out of them. And understandably. It is essential to our sanity to believe that we are 'individuals' (i.e. indivisible.) Nothing could be more frightening than the idea that some Dr Hyde part of the personality could go off on its own and start throwing objects around and causing loud bangs and crashes.

If my guess (and it is no more than that) is correct, then the 'poltergeist' lives in the right half of the brain. And for some reason, highly disturbed adolescents proceed to function like split brain patients, in the sense that the two halves go their separate ways.

This, of course, still fails to explain *how* a poltergeist can cause objects to fly through the air or burst into flame: i.e. fails to explain (a) where the energy comes from, (b) how the 'other self' makes use of it. But if you would like my guess, which I will throw in for good measure, it is that the energy somehow comes from the earth. If my poltergeist theory is correct, then the right brain is responsible for such 'paranormal' effects as dowsing, which causes a twig or divining rod to twist violently in the hands. Any good dowser knows that this energy — whatever it is — can be so powerful that it can throw the dowser on his back, or send him into convulsions. It *sounds* as if it could be the same energy involved in poltergeist activity. And if the right brain is sensitive to it — can somehow 'pick it up'— then it is not too difficult to believe that it could also use it to make objects fly around. But that, I will concede, is one of my more way-out guesses. Let us return to less controversial matters.

It would seem more-or-less accurate to say that the left brain is a scientist, the right is an artist. It also seems probable, if my poltergeist speculation has any foundation, that the right brain could be regarded as the gateway to the unconscious mind. And here I feel I must hedge myself around with qualifications, since my old friend Stan Gooch has gone on record as believing that the actual seat of the unconscious mind is the cerebellum, the older part of the brain that lies below the cerebral cortex. He may well be right; yet it still seems to me arguable that the right cerebral hemisphere plays its own important role in our unconscious activities. The one thing that seems clear is that the conscious mind is hardly thicker than the icing on a large Christmas cake, while the unconscious mind has many layers. So while, in the rest of this article, I shall refer only to the right brain, let it be understood that I am keeping an open mind about the rest of the brain and its functions.

At the time I read Ornstein's book, I was working on a biography of Wilhelm Reich. I have always been vaguely anti-Freudian, feeling that Freud's insistence that sex is the basis of *all* neurosis is as preposterous as Marx's insistence that all human creative activity can be reduced to terms of economics. In studying the history of psychoanalysis, I became increasingly convinced that Freud's error lay in regarding the unconscious as some kind of monster. As is well known, Freud stumbled on the discovery of the unconscious as a result of working with Charcot in Paris. Charcot had restored hypnosis to respectability, and he noted the similarity between hypnosis and hysteria. A hysterical woman who believes she is paralyzed can actually become paralyzed. And hypnosis can produce exactly the same effect. Charcot thought that hypnosis is a form of hysteria. Freud saw deeper. He recognized that if there is a part of the mind that can cause paralysis, phantom pregnancies and so on, then it must be far more powerful than the conscious mind. Both hypnosis and hysteria are effects produced upon this 'other' mind — the unconscious. So far so good. But Freud's next assumption was less reasonable: that if this unconscious mind is more powerful than the conscious mind, then we are all helpless puppets in the hands of this invisible monster. This is equivalent to saying that because a ship is far bigger and more powerful than the captain, the captain is not really in control — he only thinks he is.

It seemed to me that the relation between the conscious and the unconscious is more like the relation between Laurel and Hardy in the old movies. Ollie — consciousness — is basically the boss. Stan takes his cues from Ollie. If Ollie looks cheerful, Stan is positively ecstatic. *Stan always over-reacts.*

So if we wake up on a rainy Monday morning, and think gloomily: 'How am I going to get through this boring day?,' the unconscious mind begins to feel depressed. An hour later, we feel miserable and exhausted — *because the unconscious mind controls our vital energies.* This confirms our feeling that this is 'one of those days', so Stan becomes more depressed than ever…. In short, there is a build-up of negative feedback.

Consider, on the contrary, what happens to a child on Christmas day. He wakes up full of delightful anticipation: Stan takes the hint and sends up energy. And throughout the day, the mood of delight is reinforced by all the usual accompaniments to Christmas — carols on the radio, Christmas programmes on TV, fairy lights on the Christmas tree and so on. By bed time, the child may feel that it has been one of those perfect days where everything has gone right. He thinks this is the 'Christmas spirit;' in fact, it is the close and friendly cooperation of Ollie and Stan.

I would suggest that this 'tennis playing' mechanism — the feedback between Ollie and Stan — explains neurosis far more convincingly than Freud's explanations about sexual hang-ups festering in the unconscious. We can all recognize the mechanism in ourselves — how pleasant anticipation revitalizes us; how self-pity and boredom deprive us of our natural powers. Norman Vincent Peale may not have been a great intellect, but he understood something about the human mind that Freud managed to overlook.

It was at this point — about the second chapter of my book on Reich — that it struck me that this theory of neurosis works just as well if you substitute the right and left brain for Stan and Ollie. For example, as a writer, I am thoroughly familiar with the 'tennis playing' mechanism of positive and negative feedback. My instrument of communication is words — a left brain function. But what I write *about* are patterns, insights, intuitions — a right brain function. When I started to write, in my early teens, I used to find it hard and depressing work. The words were always killing the intuitions, squashing them flat. In fact, it seemed to me then that analysis is the enemy of insight. But as the years went by, I persevered, and gained a certain command over words. Sometimes, particular insights would defy me, and refuse to be turned into words. But then I learned to keep on trying — sometimes for months or years — until I saw how it could be done.

When I am writing well, there is an interesting balance between the intuitions and the words. And 'I' seem to somehow straddle the two, gently encouraging the intuitions, gently translating them into language and allowing them to flow on to the paper. If I get tired or frustrated, this balance is upset. I try *too* hard, the intuitions dwindle, and the words become clumsy and inappropriate. But some days, I am positively brilliant. I turn the intuitions into words so neatly that the right brain gets excited to see itself expressed so well; it shouts 'Yes, yes, that's it!,' and sends up more intuitions. And my left brain, pleased to be praised, makes an even greater effort, and catches the intuitions as they come pouring out. And suddenly, the tennis match is worthy of Wimbledon, both sides playing with unaccustomed brilliance. This is the state called 'inspiration'.

All this makes it clear that our basic problem as human beings is, in effect, to get both players into a mood of warm cooperation. It would seem that our two aspects have two quite different functions. The left brain is the 'front man;' its job is to cope with practical problems, to stand on guard, prepared for emergencies. Its chief instrument is crude will-power. It always seems to be in a hurry. And if we allow it to get too dominant, we end in a state of permanent tension.

The right seems essentially to look *inward*. It is concerned with patterns, with over-all meanings and values. It is the part of us that appreciates music and poetry and beautiful scenery. And for this, it needs to be left alone. If the left starts muttering '*Do* hurry up,' the right cannot function properly: if the phone keeps on ringing or your husband — or wife — keeps on nagging, the right quickly gives up. It is basically shy and easily discouraged. The right has very little sense of time — although it has quite enough for its purposes. (It can, for example, wake you up at precisely a quarter past seven in the morning....) It needs to be allowed to amble along comfortably at its own pace.

But the real business of the right seems to be to add a dimension of *meaning* to our lives. When I have finished my day's writing, at about five in the afternoon, I take a hot bath, then pour myself a glass of white wine and switch on the evening news. Then, at six fifteen or so, I pour another glass of wine, and put on a gramophone record, and play myself music until dinner is ready. If I am successful, the 'verbal me' relaxes and goes off duty, and another aspect of me begins to voyage in the world of music. 'Verbal me' retires quietly to a corner and dozes, and 'I' become a being with a completely different kind of awareness — for example, with a strong sense of the reality of history, of the fact that Mozart and Beethoven and Schubert *really existed*. During the day, when I am writing, I can *say* Mozart existed, yet in an odd sense, I don't believe it. I don't believe it even though it's true.

This change in my 'centre of gravity' from left to right is an interesting phenomenon. My usual sense of identity involves my ego, my conscious 'me'. If I become deeply absorbed in music ('Happiness is absorption' said T. E. Lawrence), I become aware that this conscious ego is not really me. He is only the front-man, only a complicated series of responses. The 'real me' seems to be a voiceless observer who lives behind the scenes of everyday consciousness. Whether this is the genuine 'real me' is anybody's guess, for I can easily imagine a yet further retreat 'inside' myself, to a level where non-verbal me would also seem to be a particular set of responses.

This experience of non-verbal me makes me aware that my so-called ego is *not* me. So, for example, I may be reacting to some annoyance or crisis with the appropriate anger or anxiety, while another level of me looks on, totally uninvolved. When I was young, this self-division worried me, since it seemed to suggest that 'I' am an illusion. Now I regard this recognition that 'I' am an illusion as a piece of good news, since it makes me aware that my real existence is to be found on a deeper level, and that my main purpose in life should be to learn to relax into that deeper level, while maintaining my faculty of analysis and verbalization.

As I expounded my 'alternative theory of neurosis' in my book on Reich — a theory, oddly enough, which is by no means in opposition to Reich's own brand of Freudianism — it struck me that this left-brain ego seems to be emerging as something of a villain. (This, of course, is the view held by D. H. Lawrence, who called it 'head consciousness;' Reich is also basically a Lawrentian.) In civilized man, it can usually be found in the role of nagging housewife, interrupting his spontaneity, questioning his intuitions, filling him with self-doubt and inner conflict. To put it crudely, you could say it is as if you had Bertrand Russell in one side of your head and D. H. Lawrence (or Walt Whitman) in the other; and the result is non-stop hostility.

But the more I thought about it, the more I saw that this view is fundamentally mistaken. 'Head consciousness' — dominance of the left-brain ego — *is* the cause of many of the problems of modern man. Yet the answer is *not* to hand over full control to the 'intuitive self'. Consider, for example, what happens in 'stage fright'. The rational-self is something of a hysteric; faced with any important problem, it is likely to over-react. It does this when you are confronted with a large audience and proceeds to 'interfere'. The familiar negative-feedback mechanism occurs, and you find yourself blushing and stammering. *And yet*, every great actor will tell you that some degree of nervousness is essential to a great performance as distinguished from a merely good one. Instead of 'interfering', it stimulates the two 'selves' to a new level of cooperation. The actor who is completely at his ease, completely relaxed, seldom turns in more than a workmanlike performance.

And now it should be possible to grasp the real importance of the left-ego. It is, and is intended to be, the controller. Consider what happens in hypnosis. The subject is apparently reduced to sleep; yet an EEG machine shows that he is awake. What happens, I would suggest, is that the hypnotist has put the left-brain to sleep, while the right remains awake. (The nature of hypnosis is still not understood; this is my own theory.) An interesting thing now happens. The subject is capable of more remarkable feats in the hypnotic state than when normally awake. The hypnotist might, for example, tell him that he will now lie with his shoulders on one chair and his legs on another, while a strong man will stand on his stomach; yet he will remain as rigid as a board. And, incredibly, the subject does precisely that. This is, of course, the phenomenon that Charcot observed — the amazing powers of that 'other self', when not constrained and undermined by the left brain. Then why can the subject not perform such feats when in his conscious state? *Because he doesn't believe he can.* When the hypnotist tells the 'other self' to perform some unusual feat, he is the voice of authority, and the other self responds like a well-trained soldier. Its own left-ego lacks that authority; it is manifestly nervous and unsure of itself. If, in fact, the left-ego could somehow generate that authority, the powers it could release might well be described as superhuman.

Lawrence, then, was mistaken. It is not true that head-consciousness has become too dominant. It is not dominant enough. The trouble lies not in the dominance of one side or the other, but in the failure of cooperation between the two. Think of a man defusing an unexploded bomb. The conscious ego, the 'look out', is totally in control; yet his concentration involves a high degree of 'inwardness'. His two egos are now like the two faces of Janus, one looking outward, the other inward, yet each perfectly aware of the other's activities. Moreover, the right is involved in its proper function of *supplying energy*, while the left makes use of that energy. There is no leakage.

Which makes us immediately aware that one of the main problems of everyday life is a constant energy leakage, as if the connection between your hosepipe and the garden tap was loose, allowing half the water to escape in the form of spray around the tap. If I am deeply absorbed in some task, there is a steady flow of effectively-utilized energy. But if I am tense or nervous, or simply in too much of a hurry (a left-brain characteristic), half the energy leaks away. In people suffering from anxiety neurosis — what used to be called neurasthenia — inner tension and self-mistrust have reached such a pitch that 90 per cent of the energy gets lost, and the slightest effort exhausts the patient.

And who is to blame? Again, the left-brain ego. He, so to speak, clamps the hosepipe to the tap and tightens the link. When deeply intent on some serious purpose, or galvanized by emergency, he makes sure there is a good seal, and little energy gets wasted: But in responding to everyday problems, he has become lazy and inefficient, so half the energy gets lost.

Again, the solution is quite clear: *increased control* on the part of the left-brain ego. It is true that learning to stop worrying, to stop over- reacting to trivialities, is important; the psychiatrist tells his obsessive patient 'Relax and let it all hang out'. Yet the real problem with such people is not too much control, but too little. There is plenty of anxiety — far too much of it. But not enough deliberate, conscious effort.

One of our chief problems is that what we tend to substitute for effort is stimulus. Apart from the commands that emanate from the left-ego, the 'other self' is trained to respond to various stimuli, all kinds of stimuli from food and alcohol and sex to music and beautiful scenery. If ten months of hard work at the office have left me over-tired, bored, mechanical, then I take a holiday and allow a new set of stimuli to set up a positive feedback with my 'other self'. This is, in fact, a confession that the 'I,' the left-ego, has abnegated control, and is relying on external stimuli to arouse its companion to cooperation. Yet if you were to tell such a person that a greater effort of self-control would do him more good in the long run than a holiday, he would be horrified, for it seems to him that such an effort might well cause him to 'snap'. He would require a high degree of insight to recognize that greater ego-control does *not* mean simply 'pushing himself' harder while remaining in the same negative frame of mind....

This attempt to use 'stimuli' in the place of control is perhaps our most dangerous human characteristic. Just about every major human ill can be traced to it. A bored child switches on television. A bored adult lights another cigarette or pours himself a stiff drink. The bored Don Juan looks around for another girl to seduce. Each new challenge arouses the automatic response of the 'other self', which responds with a flood of vital energy. And this is by no means a modern ailment. Men have always used war and conquest as a stimulant. That sonnet of Rupert Brooke — of thanksgiving for the outbreak of the First World War — is one of the saddest confessions of civilized man:

> Now God be thanked, Who has matched us with His hour,
> And caught our youth, and wakened us from sleeping,
> With hand made sure, clear eye, and sharpened power,
> To turn, as swimmers into cleanness leaping,
> Glad from a world grown old and cold and weary....

In other words, thank God for the war, which has rescued me from my own sense of inadequacy. But at least Brooke had some excuse; intelligent adolescents are notoriously subject to self-division. Grown men should know better.

The real lesson is that if we knew enough about ourselves, and if the conscious ego could achieve the necessary 'authority', we wouldn't need these dangerous stimuli. It should be totally unnecessary, for example, to call in a hypnotist to stop you from smoking: this is like calling in the man from next door to chastise your children.

Clearly, the implications of this insight are of tremendous importance. Yet I must again emphasize that I am not being dogmatic about its physiological aspect. At first, I spent a great deal of time reading works on brain physiology, in an attempt to place it all on a more solid foundation. Is there, for example, some known connection between the right cerebral hemisphere and the cerebellum and limbic region? But the textbooks were vague and sometimes self-contradictory; and when I asked Ornstein personally, he said I might as well ask whether there is a connection between the right hemisphere and the big toe. It seems fairly clear that the state of our knowledge of the brain is about equivalent to, say, the ancient Egyptian knowledge of anatomy. At which point, it struck me that this is unimportant. What I learned of the functions of the right and left brain from reading Sperry, Gazzaniga and the rest had merely made me clearly conscious of certain aspects of my inner-being that are perfectly obvious to self-observation. I discovered, for example, that that remarkable man Gurdjieff knew all about these 'two selves' (he called them essence and personality) as long ago as 1920, and even told a London audience that they are located in different parts of the brain. Having spent more than a year looking into this interesting matter, I am fairly firmly convinced that

162

'essence and personality' *do* correspond pretty accurately to the right and left hemispheres. But it hardly matters. What matters is the insight into the functioning of the 'two selves'.

And this, I think, is very important indeed — so much so that the above comments have hardly touched on its implications. The most exciting of these, for me at any rate, is the notion that the powers of that 'other self' are far greater than we realize, and yet that they might nevertheless be accessible to conscious control.

Some of the implications, I agree, look gloomy, seeming to confirm the grumpiest criticisms of Jean Jacques Rousseau, D. H. Lawrence and others who feel that civilization is sending us to hell by the shortest route. But this is a superficial view. In fact, it would be impossible to get gloomier than Freud's *Civilization and Its Discontents*, based on the Frankenstein's monster view of the unconscious. The left-right view of the human entity gives altogether firmer grounds for optimism about man's future. It suggests that our real trouble is not that we are at the mercy of sinister dark forces, but that we are enfeebled by a completely unjustified lack of self-confidence. The problem lies in my attitude towards myself, my tendency to premature defeat, my failure to grasp that I am, in fact, in control. I could be compared to an excellent army with incompetent and inexperienced officers. And this is a far better situation than an army with good officers and hopeless soldiers. Inexperience is fairly easy to cure. Moreover, the thought of inexperienced officers — reminding us of the young officers at the beginning of *War and Peace* — makes us aware that human beings are young and inexperienced in the evolutionary sense, and that therefore these problems are — with luck — little more than teething pains.

For me, the interesting question is how these insights can be used. If I am correct, this theory of the relation between right and left provides a new — empirical — foundation for psychology, and makes most of the theories of earlier psychologists — Freud, Jung, Adler et al. — redundant. That sounds such an enormous claim that even I feel startled by it, and find myself wondering if I have got it wrong somewhere. Yet the more I re-examine the question, the more convinced I become that the insight is basically valid. The unconscious may be mysterious, but it is not alien or hostile.

I soon became convinced that if the theory is correct, then certain consequences should follow. For example, a deliberate and conscious effort of control, based upon a change of attitude, ought to bring about an immediate change in the quality of consciousness. To use my earlier simile; if we take the trouble to tighten the link between the tap and the hosepipe so that leakage becomes minimal, then our available water pressure — vital energy — ought to rise dramatically. A few days of constant effort quickly demonstrated that this is so. I have spent my life examining this question of intensity of consciousness and how to achieve it — as my books, from *The Outsider* onward, make clear.

ACTIVE IMAGINATION

From *The Lord of the Underworld — Jung and the Twentieth Century*, 1984

Active imagination is certainly one of the most interesting and exciting of all Jung's ideas. But those who wish to leam more about it will have a frustrating time searching through the Collected Works; the General Index lists a few dozen references, but most of these turn out to be merely passing mentions. The earliest — and perhaps most complete — description of the method occurs in the essay on 'The Transcendent Function', written in 1916; yet here Jung does not even mention it by name. Moreover, he left the essay in his files until someone asked him for a contribution to a student magazine in 1957. It appears in Volume Eight of the Collected Works, together with a preliminary warning: 'The method is...not without its dangers, and should, if possible, not be employed except under expert supervision.'

Yet if the method is as effective as Jung claims — in his autobiography — then such a danger should not be taken too seriously. After all, *if* active imagination really works, then Jung has solved a problem that tormented so many of the 'outsiders' of the nineteenth century, and should have provided mankind with a vital key to its future evolution. In a letter of 1871 Rimbaud wrote about the poet's need to induce visions: 'I say that one must be a *visionary* — that one must make oneself a VISIONARY.' He goes on: 'The poet makes himself a *visionary* through a long, immense and reasoned *derangement of all the senses*. All forms of love, of suffering, of madness, he seeks himself....' And in *A Season in Hell*, he claims to have succeeded in inducing this derangement: 'I accustomed myself to simple hallucination:

I really saw a mosque in place of a factory, angels practising on drums, coaches on the roads of the sky; a drawing room at the bottom of a lake: monsters, mysteries….'

But when expressed in this form, we can see that it is basically the old romantic craving for wonders, marvels and ecstasies, the craving expressed in the very title of Poe's *Tales of Mystery and Imagination*. We find it in the dim, misty landscapes of Novalis and Tieck, in the grotesqueries of Hoffmann and Jean Paul, in the horrors of Poe and Sheridan Le Fanu, in the courtly day-dreams of the Pre-Raphaelites, in Aubrey Beardsley's erotic imagery (and it was Beardsley who outraged readers of the *Yellow Book* with the image of a grand piano in a field) and in the shock tactics of the surrealists and the Dadaists. It all seems to amount to Yeats's attempt to escape the 'foul rag and bone shop of the heart' with a kind of ladder of wishful thinking. Clearly, if Jung has really created a usable technique for 'making oneself a visionary' and seeing angels practising on drums and drawing rooms at the bottom of a lake, then this alone would qualify him as one of the most significant figures of our century.

It was in the autobiography that Jung made clear for the first time how he came to recognize the existence of active imagination: how the break with Freud brought him to the verge of total nervous collapse, and so allowed him a glimpse of the delusions suffered by psychotic patients. It was fortunate for Jung that the vision of Europe drowned in blood came true in the following year, bringing the recognition that an 'illusion' is not necessarily untrue. 'I see too deep and too much' says the 'Outsider' hero of Barbusse's *L'Enfer*, and this was precisely what was happening to Jung.

When the mind is under this kind of severe stress, its natural tendency is to put up frantic resistance. Jung recognized that he was in the same position as Nietzsche and Hölderlin, and that, like them, he might lose his sanity; the result was a grim determination not to 'let go'. Then, in December 1913, sitting at his desk in a state of turmoil and pessimism, he made the momentous decision to 'let go' and see what happened. The result was not total breakdown: it was the astonished recognition that the force that had been trying to make him let go was a stranger inside his own head, and that the stranger was in perfect control of the situation. It was a blinding recognition of the 'hidden ally'. In Hudson's terms, what was happening was that the 'subjective mind' was saying to the 'objective mind': 'Look, for heaven's sake stop struggling to maintain this iron curtain between us, because you're wasting your strength in fighting yourself.' It could be compared to a wife saying to her husband, who is exhausted by driving: 'Get in the back and have a nap while I drive.' Jung was sensible enough to let go of the steering wheel, and the result was the 'waking dream' of the cave with the corpse of Siegfried.

In a book called *Access to Inner Worlds* I have described how a similar experience happened to an American living in Finland, Brad Absetz. After the death of their child through cancer, his wife collapsed into severe depression. She used to lie on a bed for hours, plunged in negative fantasies and self-reproaches; Brad Absetz lay beside her, waiting for her to emerge, so he could be there to help her. He lay in a state of vigilance, waiting for the slightest indication that she was 'coming round'; at the same time, he was physically relaxed. One day, as he lay there, he experienced an overwhelming sense of lightness and relief, almost as if he were floating up off the bed. This was his own equivalent of Jung's 'letting go'. And what now happened was that that 'other person' inside his head began to express itself. As he stood by the buffet table, waiting to help himself to lunch, his arm began to twitch; he recognized this as a signal that it wanted to do something, and allowed it to reach out and take whatever food it liked. It took food that he would not normally have taken. This continued for weeks, and in a short time, he had lost weight, and felt healthier than ever before. One day his small daughter asked him to make her a drawing with coloured crayons; again, the hand began to twitch, and he allowed it to do what it liked. The result was an astonishing series of drawings and paintings, incredible 'psychedelic' patterns, every one totally different from all the others. His 'other self' took over and wrote poetry, while he merely looked on; it made metal sculptures; it performed his everyday tasks — like bee-keeping — in a simple, ritualistic manner that renewed his vitality. In the parliament of Brad's mind, the Member for the Unconscious had been given his proper say, and the result was a life that was in every way more harmonious and relaxed. He had, to a large extent, achieved 'individuation'.

Brad Absetz was in no danger of insanity when he 'let go', but he was under severe stress. His subjective mind, left to its own devices, showed him the way out of the impasse. (The method — of lying totally relaxed, but in a state of wide-awake vigilance — could be regarded as the simplest and most effective of all mental therapies.)

In 1913, Jung was in a rather worse state; so when he 'let go', the image-making powers of the subjective mind flooded into consciousness. He called the result 'active imagination', but we can see that it was not imagination in the ordinary sense of the word: the deliberate evocation of mental images or states. What Jung had achieved was a *new balance* between the ego and the unconscious, in which the unconscious was recognized as an equal partner. This explains why, from then on, Jung frequently had 'visions', like the one of the crucified Christ at the end of his bed.

We can at once see the difference between Jung's concept of active imagination and Rimbaud's. Rimbaud *talked* about surrendering to suffering and madness; but in effect, his ego remained in charge. He attempted a 'reasoned derangement of the senses' with drugs and alcohol, but since his ego was strong, these failed to produce individuation and 'access to inner worlds'. (I am inclined to regard his statement that he accustomed himself to seeing mosques instead of factories, etc., as wishful thinking, poetic license.) The real 'breakthrough' tends to occur in moments of desperation, or under extreme stress, and is a kind of inspired surrender. (Ramakrishna achieved a similar breakthrough when he attempted suicide with a sword, and was suddenly overwhelmed by a vision of the Divine Mother.)

Now we can begin to see why, although Jung regarded active imagination as the key to 'individuation', he said very little about it. There was very little to say. In the essay on 'The Transcendent Function' he writes: 'In the intensity of the emotional disturbance itself lies the value, the energy which he should have at his disposal in order to remedy the state…'

He adds: 'Nothing is achieved by repressing this state or devaluing it rationally.' In other words, the patient suffering from severe mental stress is already ideally placed to begin to develop active imagination.

Jung's instructions follow:

In order, therefore, to gain possession of the energy that is in the wrong place, he must make the emotional state the basis or starting point of the procedure. He must make himself as conscious as possible of the mood he is in, sinking himself in it without reserve and noting down on paper all the fantasies and other associations that come up. Fantasy must be allowed the freest possible play, yet not in such a manner that it leaves the orbit of its object…by setting off a kind of 'chain-reaction' process. This 'free association', as Freud called it, leads away from the object to all sorts of complexes….

He utters a similar warning in the introduction he wrote to the essay in 1958: that 'one of the lesser dangers [of the method] is that [it] may not lead to any positive result, since it easily passes over into the so-called "free association" of Freud, whereupon the patient gets caught in the sterile circle of his own complexes….' We can see that, for example, if Brad Absetz had lain on the bed 'free associating', he would never have achieved the break-through; what was so important was the combination of total relaxation with mental *vigilance* and alertness. 'The whole procedure', says Jung, 'is a kind of enrichment and clarification of the affect [powerful feeling-state], whereby the affect and its contents are brought nearer to consciousness'. In some cases, says Jung, the patient may actually *hear* the 'other voice' as an auditory hallucination — a comment that will convince split-brain psychologists that Jung is talking about the right and left cerebral hemispheres.

All this may leave readers who were hoping to learn how to practise active imagination feeling a little frustrated. Let us see if the matter can be clarified.

The essence of Jung's original experience — of 'waking dreams' — was the *recognition* of the reality of the 'hidden ally'. The 'letting go' that revealed this ally was a rather frightening process — like letting yourself fall backwards, hoping someone is standing there to catch you (a game many of us used to play as children). Once you have discovered that there is someone waiting to catch you, the fear vanishes and turns into a sense of confidence and reassurance.

We could say, then, that the correct starting point for active imagination is the recognition that there is someone standing there behind you. In a remarkable book called *The Secret Science at Work*, Max Freedom Long describes his own methods — based upon those of the Hunas of Hawaii — for contacting the 'hidden ally' (which he calls the 'low self'); Long's group began referring to the 'other self' as George, and found that it could be engaged in a dialogue (and could also answer questions by means of a pendulum).

Once the *real existence* of the 'other self' has been recognized, the next question is to tease it into expressing itself. In a letter of 1947, Jung explained his technique to a Mrs O-:

> The point is that you start with any image, for instance just with that yellow mass in your dream. Contemplate it and carefully observe how the picture begins to unfold or change. Don't try to make it into something, just do nothing but observe what its spontaneous changes are. Any mental picture you contemplate in this way will sooner or later change through a spontaneous association that causes a slight alteration of the picture.... Hold fast to the one image you have chosen and wait until it changes by itself. Note all these changes and eventually step into the picture yourself, and if it is a speaking figure...then say what you have to say to that figure and listen to what he or she has to say.

In his Tavistock Lectures of 1935 (Collected Works, vol. 18) Jung gives an example of how one of his patients finally achieved active imagination 'from cold', so to speak. He was a young artist who seemed to find it practically impossible to understand what Jung meant by active imagination. 'This man's brain was always working for itself'; that is to say, his artistic ego would not get out of the driving seat. But each time the artist came to see Jung, he waited at a small station, and looked at a poster advertising Mürren, in the Bernese Alps; it had a waterfall, a green meadow and a hill with cows. He decided to try 'fantasizing' about the poster. He stared at it and imagined he was in the meadow, then that he was walking up the hill. Perhaps he was in a particularly relaxed mood that day, or perhaps his artistic imagination now came to his aid instead of obstructing him. (We can imagine his right brain saying: 'So *that's* what you wanted! Why didn't you say so?') A waking dream took over. He found himself walking along a footpath on the other side of the hill, round a ravine and a large rock, and into a little chapel. As he looked at the face of the Virgin on the altar, something with pointed ears vanished behind the altar. He thought 'That's all nonsense', and the fantasy was gone.

He was struck by the important thought: perhaps that was not fantasy — perhaps it was really there. Now presumably on the train, he closed his eyes and conjured up the scene again. Again he entered the chapel, and again the thing with pointed ears jumped behind the altar. This was enough to convince him that what he had seen was not mere fantasy, but a genuine glimpse of an *objective reality* inside his own head, 'access to inner worlds'. This, says Jung, was the beginning of a successful development of active imagination.

What becomes very clear here is that there is a certain 'turning point', and that this is the moment when the subject suddenly realizes that this is not mere personal fantasy, but that he is dealing with an objective reality — the reality we occasionally encounter in dreams, when some place seems totally real.

The basic procedure, then, seems to be: lie still — as Brad Absetz did — and become perfectly relaxed and yet fully alert. Place yourself in a *listening* frame of mind, waiting for 'George' to speak. That is to say, assume that there is someone there who has something to communicate, and ask him to go ahead and say it. If what he 'says' is an image, then contemplate it as you might contemplate a painting in an art gallery, and ask him, so to speak, to go on.

Julian Jaynes's book *The Origin of Consciousness in the Breakdown of the Bicameral Mind* may be found a useful accessory in this quest for 'the turning point'. Jaynes believes that our remote ancestors of four thousand years ago did not possess 'self-consciousness' in the sense that we do; they could not decide a course of action by 'questioning themselves', because their minds were turned outward, so to speak. Decisions were made for them by 'voices' that came into their heads, and which they mistook for the voices of the gods; in fact, it was the other half of the brain, the 'other self'. Later, Jaynes believed, war and crisis forced man to develop self-awareness, so he no longer had need of auditory hallucinations.

We may object to this theory on the grounds that modern man is *still* 'bicameral' (with two minds), and that therefore it seems more probable that ancient man was 'unicameral', in a relaxed, 'instinctive' state of oneness with nature, like a cow. But this objection makes no real difference to the substance of the theory, which springs from the scientific recognition that we actually possess a 'second self' in the brain, and that thousands of people experience this second self in the form of auditory and visual hallucinations — what Jung called 'projections'.

In her book *Encounters with the Soul: Active Imagination*, the Jungian psychotherapist Barbara Hannah insists that ancient man's encounters with 'God' (in the Old Testament, for example) are instances of active imagination: that is, of the action of the 'bicameral mind'. She cites two highly convincing examples of the 'auditory method of active imagination' from 2200 B.C. and from A.D. 1200, then reprints an important modern document, the account of a patient called Anna Marjula, of how she was cured through the practice of active imagination. The case helps to throw light on what Jung meant by active imagination.

Anna Marjula was the daughter of a lawyer, and Jung thought the origin of her neurosis could have been sexual — seeing her father masturbating when she was a small girl; the father later revealed a certain physical interest in his daughter. She was a shy, nervous child, tormented by feelings of inferiority, and the death of her mother was a shattering experience. She was a fine musician, and wanted to become a concert pianist. Working for her examination, at the age of twenty-one, she became over-tense and spiritually exhausted. On the night before the examination, she had a 'vision'. A voice told her to sacrifice ambition, and to be perfectly willing to accept failure. (This, we can see, was the best advice her subjective mind could have offered her.) Her willingness to accept possible defeat brought religious ecstasy; at this point, the 'voice' told her that she was not destined to become famous herself, but that her real vocation was to become the mother of a man of genius. She should look around for someone who would be the right father for a man of genius, and offer herself to him without physical desire. If she could succeed in conceiving a child without any feeling of pleasure, the result would be a man of genius.

In fact, the patient never met the right man, and as she entered her forties, a conviction of having 'missed the boat' caused severe psychological problems. She was fifty-one when she became Jung's patient.

The analyst — Jung's wife — suggested that the original 'vision' was a deception of the 'animus', and that the patient should try to use active imagination to approach a more positive female archetype, the Great Mother. Clearly, the patient already had a predisposition to 'visions' and her psychological tensions provided the psychic energy for active imagination. The result was a remarkable series of conversations with the 'Great Mother', in which the patient experienced the Mother as another person — as Jung experienced Philemon. The eventual result, according to Barbara Hannah, was a happy and serene old age.

Another Jungian analyst, J. Marvin Spiegelman, set out to conquer the techniques of active imagination at the age of twenty-four, with 'fantasies' of a cave, in which he encountered a mother, daughter and a wise old man. One day, a knight appeared and carried off the mother and daughter. The knight explained that he had certain tales to tell, and that there were 'several others in his realm' who also wished to dictate their stories. Spiegelman then spent several years taking down various stories dictated by the knight, a nun, a nymphomaniac, an old Chinaman and various others: these were published in four volumes. Clearly, Spiegelman had used the same technique as Brad Absetz — allowing the 'other self' to overcome its shyness and express itself — and the results were in many ways similar.

In the fourth volume of the series, *The Knight*, Spiegelman makes an observation of central importance: that the successful practice of active imagination 'regularly leads to the occurrence of synchronistic events, in which one is related to the world in a deep, mystical way'. What happens, Spiegelman suggests, is that the inner work somehow changes one's relationship to the world. He then tells the important story of the Rainmaker, originally told to Jung by Richard Wilhelm. Wilhelm was in a remote Chinese village that was suffering from drought. A rainmaker was sent for from a distant village. He asked for a cottage on the outskirts of the village, and vanished into it for three days. Then there was a tremendous downpour, followed by snow — an unheard-of occurrence at that time of year.

Wilhelm asked the old man how he had done it; the old man replied that he hadn't. 'You see', said the old man, 'I come from a region where everything is in order. It rains when it should rain and is fine when that is needed. The people are themselves in order. But the people in this village are all out of Tao and out of themselves. I was at once infected when I arrived, so I asked for a cottage on the edge of the village, so I could be alone. When I was once more in Tao, it rained.'

By being 'in Tao and in themselves', the old man meant what Jung meant by individuation. That is to say, there was a proper traffic between the two selves — or the two halves of the brain. The people in the rainless village were dominated by the left-brain ego — which, while it is unaware of the 'hidden ally', is inclined to over-react to problems. This in turn produces a negative state of mind that can influence the external world.

This throws a wholly new light on the idea of synchronicity, and also of magic. One could say that, according to the Chinese theory, the mind is intimately involved with nature. Synchronicity is not therefore the active intervention of the mind in natural processes: rather, a natural product of their harmony. (So when we are psychologically healthy, synchronicities should occur all the time.) Our fears and tensions interfere with this natural harmony; when this happens, things go wrong.

We can see that this also changes our concept of the nature of active imagination. It is *not* some kind of 'reasoned derangement of the senses', directed by the ego. It is an inner harmony based on the recognition of the 'hidden ally', which leads to a process of cooperation between the 'two selves'.

But here again, a warning must be uttered. A remarkable American physician, Howard Miller, has pointed out that human beings already possess a form of active imagination. I can close my eyes and conjure up a beach on a hot day, imagine the warm sand under my feet, the sun on my face, the sound of waves; then, in a split second, I can change to a winter day on a mountain, with snow underfoot and on the branches of the trees, and a cold wind on my face.... But Miller points out that the 'control panel' of such imaginings is the ego itself. *I* decide on the change of scene, and my imagination obliges.

What Miller is saying, in effect, is that the right brain is the orchestra and the left brain is the conductor. If, for example, I relax and read poetry, or listen to music, I can induce all kinds of moods, and eventually achieve a state in which I can change my mood instantly: I can turn, let us say, from Milton's *L'Allegro* to *Il Penseroso*, and conjure up with total realism a summer scene with merrymakers and then the 'dim religious light' of abbeys and churches and pinewoods. The right and left brains can eventually achieve the same relationship as a great conductor with his orchestra — the orchestra that has come to respond to his most delicate gesture. But such a state of harmony depends on the initial recognition that *I* am the conductor. *I* must take up my baton, tap the music stand and say 'Gentlemen, today we do the Jupiter Symphony....' The greatest danger of active imagination is that the subject should assume it means handing over his baton to the orchestra — which is obviously an absurdity. Active imagination is a state of cooperation in which the ego must remain the dominant partner.

Western man is in the position of a conductor who is unaware that he possesses an orchestra — or is only dimly and intermittently aware of it. Active imagination is a technique for becoming aware of the orchestra. This is 'individuation'. And it is clearly only a beginning. The next task is to develop a random collection of musicians into a great orchestra. This is the real task of the conductor. And this seems to be what Jung meant when he said, towards the end of his life: 'Consciousness is the supreme arbiter.'

HUMAN EVOLUTION

From A *Criminal History of Mankind*, 1983

Since his advent so many millions of years ago, man has shown himself to be the most remarkable creature who has ever walked the earth. With none of the advantages of the big predators, he taught himself to survive by the use of intelligence. But even so, the stream of evolution from Ramapithecus, through Australopithecus and *Homo habilis* was like a broad, meandering river. Man developed because he learned the use of weapons and tools; but his development was slow because he had not yet learned to use that most valuable of all tools, his mind.

With *Homo erectus*, the river entered a valley and became a fast-flowing stream. A million and a half years later — which, in geological time, brings us almost to the twentieth century — came Neanderthal and Cro-Magnon man, and it is as if the river entered a gorge and suddenly turned into a torrent. The pace quickened again with the beginning of agriculture. With the building of the cities, the gorge narrowed and the rapids became dangerous.

It would hardly seem possible that evolution could flow faster still, but that is what happened at some time between the founding of the cities and the civilizations of ancient Crete and Mycenae. The sheer danger of the rapids created a new level of alertness and determination. Roaring along at top speed between narrow walls, man was forced to concentrate as he had never concentrated before. Bodies struggled in the water; wrecks drifted past him; but the noise and exhilaration swallowed up the screams of the drowning. A man who steers his raft with his jaw set and all his senses strained to the utmost has no time for compassion.

As he developed determination, man also developed ruthlessness. The narrowing of the senses became a habit — so that whenever he found himself in a quieter patch of water, protected by some buttress from the torrent, he no longer knew how to relax and enjoy the relative calm.

This explains why man has ceased to be the gentle vegetarian described by Leakey and Fromm. But he has no reason to envy those other animals who are still drifting placidly down broad rivers. For he has developed a faculty that outweighs all the danger, all the misery and violence. He has learned to steer.

When he learned to use his mind, this ability to steer made him also the first truly creative and inventive creature. He has poured that narrow jet of energy into discovery and exploration. But the sheer force of the jet has meant that whenever it has been obstructed — or whenever men have lacked the self-discipline to control it — the result has been chaos and destruction. Crime is the negative aspect of creativity.

Throughout history, the ruthless — from Sennacherib to Hitler — have ended by destroying themselves, for their tendency to violence makes them bad steersmen. It is true that their crimes seem to dominate human history. But, as we shall see, it is the good steersmen who play the major part in the story of mankind.

A REPORT ON
THE VIOLENT MAN

From *A Criminal History of Mankind,* 1983

On 13 December 1937, the Imperial Japanese Army marched into Nanking, in Central China, and began what has been described as 'one of the most savage acts of mass terror in modern times' — a campaign of murder, rape and torture that lasted for two months. Chinese soldiers had divested themselves of their uniforms and mixed with the civilian population, in the belief that the Japanese would spare them if they were unarmed. The Japanese began rounding them up and shooting them in huge numbers, using machine-guns. The bodies — some twenty thousand of them — were thrown into heaps, dowsed with petrol, and set alight; hundreds who were still alive died in the flames. Because they were indistinguishable from the soldiers, male civilians were also massacred. Women were herded into pens which became virtually brothels for the Japanese soldiers; more than twenty thousand women between the ages of eleven and eighty were raped, and many disembowelled. Many who were left alive committed ritual suicide, the traditional response of Chinese women to violation. Boys of school age were suspended by their hands for days, and then used for bayonet practice. Rhodes Farmer, a journalist who worked in Shanghai, came into possession of photographs of mass executions of boys by beheading, of rapes of women by Japanese soldiers, and of 'slaughter pits' in which soldiers were encouraged to develop their killer-instinct by bayoneting tied prisoners. When published in the American magazine *Look*, they caused worldwide condemnation, and the Japanese commander was recalled to Tokyo. The odd thing was that these photographs were taken by the Japanese themselves;

for they regarded the atrocities as simply acts of revenge. In two months, more than fifty thousand people died in Nanking, and towards two hundred thousand in the surrounding countryside. (In 1982 — when the Chinese were quarrelling with the Japanese about their 'rewriting' of history — the official Chinese figure was three hundred and forty thousand.)

Some six hundred miles to the north-west of Nanking, the city of Peking was already in Japanese hands. But the village of Chou-kou-tien, thirty miles to the south-west, was still held by Chinese Nationalists, and there a team of international scientists were collaborating on a project that had created immense excitement in archaeological circles. In 1929, a young palaeontologist named Pie Wen-Chung had discovered in the caves near Chou-kou-tien the petrified skull of one of man's earliest ancestors. It looked more like a chimpanzee than a human being, and the Catholic scientist Teilhard de Chardin thought the teeth were those of a beast of prey. It had a sloping forehead, enormous browridges and a receding chin. But the brain was twice as big as that of a chimpanzee. And as more skulls, limbs and teeth were discovered, it became clear that this beast of prey had walked upright. At first, it looked as if this was a cross between ape and man — what earlier anthropologists such as Haeckel had called 'the missing link'. Nearly half a century earlier the missing link theory had apparently been confirmed when the bones of an 'ape-man' had been discovered in Java. The ape-man of Peking clearly belonged to the same species. But the caves of the Chou-kou-tien hills yielded evidence that this was no missing link. Peking man had constructed hearths and used fire to roast his food — his favourite meal seems to have been venison. He was therefore more culturally advanced than had been supposed. This creature, who lived more than half a million years ago, was a true human being.

He was also, it seemed, a cannibal. All the forty skulls discovered at Chou-kou-tien were mutilated at the base, creating a gap into which a hand could be inserted to scoop out the brains. Franz Weidenreich, the scientist in charge of the investigation, declared that these creatures had been slaughtered in a body, dragged into the caves and there roasted and eaten. By whom? Presumably by other Peking men. In other caves in the area, bones of Cro-Magnon man were discovered, and here too there was evidence of cannibalism; but Cro-Magnon man came on the scene more than four hundred thousand years later; he could not have been the culprit. The evidence of the Chou-kou-tien caves revealed that Peking man had fought against the wild beasts who occupied the caves and had wiped them out; after that, he had fought against his fellow men and eaten them. While editorials around the world were asking how civilized men could massacre the population of a large city, the Peking excavations were suggesting an unpalatable answer: that man has always been a killer of his own species.

Nowadays, that view seems uncontroversial enough; the threat of atomic annihilation has accustomed us to take a pessimistic view of the human race. But in 1937, the 'killer ape' idea met with strong resistance among scientists. According to the theory that had been current since the 1890s, *Homo sapiens* had evolved because of his intelligence. He started life as a gentle, vegetarian creature, like his brother the ape, then slowly learned such skills as hunting and agriculture and created civilization. In his book on Peking Man, Dr Harry L. Shapiro, one of the scientists at Chou-kou-tien, does not even mention the mutilations in the base of the skulls; he prefers to believe they were damaged by falling rock and layers of debris. But new evidence continued to erode the older view. As early as 1924, the palaeontologist Raymond Dart had discovered an even older species of 'ape-man', which he called Australopithecus (or southern ape-man). In the late 1940s, examining an Australopithecus site near Sterkfontein, Dart found many shattered baboon skulls. Looking at a club-like antelope thighbone, he was struck by a sudden thought. He lifted the bone and brought it down heavily on the back of one of the baboon skulls. The two holes made by the protuberances of the leg joint were identical with similar holes on the other skulls. Dart had discovered the weapon with which the 'first man' had killed baboons. It seemed to verify that similar thighbones found in the caves of Peking man had also been weapons....

In 1949, Dart published a paper containing his claim that Australopithecus — who lived about two million years ago — had discovered the use of weapons. Fellow scientists declined to take the idea seriously. In 1953, he repeated the offence with a paper called 'The Predatory Transition from Ape to Man', which so worried the editor of the *International Anthropological and Linguistic Review* that he prefaced it with a note disclaiming responsibility for its opinions. For in this paper Dart advanced the revolutionary thesis that 'southern ape-man' had emerged from among the apes for one reason only: because he had learned to commit murder with weapons. Our remote ancestors, he said, learned to stand and walk upright because they needed their hands to carry their bone clubs. Hands replaced teeth for tearing chunks of meat from animal carcases, so our teeth became smaller and our claws disappeared to be replaced by nails. Hitting an animal with a club — or hurling a club or stone at it from a distance — meant a new kind of co-ordination between the hand and eye; and so the brain began to develop.

At the time Dart was writing his paper, there was one remarkable piece of evidence for the older view that 'intelligence came first'. This was the famous Piltdown skull, discovered in a gravel pit in 1913. It had a jaw like an ape but its brain was the same size as that of modern man. Then, forty years later, tests at the British Museum revealed that the Piltdown skull was a hoax — the skull of a modern man and the jawbone of an ape; both stained by chemicals to look alike. The revelation of the hoax came in the same year that Dart's paper was published, and it went a long way towards supporting Dart's views. The brain of Australopithecus was larger than that of an ape, but it was far smaller than that of modern man.

In the early 1960s, two remarkable books popularized this disturbing thesis about man's killer instincts: *African Genesis* by Robert Ardrey and *On Aggression* by Konrad Lorenz. Both argued, in effect, that man became man because of his aggressiveness, and that we should not be surprised by war, crime and violent behaviour because they are part of our very essence. Ardrey's final chapter was grimly entitled: 'Cain's Children'. Yet both Ardrey and Lorenz were guardedly optimistic, Lorenz pointing out that man's aggressions *can* be channelled into less dangerous pursuits — such as sport and exploration — while Ardrey declared, with more hope than conviction, that man's instinct for order and civilization is just as powerful as his destructiveness. Ardrey even ends with a semi-mystical passage about a mysterious presence called 'the keeper of the kinds', a force behind life that makes for order. Yet the overall effect of both books is distinctly pessimistic.

The same may be said for the view put forward by Arthur Koestler in *The Ghost in the Machine* (1967). Koestler points out: '*Homo sapiens* is virtually unique in the animal kingdom in his lack of instinctive safeguards against the killing of conspecifics — members of his own species.' (He might have added that he is also one of the few creatures who has no instinctive revulsion against cannibalism — dogs, for example, cannot be persuaded to eat dog meat.) Koestler's explanation is that the human brain is an evolutionary blunder. It consists of three brains, one on top of the other: the reptile brain, the mammalian brain and, on top of these, the human neo-cortex. The result, as the physiologist P. D. Maclean remarked, is that when a psychiatrist asks the patient to lie down on the couch he is asking him to stretch out alongside a horse and a crocodile. The human brain has developed at such an incredible pace in the past half million years that physiologists talk about a 'brain explosion' and compare its growth to that of a tumour. The trouble, says Koestler, is that instead of *transforming* the old brain into the new — as the forelimb of the earliest reptiles became a bird's wing and a man's hand — evolution has merely superimposed a new structure on top of the old one and their powers overlap. We are a 'mentally unbalanced species', whose logic is always being undermined by emotion. 'To put it crudely: evolution has left a few screws loose between the neo-cortex and the hypothalamus', and the result is that man has a dangerous 'paranoid streak' which explains his self-destructiveness.

Inevitably, there was a reaction against the pessimism. In *The Anatomy of Human Destructiveness* (1974), the veteran Freudian Erich Fromm flatly contradicts Dart, Ardrey and Lorenz, and argues that there is no evidence that our remote ancestors were basically warlike and aggressive. 'Almost everyone reasons: if civilized man is so warlike, how much more warlike must primitive man have been! But [Quincy] Wright's results [in *A Study of War*] confirm the thesis that the most primitive men are the least warlike and that warlikeness grows in proportion to civilization.' And in a television series called *The Making of Mankind* (broadcast in 1981), Richard Leakey, son of the anthropologist Louis Leakey (whose investigations into 'southern ape-man' had been widely cited by Ardrey to support his thesis) left no doubt about his opposition to the killer ape theory. Everything we know about primitive man, he said, suggests that he lived at peace with the world and his neighbours; it was only after man came to live in cities that he became cruel and destructive. This is also the view taken by Fromm in *The Anatomy of Human Destructiveness*.

Yet even the title of Fromm's book suggests that Ardrey, Lorenz and Koestler were not all that far from the truth. 'Man differs from the animal by the fact that he is a killer,' says Fromm, 'the only primate that kills and tortures members of his own species without any reason....' And the book is devoted to the question: why is man the only creature who kills and tortures members of his own kind?

Fromm's answer leans heavily upon the views of Freud. In *Civilization and Its Discontents* (1931), Freud had argued that man was not made for civilization or civilization for man. It frustrates and thwarts him at every turn and drives him to neurosis and self-destruction. But Freud's view of our remote ancestors implied that they spent their time dragging their mates around by the hair and hitting their rivals with clubs, and that it is modern man's inhibitions about doing the same thing that make him neurotic. Fromm, in fact, is altogether closer to the views that had been expressed thirty years earlier by H. G. Wells. In one of his most interesting — and most neglected — books, *'42 to '44*, written in the midst of the Second World War, Wells tried to answer the question of why men are so cruel and so destructive. 'We now know that the hunters of the great plains of Europe in the milder interglacial periods had the character of sociable, gregarious creatures without much violence.' Like Fromm and Leakey, Wells believed that the trouble began when men moved into cities, and were 'brought into a closeness of contact for which their past had not prepared them. The early civilizations were not slowly evolved and adapted *communities*. They were essentially jostling crowds in which quite unprecedented reactions were possible'. Ruthless men seized the power and wealth and the masses had to live in slums. This is Wells's explanation of how man became a killer.

What puzzles Wells is the question of human cruelty. He makes the important observation that when we hear about some appalling piece of cruelty our reaction is to become angry and say, 'Do you know what I should like to do to that brute?' — a revelation 'that vindictive reaction is the reality of the human animal'. When we hear of cruelty, we instantly feel a sense of the *difference* between ourselves and the 'brute' who is responsible. And it is precisely this lack of fellow-feeling that made the cruelty possible in the first place.

It has to be acknowledged that 'fellow-feeling' is *not* the natural response of one human being to another. We feel it for those who are close to us; but it requires a real effort of imagination to feel it for people on the other side of the world — or even the other side of the street. Sartre has even argued, in his *Critique of Dialectical Reason*, that all men are naturally enemies and rivals. If a man goes for a country walk, he resents the presence of other people; nature would be more attractive if he was alone. When he joins a bus queue, every other person in it becomes a rival — the conductor may shout 'No more room' as he tries to climb on board. A crowded city or supermarket is an unpleasant place because all these people want *their* turn. If a man could perform magic by merely thinking, he would make others dissolve into thin air — or perhaps, like Wells's 'man who could work miracles', transport them all to Timbuktu.

This is a point that was made with brutal explicitness in Colin Turnbull's study of a 'dispossessed' African tribe, *The Mountain People*. Since the Second World War, the Ik have been driven out of their traditional hunting grounds by a government decision to turn the land into a game reserve. They became farmers in a land with practically no rain. The result of this hardship is that they seemed to lose all normal human feelings. Children were fed until the age of three, then thrown out to fend for themselves. Old people were allowed to starve to death. In the Ik villages, it was every man for himself. A small girl, thrown out by her parents, kept returning home, looking for love and affection; her parents finally locked her in and left her to starve to death. A mother watched with indifference as her baby crawled towards the communal camp fire and stuck its hand in; when the men roared with laughter at the child's screams, the mother looked pleased at providing amusement. When the government provided famine relief, those who were strong enough went to collect it, then stopped on the way home and gorged themselves sick; after vomiting, they ate the remainder of the food. One man who insisted on taking food home for his sick wife and child was mocked for his weakness.

Some writers — like Ardrey — have drawn wide conclusions from the Ik — such as that human values are superficial and that altruism is not natural to us. This is illogical. We could draw the same conclusions from the fact that most of us get bad tempered when we become hungry and tired. In the case of the Ik, the 'culture shock' was particularly severe; as hunters, they practised close co-operation, involving even the women and children; to be suddenly deprived of all this must have left them totally disoriented. But then, the important question about human beings is not how far we are capable of being disoriented and demoralized — losing self-control — but how far we are capable of going in the opposite direction, of using our intelligence for creativity and organization. Negative cases, like the Ik, prove nothing except what we already know: that human beings are capable of total selfishness, particularly when it is a question of survival. In fact, many primitive peoples practise infanticide and geronticide. In *The Hunting Peoples* (p. 329) Carleton S. Coon describes how, among the Caribou Indians of Hudson Bay, old people voluntarily commit suicide when the reindeer herds fail to appear and starvation threatens. When the old people are all dead, girl babies will be killed. 'This is a heartrending business because everybody loves children.' John Pfeiffer, the author of *The Emergence of Man*, describes (p. 316) how, among the aborigines of Australia, infanticide is the commonest form of birth control, and that between 15 and 50 per cent of infants are killed; it is the mother's decision and the mother's job, and she kills the baby about an hour after birth as we drown unwanted kittens.

There is another, and equally instinctive, element that helps us to understand human criminality; xenophobia, dislike of the foreigner. In *The Social Contract*, Ardrey points out that xenophobia is a basic instinct among animals, and that it probably has a genetic basis. All creatures tend to congregate in small groups or tribes and to stick to their own. Darwin even noticed that in a herd of ten thousand or so cattle on a ranch in Uruguay the animals naturally separated into sub-groups of between fifty and a hundred. When a violent storm scattered the herd, it re-grouped after twenty-four hours, the animals all finding their former group-members. And this instinctive tendency to form 'tribes' is probably a device to protect the species.

If some favourable gene appears, then it will be confined to the members of the group and not diluted by the herd. A study by Edward Hall of the black ghetto area of Chicago revealed that it was virtually a series of independent villages. And even in more 'mobile' social groups the average person tends to have a certain number of acquaintances who form his 'tribe' — Desmond Morris suggested in *The Human Zoo* the number of between fifty and one hundred, figures that happen to agree with Darwin's observation about cattle. The group may adopt his own modes of dress, catch-phrases, tricks of speech. (Frank Sinatra's 'in-group' was significantly known as 'the rat pack'.) They enjoy and emphasize the privilege of belonging, and adopt an attitude of hostility to outsiders. Hall's study of Chicago showed that there was often gang warfare between the ghetto communities.

This helps to explain how the Nazis could herd Jews into concentration camps. Hitler's racist ideology would not have taken root so easily were it not for the natural 'animal xenophobia' that is part of our instinctive heritage. In his book on the psychology of genocide *The Holocaust and the German Elite*, Professor Rainer C. Baum remarks on the *indifference* of the German bureaucrats who were responsible for the concentration camps and the banality of the whole process. They were not frenzied anti-semites, lusting for blood; what was frightening about them was that they had no feeling about the women and children they herded into cattle trucks. And if we assume that this was due to the evil Nazi ideology, we shall be oversimplifying. Human beings do not need an evil ideology to make them behave inhumanly; it comes easily to us because most of us exist in a state of self-preoccupation that makes our neighbour unreal. The point is reinforced by the massacre of Palestinians that took place in two refugee camps, Sabra and Shatila, in September 1982. Palestinian fighters had agreed to be evacuated from Beirut — after a siege — on the understanding that their women and children would be safe. On Saturday, 18 September the world became aware that Christian phalangists had massacred hundreds of women and children — as well as a few male non-combatants — in the camps, and that the phalangists had been sent into the camps by the Israelis. While the slaughter was going on, the US envoy sent Israel's General Sharon a message: 'You must stop this horrible massacre.... You have absolute control of the area and are therefore responsible....'

What shocked the world — including thousands of Israelis, who demonstrated in Tel Aviv — was that it should be Jews, the victims of the Nazi holocaust, who apparently countenanced the massacre. But Baum's analysis applies here as well as to Belsen and Buchenwald; it was not a matter of 'evil' but of indifference. Most of the mass-murderers in history have simply placed their victims in a different category from their own wives and children, just as the average meat eater feels no fellowship for cows and sheep.

In our humanitarian age, these horrors stand out, and we draw the lesson: that to be truly human demands a real effort of will rather than our usual vague assumption of 'mutual concern'. Five thousand years ago, no one made that assumption; they were governed by the law of xenophobia and recognized that mutual concern only exists between relatives and immediate neighbours.

As we shall see, there is evidence of a slowly increasing criminality from about 2000 B.C. The old religious sanctions began breaking down at this period; the force that made men come together into cities in the first place was unable to withstand the new stresses created by these 'jostling crowds'. In his book on *Animal Nature and Human Nature*, Professor W. H. Thorpe comments on the rarity of inter-group aggression between chimpanzees and gorillas, and speculates on why human beings are so different. But he then answers his own question by pointing out that, while there is very little violence between groups of animals in the wild, this alters as soon as they are kept in captivity and subjected to unnatural conditions such as shortage of food and space; then, suddenly, they become capable of killing one another. This is what happened to man when he became a city dweller. The need to defend food-growing 'territory' from neighbours in nearby cities made man into a warlike animal. Moreover, cities had to be defended by walls, and this eventually introduced an entirely new factor: overcrowding. And this, it now seems fairly certain, was the factor that finally turned man into a habitual criminal.

It is only in recent years that we have become aware of the role of overcrowding in producing stress and violence. In 1958, a scientist named John Christian was studying the deer population on James Island, in Chesapeake Bay, when the deer began to die in large numbers. There were about three hundred on the island; by the following year, two hundred and twenty of these had died for no apparent cause. Post mortems revealed that the deer had enlarged adrenal glands — the gland that floods the bloodstream with the hormone called adrenalin, the stress hormone. James Island is half a square mile in size, so each deer had more than five thousand square yards of territory to itself. This, apparently, was not enough. The deer needed about twenty thousand square yards each. So when numbers exceeded eighty, they developed stress symptoms, and the population automatically reduced itself.

A psychologist named John B. Calhoun has made a similar observation when breeding wild Norwegian rats in a pen. The pen was a quarter of an acre and could have held five thousand rats. With a normal birthrate, this could have swelled tenfold in two years. Yet the rat population remained constant at a mere two hundred.

Calhoun was later to perform a classic experiment with his Norwegian rats. He placed a number of rats into four interconnecting cages. The two end pens, which had only one entrance, were the most 'desirable residences' — since they could be most easily defended — and these were quickly taken over by two highly dominant rats with their retinue of females. All the other rats were forced to move into the two centre cages, so that these soon became grossly overcrowded. There were also dominant males in these two centre cages (it was Calhoun who observed that the number of dominant rats was one in twenty — five per cent), but because of the overcrowding, they could not establish their own territory. And as the overcrowding became more acute, the dominant rats became criminals. They formed gangs and indulged in rape, homosexuality and cannibalism. In their natural state, rats have an elaborate courting ritual. The criminal rats would force their way into the female's burrow, rape her and eat her young. The middle cages became, in Calhoun's words, a 'behavioural sink'.

Ever since Lorenz's *On Aggression*, ethologists have warned about the dangers of drawing conclusions about human behaviour from animal behaviour; but in this case, it is impossible to see how it can be avoided. We have always known that our overcrowded slums are breeding grounds of crime. Calhoun's experiment performed at the National Institute of Mental Health in Maryland — shows us why: the dominant minority are deprived of normal outlets for their dominance; it turns into indiscriminate aggression. Desmond Morris remarks in *The Human Zoo*: 'Under normal conditions, in their natural habitats, wild animals do not mutilate themselves, masturbate, attack their offspring, develop stomach ulcers, become fetishists, suffer from obesity, form homosexual pair-bonds, or commit murder. Among human city dwellers, needless to say, all of these things occur.' Animals in captivity also develop various 'perversions' — which leads Morris to remark that the city is a human zoo. And the reason that a 'zoo' breeds crime is that dominance is deprived of its normal outlets and turns to violence. As William Blake says: 'When thought is closed in caves, then love shall show its root in deepest hell.'

Yet the warning about extrapolating from animal to human behaviour deserves serious consideration. Why is not every large city in the world a 'sink' of violence and perversion? It is true that many of them are; yet others, such as Hong Kong, where you would expect to find the 'dominant rat syndrome', have a reasonably low crime rate.

Ardrey provides one interesting clue in the chapter on 'personal space' in *The Social Contract*. He describes an experiment carried out by the psychiatrist Augustus Kinzel in 1969. Prisoners in a Federal prison were placed in the centre of a bare room, and Kinzel then advanced on them slowly, step by step. The prisoner was told to call 'Stop!' when he felt that Kinzel was uncomfortably close. Non-violent prisoners seemed to need a 'personal space' of about ten square feet. But prisoners with a long record of violence reacted with clenched fists long before Kinzel was that close; these prisoners seemed to need a 'personal space' of about forty square feet.

This seems to support the 'personal space' theory. But it still leaves unanswered the question: why do some criminals need more than others? And the answer, in this case, requires only a little commonsense. When I am feeling tense and irritable, I tend to be more 'explosive' than when I am relaxed; so much is obvious. My tension may be due to a variety of causes — hunger, overwork, a hangover, general frustration and dissatisfaction. The effect, as John Christian discovered with his Sika deer, is to cause the adrenal glands to overwork; the result of long-term stress in animals is fatty degeneration of the liver and haemorrhages of the adrenals, thyroid, brain and kidneys. The tension causes fear-hormones to flood into the bloodstream. In *The Biological Time Bomb* (p. 228) Gordon Rattray Taylor mentions that this is what causes the mass-suicide of lemmings, who are also reacting to over-population. He also describes how American prisoners in Korea sometimes died from convulsive seizures or became totally lethargic; the disease was named 'give-up-itis'.

But then, we are all aware that our attitudes determine our level of tension. I *allow* some annoyance to make me angry or impatient. When the telephone has dragged me away from my typewriter for the fifth time in one morning, I may say: 'Oh dammit, NO!' and experience rising tension. Or I may take the view that these interruptions are tiresome but unavoidable, and deliberately 'cool it'. It is my decision.

It seems, then, that my energy mechanisms operate through a force and counter-force, like garage doors on a counterweight system. Let us, for convenience, refer to these as Force T — the T standing for tension — and Force C, the C for control. Force T makes for destabilization of our inner being. Force C makes for stabilization and inhibition. I experience Force T in its simplest form if I want to urinate badly; there is a force inside me, making me uncomfortable. And if I am uncomfortable for too long, the experience ceases to be confined to my bladder; my heartbeat increases, my cheeks feel hot. My *energies* seem to be expanding, trying to escape.

Consider, on the other hand, what happens when I become deeply interested in some problem. I deliberately 'damp down' my energies, I soothe my impatience, I focus my attention. I *actively apply a counter-force* to the force of destabilization. And if, for example, I am listening to music, I may apply the counter-force until I am in a condition of deep 'appreciation', of hair-trigger perception.

When we look at it in this way, we can see that the two 'forces' are the great governing forces of human existence. From the moment I get up in the morning, I am subjecting myself to various stimuli that cause tensions, and I am continually monitoring these tensions and applying 'Force C' to control them and — if possible — to canalize them for constructive purposes. Biologists are inclined to deny the existence of free will; yet it is hard to describe this situation except in terms of a continuous act of choice. The weak people, those who make little effort of control, spend their lives in a permanent state of mild discomfort, like a man who wants to rush to the lavatory. Blake says in *The Marriage of Heaven and Hell*: 'Those who restrain their desire do so because theirs is weak enough to be restrained', and this is one of the few statements of that remarkable mystic that is downright wrong-headed. (Admittedly, he is putting it into the mouth of the devil.) Beethoven was notoriously explosive and irascible; but his 'inhibitory force' was also great enough to canalize the destabilizing force into musical creation.

It is obvious that Sika deer, Norwegian rats, lemmings, snow-shoe hares and other creatures that have been observed to die of stress, lack control of the inhibitory force. Certainly all creatures must possess some control of this force, or they would be totally unable to focus their energies or direct their activities. But in animals, this control is completely bound up with external stimuli. A cat watching a mouse hole, a dog lying outside the house of a bitch on heat, will show astonishing self-control, maintaining a high level of attention (that is, focused consciousness) for hours or even days. But without external stimuli, the animal will show signs of boredom or fall asleep. Man is the only animal whose way of life demands almost constant use of the inhibitory faculty.

We can see the problem of the Ik: they had no reason to develop the inhibitory faculty where personal feelings were concerned. As hunter-gatherers, their lives had been very nearly as uncomplicated as those of the animals with whom they shared their hunting grounds. Placed in a situation that required a completely different set of controls, they became victims of their own destabilizing forces.

All of which suggests that, in the case of Kinzel's prisoners, 'personal space' was not the real issue. This can be grasped by repeating his experiment. The co-operation of a child will make the point even clearer. Ask the child to stand in the centre of the room, then go on all fours and advance towards him, making growling noises. The child's first reaction is amusement and pleasurable excitement. As you get nearer, the laughter develops a note of hysteria and, at a certain distance, the child will turn and run. (It may be an idea to conduct the experiment with the child's mother sitting right behind him, so that he can take refuge in her arms.) More confident children may run *at* you — a way of telling themselves that this is really only daddy.

Now reverse the situation, and take his place in the centre of the room, while some other adult crawls towards you and makes threatening noises. You will observe with interest that although you have set up the experiment, you still feel an impulse of alarm, and a release of adrenalin. To a large extent, the destabilizing mechanism is automatic.

You will also have the opportunity to note the extent to which you can apply the control mechanism. The imagined threat triggers a flight impulse and raises your inner tension. One way of releasing this tension is to give way to it. If you refuse to do this, you will be able to observe the attempts of your stabilizing mechanism — the C Force — to control the destabilizing force. You will observe that you still have a number of alternatives, depending on *how far* you choose to exert control. You can allow yourself to feel a rush of alarm, but refuse to react to it. You can actively suppress the rush of alarm. You may even be able, with a little practice, to prevent it from happening at all.

I had a recent opportunity to observe the mechanism at an amusement park, where a small cinema shows films designed to induce vertigo. The audience has to stand, and the screen is enormous and curved. Carriages surge down switchbacks; toboggans hurtle across the ice and down ski-slopes; the watchers soon begin to feel that the floor is moving underneath their feet. After twenty minutes or so I began to feel that I'd got the hang of it, and could resist the impulse to sway. Even so, the end of the film took me unaware; a car hurtles off a motorway at a tremendous speed and down the exit lane, ramming into a vehicle waiting to pull out into the traffic. My foot went automatically on the brake, and I staggered and fell into the arms of the unfortunate lady standing behind me.

What had happened is that the suddenness of the final crash pushed me beyond the point at which I had established control. Yet for the previous twenty minutes I had been establishing a higher-than-usual degree of control. Under circumstances like this — and something similar happens to city dwellers every day — we are inclined to feel that all control is 'relative' and perhaps therefore futile. And this mistake — which is so easy to make — is the essence of the criminal mentality. The criminal makes the *decision* to abandon control. He can see no sound reason why he should waste his time establishing a higher level of self-control. Let other people worry about that. The result is bad for society, but far more disastrous for himself. After all, society can absorb a little violence, but for the destabilized individual it means ultimate self-destruction.

When we observe this continual balancing operation between Force T and Force C, we can grasp its place in the evolution of our species. When deer and lemmings are overcrowded, the result is a rise in the destabilizing force which causes the adrenal glands to overwork; beyond a certain point of tension, this results in death. There is no alternative — no possibility of developing the stabilizing force. They lack the motivation. When men came together to live in cities, their motive was mutual protection. One result was the development of the abnormalities listed by Desmond Morris and the creation of the 'criminal type'. But it also led to an increase in the stabilizing force, and to a level of self-control beyond that of any other animal.

It was through this development that man made his most important discovery; that control is not simply a negative virtue. Anyone who has been forced to master some difficult technique — such as playing a musical instrument — knows that learning begins with irritation and frustration; the task seems to be as thankless as breaking in a wild horse. Then, by some unconscious process, control begins to develop. There is a cautious glow of satisfaction as we begin to scent success. Then, quite suddenly, the frustration is transformed into a feeling of power and control. It dawns upon us that when a wild horse ceases to be wild, it becomes an invaluable servant. The stabilizing force is not merely a defence system, a means of 'hanging on' over bumpy obstacles. It is a power for conquest, for changing our lives.

Once man has made this discovery, he looks around for new fields to conquer. This explains why we are the only creatures who seek out hardship for the fun of it: who climb mountains 'because they are there' and try to establish records for sailing around the world single-handed. We have discovered that an increase in Force C is a pleasure in itself. The late Ludwig Wittgenstein based his later philosophy upon a comparison of games and language, and upon the assertion that there is no element that is common to all games — say, to patience, and football, and sailing around the world single-handed. We can see that this is untrue. All games have a common purpose: to increase the stabilizing force at the expense of the destabilizing force. All games are designed to create stress, and then to give us the pleasure of controlling it. (Hence the saying that the Battle of Waterloo was won on the playing fields of Eton.) Man's chief evolutionary distinction is that he is the only creature who has learned to thrive on stress. He converts it into creativity, into productive satisfaction. The interesting result is that many people who are subject to a high level of stress are unusually healthy. A medical study at the Bell Telephone Company showed that three times as many ordinary workmen suffered from coronaries as men in higher executive positions. The reason, it was decided, is that higher executives have more 'status' than ordinary workmen, and this enables them to bear stress. An equally obvious explanation is that the executive has achieved his position by developing the ability to cope with problems and bear stress. A British study of people whose names are listed in *Who's Who* showed a similar result: the more distinguished the person, the greater seemed to be his life expectancy and the better his general level of health. And here we can see that it is not simply a negative matter of learning to 'bear stress'. The Nobel Prize winners and members of the Order of Merit had reasons for overcoming stress, a sense of purpose. The point is reinforced by a comment made by Dr Jeffrey Gray at a conference of the British Psychological Society in December 1981: that there is too much emphasis nowadays on lowering stress with the aid of pills. People should learn to soak up the worries of the job and build up their tolerance to pressure. Rats who were placed in stress situations and given Librium and Valium reacted less well than rats who were given no drugs. The latter were 'toughened up' and built up an immunity to stress. The lesson seems to be that all animals can develop resistance to stress; man is the only animal who has learned to use stress for his own satisfaction.

All this enables us to understand what it is that distinguishes the criminal from the rest of us. Like the rats fed on Valium, the criminal fails to develop 'stress resistance' because he habitually releases his tensions instead of learning to control them. Criminality is a short-cut, and this applies to non-violent criminals as much as to violent ones. Crime is essentially the search for 'the easy way'.

Considering our natural lack of fellow feeling, it is surprising that cities are not far more violent. This is because, strangely enough, man is not innately cruel. He is innately social; he responds to the social advances of other people with sympathy and understanding. Any two people sitting side by side on a bus can establish a bond of sympathy by merely looking in each other's eyes. It is far easier to write an angry letter than to go and say angry things to another person — because as soon as we look in one another's faces we can see the other point of view. The real paradox is that the Germans who tossed children back into the flames at Oradour were probably good husbands and affectionate fathers. The Japanese who used schoolboys for bayonet practice and disembowelled a schoolgirl after raping her probably carried pictures of their own children in their knapsacks.

How is this possible? Are human beings really so much more wicked than tigers and scorpions? The answer was provided by a series of experiments at Harvard conducted by Professor Stanley Milgram. His aim was to see whether 'ordinary people' could be persuaded to inflict torture. They were told that the experiment was to find out whether punishment could increase someone's learning capacity. The method was to connect the victim to an electric shock machine, then ask the subject to administer shocks of increasing strength. The 'victim' was actually an actor who could scream convincingly. The subject was told that the shock would cause no permanent damage but was then given a 'sample' shock of 45 volts to prove that the whole thing was genuine. And the majority of these 'ordinary people' allowed themselves to be persuaded to keep on increasing the shocks up to 500 volts, in spite of horrifying screams, convulsions and pleas for mercy. Only a few refused to go on. In writing up his results in a book called *Obedience to Authority*, Milgram points the moral by quoting an American soldier who took part in the My Lai massacre in Vietnam and who described how, when ordered by Lieutenant Calley, he turned his sub-machine gun on men, women and children including babies. The news interviewer asked: 'How do you, a father, shoot babies?' and received the reply: 'I don't know — it's just one of those things.'

And these words suddenly enable us to see precisely why human beings are capable of this kind of behaviour. It is because we have *minds*, and these minds can overrule our instincts. An animal cannot disobey its instinct; human beings disobey theirs a hundred times a day. Living in a modern city, with its impersonality and overcrowding, is already a basic violation of natural instinct. So when Lieutenant Calley told the man to shoot women and children, he did what civilization had taught him to do since childhood — allowed his mind to overrule his instinct.

The rape of Nanking illustrates the same point. Rhodes Farmer wrote in *Shanghai Harvest, A Diary of Three Years in the China War* (published in 1945): 'To the Japanese soldiers at the end of four months of hard fighting,

Nanking promised a last fling of debauchery before they returned to their highly disciplined lives back home in Japan.' But this shows a failure to understand the Japanese character. The *Japanese Yearbook* for 1946 comes closer when it says: 'By 7 December, the outer defences of Nanking were under attack, and a week later, Japanese anger at the stubborn Chinese defence of Shanghai burst upon Nanking in an appalling reign of terror.' In fact, the Chinese resistance — ever since their unexpected stand at Lukouchiao in July 1937 — had caused the Japanese to 'lose face', and they were in a hard and unforgiving mood when they entered Nanking. But then, we also need to understand why this loss of face mattered so much, and this involves understanding the deep religious traditionalism of the Japanese character. The historian Arnold Toynbee has pointed out, in *East to West* (pp. 69—71) that if the town of Bromsgrove had happened to be in Japan, the Japanese would know exactly why it was so named, because they would have maintained a sacred grove to the memory of the war-god Bron. And there would probably be a Buddhist temple next door to the pagan shrine, and the priest and the parson of the temple would be on excellent terms. When, in the nineteenth century, the Japanese decided to 'Westernize', they poured all this religious emotion into the cult of the emperor, who was worshipped as a god. The war that began in 1937, and ended in 1945 with the dropping of two atom bombs, was an upsurge of intense patriotic feeling similar to the Nazi upsurge in Germany. The outnumbered Japanese troops felt they were fighting for their emperor-god, and that their cause was just. This is why the stubborn Chinese resistance placed them in such an unforgiving frame of mind. Like Milgram's subjects, they felt they were administering a salutary shock-treatment; but in this case, anger turned insensitivity into cruelty.

Wells, oddly enough, failed to grasp this curiously impersonal element in human cruelty. Having seized upon the notion that slum conditions produce frustration, he continues with a lengthy analysis of human cruelty and sadism, citing as typical the case of Marshal Gilles de Rais, who killed over two hundred children in sexual orgies in the fifteenth century. In fact, de Rais's perversions throw very little light on the nature of ordinary human beings, whose sexual tastes are more straightforward. The Japanese who burnt Nanking, the Germans who destroyed Oradour, were not sexual perverts; they had probably never done anything of the sort before, and would never do anything of the sort again. They were simply releasing their aggression in obedience to authority.

Fromm is inclined to make the same mistake. He recognizes 'conformist aggression' — aggression under orders — but feels that human destructiveness is better explained by what he calls 'malignant aggression' — that is, by sadism. Sadism he defines as the desire to have absolute power over a living being, to have a god-like control. He cites both Himmler and Stalin as examples of sadism, pointing out that both could, at times, show great kindness and consideration. They became ruthless *only when their absolute authority was questioned*. But this hardly explains the human tendency to destroy their fellows in war. So Fromm is forced to postulate another kind of 'malignant aggression', which he calls 'necrophilia'. By this, he meant roughly what Freud meant by 'thanatos' or the death-urge — the human urge to self-destruction. Freud had invented the 'death wish' at the time of the First World War in an attempt to explain the slaughter. It was not one of his most convincing ideas, and many of his disciples received it with reservations — after all, anyone can see that most suicides are committed in a state of muddle and confusion, in which a person feels that life is not worth living; so the underlying instinct is for more life, not less. Even a romantic like Keats, who feels he is 'half in love with easeful death', is in truth confusing the idea of extinction with that of sleep and rest. If human beings really have an urge to self-destruction, they manage to conceal it very well.

Fromm nevertheless adopts the Freudian death-wish. He cites a Spanish Civil War general, one of whose favourite slogans was 'Long live death!' The same man once shouted at a liberal intellectual: 'Down with intelligence!' From this, Fromm argues that militarism has an anti-life element that might be termed necrophilia. But he demolishes his own case by citing two genuine examples of necrophilia from a medical textbook on sexual perversion: both morgue attendants who enjoyed violating female corpses. One of them described how, from the time of adolescence, he masturbated while caressing the bodies of attractive females, then graduated to having intercourse with them. Which raises the question: is this genuinely a case of necrophilia, which means sexual desire *directed towards death*? Many highly-sexed teenage boys might do the same, given the opportunity. It is not an interest in death as such, but in sex. A genuine necrophile would be one who preferred corpses because they were dead. One of the best known cases of necrophilia, Sergeant Bertrand (whom I discussed in Chapter 6 of my *Origins of the Sexual Impulse*) was not, in this sense, a true necrophile; for although he dug up and violated newly buried corpses, he also had mistresses who testified to his sexual potency. He is simply an example of a virile man who needed more sex than he could get.

So Fromm's whole argument about 'necrophilia', and his lengthy demonstration that Hitler was a necrophiliac, collapses under closer analysis. The Spanish general was certainly not a necrophile by any common definition: he was using death in a rather special sense, meaning idealistic self-sacrifice for the good of one's country. He certainly has nothing whatever in common with a morgue attendant violating female corpses. Hitler was undoubtedly destructive, but there is no evidence that he was self-destructive or had a secret death wish. On the contrary, he was a romantic dreamer who believed that his thousand-year Reich was an expression of health, vitality and sanity. Fromm's 'necrophilia', like Wells's notion of cruelty, fails to provide a satisfactory explanation of human cruelty; it is not universal enough.

The notion of 'losing face' suggests an interesting alternative line of thought. It is obviously connected, for example, with the cruelty of Himmler and Stalin when their absolute authority was questioned. They were both men with a touchy sense of self-esteem, so that their response to any suspected insult was vindictive rage. Another characteristic of both men was a conviction that they were always right, and a total inability to admit that they might ever be wrong.

Himmlers and Stalins are, fortunately, rare; but the type is surprisingly common. The credit for recognizing this goes to A. E. Van Vogt, a writer of science fiction who is also the author of a number of brilliant psychological studies. Van Vogt's concept of the 'Right Man' or 'violent man' is so important to the understanding of criminality that it deserves to be considered at length, and in this connection I am indebted to Van Vogt for providing me with a series of five talks broadcast on KPFK radio in 1965. Like his earlier pamphlet *A Report on the Violent Male*, these have never been printed in book form.*

In 1954, Van Vogt began work on a war novel called *The Violent Man*, which was set in a Chinese prison camp. The commandant of the camp is one of those savagely authoritarian figures who would instantly, and without hesitation, order the execution of anyone who challenges his authority. Van Vogt was creating the type from observation of men like Hitler and Stalin. And, as he thought about the murderous behaviour of the commandant, he found himself wondering: 'What could motivate a man like that?' Why is it that some men believe that anyone who contradicts them is either dishonest or downright wicked? Do they really believe, in their heart of hearts, that they are gods who are incapable of being fallible? If so, are they in some sense insane, like a man who thinks he is Julius Caesar?

*This was, eventually, published in 1992 by Paupers' Press. CS.

Looking around for examples, it struck Van Vogt that male authoritarian behaviour is far too commonplace to be regarded as insanity. Newspaper headlines tell their own story:

HUSBAND INVADES CHRISTMAS PARTY AND SHOOTS WIFE
Grief stricken when she refused to return to him, he clams.

ENTERTAINER STABS WIFE TO DEATH — UNFAITHFUL HE SAYS
Amazed friends say he was unfaithful, not she.

WIFE RUN OVER IN STREET
Accident says divorced husband held on suspicion of murder.

WIFE BADLY BEATEN BY FORMER HUSBAND
'Unfit mother,' he accuses. Neighbours refute charge and call him a troublemaker.

HUSBAND FOILED IN ATTEMPT TO PUSH WIFE OVER CLIFF
Wife reconciles, convinced husband loves her.

Marriage seems to bring out the 'authoritarian' personality in many males, according to Van Vogt's observation. He brought up the question with a psychologist friend and asked him whether he could offer any examples. The psychologist told him of an interesting case of a husband who had brought his wife along for psychotherapy. He had set her up in a suburban home, and supported her on condition that she had no male friends. Her role, as he saw it, was simply to be a good mother to their son.

The story of their marriage was as follows. She had been a nurse, and when her future husband proposed to her she had felt she ought to admit to previous affairs with two doctors. The man went almost insane with jealousy, and she was convinced that was the end of it. But the next day he appeared with a legal document, which he insisted she should sign if the marriage was to go ahead. He would not allow her to read it. Van Vogt speculates that it contained a 'confession' that she was an immoral woman, and that as he was virtually raising her from the gutter by marrying her, she had no legal rights....

They married, and she soon became aware of her mistake. Her husband's business involved travelling, so she never knew where he was. He visited women employees in their apartments for hours and spent an unconscionable amount of time driving secretaries home. If she tried to question him about this he would fly into a rage and often knock her about. In fact, he was likely to respond to questions he regarded as 'impertinent' by knocking her down. The following day he might call her long distance and beg her forgiveness, promising never to do it again.

His wife became frigid. They divorced, yet he continued to do his best to treat her as his personal property, determined to restrict her freedom. When this caused anger and stress, he told her she ought to see a psychiatrist — which is how they came to Van Vogt's friend.

The case is a good example of what Van Vogt came to call 'the violent man' or the 'Right Man'. He is a man driven by a manic need for self-esteem — to feel he is a 'somebody'. He is obsessed by the question of 'losing face', so will never, under any circumstances, admit that he might be in the wrong. This man's attempt to convince his wife that she was insane is typical.

Equally interesting is the wild, insane jealousy. Most of us are subject to jealousy, since the notion that someone we care about prefers someone else is an assault on our *amour propre*. But the Right Man, whose self-esteem is like a constantly festering sore spot, flies into a frenzy at the thought, and becomes capable of murder.

Van Vogt points out that the Right Man is an 'idealist' — that is, he lives in his own mental world and does his best to ignore aspects of reality that conflict with it. Like the Communists' rewriting of history, reality can always be 'adjusted' later to fit his glorified picture of himself. In his mental world, women are delightful, adoring, faithful creatures who wait patiently for the right man — in both senses of the word — before they surrender their virginity. He is living in a world of adolescent fantasy. No doubt there was something gentle and submissive about the nurse that made her seem the ideal person to bolster his self-esteem, the permanent wife and mother who is waiting in a clean apron when he gets back from a weekend with a mistress....

Perhaps Van Vogt's most intriguing insight into the Right Man was his discovery that he can be destroyed if 'the worm turns' — that is, if his wife or some dependant leaves *him*. Under such circumstances, he may beg and plead, promising to behave better in the future. If that fails, there may be alcoholism, drug addiction, even suicide. She has kicked away the foundations of his sandcastle. For when a Right Man finds a woman who seems submissive and admiring, it deepens his self-confidence, fills him with a sense of his own worth. (We can see the mechanism in operation with Ian Brady and Myra Hindley.) No matter how badly he treats her, he has to keep on believing that, in the last analysis, she recognizes him as the most remarkable man she will ever meet. She is the guarantee of his 'primacy', his uniqueness; now it doesn't matter what the rest of the world thinks. He may desert her and his children; that only proves how 'strong' he is, how indifferent to the usual sentimentality. But if she deserts him, he has been pushed back to square one: the helpless child in a hostile universe. 'Most violent men are failures', says Van Vogt; so to desert them is to hand them over to their own worst suspicions about themselves. It is this recognition that leads Van Vogt to write: 'Realize that most Right Men deserve some sympathy, for they are struggling with an almost unbelievable inner horror; however, if they give way to the impulse to hit or choke, they are losing the battle, and are on the way to the ultimate disaster...of their subjective universe of self-justification.'

And what happens when the Right Man is *not* a failure, when his 'uniqueness' is acknowledged by the world? Oddly enough, it makes little or no difference. His problem is lack of emotional control and a deep-seated sense of inferiority; so success cannot reach the parts of the mind that are the root of the problem. A recent (1981) biography of the actor Peter Sellers (*P.S. I Love You* by his son Michael) reveals that he was a typical Right Man. Totally spoiled by his mother as a child, he grew into a man who flew into tantrums if he could not have his own way. He had endless affairs with actresses, yet remained morbidly jealous of his wife, ringing her several times a day to check on her movements, and interrogating her if she left the house. She had been an actress; he forced her to give it up to devote herself to being a 'good wife and mother'. As his destructive fits of rage and affairs with actresses broke up the marriage, he convinced himself that he wanted to be rid of her, and persuaded her to go out with another man. But when she told him she wanted a divorce, he burst into tears and threatened to jump from the penthouse balcony. ('This was not the first time he had spoken of suicide. This was always his crutch in a crisis.')

The morbid sense of inferiority emerged in the company of anyone who had been to public school or university. When, at dinner with Princess Margaret, the conversation turned to Greek mythology, he excused himself as if to go to the bathroom but phoned his secretary and made her look in reference books and quickly brief him on the subject. Then he went back to the dinner table and casually dropped references to mythology into his conversation. His son adds: 'I saw him engage in this ploy on many occasions.'

Another typical anecdote shows the borderline between normal and 'Right Man' behaviour. The children's nanny was a strong-minded woman of definite opinions; one evening, Sellers had a violent disagreement with her and stormed out of the house; he went and booked himself into the RAC Club for the night. From there he rang his wife and said: 'What the bloody hell am I doing here? If anybody's going to leave, it's that bloody nanny.' He rushed back home, seized a carving knife and drove it into the panel of her bedroom door, shouting 'I'll kill you, you cow.' The nanny jumped out of the window and vanished from their lives.

Sellers's behaviour in storming out of the house could be regarded as normal; in leaving her on the battlefield he was acknowledging that she might be right. In the club, his emotions boil over as he broods on it; by the time he has reached home, he has convinced himself that he is right and she is wrong, and explodes into paranoid rage. Whether the threat to kill her was serious should be regarded as an open question. The Right Man hates losing face; if he suspects that his threats are not being taken seriously, he is capable of carrying them out, purely for the sake of appearances.

Van Vogt makes the basic observation that the central characteristic of the Right Man is the 'decision to be out of control, in some particular area'. We all have to learn self-control to deal with the real world and other people. But with some particular person — a mother, a wife, a child — we may decide that this effort is not necessary and allow ourselves to explode. But — and here we come to the very heart of the matter — this decision creates, so to speak, a permanent weak point in the boiler, the point at which it always bursts. The *Family Chronicle* by Sergei Aksakov provides an apt illustration: Aksakov is talking about his grandfather, an old Russian landowner.

And this noble, magnanimous, often-self-restrained man — whose character presented an image of the loftiest human nature — was subject to fits of rage in which he was capable of the most barbarous cruelty. I recollect having seen him in one of those mad fits in my earliest childhood. I see him now. He was angry with one of his daughters, who had lied to him and persisted in the lie. There he stood, supported by two servants (for his legs refused their office); I could hardly recognize him as my grandfather; he trembled in every limb, his features were distorted, and the frenzy of rage glared from his infuriated eyes. 'Give her to me,' he howled in a strangled voice.... My grandmother threw herself at his feet, beseeching him to have pity and forbearance, but in the next instant, off flew her kerchief and cap, and Stephan Mikhailovich seized on his corpulent and already aged better half by the hair of her head. Meanwhile, the culprit as well as all her sisters — and even her brother with his young wife and little son [Aksakov himself] had fled into the woods behind the house; and there they remained all night; only the young daughter-in-law crept home with the child, fearing he might take cold, and slept with him in the servants' quarters. My grandfather raved and stormed about the empty house to his heart's content. At last he grew too tired to drag his poor old Arina Vasilievna about by her plaits, and fell exhausted upon his bed, where a deep sleep overpowered him, which lasted until the following morning. He awoke calm and in a good humour, and called to his Arishka in a cheery tone. My grandmother immediately ran in to him from an adjoining room, just as if nothing had happened the day before. 'Give me some tea! Where are the children? Where are Alexei and his wife? Bring little Sergei to me!' said the erstwhile lunatic, now that he had slept off his rage.

Aksakov sees his grandfather as a 'noble, magnanimous, often self-restrained man' — so he *is* capable of self-restraint. But in this one area of his life, his control over his family, he has made 'the decision to be out of control'. It is provoked by his daughter persisting in a lie. This infuriates him; he feels she is treating him with *lack of respect* in assuming he can be duped. So he explodes and drags his wife around by the hair. He feels no shame later about his behaviour; his merriness the next morning shows that his good opinion of himself is unaffected. He feels he was *justified* in exploding, like an angry god. Like the Japanese soldiers in Nanking, he feels he is inflicting just punishment.

What is so interesting here is the way the Right Man's violent emotion reinforces his sense of being justified, and his sense of justification increases his rage. He is locked into a kind of vicious spiral, and he cannot escape until he has spent his fury. Peter Sellers's son records that his father was capable of smashing every item in a room, including keepsakes that he had been collecting for years. The Right Man feels that his rage is a storm that has to be allowed to blow itself out, no matter what damage it causes. But this also means that he is the slave of an impulse he cannot control; his property, even the lives of those he loves, are at the mercy of his emotions. This is part of the 'unbelievable inner horror' that Van Vogt talks about.

This tendency to allow our emotions to reinforce our sense of being justified is a basic part of the psychology of violence, and therefore of crime. We cannot understand cruelty without understanding this particular mechanism. We find it incomprehensible, for example, that a mother could batter her own baby to death, simply because he is crying; yet it happens thousands of times every year. We fail to grasp that she is already close to her 'bursting point' and that, as the baby cries, she feels that it is wicked and malevolent, trying to drive her to distraction. Suddenly her rage has *transformed* it from a helpless baby into a screaming devil that deserves to be beaten. It is as if some wicked fairy had waved a magic wand and turned it into a demon. We would say that it is the mother who is turned into a demon; yet her rage acts as a kind of *magic* that 'transforms' the child.

The word 'magic' was first used in this sense — meaning a form of self-deception — by Jean-Paul Sartre in an early book, *A Sketch of a Theory of the Emotions*. In later work Sartre preferred to speak of '*mauvaise foi*' or self-deception; but there are some ways in which the notion of 'magical thinking' is more precise. Malcolm Muggeridge has an anecdote that illustrates the concept perfectly. He quotes a newspaper item about birth control in Asian countries, which said that the World Health Organization had issued strings containing twenty-eight beads to illiterate peasant women. There were seven amber beads, seven red ones, seven more amber beads and seven green ones; the women were told to move a bead every day. 'Many women thought that merit resided in the beads, and moved them around to suit themselves,' said the newspaper.

This is 'magical thinking' — allowing a desire or emotion to convince you of something your reason tells you to be untrue. In 1960, a labourer named Patrick Byrne entered a women's hostel in Birmingham and attacked several women, decapitating one of them; he explained later that he wanted to 'get his revenge on women for causing him sexual tension'. This again is magical thinking. So was Charles Manson's assertion that he was not guilty because 'society' was guilty of bombing Vietnam. And Sartre offers the example of a girl who is about to be attacked by a man and who faints — a 'magical' attempt to make him go away. This is a good example because it reminds us that 'magic' can be a purely *physical* reaction. Magical thinking provides a key to the Right Man.

What causes 'right mannishness'? Van Vogt suggests that it is because the world has always been dominated by males. In Italy in 1961, two women were sentenced to prison for adultery. Their defence was that their husbands had mistresses, and that so do many Italian men. The court overruled their appeal. In China in 1950, laws were passed to give women more freedom; in 1954, there were ten thousand murders of wives in one district alone by husbands who objected to their attempts to take advantage of these laws.

But then, this explanation implies that there is no such thing as a Right Woman — in fact, Van Vogt says as much. This is untrue. There may be fewer Right Women than Right Men, but they still exist. The mother of the novelist Turgenev had many of her serfs flogged to death — a clear example of the 'magical transfer' of rage. Elizabeth Duncan, a Californian divorcee, was so outraged when her son married a nurse, Olga Kupczyk, against her wishes, that she hired two young thugs to kill her; moreover, when the killers tried to persuade her to hand over the promised fee, she went to the police and reported them for blackmail — the action that led to the death of all three in the San Quentin gas chamber. Again, this is a clear case of 'magical' — that is to say, totally unrealistic — thinking. And it shows that the central characteristic of the Right Woman is the same as that of the Right Man: that she is convinced that having her own way is a law of nature, and that anyone who opposes this deserves the harshest possible treatment. It is the god (or goddess) syndrome.

Van Vogt also believes that Adler's 'organ inferiority' theory may throw some light on right mannishness. Adler suggests that if some organ — the heart, liver, kidneys — is damaged early in life, it may send messages of inferiority to the brain, causing an inferiority complex. This in turn, says Van Vogt, could lead to the over-compensatory behaviour of the Right Man. He could well be right. Yet this explanation seems to imply that being a Right Man is rather like being colour blind or asthmatic — that it can be explained in purely medical terms. And the one thing that becomes obvious in all case histories of Right Men is that their attacks are *not* somehow 'inevitable'; some of their worst misdemeanours are carefully planned and calculated, and determinedly carried out. The Right Man does these things because he thinks they will help him to achieve his own way, which is what interests him.

And this in turn makes it plain that the Right Man problem is a problem of *highly dominant* people. Dominance is a subject of enormous interest to biologists and zoologists because the percentage of dominant animals — or human beings — seems to be amazingly constant. Bernard Shaw once asked the explorer H. M. Stanley how many other men could take over leadership of the expedition if Stanley himself fell ill; Stanley replied promptly: 'One in twenty.' 'Is that exact or approximate?' asked Shaw. 'Exact.' And biological studies have confirmed this as a fact. For some odd reason, precisely five per cent — one in twenty — of any animal group are dominant — have leadership qualities. During the Korean war, the Chinese made the interesting discovery that if they separated out the dominant five per cent of American prisoners of war, and kept them in a separate compound, the remaining ninety-five per cent made no attempt to escape.

This is something that must obviously be taken into account in considering Becker's argument that all human beings have a craving for 'heroism', for 'primacy', which seems difficult to reconcile with our fairly stable society, in which most people seem to accept their lack of primacy. This could be, as Becker suggests, because we lose the feeling of primacy as we grow up; but anyone who has ever spent ten minutes waiting for his children in a nursery school will know that the majority of children also seem to accept their lack of 'primacy'. The 'dominant five per cent' applies to children as well as adults.

Now in terms of society, five per cent is an enormous number; for example, in England in the 1980s it amounts to more than three million people. And society has no room for three million 'leaders'. This means, inevitably, that a huge proportion of the dominant five per cent are never going to achieve any kind of 'uniqueness'. They are going to spend their lives in positions that are indistinguishable from those of the non-dominant remainder.

In a society with a strong class-structure — peasants and aristocrats, rich and poor — this is not particularly important. The dominant farm-labourer will be content as the village blacksmith or leader of the church choir; he does not expect to become lord of the manor, and he doesn't resent it if the lord of the manor is far less dominant than he is. But in a society like ours, where working-class boys become pop-idols and where we see our leaders on television every day, the situation is altogether less stable. The 'average' member of the dominant five per cent sees no reason why he should not be rich and famous too. He experiences anger and frustration at his lack of 'primacy', and is willing to consider unorthodox methods of elbowing his way to the fore. This clearly explains a great deal about the rising levels of crime and violence in our society.

We can also see how large numbers of these dominant individuals develop into 'Right Men'. In every school with five hundred pupils, there are about twenty-five dominant ones struggling for primacy. Some of these have natural advantages: they are good athletes, good scholars, good debaters. (And there are, of course, plenty of non-dominant pupils who are gifted enough to carry away some of the prizes.) Inevitably, a percentage of the dominant pupils have no particular talent or gift; some may be downright stupid. How is such a person to satisfy his urge to primacy? He will, inevitably, choose to express his dominance in any ways that are possible. If he has good looks or charm, he may be satisfied with the admiration of female pupils. If he has some specific talent which is not regarded as important by his schoolmasters — a good ear for music, a natural gift of observation, a vivid imagination — he may become a lonely 'outsider', living in his own private world. (Such individuals may develop into

Schuberts, Darwins, Balzacs.) But it is just as likely that he will try to take short-cuts to prominence and become a bully, a cheat or a delinquent.

The main problem of these ungifted 'outsiders' is that they are bound to feel that the world has treated them unfairly. And the normal human reaction to a sense of unfairness is an upsurge of self-pity. Self-pity and the sense of injustice make them vulnerable and unstable. And we have only to observe such people to see that they are usually their own worst enemies. Their moods alternate between aggressiveness and sulkiness, both of which alienate those who might otherwise be glad to help them. If they possess some degree of charm or intelligence, they may succeed in making themselves acceptable to other people; but sooner or later the resentment and self-pity break through, and lead to mistrust and rejection.

The very essence of their problem is the question of self-discipline. Dominant human beings are more impatient than others, because they have more vital energy. Impatience leads them to look for short-cuts. When Peter Sellers booked into the RAC Club, he could just as easily have phoned his wife, told her to give the nanny two months wages and sack her, and then got a good night's sleep. Instead, he behaved in a way that could have caused serious problems for everybody. It is easy to see that if Sellers's life, from the age of five, consisted of similar short-cuts, by the time he was an adult he would lack the basic equipment to become a normal member of society. Civilization, as Freud pointed out, demands self-discipline on the part of its members. No one can be licensed to threaten people with carving knives.

All this places us in a better position to answer Fromm's question: why is man the only creature who kills and tortures members of his own species without any reason? The answer does not lie in his genetic inheritance, nor in some hypothetical death-wish, but in the human need for self-assertion, the craving for 'primacy'.

The behaviour of the Right Man enables us to see how this comes about. His feeling that he 'counts' more than anyone else leads him to acts of violent self-assertion. But this violence, by its very nature, cannot achieve any long-term objective. Beethoven once flung a dish of lung soup in the face of a waiter who annoyed him — typical Right Man behaviour. But Beethoven did not rely upon violence to assert his 'primacy'; he realized that his long-term objective could only be achieved by patience and self-discipline: that is to say, by *canalizing* his energy (another name for impatience) and directing it in a jet, like a fireman's hose, into his music. Long discipline deepened the canal banks until, in the final works, not a drop of energy was wasted.

When the Right Man explodes into violence, *all* the energy is wasted. Worse still, it destroys the banks of the canal. So in permitting himself free expression of his negative emotions he is indulging in a process of slow but sure self-erosion — the emotional counterpart of physical incontinence. Without proper 'drainage', his inner being turns into a kind of swamp or sewage farm. This is why most of the violent men of history, from Alexander the Great to Stalin, have ended up as psychotics. Without the power to control their negative emotions, they become incapable of any state of sustained well-being.

If we are to achieve a true understanding of the nature of criminality, this is the problem that must be plumbed to its depths: the problem of the psychology of self-destruction.

DISCOVERY
OF THE VAMPIRES

From *The Mind Parasites*, 1967

The Mind Parasites *is based upon the notion that some kind of parasite or life-vampire lives in the depths of the human mind, and steals our energies. In the opening chapter of the book, the narrator's friend Karel Weissman commits suicide. Many months after his death, the narrator discovers among his papers a secret journal, under the title* Historical Reflections. *The journal describes Weissman's realization of the existence of the mind parasites. The problem the narrator has to solve in the remainder of the book is: how can human beings fight against a parasite which already knows what they are thinking the moment they think it?*

What follows is an extract from the journal.

It was in 1990 that I entered the field of industrial psychology as the assistant of Professor Ames at Trans-world Cosmetics. I immediately discovered a curious and nightmarish situation. I knew, of course, that 'industrial neurosis' had become a serious matter — so much so that special industrial courts had been set up to deal with offenders who sabotaged machinery or killed or injured workmates. But only a few people were aware of the sheer size of the problem. The murder rate in large factories and similar concerns had increased to *twice* that of the rest of the population. In one cigarette factory in America, eight foremen and two high executives were killed in the course of a single year; in seven of these cases, the murderer committed suicide immediately after the attack.

The Industrial Plastics Corporation of Iceland had decided to try the experiment of an 'open air' factory, spread over many acres, so that the workers had no sense of overcrowding or confinement; energy fields were used instead of walls. At first, the experiment was highly successful; but within two years, the factory's rate of industrial crime and neurosis had risen to equal the national average.

These figures never reached the national press. Psychologists reasoned — correctly — that to publicize them would make things worse. They reasoned that it would be best to treat each case as one would an outbreak of fire that must be isolated.

The more I considered this problem, the more I felt that we had no real idea of its cause. My colleagues were frankly defeated by it, as Dr Ames admitted to me during my first week at Trans-world Cosmetics. He said that it was difficult to get to the root of the problem, because it seemed to have so many roots — the population explosion, overcrowding in cities, the individual's feeling of insignificance and increasing sense of living in a vacuum, the lack of adventure in modern life, collapse of religion ... and so on. He said he wasn't sure that industry wasn't treating the problem in entirely the wrong way. It was spending more money on psychiatrists, on improving working conditions — in short, in making the workers feel like patients. But since our living depended on this mistake, it was hardly up to us to suggest a change.

And so I turned to history to find my answers. And the answers, when I found them, made me feel like suicide. For, according to history, all this was completely inevitable. Civilization was getting top heavy; it was bound to fall over. Yet the one thing this conclusion failed to take into account was the human power of self-renewal. By the same reasoning, Mozart was bound to commit suicide because his life was so miserable. But he didn't.

What was destroying the human power of self-renewal?

I cannot explain quite how I came to believe that there might be a single cause. It was something that dawned on me slowly, over many years. It was simply that I came to feel increasingly strongly that the figures for industrial crime were out of all proportion to the so-called 'historical causes'. It was as if I were the head of a firm who begins to feel instinctively that his accountant is cooking the books, although he has no idea how it is being done.

And then, one day, I began to suspect the existence of the mind vampires. And from then on, everything confirmed my guess.

It happened first when I was considering the use of mescalin and lysergic acid for curing industrial neurosis. Fundamentally, of course, the effect of these drugs is no different from that of alcohol or tobacco: they have the effect of unwinding us. A man who is overworked has got himself into a habit of tension, and he cannot break the habit by merely willing. A glass of whisky or a cigarette will reach down into his motor levels and release the tension.

But man has far deeper habits than overwork. Through millions of years of evolution, he has developed all kinds of habits for survival. If any of these habits get out of control, the result is mental illness. For example, man has a habit of being prepared for enemies; but if he allows it to dominate his life, he becomes a paranoiac.

One of man's deepest habits is keeping alert for dangers and difficulties, refusing to allow himself to explore his own mind because he daren't take his eyes off the world around him. Another one, with the same cause, is his refusal to notice beauty, because he prefers to concentrate on practical problems. These habits are so deeply ingrained that alcohol and tobacco cannot reach them. But mescalin can. It can reach down to man's most atavistic levels, and release the automatic tensions that make him a slave to his own boredom and to the world around him.

Now I must confess that I was inclined to blame these atavistic habits for the problem of the world suicide rate and the industrial crime rate. Man has to learn to relax, or he becomes overwrought and dangerous. He must learn to contact his own deepest levels in order to re-energize his consciousness. So it seemed to me that drugs of the mescalin group might provide the answer.

So far, the use of these drugs had been avoided in industrial psychology, for an obvious reason: mescalin relaxes a man to a point where work becomes impossible. He wants to do nothing but contemplate the beauty of the world and the mysteries of his own mind.

I felt that there was no reason to reach this limit. A tiny quantity of mescalin, administered in the right way, might release a man's creative forces without plunging him into a stupor. After all, man's ancestors of two thousand years ago were almost colour-blind because they were in a subconscious habit of ignoring colour. Life was so difficult and dangerous that they couldn't afford to notice it. Yet modern man has succeeded in losing this old habit of colour-blindness without losing any of his drive and vitality. It is all a matter of balance.

And so I inaugurated a series of experiments with drugs of the mescalin group. And my first results were so alarming that my engagement with Trans-world Cosmetics was terminated abruptly. Five out of my ten subjects committed suicide within days. Another two had a total mental collapse that drove them into a madhouse.

I was baffled. I had experimented with mescalin on myself in my university days, but I found the results uninteresting. A mescalin holiday is all very pleasant, but it all depends whether you enjoy holidays. I do not; I find work too interesting.

But my results made me decide to try it again. I took half a gram. The result was so horrifying that I still perspire when I think about it.

At first, there were the usual pleasant effects — areas of light swelling gently and revolving. Then an immense sense of peace and calm, a glimpse of the Buddhist nirvana, a beautiful and gentle contemplation of the universe that was at once detached and infinitely involved. After about an hour of this, I roused myself from it; I was obviously not discovering what had caused the suicides. Now I attempted to turn my attention *inward*, to observe the exact state of my perceptions and emotions. The result was baffling. It was as if I was trying to look through a telescope, and someone was deliberately placing his hand over the other end of it. Every attempt at self- observation failed. And then, with a kind of violent effort, I tried to batter through this wall of darkness. And suddenly, I had a distinct feeling of *something living and alien* hurrying out of my sight. I am not, of course, speaking of physical sight. This was entirely a 'feeling'. But it had such an imprint of reality that for a moment I became almost insane with terror. One can run away from an obvious physical menace, but there was no running away from this, because it was inside me.

For nearly a week afterwards, I was in a state of the most abject terror, and closer to insanity than I have ever been in my life. For although I was now back in the ordinary physical world, I had no feeling of safety. I felt that, in returning to everyday consciousness, I was like an ostrich burying its head in the sand. It only meant that I was unaware of the menace.

Luckily, I was not working at the time; it would have been impossible. And about a week later, I found myself thinking: Well, what are you afraid of? You've come to no harm. I immediately began to feel more cheerful. It was only a few days after this that Standard Motors and Engineering offered me the post of their chief medical officer. I accepted it, and plunged into the work of an enormous and complex organization. For a long time it left me no time for brooding or devising new experiments. And whenever my thoughts turned back to my mescalin experiments, I felt such a powerful revulsion that I always found some excuse for putting it off.

Six months ago, I finally returned to the problem, this time from a slightly different angle. My friend Rupert Haddon of Princeton told me of his highly successful experiments in rehabilitating sexual criminals with the use of L.S.D. In explaining his theories, he used a great deal of the terminology of the philosopher Husserl. It immediately became obvious to me that phenomenology is only another name for the kind of self-observation I had tried to carry out under mescalin, and that when Husserl talks about 'uncovering the structure of consciousness', he only means descending into these realms of mental habit of which I have spoken. Husserl had realized that while we have ordnance survey maps that cover every inch of our earth, we have no atlas of our mental world.

Reading Husserl renewed my courage. The idea of trying mescalin again terrified me, but phenomenology starts from ordinary consciousness. So I again began making notes about the problems of man's inner world, and the geography of consciousness.

Almost at once, I became aware *that certain inner-forces* were resisting my researches. As soon as I began to brood on these problems, I began to experience sick headaches and feelings of nausea. Every morning, I woke up with a feeling of profound depression. I have always been a student of mathematics in an amateurish way, as well as a good chess player. I soon discovered that I felt better the moment I turned my attention to mathematics or chess. But the moment I began to think about the mind, the same depression would settle on me.

My own weakness began to infuriate me. I determined that I would overcome it at all costs. So I begged two months' leave of absence from my employers. I warned my wife that I was going to be very ill. And I deliberately turned my mind to these problems of phenomenology. The result was exactly as I predicted. For a few days I felt tired and depressed. Then I began to experience headaches and nerve pains. Then I vomited up everything I ate. I took to my bed, and tried to use my mind to probe my own sickness, using the methods of analysis laid down by Husserl. My wife had no idea of what was wrong with me, and her anxiety made it twice as bad. It is lucky that we have no children; otherwise, I would certainly have been forced to surrender.

After a fortnight, I was so exhausted that I could barely swallow a teaspoonful of milk. I made an immense effort to rally my forces, reaching down to my deepest instinctive levels. In that moment, I became aware of my enemies. It was like swimming down to the bottom of the sea and suddenly noticing that you are surrounded by sharks. I could not, of course, 'see' them in the ordinary sense, but I could *feel* their presence as clearly as one can feel toothache. They were down there, at a level of my being where my consciousness never penetrates.

And as I tried to prevent myself from screaming with terror, the fear of a man facing inevitable destruction, I suddenly realized *that I had beaten them*. My own deepest life forces were rallying against them. An immense strength, that I had never known I possessed, reared up like a giant. It was far stronger than they were, and they had to retreat from it. I suddenly became aware of more of them, thousands of them; and yet I knew that they could do nothing against me.

And then the realization came to me with such searing force that I felt as if I had been struck by lightning. Everything was clear; *I knew everything*. I knew why it was so important to them that no one should suspect their existence. Man possesses more than enough power to destroy them all. But so long as he is unaware of them, they can feed on him, like vampires, sucking away his energy.

My wife came into the bedroom and was astounded to find me laughing like a madman. For a moment, she thought my mind had collapsed. Then she realized that it was the laughter of sanity.

I told her to go and bring me soup. And within forty-eight hours, I was back on my feet again, as healthy as ever — in fact, healthier than I had ever been in my life. At first, I felt such an immense euphoria at my discovery that I forgot about those vampires of the mind. Then I realized that this in itself was stupid. They had an immense advantage over me; they knew my own mind far better than I did. Unless I was very careful, they could still destroy me.

But for the moment, I was safe. When, later in the day, I felt the persistent, nagging attacks of depression, I turned again to that deep source of inner power, and to my optimism about the human future. Immediately the attacks ceased, and I began to roar with laughter again. It was many weeks before I could control this laughter mechanism whenever I had a skirmish with the parasites.

What I had discovered was, of course, so fantastic that it could not be grasped by the unprepared mind. In fact, it was extraordinary good luck that I had not made the discovery six years earlier, when I was working for Trans-world. In the meantime, my mind had made slow and unconscious preparation for it. In the past few months, I have become steadily more convinced that it was not entirely a matter of luck. I have a feeling that there are powerful forces working on the side of humanity, although I have no idea of their nature.

(I made a special note of this sentence. It was something I had always felt instinctively.)

What it amounts to is this. For more than two centuries now, the human mind has been constantly a prey to these energy vampires. In a few cases, the vampires have been able completely to take over a human mind and use it for their own purposes. For example, I am almost certain that De Sade was one of these 'zombis' whose brain was entirely in the control of the vampires. The blasphemy and stupidity of his work are not, as in many cases, evidence of demonic vitality, and the proof of it is that De Sade never matured in any way, although he lived to be seventy-four. The sole purpose of his life work is to add to the mental confusion of the human race, deliberately to distort and pervert the truth about sex.

As soon as I understood about the mind vampires, the history of the past two hundred years became absurdly clear. Until about 1780 (which is roughly the date when the first full-scale invasion of mind vampires landed on earth), most art tended to be life-enhancing, like the music of Haydn and Mozart. After the invasion of the mind vampires, this sunny optimism became almost impossible to the artist. The mind vampires always chose the most intelligent men as their instruments, because it is ultimately the intelligent men who have the greatest influence on the human race. Very few artists have been powerful enough to hurl them off, and such men have gained a new strength in doing so — Beethoven is clearly an example; Goethe another.

And this explains precisely why it is so important for the mind vampires to keep their presence unknown, to drain man's lifeblood without his being aware of it. A man who defeats the mind vampires becomes doubly dangerous to them, for his forces of self-renewal have conquered. In such cases, the vampires probably attempt to destroy him in another way — by trying to influence other people against him. We should remember that Beethoven's death came about because he left his sister's house after a rather curious quarrel, and drove several miles in an open cart in the rain. At all events, we notice that it is in the nineteenth century that the great artists first begin to complain that 'the world is against them'; Haydn and Mozart were well understood and appreciated by their own time. As soon as the artist dies, this neglect disappears — the mind vampires loosen their grip on people's minds. They have more important things to attend to.

In the history of art and literature since 1780, we see the results of the battle with the mind vampires. The artists who refused to preach a gospel of pessimism and life devaluation were destroyed. The life-slanderers often lived to a ripe old age. It is interesting, for example, to contrast the fate of the life-slanderer Schopenhauer with that of the life-affirmer Nietzsche, or that of the sexual degenerate de Sade with that of the sexual mystic Lawrence.

Apart from these obvious facts, I have not succeeded in learning a great deal about the mind vampires. I am inclined to suspect that, in small numbers, they have always been present on earth. Possibly the Christian idea of the devil arises from some obscure intuition of the part they had played in human history: how their role is to take over a man's mind, and to cause him to become an enemy of life and of the human race. But it would be a mistake to blame the vampires for all the misfortunes of the human race. Man is an animal who is trying to evolve into a god. Many of his problems are an inevitable result of this struggle.

I have a theory, which I will state here for the sake of completeness. I suspect that the universe is full of races like our own, struggling to evolve. In the early stages of its evolution, any race is mainly concerned to conquer its environment, to overcome enemies, to assure itself of food. But sooner or later, a point comes where the race has progressed beyond this stage, and can now turn its attention inward, to the pleasures of the mind. 'My mind to me a kingdom is', said Sir Edward Dyer. And when man realizes that his mind is a kingdom in the most literal sense, a great unexplored country, he has crossed the borderline that divides the animal from the god.

Now I suspect that these mind vampires specialize in finding races who have almost reached this point of evolution, who are on the brink of achieving a new power, and then feeding on them until they have destroyed them. It is not their actual intention to destroy — because once they have done this, they are forced to seek another host. Their intention is to feed for as long as possible on the tremendous energies generated by the evolutionary struggle. Their purpose, therefore, is to prevent man from discovering the worlds inside himself, to keep his attention directed *outwards*. I think there can be no possible doubt that the wars of the twentieth century are a deliberate contrivance of these vampires. Hitler, like De Sade, was almost certainly another of their 'zombis'. A completely destructive world war would not serve their purposes, but continual minor skirmishes are admirable.

What would man be like if he could destroy these vampires, or drive them away? The first result would certainly be a tremendous sense of mental relief, a vanishing oppression, a surge of energy and optimism. In this first rush of energy, artistic masterpieces would be created by the dozen.

Mankind would react like children who have been let out of school on the last day of term. Then man's energies would turn inward. He would take up the legacy of Husserl. (It is obviously significant that it was Hitler who was responsible for Husserl's death just as his work was on the brink of new achievements.) He would suddenly realize that he possesses inner-powers that make the hydrogen bomb seem a mere candle. Aided, perhaps, by such drugs as mescalin, he would become, for the first time, *an inhabitant of the world of mind*, just as he is at present an inhabitant of earth. He would explore the countries of the mind as Livingstone and Stanley explored Africa. He would discover that he has many 'selves', and that his higher 'selves' are what his ancestors would have called gods.

I have another theory, which is so absurd that I hardly dare to mention it. This is that the mind vampires are, without intending it, the instruments of some higher force. They may, of course, succeed in destroying any race that becomes their host. But if, by any chance, the race should become aware of the danger, the result is bound to be the exact opposite of what is intended. One of the chief obstacles to human evolution is man's boredom and ignorance, his tendency to drift and allow tomorrow to take care of itself. In a certain sense, this is perhaps a greater danger to evolution — or at least, a hindrance — than the vampires themselves. Once a race becomes aware of these vampires, the battle is already half won. Once man has a purpose and a belief, he is almost invincible. The vampires might serve, therefore, to inoculate man against his own indifference and laziness. However, this is no more than a casual speculation....

The next problem is more important than all this speculation: How is it possible to get rid of them? It is no answer simply to publish 'the facts'. The historical facts mean nothing at all; they would be ignored. In some way, the human race has to be made aware of its danger. If I did what would be so easy — arranged to be interviewed on television, or wrote a series of newspaper articles on the subject — I might be listened to, but I think it more probable that people would simply dismiss me as insane. Yes, indeed, this is a tremendous problem. For short of persuading everyone to try a dose of mescalin, I can think of no way of convincing people. And then, there is no guarantee that mescalin would bring about the desired result — otherwise, I might risk dumping a large quantity of it in some city's water supply. No, such an idea is unthinkable. With the mind vampires massed for attack, sanity is too fragile a thing to risk. I now understand why my experiment at Trans-world ended so disastrously. The vampires *deliberately destroyed* those people, as a kind of warning to me.

The average person lacks the mental discipline to resist them. This is why the suicide rate is so high.

I *must* learn more about these creatures. While my ignorance is so complete, they could destroy me. When I know something about them, perhaps I shall also know how to make the human race aware of them.

VISION ON THE EIGER

From *The Black Room*, 1971

The Black Room *is a spy novel, about the attempt of a group of scientists to find a method of preventing brain-washing through sensory deprivation. In this extract, the hero, Kit Butler, has just emerged from his own experience of the black room.*

Butler said: 'What time is it?'

'A quarter past six on Saturday morning.'

'Saturday! I must have slept for about forty-eight hours!'

Gradwohl was tall and bony, about sixty years old. He wore a light grey suit that hung limply on him, giving the impression that it had been made for a much broader man. The height of the domed forehead was emphasized by the almost complete baldness of his head. He reminded Butler of his former house master. He said: 'Come and have some coffee. Let me say first that it is a great privilege to meet you.' His handshake was jerky, like a man tugging impatiently at a bellrope.

Butler followed him out, and down the ladder. The gunmetal door was wide open, and the smell of the morning was intoxicating. Gradwohl asked: 'How much longer do you think you could have stayed in?'

'I'm not sure. Quite a while, I think.'

'I think so too.'

'Why did you fetch me out?'

The sunlight dazzled him, so that he stumbled on a rut in the mud. Gradwohl took his elbow.

'I myself arrived only two hours ago. I drove straight up from Edinburgh. And since I was not tired, I went into Colonel Sampson's office and checked on the black rooms. I heard everything you said about false fatigue. Very important. I had come to similar conclusions myself. You are also right when you say that you all need more discipline before you can stand the black room for a long period.'

They walked around the side of the building — the back door was locked — and in through the main entrance. The smells of the morning seemed unnaturally sharp and sweet. When his eyes adjusted to the sunlight, it seemed as cold and fresh as a waterfall of snow. In comparison, the main lounge, with its dead fire and smell of stale tobacco, seemed strange and lifeless. On the table, an electric coffee percolator was bubbling; when he came close to it, the smell of coffee seemed to assault his senses, flooding his mind with memories of Paris and Berlin. He went to the window, opened it and looked down at the loch.

'Black or white?'

'White, please.'

Gradwohl's movements amused him. They were all sudden and sharp, like those of a puppet. When he poured the coffee, he kept his heels pressed tightly together, as if afraid they might run off in opposite directions. His speech, like his movements, was jerky and spasmodic, and this effect was increased by the strong German accent, that pronounced all d's as t's.

He handed Butler his coffee in a large cup, and the basin of lump sugar. Butler said: 'I'm told that you managed to stick the black room for twelve days. How did you manage that?'

Gradwohl sat down, stirring his coffee.

'That is not easy to explain. Partly by various disciplines — working out problems and so on. Partly because I have a naturally healthy subconscious mind...do you understand?'

'I think so.'

'And you know how I got it? By climbing mountains.'

'But how?'

'I can't explain how. But I can tell you about it. You know that in the thirties, Hitler's followers used to set out to climb impossible mountains?'

'No, I didn't. You mean as propaganda?'

'Quite. They developed a cult of physical courage that was sometimes stupid. They would deliberately choose almost impossible routes up mountains, and then climb them with the help of *pitons* — steel spikes that can be hammered into the rock — and *karabiners*, which are steel snap links that fit on the spikes. The major school of these Nazi daredevils lived in Munich, where my brother and I were also living. And so we began deliberately challenging them, just to prove that you didn't have to be a Nazi to climb a vertical rock face. We were both, of course, violently anti-Nazi, although we are not Jewish.' Gradwohl's accent made his words difficult to follow; it sounded almost as if he were speaking German. By concentrating hard, Butler was able to follow what was being said.

'Well, one day we heard that some of this Munich School had succeeded in climbing the north face of the Matterhorn, which rises like a wall for several thousands of feet. So Otto and I decided to go a step further, and attempt the Eigerwand — the north face of the Eiger, which is a six thousand foot wall, which had never been climbed, although several climbers had died in the attempt. Wulffian Gartner, the most daring climber in the Munich school, heard about our preparations and decided that he would do it first. So when we set up our camp in the meadows at the foot of the wall, we heard that four men had set out two days ago, and had climbed up to the third ice field. But before we had time to set out, the weather changed into ice and sleet. After another day, they decided to turn back — one of them had been injured by falling ice. On the fourth day, a thick cloud came down over the mountain, and a rescue party set out to try and reach them. We decided to join it — for although we disagreed with them politically, we didn't want to see them destroyed. We all went by train to the Eigerwand Station, then started to move across the ice by means of *pitons*. By the time we came close to them, only one of the four was still alive — Wulffian Gartner. But it was too dark to get to him. We had to return, and leave him there all night. We expected him to die, but when we reached him again the next morning he was still alive. But he was up above us, and his rope was too short to reach us. There was a great projecting rock between us, so we could get no higher. We told him to climb up to the body of one of his companions, and let it fall; then unravel the rope from the body into strands and lower it to us, so we could send him up another rope. It took him five hours and we thought he would never make it. But he did, and finally climbed down to within ten feet of us. Then the knot joining two ropes jammed in the *karabiner*, and he hung there, trying to free it with his teeth. There was nothing we could do — just stand there and watch him. Then suddenly, he looked down into my face. He said: 'Thanks for trying, anyway. I'm finished.' And I watched him die — quite suddenly, as if he had been shot.' Butler tried to disguise the shiver that passed over him. Gradwohl said: 'I watched him *decide* to die.'

'I suppose his strength was at an end.'

'What you call his strength had been at an end since the previous day. But he did not die, because he had decided there was still hope. And if he had reached our party, he would have found still more strength to make his way back to the station. No. It is what you were saying in the black room. Your will-power sustains your body from a subconscious reservoir. But if you get very exhausted, only a tremendous sense of purpose can sustain you. He had been making tremendous efforts for days, and now he suddenly decided it wasn't worth it any more.' Gradwohl sipped slowly at his coffee. 'That taught me the first lesson: that man is as strong as his sense of purpose — no more and no less. We don't notice this normally because we never see people pushing themselves to their limits.'

Butler helped himself to more coffee, and poured in cold milk. 'And did you climb the Eigerwand?'

'We did, but not that year — 1935. We decided to wait for the next year, and make the attempt just before the Olympic Games.' He paused, staring into the fireplace with its charred logs. 'We were lucky. If the weather had changed, we would have died too. And it was there that I learned the second lesson.' Butler waited for him to go on. Gradwohl seemed in no hurry. He said finally:

'We set out by night, because during the day, the sunlight causes the ice to melt, and rocks and chunks of ice keep falling down. We climbed this with *pitons* and *karabiners*, and reached the top at about eleven in the morning. Before evening, we had reached the foot of the second ice field, where we camped for the night. The mist had come down, and we were afraid that the weather would get worse. Before dawn the next day we started on again. Here we had to leave behind some of our rope and two *pitons* and steel links — we had to hammer *pitons* into a vertical wall of ice, and then swing across it on ropes to reach a ledge. It took us all day to reach the third ice field, and we decided to try to cross this before we camped for the night. This was a mistake, because we were very tired, and there is only one way off the ice field, up a kind of ramp. When we were halfway up, the wind began to rise, and I knew that we had been foolish. We couldn't go back now. We could only go on. But if the darkness came before we found a ledge, it was the end of us — because although we were used to climbing in the dark, this was a vertical wall of ice, like the side of a sky-scraper. Then, just as we were at the end of our strength, Otto saw a ledge about twenty feet to the right — which was the opposite direction from the one we wanted to go. It took us an hour to reach it, and at one point, Otto slipped and I had to haul him back up — luckily, the rope was fixed to a *piton*. The ledge was three feet wide, and had a steep slope. It was also covered with ice to a depth of six inches. It was just large enough for the two of us. We hammered *pitons* into the ice, and tied ourselves to them. We could not sleep, of course — it was too cold, and we might accidentally tear out the *pitons*. So we sat there, looking into the clouds, and praying that there would be no storm. And then, suddenly, the clouds all drifted away, and we could look down at the lights of Grindelwald, thousands of feet below. And suddenly, Otto laughed, and said: "Why are we doing this, Franz? Are we both mad?" I said: "No, we are not mad."

And I began to think about it. Why did I suddenly feel so happy, hanging there like a fly and looking at the lights? I was thinking: Thousands of comfortable people are lying down there in their beds, and they are not particularly happy, because they take their beds for granted. They are all suffering from what you call false fatigue — a mistaken feeling that life is not really worth living. And then I thought: But now I *know*, beyond all shadow of doubt, that life *is* worth living. Tomorrow, I shall be climbing up the most dangerous part of the mountain, the White Spider, and for every foot of the way, I shall be concentrating, determined not to slip, determined to reach the exit cracks. And then the absurdity of it struck me. I said to Otto: "We have climbed this mountain to remind ourselves of something we ought to know anyway — that life is only worth living when the will is concentrated." You see what I mean? Why do I need to set myself a difficult obstacle to concentrate my will? For two million years man has been climbing a mountain of evolution, and his will is so weak that he dies when he is less than a century old. That is all very well for most people, because they are so stupid. But you and I ought to know better, because our business is evolution. You are a composer, I am a philosopher. We can look back on the civilizations of the past and see how far we have climbed up the mountain. We shouldn't be drifting like the rest of the fools.'

UNCLE SAM

From *The World of Violence*, 1963

The World of Violence is a study in the contrast between the 'ivory tower' of an intellectual — in this case a mathematical prodigy — and the chaotic violence of actuality. The narrator is shaken out of his ivory tower when he sees a youth being beaten up by young hooligans. His sense of helplessness leads him to buy a gun, and to join a pistol club, merely to convince himself that intellectuals can also be men of action. The ivory tower theme is first sounded early in the book, in the narrator's story about his uncle Sam.

I must mention now a circumstance that perhaps sounds absurd — or almost meaningless — but which has been of central importance to me since I was very small. It is this: I have never liked human beings. I do not mean that I felt a Swiftian hatred for them. This was something different; an obscure discomfort, as if mixing with people was like sitting in a dentist's chair having one's teeth drilled. As a small child, and well into my early twenties, I could not even go into a shop to buy a pencil without overcoming a certain revulsion. This was not shyness or a sense of inferiority, but a feeling that human relations are somehow absurd. I have never been able to watch two people talking about the weather without a deep feeling of wonderment; I watch them closely, expecting to see their faces crumble suddenly into horrible grief.

I suppose this is partly because human relations offend my sense of economy. I learned to think mathematically at the age of six; when I had a spare moment, I worked at some problem, such as Fermat's question of a formula that will generate prime numbers. I therefore feel astonished at the amount of thought-energy that most human beings seem to waste as a matter of course. It is rather as if someone should say to a long-distance hiker: 'Well, I'm going to take my morning walk now', and then proceed to walk around in a three-foot circle, explaining that when he has done this five thousand times he has walked the equivalent of five miles.

I certainly inherited this part of my temperament from my father's Uncle Sam, and I must write about Uncle Sam at this point.

Uncle Sam abruptly retreated from the world one day, locked himself up in an attic room, and refused to see anyone for several months. This happened when I was four years of age, so I have no early memories of Uncle Sam. He was the richest member of our family — he owned a lumber business and had a great deal of money invested. My Aunt Bertha, his second wife, was a plump, cheerful woman who did not seem to be in the least worried by his eccentricities. When people asked her why Uncle Sam had retreated, she would say 'He doesn't like noise' as if this explained everything.

But the oddest part of it was that Uncle Sam's attic room was dark; two workmen bricked up the window, under his instructions, and a carpenter made a new door, twice as thick as the old one, and with a sliding hatch near the bottom, through which he could take food. He stayed in his attic for twenty years, until his death, and refused to see any of the family. There was no talk of having him certified, for everyone in the family expected to benefit in his will. When he had been in the room a few months, he allowed Aunt Bertha in to tidy up, but never saw anyone else.

As it happened, I was the first person to see Uncle Sam (except, of course, Aunt Bertha) after his 'retreat'. This happened about four years later — when I was nine. This was at the beginning of the war. I was in the habit of spending whole evenings with Aunt Bertha; she liked my company, let me listen to the radio, and made me cakes and tarts. One day there was a power-cut just as she was about to take Uncle Sam's supper upstairs, so I preceded her with a lighted candle. From behind the locked door, Uncle Sam called: 'Who's that with you?' Aunt Bertha told him, and he opened the door and invited me in. He stood there, blinking in the candlelight, wearing a long grey nightshirt. His hair and beard were astounding — he looked like an old biblical prophet. (In fact, he allowed Aunt Bertha to trim them every six months or so; but to me, it looked as if they had been uncut for years.) He peered at me, then said: 'Come in, boy.' I looked at Aunt Bertha; she seemed so pleased that I was reassured. 'Put the supper down there, Bertha. You can go.' 'What about the candle?' she protested. As if to answer her, the light at the bottom of the stairs came on, although the room itself remained in darkness. So she went and left me alone with him. I disliked the room, and had no reason to like Uncle Sam. He smelt of sweat and unwashed clothes; there was a full chamberpot under the bed. Since there was no window, there was no way for air to circulate, and every smell of the last four years seemed to have left its traces in the room, including all the meals he had eaten.

I cannot remember how long I stayed, or what we talked about, except that he asked me a few questions about my mother and father. He sat at a table, eating his meal, and finally asked me to go down and fetch him a bottle of beer. I went, glad to escape. 'Take the candle', he said. He was still eating, and I asked him if he would not need it to see his food. He said briefly: 'No'. This puzzled me so much that I stopped at the door, and asked him: 'Why don't you get a light, uncle?'

'Because I prefer to live in the dark.'

'But why?'

'Because boy, darkness is man's natural element.'

I wanted to ask him what he meant by 'element', but he told me to hurry and send up his beer. So I went downstairs again, and Aunt Bertha took up the beer.

Later, I asked Aunt Bertha about elements. Evidently Uncle Sam had said the same kind of thing to her, because she explained that water is the fish's element, and air is the bird's. This failed to satisfy me. I objected that a fish dies in the air, and a bird dies if it is held under water, but a man doesn't die when he's not in the dark. Aunt Bertha just said: 'You'd better ask him next time you see him'. I didn't, because I was not interested, although I saw Uncle Sam fairly frequently after that. I learned the truth ten years later, after his death. He left me money — as I shall tell — and a document, which is in front of me now. It consists of forty handwritten pages, and is headed: 'Letter to my Nephew Hugh'. I am going to quote the relevant pages, because they seem to me important enough to cite at length. The early pages tell the story of his first marriage, his years in India and his first business successes. By the time he was forty, in 1925, he was a member of the boards of two large companies. He writes:

'The ease with which I made my first ten thousand pounds convinced me that destiny was reserving for me some role of cardinal importance. One day, however, an incident occurred that changed my whole outlook....'

'I was on my way to a board meeting, and was confident that I could persuade the other directors to follow my advice and buy up Cardew's business before the news of his impending bankruptcy circulated in the trade. I remember feeling pleasurable anticipation as I travelled across London by tube — the congratulations, and the comments: "Dawson's done it again". It was a hot morning in spring, and the train was crowded, but I felt cheerful and full of optimism; I even decided to take Mildred to the Savoy for supper. I cannot now recall the train of thought that then occurred to me; but I remember pushing my way through the crowd on the platform, and suddenly being overwhelmed by a feeling that struck me as abruptly as a heart attack. *It was a sudden and violent hatred for all my fellow human beings.* As I stood there, surrounded by pressing bodies, loathing and contempt rose in me until I felt as if I were drowning. I looked at their faces, and they seemed alien monsters, beings of clay and corruption. It is true that I could have restrained this hatred; but it seemed to me that I had glimpsed some great truth, and I had no right to turn away. My body felt drained of strength; I got up to the street with difficulty, and wondered why fate had waited so many years to play this trick on me. It was really like a denouement in a play. As I walked through the streets, all the stupidity and pettiness of humankind were present to my mind. I recalled the *saeva indignatio* of Swift, but this seemed inadequate. I felt as if I had been transported into a city of gigantic and hairy spiders, who perspired rottenness. I began to think how sweet the earth would be if freed of all animal life, and realised that, if I were God, I would destroy all life on this planet. It has occurred to me since that my vision was a kind of religious revelation.'

'I attended my board meeting, but I found myself unable to utter a word. Loathing made me incapable of speech. But force of habit made me scrawl on a sheet of paper: "Cardew going bankrupt; suggest we move in quickly", and pass it to the chairman, then I hurried out of the room.'

'I expected that the feeling would slowly pass away, and as I went home I tried to look into myself and discover how it had come about. It was as sudden as the bursting of a boil; but how had I failed to notice the boil earlier? I am still unable to explain this, except to say that *I have always been unusually sensitive to the idea of violence.*' [My italics.]

'I was mistaken; it did not pass. I had always been fairly fond of my wife, although I had ceased to respond to her on a physical level since she had put on weight. But when I arrived home I found that she had become wholly repulsive to me. All her faults seemed magnified; her voice threw me into a rage; the sight of her face made me feel sick; the thought of ever having embraced her convulsed me with nausea. I realized that I had to escape immediately. I pleaded that I felt ill, refused to go to bed, and hurried out of the house, saying that I was going to see a doctor. Instead, I took the first train to Scotland, and stupefied myself on the journey by drinking a bottle of gin — an unusual indulgence for me, for I have always been very nearly a teetotaller. I remembered a deserted cottage on the coast of Ayrshire that I had seen when shooting grouse.... From there, I cabled Mildred that I had been called away on a business trip and would be back in a fortnight.'

'The strange state of mind persisted, but I now suspected it was pathological. Instead of disappearing, my hatred seemed to increase. It vanished only when I could be alone and forget human beings. Even the local tradesman who delivered food seemed to me a kind of monstrous vegetable, a walking fungus, wholly alien. I felt as if I had been transported from some more civilized planet on to a strange world, full of creatures.'

'....When I returned to London, a month later, it was to discover that Mildred had left me and returned to Horatio [her previous husband]. I was not sorry. I allowed her to divorce me on the grounds of desertion.'

'It was some time before I was able to rationalise my strange malady. No doubt it had some physico-cerebral origin. But it was clear to me that I had stumbled upon an apocalyptic vision of human life that was totally *useless* to me as a living man. As a painter, I might have made use of it in depicting human beings as monsters. But as a family man, it was like a weight around my neck. There were times when I felt as if I had been branded by the Lord. (For although I have never regarded myself as a religious man, I have never been able to accept the ruthless economy of the atheist, and forgo the convenience of a universal scapegoat.)'

'My business losses in 1929 occupied my mind for the next three years. Although I now felt a stranger among human beings, I no longer experienced acute discomfort when in their presence. I had lost all real interest in money, but I treated business as a game, and played it with some success in the early thirties, accumulating enough money to insure against starvation in case another "attack" should make human society completely intolerable to me. In 1932, Bertha became my cook. She had escaped from two unfortunate marriages, and showed no tendency to ask questions or to try to impose her personality on me. I was so impressed by her independence of mind that I finally proposed marriage to her, and immediately settled half my fortune on her in case I should again feel the need to "retreat". I was even able to explain to her, in guarded terms, the nature of my occasional attacks; she said she understood perfectly, because her brother had suffered from jaundice. She has been an excellent wife, and as I write this I feel nothing but affection for her.'

'And yet I was never unaware of a basic uneasiness in these days, and in 1936 a certain moral exhaustion warned me that I would shortly pay the price of another collapse of vital force and motivation. Since my physical health was also delicate, I dreaded this event. I discovered that a smell of grass or privet had the power to soothe me, and Bertha made a habit of placing boxes filled with both in my bedroom. I believe that it was some association of childhood with the smell that helped to hold back the rising tide of sickness in me.'

'One morning in 1936 I accompanied Bertha to church. Dr McNab, the well-known Scottish nonconformist, was preaching. He was a widely travelled man and, aware, perhaps, of the number of business men in his congregation, took occasion to express harsh criticism of President Roosevelt's New Deal. All at once a strange excitement came over me, for I saw in a flash the origin of my troubles. The political new deals may or may not be effectual; but the new deal for which all men wait is an alteration in God's relations towards man. This idea so excited me that I stood up halfway through the sermon and hurried outside. It was a fine autumn morning, and I sat on a stone in the churchyard and pursued my revelation. Now for the first time I understood my attacks of hatred for human beings. They are all more or less contented slaves. Certain malcontent intellectuals have taught the workers to feel dissatisfaction with their employers. But it seems to have struck no one that human beings are *grossly exploited by God*. We are expected to bear misfortune, to learn from experience (like obedient schoolchildren), to offer thanksgiving for benefits received; our role is in every way that of the slave and the sycophant. We are entrapped in the body, which we carry around like a suit of armour weighing a ton, and we have to endure with patience its stupidities and enfeeblements. The days pass quickly, devoted to eating, defecating, reproducing, and combating the irony of fate. No Egyptian slave suffered more continuous indignity under the lash of his overseer than man suffers constantly under the mismanaged government of God. (You understand, Hugh, that I use the word "God" as a convenience to describe what the Ancients would have called Fate or The Gods, and what certain modem writers have preferred to call Life.)'

'Once this became clear to me, I trembled with excitement. I experienced the astonishment that has fallen upon all thinkers when their greatest ideas have occurred to them; I understood the feelings of Newton discovering the law of gravity, of Darwin recognizing natural selection, of Karl Marx apprehending the principle of class war. Perhaps the last parallel is closest to my own case. My excitement was so great that I could not bear to wait for my wife; instead, I made my way home alone. As I walked among the Sunday morning crowds, I now understood what had happened to me on that other morning ten years earlier, in the St Paul's underground station. These people were loathsome to me because they were slaves, and accepting them as fellows made me loathsome to myself. And yet, it seemed to me, other revolutionary thinkers had succeeded in changing the state of mankind. Was it not possible that my revelation was a sign that new changes were about to occur in man's relation to his destiny?'

'As the day wore on, however, my excitement vanished, for I recognized that my analogy was a false one. Marx depended on the physical discomfort of the workers to provide the explosive power of revolution; the only precondition was to direct the attention of the workers to the employers, and propagate the idea of underprivilege. But God had concealed himself so carefully that man's agony can discover no direction or object. I had frequently been struck by the absurd logic of criminals who claim that their crimes have been an attempt to get their revenge on "society".'

'In spite of my perplexity, two facts were clear to me. One, that I strongly objected to being an exploited human being, a slave of God or chance; two, that most people have no such objection. Besides, how could I call upon human beings to revolt against an entity that I myself recognized to be an abstraction?'

'This much was clear. It then became apparent to me that I could do no more than make my individual protest, that all the higher powers within me pointed to this aim. If I could not call on the rest of the human race to protest with me, I could at least have a one-man strike.'

'The rest of the story you know. I moved into the attic and had the window bricked up. I preferred darkness, recognizing that it was important to keep my mind concentrated on its object. Besides, I had no desire to bring my mind into contact with the stupidities and half-measures that make up the literature of the human race.'

'I had been in the room three days when it came to me that only one other man in human history had felt impelled to act in the same way, as an intercessor for all mankind. In that moment, I began to shiver uncontrollably with fear and joy.'

'At first, I had an idea that, if I concentrated hard enough on the grievances of mankind, the Great Employer might try negotiation with me, might deign to treat me as a spokesman of the human race and reveal himself to me. After a few months, I recognized that this was unlikely, and contented myself with recognizing that my protest was unique in the history of the human race and that, like Christ, I also had made an attempt to treat directly with God on behalf of my fellow human insects.'

'I cannot honestly advise you to do the same, unless you feel strongly so inclined. But I have observed in you signs of a kind of perception similar to my own. Do not try to force this; but in the event of your wishing to retire into solitude, I have made provision in my will, which is in the hands of Mr Pollard of Lake and Pollard….'

There followed a sub-heading: 'Summary of my religion and philosophy', which occupied some twenty pages. The deterioration of the handwriting indicated that it had been written some time later. I shall not quote it because it seems to me that his attitude has already been explained clearly enough in the section quoted already. Only one phrase strikes me as immediately important, and this is part of a sentence that is only half decipherable; the phrase is: 'What is the *logical response* to being alive?'

There is only one thing to add. Aunt Bertha told me that, two days before he died, Uncle Sam went into a kind of trance; he refused to eat, and stared in front of him with a strange, fixed expression. But Aunt Bertha told me that she thought it was an expression of joy. A few hours before he died, he drew her attention by tugging at her dress (she was asleep in an armchair beside the bed) and indicated that he wanted a pencil. But when she handed it to him, his hand shook so that he could hardly write. Finally, after several efforts, he managed to scrawl: 'I saw it'. He then dropped back, looking exhausted, and died quietly an hour or so later. The paper disappeared after the funeral.

This puzzled me. If Uncle Sam had written: 'I saw Him', it might have made sense; he had spent twenty years waiting for a vision of God; but Aunt Bertha was quite definite about it; the final pronoun had been 'it'. I still have no idea of what he meant, although I suppose it is remotely possible that he was referring to some vision of the purpose of human life. Whatever it was that he saw, it had the effect of Aquinas's final vision; it robbed him of the desire to go on living.

PEAK EXPERIENCE

I delivered the Schumacher Lecture at Bristol University in July 1982. I was speaking without notes, so the style leaves something to be desired — although the tape-recorded version, printed in the magazine Resurgence, *has here been revised.*

I was going to write a book about Schumacher just before he died — I feel that his ideas were a natural extension, in a social direction, of my own work.

I had always been preoccupied with the problem of the person who stands alone in a society that he feels to be too big and too impersonal. This was the basic theme of *The Outsider*.

Somewhere in *The Outsider* I say that I feel the Outsider dislikes the whole idea of civilization itself, because it destroys the sense of individuality. That is, of course, a deliberate overstatement. And yet, lecturing in America not long after *The Outsider* came out, I was struck by the awful impersonality of the universities, where in many cases the classes were so big that the students had to sit in other rooms watching the lecture on a TV monitor. I could see clearly that it must be almost impossible for many of these students to get that *personal*, individual feeling that could develop into creativity.

Because this, it seems to me, is the fundamental aim of civilization. This is what it is about. It is an attempt to promote creativity in the individual, because this is the highest thing of which the individual is capable.

In the early 1960s, I received a letter from the American psychologist Abraham Maslow, who was writing to me about a book of mine called *The*

Age of Defeat. Maslow said that I was attacking the same problem that had obsessed him for years: that our civilization has a kind of *premise of defeat* — that our art, our literature, our culture seems to spring from the notion that ultimately the individual cannot make much of an impression on the civilization; he is helpless, a mere member of the crowd.

Maslow also sent me some of his papers. I must admit that when I read their rather academic titles, I delayed reading them for a long time. When I did start to read one of the papers, about six months later, I was immediately excited by Maslow's central thesis, which was this: that psychologists are always studying sick people, because sick people are always talking about their sickness, while nobody had ever thought of studying healthy people, because healthy people never talk about their health. Maslow argued that we would do better to study the healthy. He enquired among his friends, asking, 'Who is the healthiest person you know?' And then he proceeded to study a number of these healthy people, and was amazed to discover something that no one had ever discovered before, because no one had ever thought of studying healthy people: that is, most of them appeared to experience with a fair degree of frequency what Maslow called 'peak experiences'. These were just sudden bubbling, overwhelming moments of happiness. They were not in any sense *mystical* experiences. A young mother was watching her husband and kids eating breakfast, when suddenly a beam of sunlight came in through the window, and she thought, 'Aren't I lucky', and went into the peak experience. A hostess who had just given a very successful party, looking around the room at the cigarette butts trampled into the carpet, and the wine spilled on the armchairs, nevertheless suddenly went into the peak experience. Maslow said that the peak experience seemed to characterize all healthy people. It was basically a sudden powerful surge of unconscious vitality. I was immensely struck by this, and wrote to Maslow about it. I ended by writing a book about him called *New Pathways in Psychology*.

As soon as I read Schumacher's *Small Is Beautiful*, I could see that this was a logical extension of Maslow's ideas — that the healthy person is the person who does not feel overwhelmed by his environment. He doesn't feel helpless, he doesn't feel a cog in a machine; he preserves a sense of drive, of individuality and creativity. And clearly the problem for the whole civilization is this problem of how to keep things 'small' enough, so that as many people as possible can experience the sense of individuality.

I recognized that my own background in Leicester, my home town, had exercised a strong influence on me, largely because it was so claustrophobic and boring. And the same appears to be true of an enormous number of writers of the present century: James Joyce's Dublin, Bernard Shaw's Dublin, H. G. Wells's Lewisham, Arnold Bennett's Burslem, Proust's Combray — all very small places that enable their inhabitants to feel individual among other individuals. Of course, what it really amounts to is feeling yourself to be a small fish in a small pond. If you are a small fish in a big pond, you are bound to lack that sense of individuality. I recognized this when I first went to London at about the age of nineteen: the feeling of being completely lost in crowds — that if I was knocked down by a bus, nobody would care. Obviously, we all crave this sense of individuality. Now Maslow had recognized that human beings appear to evolve through a series of needs, or values; he called it 'the hierarchy of needs'.

What he meant was this: that if a person was starving and had never had a square meal in his life, then he would dream about food and imagine that perfect happiness would be to have one really good meal every day. Yet if he achieved this, the next level would emerge: the need for security, for a roof over one's head. (This is why every tramp daydreams of a country cottage with roses round the door.) If he achieves this 'territorial' level, then the next level emerges: the need for love, for a feeling of belongingness, of intimacy with another person or persons. If these needs are satisfied too, says Maslow, then the next level emerges: the need for self-esteem, the need to be respected and liked by other people. This is the level at which women invite the neighbours to coffee mornings, and men join Rotary Clubs.

If the self-esteem level is thoroughly satisfied, then, said Maslow, the next level — with luck — emerges (and he said 'with luck' because, for some reason, many people do not appear to ever reach this level): this is the creative level, what Maslow called 'self-actualization'. By this, he didn't necessarily mean art or science or some other form of creativity. Self-actualization means doing something purely for the pleasure of doing it well. In one case he cited, a woman was particularly good at fostering children, and continued to do this when her own children were grown up. Another man was skilful at putting ships in bottles, and he did it brilliantly: obviously, this satisfied the self-actualizing need in him. Self-actualization seems to be the pinnacle of the hierarchy of needs.

Fortunately, in our society, most people have achieved the first three levels anyway — the basic needs for food, for security and for some kind of warm human relationship. The need that a majority of people have still not satisfied, and that becomes increasingly urgent in a society like ours, is the self-esteem need — the need, if you like, for some kind of 'recognition', if only by a very small group of neighbours and friends. And this is obviously one of the basic problems of our civilization, with its increasing tendency to de-individuation: self-esteem. It obviously cannot be satisfied if you are in such an enormous pond that you feel alienated from everybody else — in other words, if you feel a nobody.

This is what I identified in *The Outsider* as the basic Outsider problem. Now, it seemed to me that in recognizing that it is possible to decentralize society, to live in much smaller units, Schumacher had made an immensely important contribution. He had, of course, been anticipated by idealists like G. K. Chesterton and Hilaire Belloc, who called their political philosophy 'Distributism'; it was usually summarized in the phrase 'Two acres and a cow'. Clearly, two acres and a cow would not solve the problems of the modern city-dweller. But Schumacher had seen that Distributism *could* be brought up to date — that we could live in a completely different kind of way. When I first came upon his ideas — in a television programme — they excited me so much because it was already clear to me that we have *got* to live in a completely different kind of way if we are to satisfy the basic human need for self-esteem. And, as Maslow said, unless we satisfy this need for self-esteem, it is impossible to move beyond it to the level of self-actualization — which would be the ideal level for society.

I wrote to Schumacher; we corresponded, and I went to see him at his home to discuss the idea of a book about him. (He was also a friend of Maslow.) Then, while the book was still in the planning stage, he died. It was only after *Guide for the Perplexed* came out that I realized that Schumacher, like myself, had turned away from the social aspect of the problem — which is indeed very important — towards what seems to me to be in a sense even more important: the problem of the lone individual in our society.

At the time when I wrote *The Outsider* — I was in my early twenties — hardly interested in politics, and after every lecture I gave, somebody would always ask the same question: 'This is all very well, but how could your ideas improve our society?' And I always had to admit that I couldn't see any obvious way in which they would improve our social conditions. For, as far as I could see, improving society has to start by improving the individual. It was pleasant for me to discover that this was the conclusion Schumacher came to in *Guide for the Perplexed*. And in that beautiful appendix — for anyone who hasn't read the book, I suggest you start with the epilogue — he quotes Dorothy L. Sayers on the subject of Dante; she said that Dante's *Inferno* is a picture of human society in a state of sin and corruption, and then goes on to say that these are the problems of our own society: 'Futility, lack of a living faith, drift into loose morality, greedy consumption, financial irresponsibility, self-opinionated and obstinate individualism, and violence.'

Schumacher goes on to point out that Dorothy L. Sayers wrote this thirty years ago, and that things, if anything, are now much worse. Then he goes on to say that the real problem is that we are trying to live without a religion — and I don't think for a moment that Schumacher meant a religion in the sense of some religious sect. What he meant was the kind of inner certainty which provides an anchor against the sense of alienation.

Even at the time I wrote *The Outsider*, I could see that this was the central problem. If you had an absolutely ideal society with enough material goods for everybody, it would obviously still not guarantee universal happiness. In point of fact, as a student of crime — I am writing *A Criminal History of Mankind* at the moment — I have always recognized that one of the worst consequences of an increasingly comfortable civilization is a soaring crime rate. What is worse still is that the crimes become increasingly violent and sadistic. There are certain crimes of the past two decades — particularly certain examples of mass murder — that would simply never have happened before the 1960s. There has been an increase in deliberate sadism that is obviously due to sheer frustration.

Yes, the problem begins with the individual, because in an ideal society you could still not guarantee an end to all crimes of frustration. It is obviously necessary, as Schumacher says, to think in terms of religion. Bernard Shaw was one of the first people to recognize this clearly, and to state, 'Modern man cannot live without a religion.' Arnold Toynbee made this one of the central theses in *A Study of History*. And Schumacher is the third important thinker of this century to put his finger on this basic problem.

Now religion is fundamentally something that you live by. Whitehead once said, 'Religion is what a man does with his solitude.' Religion is also the ability to induce in oneself a certain inner peace. For me, one of the most important sections in *The Outsider* deals with the novelist Hermann Hesse. (In fact, I was the first person to write about him extensively in England.) I was particularly excited by his novel *Steppenwolf*, which seemed to me to express this central problem with unparalleled clarity. Steppenwolf is a would-be writer who is fairly well-off; he lives in a comfortable room in a comfortable lodging house; he has plenty of books and gramophone records; he has a girl-friend; in fact, he seems to have most of the things that a human being needs to be happy. And yet, for some reason, Steppenwolf is not happy. His problem is a continual feeling of boredom and frustration, that inability to break through to forms of deeper mental intensity. He feels that his consciousness is somehow boring and lukewarm. In the early pages of the book, he describes his frustration and the occasional temptation to commit suicide. Then, later that day, he wanders along to a restaurant for a meal, and as he tastes his first glass of Moselle he experiences that curious sense of deep relaxation that Maslow calls the peak experience. He says, 'The golden bubble burst and I was reminded of Mozart and the stars.'

And this goes to the heart of the matter. If only there were a way in which you could push a button and induce that experience instantly — make the golden bubble burst so that you are reminded of Mozart and the stars. If only we could do that — if we could even find some drug or chemical that would do it — then we would have solved the basic problem of modern civilization. No more crime, no more war, no more frustration and hatred. Aldous Huxley, you may remember, even suggested that we should all take mescalin for that purpose: but the trouble with mescalin is that it makes you so ecstatically lazy and happy that you don't want to do anything at all. A pile of unwashed dishes looks so beautiful that nobody would ever want to wash them. So clearly, this is not the answer. Yet you can see that, if we could find a method of inducing Maslow's peak experience at will, we *would* have found the answer to this problem.

Schumacher makes another point of fundamental importance in *Guide for the Perplexed*, in the section called 'Adaequatio': that the problem is that the information that comes in through our senses is not reality. He points out that we see not only with our eyes, but with a great part of our mental equipment as well. And since this mental equipment varies greatly from person to person, there are inevitably many things some people can see while others can't. 'Or to put it differently, for which some people are adequate while others are not. When the level of the knower is not adequate to the level of the object of knowledge, the result is not factual error but something much more serious: an inadequate and impoverished view of reality.' Now there, it seems to me, Schumacher has gone to the very heart of the fundamental problem of human existence.

This problem has to do with our senses, and with the curiously 'impoverished view of reality' that we hold. And this, I could see from my *Outsider* days, was the heart of the problem. Steppenwolf solves it for a moment by taking a drink of Moselle, but wine doesn't always work, and if you rely upon it you become an alcoholic. Wine, mescalin, pot — all these chemical ways of solving the problem tend to let us down half the time. This was something Maslow discovered when he and a psychologist called Hoffer were treating alcoholics. Maslow concluded that alcoholics are very often more intelligent than the average person, and consequently they find the world more dreary and boring than most people; like Wordsworth, they find that 'the world is too much with them'. They drink because drinking gives them a brief peak experience, but it doesn't always work. Sometimes you can feel completely ecstatic on a glass of wine or beer; at other times you can drink a whole bottle of gin and still feel depressed. The alcoholic nevertheless keeps on drinking because this to him seems to be the only way back to the peak experience. And, of course, as they become more resistant to the alcohol, they need larger quantities, and the problem is complicated by a feeling of guilt....

Now Maslow started from the assumption that the alcoholic was probably more intelligent than the average person. He would ask, 'What kind of things gave you a peak experience before you became an alcoholic?' Some would mention visual things — paintings, beautiful scenery; others, poetry, music, ballet. What Maslow and Hoffer then did was to administer a psychedelic drug which produced a kind of artificial 'lift', and then would induce intense peak experiences by means of colours blending on a screen, music, poetry read aloud and so on. They discovered that they got something like an 85 per cent permanent cure rate. Why? Because the alcoholic was like a man on a kind of descending escalator, doing his best to induce peak experiences but remaining essentially passive, allowing the will to remain half-asleep — waiting, in other words, for the alcohol to carry him like a magic carpet into the peak experience. But as soon as he was carried into a far more intense peak experience by the mescalin and poetry, he would recognize clearly that the peak experience depends upon *health*, and that health in turn depends upon a powerful will-drive. Just as the body feels healthiest when you are taking plenty of exercise, so the emotions feel healthiest when the will is well exercised. And as soon as the alcoholic recognized this, he instantly ceased to be an alcoholic. In a sense you could say that he changed drugs, and used will instead of alcohol. Now this seems to me to be getting very close to a solution of the problem of 'impoverished reality'.

Graham Greene stumbled upon another clue, which he describes in an essay called 'The Revolver in the Corner Cupboard'. He describes how, in his teens, his schoolmasters became alarmed because he appeared to dislike sport and sent him to a psychiatrist. After six months of analysis, Greene was much better 'socially adjusted', but found that he was in a state of total depression. He said that everything he looked at appeared to be grey and dull. He could look at some scene which he saw *visually* to be beautiful but about which he felt nothing whatever. He was in this state of inner-deadness when he discovered in a corner cupboard a revolver belonging to his older brother. He took this on to Berkhamsted Common and played Russian roulette — put one bullet in the chambers, pointed it at his head and pulled the trigger. When there was just a click, he looked down the barrel and saw that the bullet had now come into position. So he had missed death by just one chamber. He said that he instantly experienced an overwhelming feeling of ecstasy and happiness. He said, 'It was as if a light had been turned on and I suddenly saw that life is infinitely beautiful.'

I was excited by this story, when I came across it in my early teens, because it shows so clearly what goes wrong with us. When we are bored and tired we are, so to speak, 'spread out'; the will is slack; you are passive, like an exhausted swimmer lying on a beach. The moment Greene pointed the gun at his head and pulled the trigger, he went into violent tension. And when he heard the click, he relaxed. And *that* is the essence of the peak experience. It is a tensing of the will, followed by total relaxation. A movement of contraction followed by expansion. Moreover, the relaxation doesn't work unless you become tense first. It is like those handbrakes on old cars, where you have to pull it towards you and tighten it before it can be released.

Using Greene's insight, I evolved a technique for inducing peak experiences. What I did was this: I would take a pencil and hold it up against a blank wall. I would concentrate intently on the pencil until I saw nothing but the pencil; then I'd let go completely, until I could see the whole background of the wall behind the pencil. Then I would concentrate intently on the pencil again, and then let go again and so on. When I had done that about ten times, I would begin to feel a kind of pain behind the eyes. When you feel that pain, press on as hard as you can, because you are almost there. Two or three more times and suddenly you relax totally into the peak experience. And if you do it with total conviction, it always works. Not long ago in Finland, I was explaining this technique to a class, and in the following session I explained to them about Wilhelm Reich's breathing techniques. Reich said that in order to breathe properly you must take a deep breath, then allow it to go out first of all from the chest, then from the stomach and then finally from the genitals. As Reich made his patients do this, he would say, 'Out, down, through.' I was explaining the Reichian breathing to them as we all lay around on the floor and then, on the spur of the moment, I decided to try and combine it with the 'pencil trick'. Breathing slowly and deeply, we held the pencil up against the ceiling, concentrated intently and then let go. To my astonishment, the two combined perfectly. Within a few minutes, I felt almost as if I had floated up from the floor towards the ceiling. The curious thing is that the total concentration of the pencil exercise and the total relaxation of the breathing exercise somehow combine in the most peculiar way to produce an instant peak experience. We all lay there quietly for well over half an hour, until I looked at my watch and said, 'Hey! We're missing lunch!'

But why does it work? I discovered the answer only a few years ago, when I was reading a book about the split-brain experiments of Roger Sperry and Michael Gazzaniga. I must admit it came to me as a revelation.

What it amounts to is this. If you could take off the top of your head and look down on the brain, it would look like a walnut joined together by a kind of bridge. This bridge is called the *corpus callosum*, or commissure — a block of nerve fibres. In the 1930s it was discovered that severing the commissure would prevent epileptic attacks: it appears to prevent the electrical storm from passing from one side of the brain to the other. Oddly enough, this operation appeared to make no difference whatever to the patient. No one could quite understand why this should be so. Somebody even suggested that the only purpose of the *corpus callosum* is to stop the brain from sagging in the middle. It wasn't until Roger Sperry began repeating these experiments in the 1950s that he discovered that, in fact, there *is* a basic difference in split-brain patients. The difference is that you become two people.

We have known for about a century that the left side of the brain deals with speech, reason, coping with the external world. The right side of the brain deals with pattern recognition and intuition. To put it crudely, the left side is a scientist and the right an artist. For some odd reason, the left side of the brain controls the right side of the body and vice versa — no one knows why. We could also say — I am deliberately over-simplifying — that the left cerebral hemisphere controls the right eye and the right hemisphere controls the left eye. Now if you show a split-brain patient an apple with the left eye and an orange with the right — so that one cannot see what the other is looking at and ask, 'What have I just shown you?', he will reply, 'An orange'. But if you say, 'Write with your left hand what I have just shown you', he will write, 'Apple'. And if you say, 'What have you just written?', he would reply, 'Apple'. In the same way, a patient who was shown a dirty picture with the right side of her brain blushed. When asked why she was blushing, she said, 'I don't know.' One split-brain patient tried to embrace his wife with his right hand while the left tried to push her away. Another tried to do up his flies with his right hand — connected to the logical half of the brain — while the left tried to undo them. Obviously, the two different sides of the brain had completely different intentions.

Now you observe that when the patient is asked, 'What have you seen?' it is the left side of the brain that answers the question. In other words, the person you call 'you' lives in the left side of your head. The person who lives over there in the right-hand side is a total stranger. Now you will say that this is obviously untrue because *we* are not split-brain patients. Yet, in an important sense, we are. Mozart said, for example, that melodies were always walking straight into his head fully formed. What he meant was: melodies were walking out of his right brain into the part of the brain in which *he* lived. And this is true for all of us. Although we are vaguely aware of the right brain and its activities, we are not closely *connected* to it. This explains, for example, why you become self-conscious if someone looks over your shoulder when you are writing. When you are engaged in any interesting task, you 'forget yourself' and become absorbed in what you are doing. The left and right brain enter into close collaboration, the right supplying the intuition, the left supplying the mechanical skills. When someone looks over your shoulder, the left becomes 'self-conscious' and promptly loses contact with the right. The flow of meaning stops, and you feel somehow 'stranded' in the present moment. The same thing would happen if you tried to play a piano attending *to* your fingers. You would play very badly indeed. A good pianist ignores his fingers — he attends *from* the fingers to the music. Attending *to* things is a sure way of screwing yourself up. You must attend *from* them to the meaning.

I could recognize the same process in my activity as a writer. When I first started writing, I found that trying to capture intuitions on paper seemed to strangle the life out of them. When I went back to look at what I'd written the next morning, it wasn't there anymore. The words seemed dead and lifeless. The meaning had evaporated. I even began to suspect that words are a straightjacket that cripple the intuitions. But I kept on trying, because that was all there was to do, and eventually I found that I got good at it. One day, I re-read what I'd written the night before, and it was still there. And after that, I recognized that good writing was an interplay between two halves of the brain, very much like a game of tennis. The right produces the insights and the left turns them into words. If the left verbalizes an insight with particular neatness, the right gets excited and says, 'Yes, yes, that's exactly what I meant!' And the left would say, 'Really? Thank you,' and would proceed to do it even better. And then suddenly the two of them were working together like a couple of top-class tennis players, or like two lumberjacks at either end of a double-handled saw. States like this are obviously what we call inspiration — and they consist of perfect co-operation between the right and the left.

Another interesting thing discovered by Sperry is that the left brain works much quicker than the right. The left is the go-getter. It is turned towards the external world: it copes with reality. The right, on the other hand, appears to be turned inwards, towards our inner world. Its business is to supply us with energy, with strength and purpose; hence, of course, the peak experience.

But because the left is fast and the right is slow, they find some difficulty in reaching a state of empathy. This explains why the peak experiences are relatively rare. The right saunters along slowly with its hands in its pockets; the left walks with a kind of nervous haste. The result is that there is soon a large gap between them and they can no longer hear one another. There seem to be two ways of getting the two halves to work at the same speed. One is to make the left go slower, the other is to make the right go faster. We can make the left go slower by meditation and relaxation. We can make the right go faster by deliberately working ourselves into a state of excitement — this is the aim of African drumming or the repetitive beat of pop music.

Now when this happens you can compare the situation to two trains running on parallel tracks that are suddenly running side by side, so that the people can lean out of the windows and talk to one another. Here you can see we are beginning to grasp the mechanics of the peak experience.

Our basic problem, as you can see, is that the 'you' who lives in the left side of the brain is not even aware that it has this immensely powerful co-worker. You notice this particularly when you feel tense and anxious: the more anxious you become, the more the 'you' tends to take over, and the more it becomes separated from the source of power in the right brain. The more anxious we become, the weaker we become. You can see why I say that we are, in a factual sense, all split-brain patients. In the peak experiences, or those curious moments of total happiness and relaxation, we simply recognize that we have a powerful supporter, a companion who can take half the work from our shoulders.

For here is the important point: the right half of the brain is the creator of energy. He is the one who keeps us supplied with energy and vitality. You could compare the left and right halves to Laurel and Hardy in the old films. The left brain is Ollie, the fat one and the leader of the two. The right brain is much more vague and easy-going — that's Stan. When you wake up on a dull Monday morning, 'you' wake up — that is, Ollie wakes up — and he looks out of the window and thinks, 'Oh God, it's Monday and it's raining ....' Stan overhears him and Stan is, unfortunately, immensely *suggestible*. So he promptly sinks into depression. 'Oh God, it's *Monday* and it's *raining....*' For the trouble with Stan is that he is inclined to over-react. When Ollie is cheerful, Stan is delighted, when Ollie is gloomy, Stan is almost suicidal. But since Stan is in charge of the energy supply, he stops sending up energy when he feels depressed. So when Ollie goes down to breakfast, he feels curiously low and depressed. So he cuts himself while shaving, and trips on the pavement and drops his umbrella, and thinks, 'This is just one of those days when everything goes wrong....' And again Stan overhears him and plunges into even deeper gloom. In short, you will have what you might call a negative feedback situation, in which the misery of one keeps reinforcing the misery of the other.

Conversely, when a child wakes up on Christmas morning, his 'Ollie' says, 'Marvellous, it's Christmas!' And from then on, everything reinforces his feeling of delight and optimism: the decorations on the Christmas tree, the smell of cooking, the Christmas music on the radio.... And both Stan and Ollie finally relax into such a state of trustful happiness that life seems totally transformed. Suddenly, everything is marvellous, and all the problems of yesterday appear trivial and quite unimportant. If we could cling on to this state of mind, human beings would become gods within the next century. And the key undoubtedly lies in the 'feedback mechanism' between Stan and Ollie.

Of course, it is true that there are drugs that will induce this state of intensified consciousness: Thomas De Quincey did it with laudanum. Yet neither alcohol nor drugs are a solution. Their basic effect is to produce a kind of animal consciousness. If you could get inside the skin of a cow or a dog, you would feel just as if you'd had three or four large whiskies. The world would seem pleasantly warm and real. They probably experience permanently the state that we experience only occasionally on beautifully spring mornings. You could say that animals are permanently drunk.

This, incidentally, could be the reason that animals appear to have certain paranormal powers — for example, second-sight. The wife of the Scottish poet Hugh McDiarmid told me that she always knew when he was coming back from a long journey because the dog would go and sit at the end of the lane waiting for him a couple of days before he arrived. Human beings can also achieve these powers when they relax completely; I have noticed this again and again in myself. I am totally ESP-thick until I am either very relaxed or very excited, and when that happens, the two halves are obviously in collaboration and my right begins to tell me the answers. Three or four years ago, I discovered to my astonishment that I could dowse. When a friend offered me a dowsing rod, I told him these things never work for me. He asked me to show him how I held it, and then said, 'You are holding it the wrong way. Twist the two ends in your hands so that there's a spring on the rod.' I did what he said, and walked towards a standing stone in the circle called the Merry Maidens. To my astonishment, the rod suddenly shot up. I was convinced that I had done it accidentally by twisting it, so I walked towards the next one — and it shot up again. Every time I went between the standing stones the dowsing rod twisted in my hands. It was quite obvious that something inside me was reacting to something in the ground or in the stones, but I, who live in my left brain, could feel nothing whatever. What was happening, I suspect, was that my muscles were tensing unconsciously — the striped muscles that are in the control of the right brain. The message was coming from the standing stones into my right brain, and the right brain was telling me that I was near something interesting by causing my muscles to convulse.

This seems to be confirmed by an experiment devised by Sperry. He tried flashing red and green lights at random into the blind eye — the left eye — of split-brain patients, and would ask, 'What colour have you just seen?' Of course, the split-brain patient had no idea. But if he was allowed a second guess he would always get it right, because if he said 'red' and the colour was actually green, he'd convulse as if someone had kicked him under the table. The right brain had heard the wrong guess, and was telling him so by making his muscles convulse — as in dowsing.

All this is to say that we have inside us — as Plato declared — a being who knows far more than we do, and who is perfectly willing to tell us. He is also perfectly willing to send us up any amount of energy; for where energy is concerned, he is the quartermaster whose job is to keep us supplied. Then why doesn't he always do so? Because, more often than not, the telephone line between the two halves is out of order. Tension isolates us in the left brain and separates us from the other half.

There is, of course, another side to this problem. When a man is drunk, he cannot insert the key into the keyhole. He is in a pleasant state of right-brain relaxation — he may even have a beautiful bird's-eye view of the universe — but his ability to concentrate microscopically on details no longer works. We can pay for right-brain relaxation with a certain loss of precision and accuracy, just as we pay for left-brain precision with a loss of right-brain relaxation. It is as if all of us had a telescope attached to one eye and a microscope to the other — the aim being to see into the distance and to be able to study things close-up. But when you look through a microscope, you close one eye. We tend to go around with one eye permanently closed, so we lose our distance-vision. Life becomes a kind of permanent worm's-eye view, an endless, boring close-upness, as unsatisfactory as going into a picture gallery and being forced to peer at all the pictures with your nose only an inch from the canvas. It is only in those curious moments of peak experience that we open both eyes and suddenly can see into the distance as well as what it is in front of our noses. On these occasions, we see the near and the far simultaneously.

L. H. Myers wrote a novel called *The Near and the Far* which expresses this very precisely. At the beginning of the novel, the young Prince Jali has travelled over the desert with his father to some congress of princes called by Akbar the Great. Standing on the battlements of Akbar's castle, he looks out over the desert and thinks, 'What a pity that the desert *looks* so beautiful and feels so exhausting to walk over.' It is as if there were two deserts, one of which is a glory to the eye and the other one a weariness to the foot. Isn't it a pity that we are unable to grasp the mystery and delight of the 'far'? Unfortunately, if you tried to grasp the ecstasy of the distance by rushing downstairs and out of doors, you would just get your shoes full of sand. It appears, Myers said, to be impossible to reconcile the near and the far.

Well, we can see that it is not. This is what the two halves of the brain were *intended* to do. When they work together we can grasp the near and the far simultaneously.

They have another purpose which is even more interesting. In a book called *The Occult*, I wrote about what I called 'Faculty X'. In his *Study of History*, Arnold Toynbee described the experience that led him to begin writing the book. He had been climbing Mount Taygetus in Greece, and was sitting on the ruined walls of the citadel of Mystra, staring out over the plain of Sparta, when suddenly it struck him like a revelation that a few hundred years ago a hoard of barbarians had poured over that wall and destroyed the town, and that ever since then it had been a ruin. This realization was so powerful that he could almost see the barbarians clambering over the wall. Now this sudden curious sense of total reality is what I call Faculty X. Chesterton once said that we say thank you when someone passes us the salt, but we don't really *mean* it. We say the earth is round, but we don't really *mean* it, even though it is true. But when the astronauts went into space, they could say 'the earth is round' and *mean* it. That is Faculty X. When Proust tasted a biscuit dipped in tea, it filled him with a curious feeling of delight as it flooded him with memories of his childhood. He wrote, 'I had ceased to feel mediocre, accidental, mortal.' And when he tried to remember why it had caused him such pleasure, he recalled that when he was a child in Combray, his aunt had always given him a cake dipped in her herb tea when he went to see her, and this taste had suddenly revived the whole of his childhood. That is to say, a moment before he tasted the madeleine, he could say, 'Yes, I was a child in Combray', but he wouldn't have *meant* it. As soon as he tasted the madeleine he could say it and *mean* it: Faculty X.

We can see what has happened. The unconscious part of the brain — and the right appears to be the gateway to the unconscious — has stored up memories of everything that has ever happened to us. But this library of tape recordings is not accessible to you unless you can relax sufficiently to somehow clear the telephone line. Or, to use my other analogy, get the two trains running at the same speed.

As absurd as it sounds, the reason we have two identical halves in the brain is so that we can be in two different places at the same time. We should be capable of being in the present *and somewhere else*. When we are stranded in the present, we lose all sense of perspective. We become lost in mere material reality. Our powers remain blocked and passive until we can achieve that double glimpse of the near and the far. In these moments we cease to be trapped in the worm's-eye view and achieve a bird's-eye view.

And because we are almost permanently trapped in a worm's-eye view, our instinctive feelings about the world tend to be negative. Normal consciousness can be compared to those nightmares when we try to run, but our legs seem too heavy. It is only in those moments of double-consciousness, the near and the far, that we seem to contact some source of power inside ourselves. Hence Proust's comment: 'I had ceased to feel mediocre, accidental, mortal.' *The underpinning of everyday consciousness is basically negative.*

I can recall sitting in a cinema as a child, and as the film ended suddenly realizing that I was feeling intensely happy and optimistic. I thought, 'Why am I feeling so happy?' and then remembered, 'Of course, we broke up from school today, and it's the beginning of the August holiday.' I was feeling happy, and yet the happiness had retreated into my subconscious mind. Not, please note, into the *unconscious* only into that twilight realm between consciousness and the unconscious: the subconscious. You could compare these states of subconscious optimism to a kind of underfloor lighting which creates a kind of rosy glow and makes us feel happy and relaxed. The playwright Granville Barker called it: 'The secret life'. Healthy people have their underfloor lighting permanently switched on — which is why they find it so easy to have peak experiences. But consider again Graham Greene's experience of Russian roulette. When he pulled the trigger and there was just a click, 'It was as if a light had been turned on and I saw that all life was infinitely beautiful.' He had switched on his underfloor lighting by deliberately inducing a crisis.

In the same way, I had an old friend who told me that his dog was subject to fits of depression. One day, he accidentally locked the dog in the cupboard and when it came out, it was bouncing with joy. From then on, whenever the dog became depressed, he would lock it in the cupboard for five minutes, and it would always emerge full of delight.

You see the absurdity? We feel bored or depressed, or just indifferent. A crisis presents itself and fills us with alarm. Then the crisis disappears, so the situation is basically the same as it was before the crisis presented itself. And yet we are now filled with a sense of delight. Moreover, this is not just a 'feeling'. We can *see*, now the crisis has vanished, that we have a thousand reasons for being glad to be alive. It is as if normal consciousness was somehow *blinkered*, like a blinkered horse. And crisis tears off the blinkers.

This is the absurd paradox of human existence. Man knows what he *doesn't* want far more clearly than he knows what he *does* want. As Fichte says: 'To *be* free is nothing; to *become* free is heaven.' There is something preposterous about this. It is like buying an expensive car, and discovering that it will do 90 miles an hour *in reverse* and only 10 miles an hour going forward. Nature seems to have made some kind of basic error in the human design.

Camus makes the same point in his novel *L'Étranger*. His hero Meursault, who has gone through the novel in a state of bored indifference, suddenly wakes up when he is on the point of death, about to be hanged for a murder he did not commit. As the priest tries to persuade him to repent, he suddenly loses his temper and shakes him until his teeth rattle. The result of this discharge of emotion is a sense of immense relaxation and happiness — a feeling of oneness with the universe. He makes the curious statement: 'I realized that I had been happy and I was happy still.' Is it possible to be happy and not to know it? Sperry discovered the answer to that question. It is perfectly possible for one side of the brain not to know what the other is feeling. But *real happiness*, such as Meursault experiences at the end of the novel, only happens when the left and right sides of the brain both feel the same thing.

The director of the BBC's music programme, Hans Keller, once described how, when he was in Germany in the 1930s and Jews were being put into concentration camps, he swore, 'If only I could get out of Germany alive I promise that I would never be unhappy for the rest of my life.' And, to a man whose life was in danger, it would seem obvious that it would be so easy to keep that promise. All he would have to do is to remember what it was like to expect to be arrested and thrown into a concentration camp.

In the same way, Raskolnikov, in *Crime and Punishment*, says, when he thinks he is going to be arrested and executed for murder, 'If I had to stand on a narrow ledge for ever and ever, in eternal darkness and eternal tempest, I would rather do that than die at once.' But what would he *do* on his narrow ledge? It is difficult to put into words, yet every one of us can see the answer. Dr Johnson said that when a man is to be hanged in the morning, it concentrates his mind wonderfully. When the mind is totally concentrated, full of a deep sense of purpose, the right and left brain suddenly begin to work in concert, and consciousness is transformed. Raskolnikov feels that he could stand on a narrow ledge for all eternity because he has the world inside his brain. He is like a man with the whole British Museum library inside his head. And we somehow know instinctively that this library is accessible to us when we can galvanize ourselves into a sense of urgency.

What we are now speaking about is what the Buddha meant by enlightenment. We have nearly translated this into Western terms. We are talking, in other words, about religion. Whenever we are able to relax and see life from a bird's-eye view, we recognize that we are happy and that life is intensely beautiful. This never fails to happen. Any crisis, any stimulus, will release that handbrake inside us, and enable us to go into deep relaxation and the peak experience.

Why then can we not do it except by dangerous expedients like Russian roulette or alcohol or drugs? The problem, we can see, lies in the underfloor lighting. When it is switched off, life is like a dull Sunday afternoon. Let me remind you again of Schumacher's words. 'We see not simply with our eyes but a great part of our mental equipment as well, and since this mental equipment varies greatly from person to person, there are inevitably many things that some people can see and others can't. In other words, for which some people are adequate and others not. When the level of the knower is not adequate to the level of the object of knowledge the result is not factual error but something much more serious: an inadequate and impoverished view of reality.' You could compare this impoverished view of reality to someone who went into a picture gallery lit only by dim lights, and who insists that he can see the pictures perfectly well. And so, in a sense, he can — in the sense of being able to describe any one of them. Yet if someone raised the blinds and let in the sunlight, he will suddenly recognize that he was *not* seeing the pictures. He was only half-seeing them.

And now, I think, we can begin to see our way towards the solution. At least, we have now started to define our terms fairly clearly. We know that everyday consciousness is narrow because it is restricted to left-brain awareness. It lacks that third dimension which is added by right-brain participation. Because we easily slip into boredom, our subconscious premises tend to be negative. We feel the world is basically rather a dull place. Sudden crisis has the effect of shaking the mind awake, and making us realize that the world is full of infinite potential. We were seeing the pictures with the blinds drawn.

If only we could clearly *recognize this*, if we could say it to ourselves again and again until we *know* it to be true, we could gradually reverse this negative assumption that underlies consciousness. *In short, what we must do is to re-programme our underfloor lighting.*

In the 1890s, an American newspaper editor called Thomson J. Hudson became fascinated by hypnosis, and went on to write a classic book called *The Law of Psychic Phenomena*. His interest seems to have begun when he witnessed a hypnotic session in which a rather commonplace young man was placed in a trance by a professor of physiology. The young man was a Greek scholar and the professor pointed to an empty chair and said, 'Allow me to introduce you to Socrates.' The young man bowed reverently to the empty chair. The professor told him that he could ask Socrates any questions he liked — adding that as Socrates was a spirit, the rest of them could not hear him. He asked the young man to repeat aloud what Socrates said. The young man proceeded to ask Socrates various questions, and then repeated his answers, which were so brilliant and apposite that some people present thought that perhaps the spirit of Socrates really was sitting in the chair. After Socrates, they introduced him to various other modern philosophers, and in each case the answers formed a brilliant and self-consistent system of philosophy.

What was happening, of course, is what happens when we dream that we are composing a piece of music, and actually hear magnificent music in our sleep. The right brain seems to have this capacity for sheer creativity.

Hudson observed many such cases, and concluded that we have two people living inside our heads — this was in 1893 — which he called the objective mind and the subjective mind. The objective mind looks out towards the external world and copes with everyday reality — in other words, the left brain. The subjective mind looks inward towards our inner being, and is in charge of our intuitions and our vital energy — in other words, the right brain. The subjective mind, said Hudson, is far more powerful than the objective mind. Under hypnosis, the objective mind is put to sleep, which explains why people become capable of far more under hypnosis than when they are awake. An old trick of stage hypnotists was to tell someone that he would become as stiff as a board, and that when he was placed between two chairs, with his head on one and his feet on the other, two men would jump up and down on his stomach without making him bend in the middle. And of course, he was able to do it. Yet it would have been totally impossible if he was awake. In other words, his 'subjective mind' — or right brain — could make him do extraordinary things *under the orders of the hypnotist*, and yet would not do them under the orders of his own left brain. Why not? Because the right brain believes the hypnotist, but it doesn't believe your left brain. If your left brain told it that it was going to lie between two chairs and support the weight of two men, it would sense the left brain's lack of confidence, and feel totally undermined.

The astonishing conclusion is that what is wrong with us is lack of 'left-brain confidence'. To our generation, this sounds an appalling heresy. D. H. Lawrence and Henry Miller have told us again and again that 'head consciousness' is dangerous and stupid and that we ought to trust the 'solar plexus' — by which they mean our instincts. That sounds very plausible, until we think about hypnosis. Then we can see that the problem is not that 'head consciousness' is overconfident and conceited, but that it is far too weak and diffident.

The translator, Richard Wilhelm, tells an interesting story that underlines the point. A remote Chinese village was suffering from drought, and they finally sent for a rain-maker from some distant province. When he arrived, he asked to be conducted to a house on the edge of the village and ordered them not to disturb him. For three days, no one heard or saw him. Then suddenly it began to rain heavily; in fact, it began to snow too. When the man emerged from the hut, Wilhelm asked him how he had succeeded in making rain. The rain-maker replied, 'I didn't make rain.' 'But it is raining', said Wilhelm. 'But I didn't make it rain,' said the rain-maker. 'I come from a region where everything is in order. It rains when it should and is fine when that is needed. The people are also in order and in themselves. But that was not the case for the people here. They were all out of order and out of themselves. They were not living in the way of Tao. Their attitude infected me when I arrived, so I had to go away on my own for three days until I was once more in Tao. As soon as that happened, it rained naturally.'

In other words, the people of the village had become so infected with a sense of discouragement and defeat that they were somehow making things worse. As soon as they were 'in Tao' — that is, the right and left brains were working in harmony — Nature also fell into harmony, and it began to rain.

According to Taoism, our minds can somehow influence reality. In fact, they do influence reality all the time. If our minds are out of harmony, then so is reality. Jung seems to have had the same intuition when he recognized that 'synchronicity' is not merely another name for coincidence, but is something more meaningful. Synchronicity is a type of coincidence *caused by the mind*.

Maslow, as you know, died more than 20 years ago. Since then, I have come across one other thinker who seems to me to be of comparable importance. It is unlikely that you have heard his name. He is an American doctor called Howard Miller, and he wrote to me some time in the late 1970s. In his letters, he enclosed a couple of his papers. Like Thomson J. Hudson, Miller had become deeply interested in the mystery of hypnosis. One of his patients had been terrified of dental injections, and when he read in a newspaper an advertisement by a dentist that said he could draw teeth under hypnosis, Miller took his patient along to see him. The dentist placed her under hypnosis and then, to Miller's surprise, said, 'What is more, when I pull out the tooth you will not bleed.' This struck Miller as preposterous; you can't tell a person not to bleed. Yet indeed when the tooth came out the patient did not bleed.

Miller began to try it on his own patients. He discovered that he was good at hypnosis, and tried hypnotizing terminal cancer patients. He began to obtain astonishing remissions, which convinced him once again that there is something in the brain which is far more powerful than the ordinary conscious self.

However, Miller went a very important stage beyond Hudson. Miller asked himself, 'What is it that actually gives the order to the autonomic nervous system and prevents the bleeding?' His answer was, 'The hypnotist is *replacing* the "you" in your brain and giving the orders in its place. Which means that if the "you" in your brain could give the orders with sufficient authority, you could stop bleeding without the intervention of a hypnotist.'

(Incidentally, there is a hypnotist in the Wirral called Joe Keeton who is curing cancer patients by means of hypnosis — completely and totally curing them. He even had remarkable success with a girl whose heel had been completely destroyed in a motorcycle accident: he somehow caused her to regrow the heel under hypnosis. He believes that what he is doing is simply getting through deep into the autonomic nervous system and reactivating certain healing powers which all human beings possess.)

Now Miller said that the key to all this is the 'you', the person who lives in the cerebral hemispheres of the brain and which he calls 'the unit of pure thought'. (Miller holds the somewhat paradoxical view that the brain is a mere *amplifier* of thought, which somehow originates beyond the brain. This is why he calls the creator of thought 'the unit of pure thought'.)

I read all this, and thought, 'Very interesting, but it isn't new. All Miller has done is to rediscover what the philosopher Husserl called the "transcendental ego".' So I wrote back to Miller, thanking him for his papers and telling him about Husserl. He was obviously disappointed by my response.

About three months later, I had finished a very hard day's writing and I went out for a walk on the cliff. Now I have got used to the fact that if I have been writing hard and I go for a walk, I can't relax fully. My brain goes grinding on, and somehow I just don't enjoy the scenery. And I discovered a long time ago that the best way to induce a state of appreciation is to play a kind of 'Russian roulette' with myself. What I do is to tense myself as fully as I possibly can, and then when I am fully, totally tense, I let go. And when I do that, suddenly I can *see* the scenery, and I feel completely relaxed. Well, I did this on this particular occasion, and then found myself thinking, 'What precisely did you just do? What part of you gave the order?' And I answered, 'It was just *me* — my left brain.' Then I thought, 'No, surely, that is impossible. The left brain is just my logical self, and everyone knows that it is the villain — the person who stands in the way of inspiration.' I brooded about it for the rest of my walk, and came to the conclusion that it *was* my left brain that had given the order. And my right had relaxed because the left gave it with sufficient determination and authority. Then, suddenly, I realized that Miller was completely right. I wrote to him that evening to tell him so. And I re-read his paper — 'What Is Thought?' — with far more attention.

What Miller points out is that the brain is basically an enormous computer. It was the surgeon Wilder Penfield who discovered that if, during brain surgery, he accidentally touched a point in the temporal cortex, the patient was suddenly flooded with detailed memories of his childhood. The experiment makes it very clear that our brain is an enormous library.

In the same way, when a tune gets stuck in your head, you feel as if your brain contains a gramophone record that has got stuck in the groove. We have, in other words, a feeling that we have no control over our own mental states.

Yet, said Miller, let us try a different experiment. Try closing your eyes and conjure up a mental image. You will quickly realize that you can, *on demand*, evoke from the brain any image you desire and cause it to be projected on a kind of inner mental screen. Order your brain to produce an image of yourself on the beach, see yourself there in total reality, visualize the colour of your bathing suit, the feel of the sand, the heat of the sun.... Now instantly *order* the scene to be changed; ask a new film to be brought out. Imagine yourself at the base of a very tall mountain, look up to its summit, feel the sting of the frosty air, hear the feet crunching on the icy snow — and now on command, dissolve the entire mountain.

If you take the trouble, you can become aware of the distinction between your 'observer' and the scene you are observing. These scenes were being called into existence by the *thought* that preceded them. Your 'unit of pure thought' gave the order and your brain obeyed. You *are* in control of the computer.

What is wrong with human beings is basically that we do not *realize* that we are in control. 'Lack of this awareness', says Miller, 'has kept us from picking up the reins and taking control of our own brains'. The situation could be compared to a man sitting in the cinema, watching a film that seems completely scrambled and haphazard, and wondering what on earth has gone wrong in the projection room. He goes up into the projection room and discovers that, in fact, there is no one there. And then, with a sudden shock, he remembers: *he* himself is the projectionist. We can only take control of our brains, says Miller, when we recognize that we are the projectionists.

Now I would suggest that we have stumbled upon two basic ideas that might form the foundation of a new religion. The first of these is the recognition that the 'you' is basically the master of consciousness: it is in charge of what goes on inside our heads. The second is that the way in which we can establish contact with the enormous powers of the 'hidden self' is by *reprogramming the subconscious mind* into a positive instead of a negative attitude. The Hindu saint Ramakrishna did it accidentally. He was in a state of misery and despair because his inner life had become dull and inert. In desperation, he seized a sword, and was about to drive it through his heart when he said, 'Suddenly, the Divine Mother revealed herself, and I was overwhelmed by waves of shining light.' The ecstasy was so intense that he became unconscious. He had experienced the state called *samadhi*. And from this time on, he only had to hear the name of the Divine Mother to go into *samadhi*. In other words, the experience had totally reprogrammed his subconscious mind, and he could induce *samadhi* by pushing a kind of mental button.

Now I think you should be able to see what I mean about reprogramming the subconscious. Whenever you experience any kind of delight, whenever you experience those momentary visions of intensity, it is important to hang on to them and use the insight to re-programme your subconscious, because *this* is the best time to do it. Provided you do it in the moment of vision or insight, the subconscious can be totally reprogrammed. What you are trying to do is to *grasp* that 'bird's-eye vision' so that you can never forget it. It could be compared to trying to take a kind of aerial photograph, remembering all the salient points of the landscape below you before you plunge back to earth again.

One more example. When I was lecturing in Vancouver at Simon Frazer University, I spent a whole week talking to my students about these things, and at the end of that time I felt exhausted. I had been trying to teach them the 'pen trick' — the trick of driving yourself to a point of concentration where the brain almost rebels, and then deliberately forcing yourself one stage further. I told them about a friend of mine, Bill Powell, who used to climb Nelson's Column in Trafalgar Square. He used to do this by putting a huge belt around the column and then edging his way up until his feet were level with the belt. He would then hitch the belt up, momentarily bending his knees and then walking up again until he was level with the belt. Bill said, 'The trouble is, when you are halfway up, your knees hurt like mad and you just want to relax. But, of course, if you do, you would go straight down to the bottom.' Well, it's the same with the discipline of the mind. And I told my students, 'When it hurts, for God's sake *don't* let go. You are nearly there.'

A couple of hours later, driving home to the motel where I was staying, I could look down on the whole of Vancouver and its bay. The lights were just coming on, and it looked beautiful. I found myself thinking, 'Isn't it absurd. It looks beautiful but I am too bloody tired to appreciate it.' And then suddenly I thought, 'Wilson, you fool, you have been telling them all day that when they are in this state, they are almost there.' I made a tremendous effort, and it happened instantly: the whole bay seemed to explode and become suddenly incredibly beautiful.

The absurd thing was that I had almost forgotten. I was allowing my brain to churn on mechanically, merely looking forward to getting back home and pouring myself a drink. This is the danger: giving way to our *automatic mechanisms*. Yet because I knew, intellectually, that I could do it, I was able to side-step the mechanisms and achieve the peak experience. And I did it basically by suddenly *remembering* to make the additional effort.

We *can* do it. The power is already there in the brain. Everything is already there inside us. The Buddha was right: the key to peace lies inside us and always has. And now we can begin to understand it in Western scientific terms, it means that 'enlightenment' is no longer one of those mystical words with no precise meaning.

One final thought. Maslow discovered that when he began to talk to his students about peak experiences, they began to remember all kinds of occasions on which they'd had peak experiences — occasions that they'd almost forgotten about. And as soon as they began to remember and discuss peak experiences, *they began having peak experiences all the time.*

Merely talking and thinking about it had reprogrammed the subconscious.

Most Western thinkers seem to agree that the world is in an appalling state, and that the correct attitude is pessimism tempered by cautious hope. For my own part, I believe that man has arrived at the most interesting point in his evolution, and that the future has never looked more promising. It is because Schumacher shared that sense of optimism that I hold his memory in so much affection.

THE HUMAN CONDITION

A Postscript to the Schumacher Lecture, 1984

The Schumacher lecture seems to me one of the clearest and most compressed summaries of my ideas. Its conclusion — that the basic method of crating 'affirmation consciousness' is by 'reprogramming the subconscious' — goes to the heart of the matter. But how is this reprogramming to be accomplished? To explain this requires a summary of my view of 'the human condition'.

From the moment they are born, human beings are entangled in subjective emotions. Our senses do their best to give us a clear and accurate picture of the world around us. But their testimony is always being undermined by the fluctuation of our feelings, which offer us a different 'truth' every ten minutes. When you are hungry, food is self- evidently 'good'. When you are being violently sick, it seems disgusting. When a man is in love, the girl seems the most desirable creature in the world; when she is suing for divorce, she seems repulsive.

While fluctuations as great as this are the exceptions, dozens of smaller ones occur every day. As my feelings ebb and flow, my attitude towards the world changes continually. I may feel that life is infinitely exciting at ten in the morning and that it is dreary and repetitious by four in the afternoon. The commonest of all experiences is to look forward to something and then find it rather disappointing. Occasionally it is the other way round: something we had expected to be unpleasant and boring turns out to be rather enjoyable. But it all seems to be totally unpredictable. This un-predictableness also affects my powers of action. Something I decide to do at ten in the morning seems quite futile at four in the afternoon. Decision-making in such a world can be as frustrating as Alice's game of croquet with flamingos instead of mallets and balls that uncurl themselves and run away. This is why so many philosophers have concluded that life is 'vanity of vanities', and that the best way to avoid disappointment is to abandon all hope and expect the worst.

As we grow up and develop the power of reason, we do our best to make adjustments for these changes of mood. In many ways we succeed. We learn to smile at people we dislike. We resist various temptations. We eat food we know to be good for us even though we enjoy it less than food that is bad for us. Yet we still go on making judgements that betray total subjectivity. One man detests sport and regards people who enjoy it as idiots. Another hates pop music and is convinced that people who enjoy it must be tone deaf. Another believes that a certain political party is a collection of crooks and charlatans. If someone suggests to these people that their prejudices are purely subjective, they will become indignant, for they are convinced that their views are based on logic and reason. All this amounts to what William James called 'a certain blindness in human beings'.

It may seem that this blindness does no real harm. If I dislike sport, I can watch some other television channel. If I hate pop music, I can avoid listening to it. If I distrust a certain political party, I can vote for its rival. But the real objection to the 'blindness' is that it causes us to waste our lives by keeping us trapped in a narrow and trivial state of consciousness. And this suddenly dawns upon us when some serious challenge or crisis threatens us with major disruption — perhaps even with death. Quite suddenly, we see life from a 'bird's-eye view', and we *know*, beyond all doubt, that life without this threat would be a continual delight. This is the feeling of 'absurd good news'.

The worst of it is that we know perfectly well that, as soon as the threat is past, we shall sink back into the old state of narrowness and blindness. It is then that we grasp the damage caused by 'subjectivity', and the way it ruins our lives. For we can *see* that, objectively speaking, we have a thousand reasons for congratulating ourselves. It is true that there are many people in the world with real cause for misery: poverty, starvation, physical pain. But most people in the civilized world enjoy a fairly high degree of comfort and security. They ought to regard their lives as a perpetual holiday. The 'blindness' makes us incapable of grasping how lucky we are.

This recognition struck me forcibly during the period of 'panic attacks' (described in the introductory chapter of *Mysteries*.) Plunged into a state of depression, weighed down with a heavy feeling of foreboding, I asked myself whether there was any objective reason to feel so miserable, and the answer was obviously no. In fact, it took very little reflection to see that I ought to be ecstatically happy. So I was in the strange position of recognizing, logically, that I ought to be bubbling with optimism while my subconscious mind sent back messages of gloom and foreboding. I discovered that, with a tremendous effort, I could *impose* my objective perceptions on my subjective feelings, and heave myself bodily into a state of optimism. Half an hour later, the foreboding was back again; but at least I had come to recognize that it could be made to go away.

For this reason I regard the panic attacks as one of the most important experiences of my life. They taught me something that I could never have grasped otherwise: that we do not have to accept the continual switchback of emotions that dominates everyday consciousness. It was a startling discovery — rather like realizing that when clouds obscure the sun, you do not have to wait for them to drift away: you can *blow* them away. The final arbiter is *the mind itself.*

I expressed it by saying that consciousness has a 'bass line' of subjectivity and an 'alto line' of objectivity. It could be compared to Brooklyn Bridge, with the roadway down below, and the superstructure soaring in a gigantic arch up above. It seems natural for human beings to follow the roadway. Yet in our moments of intensity, we see that this is laziness. If we want to understand what consciousness is *for*, we have to follow the superstructure.

The panic attacks made me understand that *'everyday consciousness' is a form of depression.* Because we accept its judgements as natural and inevitable, we drift along without making any real effort. But if we begin to question its judgements, to resist its moods, to reject its over-simplifications, we gradually begin to understand the kind of consciousness we were intended to experience.

Even a brief experience of objective consciousness brings a fascinating insight: that subjective consciousness is somehow *incomplete.* It never achieves its natural state of fulfilment. It could be compared to an engine that has been allowed to deteriorate until it works at only a fraction of its true efficiency. The washers are loose, the piston-rings are worn, the gaskets are burnt, the plugs are oiled-up. So most of the energy it produces escapes in leakages.

But the odd thing about the engine called the human mind is that it is self-repairing. The moment some intense stimulus causes it to build up a higher pressure than usual, it seals its own leaks, and begins to work at a far greater level of efficiency. The result is a revelation. Quite suddenly, reality becomes more 'real'. There is a curious effect as if all the colours of the world have become deeper and richer, and as if everything had become somehow more solid, more hard and real. But what is most surprising is the sudden clear recognition that this 'ordinary' consciousness, which we have always taken for granted as the only kind of consciousness, is a poor substitute for the real thing. Mystics have always experienced this insight, and found it hard to put into words simply because all our language is based upon the premise that 'ordinary consciousness' *is* the real thing. A writer named R. H. Ward, who experienced a glimpse of this higher type of consciousness when lying in the dentist's chair, described the sensation as follows: '...I passed, after the first few inhalations of the gas, directly into a state of consciousness already far more complete than the fullest degree of ordinary waking consciousness....' *

In my own experiences of these states — which, I hasten to add, have never achieved the intensity described here by Ward — there has always been a clear recognition that ordinary consciousness is limited by its lack of energy, like an electric light when the power is low. The sensation could also be compared to driving a car with a heavily frosted windscreen, in the centre of which you have scraped a circular hole that gives you a certain limited view. But until the heater has defrosted the windscreen, you are forced to lean forward, peering through the hole, driving at five miles an hour in low gear. The problem, of course, is that the small hole limits what you see, so you are only receiving enough information to stay on the road and avoid hitting something. Ordinary consciousness has this same narrow quality, so it can only offer us the most essential, basic information. Glimpses of Ward's 'completer' state of consciousness make us aware that they are not really 'higher' forms of awareness, but merely a step in the direction of true 'normality' — with the windscreen completely clear of frost.

This recognition about the nature of consciousness is in no way abstract or 'mystical'. It can be arrived at by reason. Consider what happens when I am faced with some problem or inconvenience. I am galvanized into brooding on how it can be solved; I concentrate my forces. This has the effect of switching on a kind of red light in my subconscious mind, an 'underground' sense of vigilance and anxiety. When I solve the problem, the red light changes to green, and I experience a sensation of relief and delight. If the red light has been on for a long time, then the relief and delight will also last a long time. I may wake up every morning for day after day with the feeling 'Thank God *that's* solved'. But sooner or later, the relief fades, and I take the solution of the problem for granted. What happens? I am not actually ungrateful for my new state of non-anxiety. But I 'put it into storage', so to speak. I consign it to the realm of the 'taken for granted', a kind of 'forgetfulness'. For I am already focusing on new problems and how

* *A Drug-Taker's Notes*, p. 26.

to solve them. And in due course, my gratitude for solving them will also be put into storage in the realm of 'forgetfulness'.

Now in a sense, this seems absurd. If a threat is really overwhelming, I tell myself that 'if only' I can solve it, I shall never cease to feel relieved.... And I can see that this is perfectly possible. A mother whose child is dangerously ill may tell herself that, if he recovers, she will never cease to offer prayers of thanksgiving. And she may well keep her promise. The fact remains that it is extremely difficult to keep a sense of relief and gratitude alive for a long period, simply because *we require our consciousness for other things.* So to some extent, 'forgetfulness' is a necessity of existence.

This means that all of us have a vast cupboard full of reasons for gratitude, all labelled and preserved, but out of sight. When a man owns his first car, he looks at it with pride every morning. By the time he buys his fourth car, he is taking it for granted; his gratitude is now packed away in the storage cupboard. But if he gets into debt, and has to contemplate selling his car, his sense of its value is once again reactivated. The storage cupboard is not a graveyard; all its contents can be taken out for inspection and 'reactivated'.

So in a perfectly logical sense, we have a thousand reasons for feeling relief and delight. Moreover, our species has accumulated another million. If we could look backwards through time and see our ancestors in the Pleistocene era, six hundred thousand years ago, crouching, half-starved, in caves while the snowdrifts piled up outside, we would recognize just how many triumphs, how many conquests, how many problems solved, are represented by a modern city.

Yet clearly, it would be impossible for us to be 'mindful' of even a tiny percentage of these 'reasons for delight'. Is not this in itself a sufficient explanation for the narrowness of everyday consciousness?

The answer is no. For here we come to the most interesting part of the story. Again and again, these half-forgotten 'reasons for delight' emerge from the storage cupboard of their own accord, and 'reactivate' themselves. It happens most frequently when I solve another problem. The feeling of relief causes the 'green light' to glow in my subconscious mind, and quite suddenly, it has ceased to be a *particular* feeling of delight, and has turned into something far more broad and general. Suddenly, *all* life seems good — even a life crowded with problems. But there is even more to it than that. We experience a strange sense of excitement and optimism as we realize that this sense of delight is always accessible to consciousness. There is no need to wait for the solution of yet another problem. *We can do it ourselves.*

How? The answer becomes clear if we study the mechanism of the delight experience — what Maslow calls the peak experience. I have said that when we are confronted with some problem or anxiety, a 'red light' goes on in the subconscious. When the problem is overcome, a green light goes on. In fact, a whole range of coloured lights are switched on until the subconscious mind looks like the Blackpool illuminations. We might refer to this as 'underfloor lighting'.

What has happened? If we think in terms of the 'Laurel and Hardy theory of consciousness' (described elsewhere in this book), Ollie has passed on the good news to Stan — the right brain — and Stan switches on the underfloor lighting. Note that Ollie merely has to *tell* Stan. Or rather, Ollie tells himself ('Thank God, everything's all right after all!'), and Stan overhears. The moment the underfloor lighting is switched on, consciousness takes on a third dimension. Husserl says: 'The natural wakeful life of the ego is a perceiving.' And this 'perceiving' consciousness is flat, two dimensional. The moment I am flooded with joy or relief, *everything* is affected. Reality becomes more real. Everything I look at is seen to be more meaningful, more interesting, than I had realized when my consciousness was 'flat'. I see that I have a thousand reasons for delight and optimism.

As soon as this happens, I am struck by an exhilarating realization. If this is *true*, if reality is really 'three dimensional', then I do not have to wait for the solution of some problem, or the disappearance of some crisis, to feel delight. I have a permanent reason in the fact that reality is three-dimensional. If I can grasp this, I can get rid of two-dimensional consciousness once and for all.

But if two-dimensional consciousness is 'dispensable', then why do we have it? In the '3-D' states, the answer is quite plain. Because everyday consciousness is quite unnecessarily *negative*. It is almost entirely a matter of bad habits. We are always working ourselves up into states of anxiety about trivialities. So we spend a large part of our lives in an unnecessary state of 'discouragement' and disenchantment. The result is an effect of 'negative feedback', with discouragement producing a flat, bored state of perception, and this state of perception confirming us in the view that nothing is really worth the effort.

The source of this problem is the 'emotional body'. Anyone who pays attention to the ebb and flow of mood and feeling becomes aware that we possess an emotional as well as a physical body. But while the physical body reaches maturity at the age of twenty or so, the emotional body in most of us remains in a state of arrested development from about the age of ten. This is one of the penalties of civilization, which protects us from the cradle to the grave. Our ancestors had a far harder time of it, and had to acquire a far higher degree of self-discipline, enabling the emotional body to reach a higher level of maturity (say, fifteen instead of ten years of age). Prod most civilized men, and you find a child just below the surface.

All this explains why we have a craving for adventure, for excitement, even for danger and discomfort; we know instinctively that this is the most direct way of forcing the emotional body into some kind of maturity, and preventing it from ruining our lives.

But the insights of 'three-dimensional consciousness' are themselves a direct method of overcoming the problem. If we make the effort to grasp their meaning, the result is the flash of what is traditionally called 'enlightenment'. It suddenly becomes self-evident that knowledge itself can break this vicious circle of negativity. Once 3-D awareness has achieved even a toe-hold, it can gradually dislodge the old bad habit of 2-D awareness.

The chief danger here is failure to grasp exactly what is happening when we experience 3-D consciousness. If it comes as a result of a holiday, or some relief from anxiety, or a sudden reason for celebration, we may feel that it is merely a temporary break from 'normality', and that, like a pleasant weekend, it has to be followed by a return to the old dreary routine. Worse still, we may experience the feeling 'This is too good to last', and expect it to vanish like a dream. This, in fact, is how most of us tend to react to glimpses of 'completer consciousness'. This particular problem can be solved by thoroughly absorbing the arguments of the preceding pages. In a sense, that is the least of our problems.

'Completer consciousness' involves another insight that seems to contradict our everyday assumptions. When I open my eyes in the morning, it is natural for me to feel that I have emerged from an 'inner' world of unconsciousness into the 'real' world that I share with my fellow human beings. I am now, so to speak 'in' that external world, and shall stay in it until I close my eyes tonight and sink back into my inner world.

In flashes of objective consciousness, we can see that this is a misconception. There is a world 'out there', stretching around me as far as the eye can see; and there is an equally vast world 'in here'. In *Heaven and Hell*, Aldous Huxley pointed out that 'like the earth of a hundred years ago, our mind still has its darkest Africas and Amazonian basins'. He was discussing the strange insights that came to him as a result of taking the psychedelic drug mescalin. But this 'inner world' may be understood in an altogether more practical and down-to-earth sense. In 1933, Dr Wilder Penfield, a neurosurgeon, was performing a brain operation on a conscious patient, using only local anaesthetic, when he happened to touch the temporal cortex with an electric probe. The patient instantly recalled in detail an event from his childhood; in fact, he virtually re-lived the event. Penfield performed the same experiment over many years, and found that it always had the same effect; part of the vast memory archives of the brain suddenly disgorged their content.

As pointed out elsewhere in this book,* Proust had the same experience when he tasted a cake dipped in herb tea, and was suddenly flooded with a sense of the reality of his childhood. Proust makes the interesting comment: 'I had ceased to feel mediocre, accidental, mortal....' Three-dimensional consciousness had produced the 'god-like sensation', the sudden recognition that we *all* underestimate ourselves and our powers.

When some crisis has disappeared, and we heave a sigh of relief, the feeling of 'absurd good news' is accompanied by a sense of the reality of this world inside my head. In fact, when I relax deeply, I am aware of sinking into this world inside my head. Most children can do it easily; you can watch a child stick his thumb into his mouth, gaze into the fire and float off into that inner world on a kind of magic carpet. Some adults retain this capacity. In his book on Shelley, Thomas Jefferson Hogg remarks that the poet was always reading — over meals, in bed, even walking along the street — and that he became totally absorbed in the book, to the exclusion of the outside world. He also had a capacity to fall asleep at any moment like a baby; he would often move from his chair to the floor, curl up like a cat and sleep deeply. Like most poets, Shelley was very much a 'right brainer', and 'access to inner worlds' came easily to him.

Once we have grasped this concept of an 'inner world', we can see that we *always* inhabit it, even when we feel most trapped in external reality. And when I intensely enjoy any experience, it is because I am simultaneously in two worlds at once: the reality around me and the reality inside me. When a man deeply enjoys a book, it is as if he has taken the book into a cave inside himself, where he can be free from interruption. When he is absorbed in playing golf, he has taken the golf course inside him. When he is absorbed in making love, he has taken the girl inside him. The deeper he can retreat into that inner world, the more he can enjoy his experience of the outer world. Conversely, when he feels trapped in the outer world by boredom or tension, all his experience becomes unsatisfying and superficial. In order to begin to understand the mechanism of 3-D consciousness, we need to recognize the independent reality of that inner world, and to grasp the error of the view that we are creatures of the physical world around us.

*'Magic, the Science of the Future'.

We should also note that Shelley's capacity for 'absorption' meant that he could 'enter into' a book and abandon himself to its reality. When a man is in a state of boredom or tension, he cannot 'enter' the book, and so cannot experience its reality. What do I do if I read some description by Dickens or Balzac and feel so absorbed that I actually seem to be there? I somehow add my own experience to the description, so it 'becomes real'. This is what Proust did spontaneously as he tasted the cake dipped in tea. This is what Arnold Toynbee did spontaneously as he sat in the citadel of Mistra and became aware of the reality of its destruction. In short, we are speaking of the capacity I have labelled 'Faculty X'.

As soon as we experience the flash of 'three-dimensional consciousness', we recognize that this *is* 'normal' consciousness — or at least, a step in the right direction. Ordinary consciousness is a mistake. It is an error that has been created by our 'intermediate' stage of evolution. Left-brain awareness — the ability to examine the world through a magnifying glass — is essential, but its 'close-upness' has deprived us of meaning. We are stranded in an oversized world of magnified objects, and we can see the trees but not the wood. And at this point, the emotional body intervenes, with its negativity and self-pity and mistrust, and turns the wood into a forest of nightmare. This is the state that Sartre calls 'nausea', and that I have called 'depression'. It can be overcome only by recognizing that it *is* a mistake. And the 'absurd good news' is the recognition that this insight, in itself, can transform subjective into objective consciousness. The bogies created by the mind can be destroyed by the mind.

ADDITIONS TO THE ORIGINAL 1985 EDITION

1. 'Inside the White Tower' from *Spider World: The Tower*
[Chosen by Nicolas Tredell]

2. 'Below the Iceberg' from *Below the Iceberg,
Anti-Sartre and Other Essays*
[Chosen by Vaughan Rapatahana]

3. 'The Seventh Degree of Consciousness' from
The Books in My Life
[Chosen by Geoff Ward]

4. 'The Fifth Window' from *The Misfits*
[Chosen by Gary Lachman]

5. 'The Psychology of Optimism' from *Adbusters: Journal of the Mental
Environment*, vol. 14, no. 1
[Chosen by Colin Stanley]

6. 'The Future of Mankind' from *A Criminal History of Mankind*,
2005 edition.
[Chosen by Colin Stanley]

INSIDE THE WHITE TOWER

From *Spider World: The Tower*
Grafton, 1987

Extracted from the first volume of the science fantasy tetralogy. The hero Niall finds his way into the city of the death spiders and gains entry to the mysterious white tower. Here a human simulation called Steeg explains that the tower is a museum for the history of the Earth before it was evacuated by humans when a radioactive comet approached. The following is Niall's history lesson…

Niall positioned himself once more on the bed underneath the blue metal canopy; again, the light came on as soon as his body sank into its yielding surface. Then the enormous sense of peace and relaxation once more washed gently through his nervous system, bringing an upsurge of tremendous joy. But this time there was no desire to sleep. He was conscious of some point above his head, like an eye looking down from behind the opaque glass and conveying images directly into his brain. It was a strange process, not unlike dreaming. At the same time, a voice seemed to speak inside his chest, although it was not using human language; instead, it was evoking in him the insights and responses that language would have aroused.

When he closed his eyes, he saw the spider city spread out before him as he had first seen it from the gap in the hills: that city of immense square towers — which he now knew were called skyscrapers — with the great river dividing it into two. Then, as if he was rising vertically into the air, the city was below him. Moments later, he could see the sea, and the harbour with its great stone blocks. Then both the city and the harbour dwindled below him until they were reduced to one single point in a broad green plain. He could see the land on the other side of the ocean, and the red desert beyond the mountains. Somewhere there was the burrow, where his dead father lay. As soon as he tried to see it more clearly, the mental image became static and he was able to trace the contours of the great plateau, and of the great salt lake south of Dira. Then, once more, he was rising, so that he could see the lands to the south of the salt lake and to the north of the spider city. His speed increased until he could see the curve of the earth's surface, and the green lands below began to blend into a light blue, while the sea itself became darker. Soon he could see the earth as a furry ball, turning slowly in space. The stars looked enormous and brilliant, as if made of a kind of crystallized ice that was illuminated from inside. To his right, the sun was a ball of exploding radiance that hurt his eyes, so he had to look away. The moon was now a vast silver globe — it seemed strange to realize that it was a sphere when he had seen it all his life as a flat golden plate floating through the clouds. And although only part of its surface was illuminated by the sun, he could clearly see its darkened areas by the brilliant light of the stars.

Then they were out in space, up above the plane of the solar system, so far that the sun itself was hardly larger than an eyeball. One by one, Niall was made aware of the planets in their elliptical orbits: of Mercury, that tiny ball of red hot iron whose surface is as cracked as a wizened apple, of Venus, swathed in its atmosphere of sulphurous mist, of Mars with its frozen red deserts, of Jupiter, the vast red giant made of bubbling liquid, of the grey wanderer Saturn, whose immense bulk consists mainly of frozen hydrogen, and of Uranus, Neptune and Pluto, whose temperatures are so low that they are little more than floating balls of ice. Niall felt chilled and overawed by the sheer size of the solar system. From the orbit of its outermost planet, Pluto, the sun looked the size of a pea, while the earth was an almost invisible pinhead.

When Niall's attention returned to the present, he realized with a shock that he had forgotten who he was. This experience had absorbed him so completely that his identity seemed slightly absurd. In the past, he had frequently 'lost himself' in daydreams, or in stories told by his mother or grandfather. These had ignited his imagination; but compared with this experience, they seemed no more than a spark compared to a bonfire. It left him stunned and breathless, feeling like a man who has suddenly awakened from a dream. Immense forces were stirring inside him. He longed to ask a thousand questions, to be allowed to visit every planet in turn, then to voyage through space to other stars and solar systems. He experienced something like despair at the thought that knowledge was infinite and his own life so short.

As these thoughts disrupted his inner peace like an earthquake, the wordless voice inside him seemed to advise him to be patient. The negative emotions were dissolved away; instead he experienced a consuming appetite for knowledge, a desire to devote the rest of his life to learning and understanding.

'Ask any questions you like,' the old man's voice said. 'The Steegmaster contains the sum of all human knowledge. It is for you to decide what you want to know.'

'Could you tell me about the earth before the spiders came, and about the men who built this city?'

'For that we need to go back nearly five thousand million years, to the birth of the solar system ....'

As he closed his eyes again, the voice was no longer coming from the old man but from inside him. Now he was watching a blinding explosion that seemed to fill all space, and that hurled great spirals of gas away from its centre like the arms of an octopus. The explosion seemed to go on forever, sending wave after wave of searing, destructive energy into space. Then, very slowly, it subsided, and its own gravity turned the initial explosion into an implosion. The remaining gases, sucked back together again, began to rotate in an immense whirlpool. Gradually, in the freezing cold of space, it lost its heat until the gases condensed into drops of liquid. Half a billion years later, these droplets had condensed into ten planets. Some, like Mercury, were too hot to retain an atmosphere; some, like Mars, were too small and too cold. Only the earth, nearly a hundred million miles away from the sun, was neither too hot nor too cold.

The formation of the planet was as violent as its birth. Comets and fragments of planets crashed into it, churning it into a mass of boiling mud. It took two billion years for the earth to cool from a seething inferno into a planet with seas and continents. By then, it had shrunk to about a thousandth of its original size. And the sun had also been shrinking steadily, until it reached a point where nuclear reactions began and it turned from a dark globe into a dull red mass, then into a raging atomic furnace. Its ultra-violet rays penetrated the earth's thin atmosphere — mostly of hydrogen and ammonia —— and caused violent electrical storms. And as the gases and water vapour were subjected to this bombardment, the first complex molecules began to form — the sugars and amino-acids. There also appeared a molecule called DNA — deoxyribonucleic acid — which had the peculiar property of duplicating itself. It was DNA that created the first form of life on earth – the bacteria. The bacteria possessed only one simple instinct — to gobble up the organic compounds floating around them in the warm seas, and so steal their energy. Life began as an energy-vampire.

At this early stage, life was almost destroyed by its own success. Bacteria flourished so abundantly that they had soon eaten up most of the organic compounds in the sea. Life would have vanished as quickly as it started if one of these bacteria had not discovered a new trick: manufacturing its own food by absorbing the energy of the sun. By this process — known as photosynthesis — the bacteria learned to make sugar from carbon dioxide and water. They absorbed the sunlight through a chemical called chlorophyll, and the chlorophyll gave these tiny organisms a green colour. Soon, the rocks around earth's continents — there were four immense continents at this time — were stained with a green, slimy substance, the first algae. And the blue-green algae drank the carbon dioxide from the earth's atmosphere and turned it back into oxygen.

Another immense period of time drifted past, during which the earth's atmosphere became increasingly rich in oxygen. Once more, life was in danger of destroying itself through its own success — for to plants, oxygen is a poison, and an earth that contained only plants would die from lack of carbon dioxide. But before this could happen, a new life form appeared — a form that could absorb oxygen and change it into carbon dioxide. These tiny blobs of swimming jelly were the first animals.

As Niall looked down on the earth of a billion years ago, he saw a peaceful and static planet whose warm seas lapped gently on the shores of the barren continents — or rather, on the shores of the barren continent, for the four continents had now drifted together to form one immense land mass known to geologists as Pangaea. On this placid globe, nothing ever changed. For, oddly enough, there was no death. These primitive amoebas and worms and algae shed their old cells and grew new ones, and went on living for ever.

And then, somehow, life invented death, and all the amazing complexities of evolution became possible. What happened is that these simple living creatures learned how to reproduce themselves, so the parent could die, and the young take over.

A creature that goes on living for millions of years falls into a lazy rhythm of existence. It knows how to survive, and that is enough. But when a new creature is born, it knows nothing whatever. It has to fight to establish a foothold. And it has to develop the power to *remember* what it has learned. An immortal creature has no need of memory; it learned the basic tricks of survival millions of years ago ... A new-born creature has to pack its learning into a very short period, otherwise it will not survive. The ancient, immortal organisms were mere vegetables; the new life forms were fighters and learners.

And with the invention of death, history begins. These new organisms were no longer identical; they had individuality. And their individuality meant that they explored new environments, and so began to change in themselves. New types began to evolve, new species. Sometimes, an accidental change in the DNA — some careless piece of duplication that gave the creature an extra eye or a finger — made it better able to adapt to its environment than its brothers and sisters; so it survived while they died out. Blobs of jelly turned into worms and fishes and molluscs. And some of those fishes were so spectacularly successful there was no need for further change. The giant shark arrived on earth nearly four hundred million years ago, and his descendants resemble him in every particular.

But it is a basic law of life that, in some paradoxical sense, the less successful species are the most successful. For they go on struggling and evolving while the successful ones remain static. At roughly the same time the giant shark appeared on earth, certain fishes with large fleshy fins made a habit of struggling up onto the beach to escape their enemies and relax in the sunlight. They were not particularly well adapted to life out of water; if the tide went out, their fleshy fins were hardly powerful enough to enable them to struggle back to the sea. And their lungs found a diet of undiluted air painfully difficult to cope with — many of them lost consciousness and suffocated before they could regain the sea. Yet the land was so much safer than the sea — for it had no other living creatures — that these early amphibians preferred to risk exhaustion and death to taking their chance among the sharks. They became the first reptiles. And after another two hundred million years of evolution, the reptiles had become the lords of the earth. The plant-eating dinosaurs were the largest creatures the earth has ever known — the brontosaurus was often twenty-five yards long and weighed thirty tons. The meat-eating dinosaurs — like tyrannosaurus — were the fiercest creatures the earth has ever known. And the flying dinosaurs — the archaeopteryx and the pterodactyl — became the most mobile creatures the earth had ever known. For a hundred and fifty million years, the dinosaurs dominated. And then they became the victims of their own success. Some great catastrophe — probably a giant meteor — ploughed into the earth sixty-five million years ago and threw up a cloud of steam that turned the atmosphere into a greenhouse. The temperature soared, and the plant-eating dinosaurs, with their huge bodies, died of excess heat. The flesh-eaters, which lived off the plant-eaters, died of starvation. And, for the first time, the warm-blooded animals had a chance to multiply and flourish. The death of the dinosaurs set the scene for the appearance of man.

Man's earliest mammalian ancestor was a rodent — a tiny tree shrew with a long tail and a flexible spine. Over ten million years or so ago, they developed a flexible thumb opposite their fingers to aid them in climbing trees. The shrew developed into a monkey. Ten million more years, and the monkey had become an ape. And a mere five million years ago the chimpanzee developed into two new types of ape: the gorilla and the ape-man. And the ape-man arrived on earth in time for a twelve-million-year drought known as the Pliocene era. As the vegetation decreased, the ape-man came down from his trees to spend an increasing amount of time on the ground, digging for roots and worms. He began to develop his earliest and most interesting talent — walking upright on his hind limbs. And since he could no longer rely on the forest to provide him with food, he had to learn to generalize — to scratch some kind of a living from any environment — desert, woodland, mountains, frozen tundra. And in order to cope with these new problems, he developed the largest brain of any living creature.

When, about three million years ago, the weather changed, the ape-man had become the world's most adaptable animal. Suddenly there were lakes and rivers and vast plains of grass; and on these plains were herds of grass-eating animals. The ape-man had always been capable of cooperation with others of his kind, but there been little opportunity for it in the drought of the Pliocene. Now cooperation became a necessity. A single man stood no chance against the mammoth, the cave bear, the woolly rhinoceros, the giant red deer and the sabre-toothed tiger; but a group of hunters, lying in ambush with spears and bone clubs, were a match for most animals. The upright posture gave man an immense advantage. And the skill required in hunting developed his brain at an incredible rate. The early ape Ramapithecus had a brain that weighed about four hundred grams. The brain of the hunter was half as big again. And in a mere two million years, *Homo erectus* had a thousand-gram brain. Then, only half a million years ago, it increased its size yet again by fifty per cent. This remains the average brain size of modern man.

Homo erectus invented the hand axe for skinning animals, but in a million years he made no attempt to develop this simple tool — for example, to provide it with a handle and use it as a weapon. About three-quarters of a million years ago, a group of *Homo erectus* arrived in Europe from Africa and Asia and evolved into *Homo sapiens*, the species to which modern man belongs. This new type of man did not know how to make fire, but when lightning set the forests alight, he carefully preserved the fire and kept it burning year after year. He used it to set fire to the undergrowth and drive animals into traps or over clifftops; he also used it for cooking. The great ice ages came and he used the fire to keep warm in his caves. It may have been fire that produced the 'brain explosion' of half a million years ago, for it obliged man to live in integrated societies and forced him to learn the disciplines of a social animal. A small tribe of twenty or thirty human beings can live as simply as a herd of cattle. But a group of a hundred or two hundred has to learn to organize itself. Laws and customs become necessary. Above all, he has to learn good manners. The primitive grunts that had once served to communicate had to evolve into a more sophisticated language.

There were two main sub-species of human beings about a hundred and twenty thousand years ago. One looked like modern man and was found mainly in Africa. The other, Neanderthal man, was more primitive and ape-like, yet in many ways, just as intelligent. He invented the bow and arrow, which meant that hunters could kill their prey from a distance. His women decorated themselves with red ochre. Moreover, he worshipped the sun and believed in an afterlife — or at least, we can make this assumption from the fact that he manufactured stone spheres and discs and buried his dead with some form of ritual involving flowers. For more than fifty thousand years, Neanderthal man was the dominant human species. And then, suddenly, he disappeared. And his disappearance corresponds with the sudden rise of his more 'human' brother, Cro-Magnon man. It seems probable that our ancestors wiped out their Neanderthal rivals between thirty and forty thousand years ago and took over the continent of Europe for themselves.

Compared to Neanderthal men, Cro-Magnon men were supermen. They learned to communicate by speaking in sentences instead of grunts. Their priests — or shamans — used a kind of magic to aid the hunters, drawing pictures of their prey on the walls of caves and performing certain rituals to induce them to walk into the hunter's ambush. They even developed the first form of writing, scratching marks on bone to enable them to predict the phases of the moon and the march of the seasons. They learned to make boats to cross rivers, and were soon using them to cross the seas. Now they could speak, men who lived hundreds of miles apart could trade with one another, exchanging flints, pottery and animal skins. They learned to domesticate animals — the wolf (which became the dog), the horse, the goat, and to breed cattle and sheep. About ten thousand years ago, they began to develop agriculture, learning to grow wheat and barley. And it was not long after this that they built the first walled cities, and man embarked on a new stage of his evolution.

Chosen by Nicolas Tredell, author of *Novels to Some Purpose: the fiction of Colin Wilson.* (Paupers' Press, 2016).
Tredell writes: '…it seems to me that this, very effectively, in its diction, imagery, rhythm and structure, evokes Niall's elevation to a state of heightened and widened consciousness and conveys the dynamism and excitement of the evolutionary narrative that is so crucial and central in Wilson's thinking.'

BELOW THE ICEBERG

From *Below the Iceberg, Anti-Sartre and Other Essays*, 1998

The editor has asked me to choose what I regard as the most important of my non-fiction books. I reply without hesitation: *Beyond the Occult*. This was first published in 1988, and unites two main currents in my thinking: the 'existentialist' ideas developed in *The Outsider*, and the ideas that developed from my study of 'the occult'. *Beyond the Occult* is my most important synthesis.

Oddly enough, I had no desire to write it. It came about because I was approached by an old friend who had been the editor of many of my early books — among them, *The Space Vampires* and *A Criminal History of Mankind*. He was now working for another publisher and wanted to commission another 'occult' book from me. I was anxious to oblige, but had no desire to write another book about 'the occult'. Finally, I allowed myself to be persuaded. In retrospect, I have never been so satisfied with any decision I have ever made.

Thirty years earlier, in 1956, my first book *The Outsider* had appeared, and brought me an overnight notoriety that I found astonishing and exhausting. Since the ideas of *The Outsider* play such an important part in *Beyond the Occult*, I must begin by trying to explain them.

Ever since childhood, I had been baffled by a strange phenomenon: how we can want something badly, and then feel bored almost as soon as we get it. I had noticed it particularly at Christmas time. For months before Christmas Day, I would look forward to owning some long-coveted toy; yet a few hours after receiving it, I was already beginning to 'take it for granted', and even to find it slightly disappointing. I noticed the same thing about school holidays — how eagerly I would look forward to them during the school term, and how easily I became bored with them. I glimpsed the solution to this problem when I was still a thirteen-year-old schoolboy. One day, at the beginning of the six-week-long August holiday, I went to a church bazaar, and bought for a few pence some volumes of an encyclopaedia called *Practical Knowledge for All*. It contained 'courses' on every imaginable subject, from accountancy, aeronautics, astronomy, biology, botany and chemistry to philosophy and zoology. I had been fascinated by astronomy and chemistry since the age of ten, and now I conceived the preposterous idea of trying to summarize all the scientific knowledge of the world in one single notebook. I gave it the grandiose title of *A Manual of General Science*, and wrote steadily throughout that August holiday, filling four notebooks with my round, schoolboy handwriting. And I noticed that I never became bored. Learning — and writing — about geology, biology and philosophy — from *Practical Knowledge for All* — kept me happier than I had ever been in my life, and I continued writing the book over Christmas, when I began the seventh volume — devoted to mathematics. All the time I was writing this book, I had an almost drunken sensation of the sheer immensity of the *world of ideas*, which seemed to stretch, like some marvellous unknown country, to a limitless horizon. Every day, when I began writing, I felt like a traveller preparing to discover new lakes and forests and mountain ranges. I felt sorry for the other boys at school, who were ignorant of this magical kingdom where I spent my evenings and weekends. I had learned a basic lesson: that the secret of avoiding boredom is to have a strong sense of purpose. Unfortunately, when I had finished the book, the problem of boredom returned, for I had no idea of what to do next. I spent one long school holiday trying to read all the plays of Shakespeare and his major contemporaries — Marlowe, Jonson, Middleton and the rest. During another holiday I read works by all the major Russian writers — Aksakov, Pushkin, Gogol, Tolstoy, Dostoevsky and Chekhov. During yet another, I studied the history of art, and discovered van Gogh and Cézanne. Yet because I was merely reading, and not writing about them, even this left me bored and dissatisfied.

When I was sixteen I came upon another important clue. It was soon after the end of the war, and a British publisher had started to reissue the novels of Dostoevsky. I bought *Crime and Punishment* with my pocket money. In the Translator's Preface, I read Dostoevsky's letter to his brother Mikhail describing how he — and other condemned Revolutionaries — were taken out on the Semyonovsky Square to be shot.

They barked orders over our heads, and they made us put on the white shirts worn by persons condemned to execution. Being the third in the row, I concluded I had only a few minutes of life before me. I thought of you and your dear ones, and I contrived to kiss Plestcheiev and Dourov, who were next to me, to bid them farewell. Suddenly, the troops beat a tattoo, and we were unbound, brought back to the scaffold, and informed that his Majesty...had spared our lives.

One of his fellow prisoners went insane. It struck me that if Dostoevsky had been offered his pardon *on condition that he promised never to be bored for the rest of his life*, he would have accepted gladly, and been quite certain that it should be possible — indeed, that it should be easy. And it seemed to me that he would obviously be correct. Surely, someone who had been through such a crisis would only have to *remember* being in front of the firing squad in order to be ecstatically happy? In fact, it was this episode — and the years in Siberia that followed — that turned Dostoevsky into a great writer. Before he was arrested, he was a good but minor writer — in the tradition of Dickens and Gogol — but as a human being he was touchy and self-obsessed to the point of paranoia. His arrest — and long imprisonment in Siberia — made him aware that even to be alive is in itself a cause for rejoicing. The result of his new insight is expressed in a passage in *Crime and Punishment*, where the hero is afraid that he may be executed for his murder of an old woman, and thinks: 'If I had to stand on a narrow ledge for ever and ever, in eternal darkness and tempest, I would still rather do that than die at once.' He had seen that 'life failure' — to be bored, miserable, tortured by guilt — is a form of childish *spoiltness*.

In my mid-teens, my problem was not simply boredom with my working-class existence (my father was a boot- and shoe-worker who earned about £3 a week). It was a longing to escape from it and to retreat into that magical world of the mind that I had discovered when writing the *Manual of General Science*. This was intensified by my discovery — through *Practical Knowledge for All* — of the realm of English poetry. I left school when I was sixteen, and for a few months worked in a factory, while I prepared to take the mathematics exam a second time. Factory work made me so miserable that I spent my evenings and weekends reading poetry — all kinds of poetry, from Chaucer's *Canterbury Tales* to T. S. Eliot's *Waste Land*. I quickly discovered that, after half an hour immersed in the world of Keats or Shelley or Wordsworth, my rage and despair had turned into a gentle sense of melancholy, which was slowly transformed into a sense of happiness and optimism, as if I was floating *above* the world, looking down on it like a bird. When, in the writings of Richard Wagner, I later came across the phrase: 'art, that makes life seem like a game, and withdraws us from the common fate', I understood instantly what he meant.

The only problem with this state of mind — the 'bird's eye view' — was that it made it twice as difficult to go back to work the following morning and accept the 'worm's eye view' of boredom and triviality. Years later, when I read Thomas Mann's novel *Buddenbrooks*, I recognize my own problem in the episode where young Hanno Buddenbrook goes to the opera to see Wagner's *Lohengrin*, and is transported into ecstasy, so that he feels he is walking on clouds. But when, the next morning, he has to get up in the freezing dawn and make his way to school through the dark, icy streets, his despair is twice as deep because he has experienced ecstasy the night before.

It then seemed to me that the problem of human existence can be expressed very simply. At long intervals, we experience moments of strength and happiness in which we feel that we have the power to *change* the world and our own lives. But such moments are brief. For most of the time we experience the sense of being victims of circumstance, like dead leaves carried along by a river, with no ability to choose our course. And when circumstances become especially difficult, it is easy to imagine that fate will afflict us with a series of misfortunes, like Job, that will destroy all our security and leave us completely helpless.

As I read my favourite writers — Plato, Hoffmann, Shelley, Nietzsche, Dostoevsky, Eliot — or listened to the music of Beethoven, or looked at the paintings of van Gogh, it seemed to me that all shared an awareness of this problem. Plato said that the universe is divided into a world of *being* and a world of *becoming*. The world of 'becoming' is this everyday world of matter, of endless change, in which we are trapped. The world of 'being' is the world of intellect and ideas, the world of truth and values that lies hidden behind the façade of the material world. As he prepares to commit suicide, Socrates declares that the philosopher spends his life trying to live in the world of true being, and that therefore he should welcome death, which finally frees us from the endless distractions of the world of mere 'becoming'. This, I realized, was why so many romantics were fascinated with death. Yet I still found the idea of death stupid and repellent. It was an attempt to *escape* from reality. And the moments of ecstasy, of 'bird's eye vision', seemed to promise that life itself could be lived on a level of continuous joy and affirmation.

When, in my late teens, I began to write a novel, it was inevitable that it should be about this problem of the bird's eye view and the worm's eye view.

The hero of *Ritual in the Dark* is a young man who has spent years working in boring jobs, and whose strongest desire is to have the freedom to read and think and listen to music. Then he receives a small legacy which enables him to rent a cheap room and spend his days in libraries and art galleries. And he finds that this kind of 'freedom' is curiously boring. Then he becomes accidentally involved with a man he suspects of being a murderer — and feels ashamed that, now he has something to maintain his 'interest', he no longer feels bored. He is ashamed because it has taken an external stimulus to suddenly renew his sense of being fully alive, when he feels *that he ought to be able to do it himself.* Surely he ought to wake up every morning with a feeling of immense gratitude for not having to go to an office? What is *wrong* with the human mind that it seems so incapable of freedom?

It was while I was writing this novel that I decided to break off and try to express some of its basic ideas in a volume of philosophy. Inevitably, this book was about 'Outsiders', people who felt a longing for some more purposeful form of existence, and who felt trapped and suffocated in the triviality of everyday life. It was a book about 'moments of vision', and about the periods of boredom, frustration and misery in which these moments are lost. It was about men like Nietzsche, Dostoevsky, van Gogh, T. E. Lawrence and William Blake, who have clear glimpses of a more powerful and meaningful way of living, yet who find themselves on the brink of suicide or insanity because of the frustration of their everyday lives. The problem of the Outsider is summarized in the life of Vincent van Gogh. His painting called *The Starry Night* is full of mystical vitality and affirmation; yet van Gogh committed suicide and left a note that read: 'Misery will never end.'

Here, then, is the vital question. *Was the tragedy of Nietzsche and van Gogh inevitable, or should there be some way in which human beings can live on a higher level of intensity?*

My own conclusion was that tragedy was *not* inevitable. Many Outsiders caused their own downfall through self-pity — in other words, they *allowed* themselves to become weak. Why? Because they are inclined to feel that life is futile and meaningless — or at least, that it is so difficult that it is not worth the effort. In the twentieth century, this feeling has been expressed most clearly in the works of Samuel Beckett.

It is recorded that when he was a young man, Beckett stayed in bed all day because he could see no reason to get up. And his works are a part of a long tradition of 'defeatism' that goes back to *Ecclesiastes*, with its 'Vanity of vanities, all is vanity', and 'There is nothing new under the sun.' This is the feeling that haunts so many Outsiders, particularly when they become tired and discouraged. It was expressed with a certain gloomy power in the philosophy of Schopenhauer. I labelled this sense of boredom and futility 'the Ecclesiastes effect'.

This sense of meaninglessness was also expressed by a Greek philosopher who died fifty years before Plato was born. Heraclitus argued that the world of 'becoming' is the *only* reality: everything changes constantly. Permanence is an illusion of the senses. Therefore man can make no real 'mark' on the world, for any 'mark' we make vanishes again as quickly as the tide washes away words written in the sand. This view also implies, of course, that there is no such thing as good or evil, and that 'values' are an illusion.

This is certainly the feeling we get when we are exhausted with effort, and life seems to be an endless vista of problems and complications. Yet the truth is that it is impossible to be a genuine follower of Heraclitus. According to Heraclitus, death is inevitable, and it is therefore no use making any efforts. Yet if Heraclitus had fallen into the river, he would have struggled to get out again. And if someone had put a knife to his throat and asked: 'Shall I cut your windpipe and save you the trouble of living?' he would have shouted: 'No!'

Still, Heraclitus has undoubtedly put his finger on our most basic problem: that everything we do is soon undone by time. Life is basically repetition. In *The Myth of Sisyphus*, Camus writes: 'Rising, streetcar, four hours of work, meal, sleep, and Monday, Tuesday, Wednesday, Thursday, Friday, and Saturday, according to the same rhythm.... But one day, the "why?" arises, and everything begins in that weariness tinged with amazement.' Camus calls this sudden revelation 'the Absurd', a word he borrowed from his friend Sartre, who also coined a word for man's reaction to the Absurd: 'nausea'. Nausea is the sudden recognition that we are 'unnecessary', and that the world of matter that surrounds us is the only reality. 'Meaning' is an illusion.

Yet, like Heraclitus, Sartre and Camus contradicted themselves. Sartre recorded that he had never felt so free as when he was working for the French Resistance, and was likely to be arrested and shot at any moment. And, on the evening before his execution, the hero of Camus's novel *L'Étranger* is overwhelmed by a feeling of happiness and affirmation that sounds like van Gogh's starry night. He writes: 'I had been happy and I was happy still.'

And this, obviously, brings us back to Dostoevsky facing the firing squad. He suddenly knows that life is not pointless and meaningless. And we all know the same thing whenever we are faced with any serious problem or crisis. We know that the statement 'Life is meaningless' or 'Nothing is worth doing' is the self-indulgence of a philosopher who is both lazy and weak.

But moments of crisis are not the only moments in which we recognize that the philosophy of Heraclitus and Samuel Beckett is nonsense. The same thing happens in all moments of sudden happiness — the feeling we experience on a spring morning, or when setting out on holiday. In *Seven Pillars of Wisdom*, T. E. Lawrence describes such an experience:

> We started on one of those clear dawns that wake up the senses with the sun, while the intellect, tired of the thinking of the night, was yet abed. For an hour or two, on such a morning, the sounds, scents, and colours of the world struck man individually and directly, not filtered through or made typical by thought: they seemed to exist sufficiently by themselves, and the lack of design and carefulness in creation no longer irritated.

This is the basic poetic vision, the sheer affirmation experienced by Wordsworth and Shelley and William Blake. And Lawrence has also identified the problem: the 'tired intellect' which questions everything. Elsewhere he referred to it as his 'thought-riddled nature'.

It is the 'thought-riddled nature' that causes Outsiders to see life as meaningless. They are in the position of someone who wears sun glasses and complains that the world is dark. But if thought has caused this problem, surely it is capable of identifying and overcoming the problem?

Let me again define this problem. It is the feeling that 'nothing is worth doing', that life is so complicated and the world in such a state of endless flux that all our actions are futile. It is the feeling that we cannot *do*.

Yet this feeling vanishes — and is seen to be an illusion —every time we experience the 'spring morning feeling' described by T. E. Lawrence. Optimism gives us the certainty that action *is* worthwhile, and that the use of the intellect can bring freedom. We only have to look around us to see the truth of this assertion. We are living in a world that has been completely transformed, in the course of little more than a century, by science and optimism. In fact, since the days of the cave man, human effort and optimism have steadily transformed the world. Individual men have died in failure and misery, yet the efforts of the human race have altered our lives until we are no longer mere animals, living and reproducing and dying. We are slowly learning to become something a little more like gods.

This, then, is the basic philosophy I reached after *The Outsider*. Dr. Johnson once said: 'When a man knows he is to be hanged in a fortnight, it concentrates his mind wonderfully.' The pessimism of Heraclitus and Samuel Beckett is basically due to a *lack of concentration*. Our sense of futility, the feeling that life is just 'one damned thing after another', is an illusion due to fatigue.

But how can we rescue ourselves from this feeling? First of all, we have to study it and *understand* it, as I tried to study and understand it in *The Outsider*. Our most important ally in this battle is the imagination. If you can imagine the feelings of Dostoevsky as he stood in front of the firing squad, then you are already learning to overcome the petty annoyances and childish weaknesses that make most people unhappy. The truth is that we have no *right* to be unhappy. It is an insult to the spirit of life. A man who is dying of AIDS knows that, if only he could be cured, he would live his life on a far higher level of purpose and optimism.

Until the late 1960s, I had considered myself a kind of 'existentialist' philosopher, who was attempting to rescue existentialism from the pessimism of Sartre, Camus and Heidegger. But at this point, I came upon a new subject of study that turned my thoughts in an entirely different direction. An American publisher asked me if I would be interested in writing a book about 'the occult'. It was not a subject that interested me greatly. As a child I had been fascinated by 'spiritualism' and the question of whether there is life after death. But as soon as I began to study chemistry, physics and astronomy, this interest seemed to evaporate like a dream.

After the request from the publisher, I began to give the matter some new thought. I also began to ask people of my acquaintance whether they had ever had any 'paranormal' experiences, and I was surprised by the number who said yes.

One friend was a concert pianist called Mark Bredin. He told me how he had been returning, very late at night, from a concert in central London, and traveling in a taxi along the Bayswater Road. Suddenly, he knew *with absolute certainty* that at the next traffic light, a taxi would try to 'jump' the light, and would hit them sideways. He wondered if he ought to warn his driver, but felt that he might be regarded as slightly mad. And at the next traffic light, a taxi tried to 'beat' the light at Queensway and hit them sideways.

It seemed to me that there was a certain parallel between Mark's experience and that of T. E. Lawrence in the early dawn. Both had been tired, and the 'intellect' was therefore asleep. But what peculiar power could make Mark aware of something that would happen *in the future*?

I had already recognized that the mind possesses the power to escape from pessimism and defeat by meditating on a firing squad. But this was something altogether more strange and unusual.

Another friend, the historian A. L. Rowse, told me how he had been leaning out of a window in Oxford. The window frame was very heavy, and it occurred to him that if it fell, it might easily kill him. Since he was in a bad mood, he thought: 'Let the damn thing fall!' A few moments later, just after he had withdrawn his head, the window fell.

Rowse also told me how, one quiet afternoon, he had a sudden premonition that if he went into the college library, he would find two young men embracing. He crossed two quadrangles and walked into the library — and saw the two young men embracing.

Even stranger was an experience described to me by a middle-aged friend named Kay Lunnis, who spent several days a week in our house, helping to look after our children. Kay described how she had once been seriously ill, and had felt herself rise up above her body so she could look down on it; then she had descended and re-entered her body.

A few years earlier I would have at least considered the possibility that this was some kind of hallucination due to fever. But in gathering material for *The Occult*, I had come across far too many cases of 'out-of-the-body experiences' to doubt that it was possible. Another friend, Lyall Watson, had described how, when his vehicle overturned in Kenya, he suddenly found himself hovering above the bus, and looking at the head and shoulders of a boy who had been hurled halfway through the canvas roof. It occurred to him that if the bus rolled any further, the boy would be crushed. A few minutes later, he recovered consciousness in the driving seat, got out of the vehicle and rescued the boy, who was in exactly the position he had seen a few moments earlier.

Now, if these friends were telling the truth — and I was strongly inclined to believe that they were — then human beings possess at least two 'powers' that were unsuspected by Heraclitus, Schopenhauer and Samuel Beckett: the power to 'see' the future, and the power to 'leave the body'.

Now quite clearly, if this were true, then it should be taken into account in any attempt to create a 'philosophy of human existence'. Such a philosophy demands that we try to understand 'what man is'. And if, in certain moments, man can see into the future, then he is certainly more than Heraclitus assumed.

Inevitably, I also had to reconsider the question of life after death. Another friend, Professor G. Wilson Knight, was a convinced spiritualist, and told me a circumstantial story that seemed to prove beyond all doubt that his mother had survived death. Now Dostoevsky had once remarked that if there is such a thing as life after death, it would be the most important thing that human beings could possibly know. And Dostoevsky was the most profound of the 'existential' philosophers. In *The Brothers Karamazov*, Ivan Karamazov argues that the world is so full of suffering that no 'religion' can justify it; Ivan says that he wants to 'give God back his entrance ticket'. Here he is expressing the philosophy of Heraclitus and *Ecclesiastes* and Sartre — that in a world dominated by brute matter, 'man is a useless passion' who is doomed to defeat. Yet Dostoevsky recognized that if there is life after death, this fact would change everything.

This, then, is why I regarded the evidence of the paranormal as so important. According to modern Western philosophy, which begins with Descartes, it is the philosopher's duty to 'doubt everything' until he has achieved some area of ultimate certainty — no matter how small — on which he can take his stand. Unfortunately, this method has failed to yield *any* kind of certainty. It led Bishop Berkeley to doubt the existence of the material world and David Hume to doubt cause and effect, and even the existence of the 'self'. It led Sartre to conclude that 'it is meaningless that we live and meaningless that we die', and Camus to regard human life as 'absurd'. The most fashionable of modern French philosophers, Jacques Derrida, is quite simply a descendant of Heraclitus, who believes that there is no such thing as 'underlying meaning' (which he calls 'presence') in the universe; the only reality is the endless flux of matter.

When *The Occult* appeared in 1971, it soon became apparent that many people who had regarded me as a kind of maverick existentialist now believed that I had turned to more trivial topics, and abandoned the rigour of my 'Outsider' books. To me, such a view was incomprehensible. It seemed obvious to me that if the 'paranormal' was a reality — as I was increasingly convinced that it was — then any philosopher who refused to take it into account was merely closing his eyes.

To begin with, most modern philosophers seem united in denying that man has a central 'self' (or soul). The Scottish philosopher David Hume started this revolution in the eighteenth century when he declared that, 'when I enter most intimately into what I call *myself*, I always stumble on some particular perception or other.... I never catch *myself at* any time'. Sartre declared that man has no 'self'; what he thinks of as 'himself' is really created by the outside world, 'the gaze of others'. And this is the position that has been accepted by French philosophers ever since. Derrida, who is celebrated for his theory of 'deconstruction', believes that the 'self' is a delusion that has been created by 'metaphysical' philosophers, whom he rejects with contempt.

Sartre's close ally Simone de Beauvoir expressed the same notion when she wrote (in *Pyrrhus and Cineas*): 'I look at myself in vain in a mirror, tell myself my own story, I can never grasp myself as an entire object, I experience in myself the emptiness that is myself, I feel that I am not.' In other words, man is a purely *superficial* creature; the sense of selfhood is like a mere reflection on the surface of a pond. Sartre carried this view to its logical conclusion when he declared that there is no such thing as the 'unconscious mind'.

Yet as soon as we begin to study the paranormal, we immediately encounter the existence of all kinds of powers that contradict Sartre and Simone de Beauvoir. Far from being a mere reflection on the surface of a pond, man seems to be like an iceberg whose most important part is hidden below the surface. Of course, Freud and Jung had already told us about the 'unconscious' (the word was actually invented by Leibniz). But it would seem that even they underestimated its powers. Even the anecdotes I have recounted above seem to indicate that the part of the 'self' hidden below the water-line possesses virtually magical powers.

And of course — as Dostoevsky recognized — the ultimate contradiction of the view that we possess 'no self' would be an actual proof of life after death, for without a self, there would be nothing to survive death. This ultimate proof eludes us; but the existence of other paranormal powers seems to leave no doubt of the truth of the 'iceberg' view of the human mind.

Moreover, it seems clear that some of these powers that lie below the surface seem to contradict the 'scientific' view of man. Science tells us that the future has not yet happened; therefore we can only guess what is going to happen. Yet when he was deeply relaxed, Mark Bredin had a clear premonition of what would happen when his taxi reached the next traffic light.

Robert Graves, the friend to whom *The Occult* was dedicated, drew my attention to another curious example of these unknown powers. It is described in one of his autobiographical stories called 'The Abominable Mr. Gunn'. In Graves's class at prep school there was a boy called F. F. Smilley, who was apparently a mathematical prodigy, a 'lightning calculator'. When the master (Mr. Gunn) had given the boys a difficult mathematical problem, Smilley simply wrote down the answer. He explained that he had not had to work it out, because it had just 'come to him'. Mr. Gunn accused him of looking up the answer in the back of the book. Smilley denied this, and pointed out that the answer in the back of the book had two figures wrong. Mr. Gunn regarded this as impertinence, and sent Smilley to the headmaster to be caned. After that, he bullied Smilley into doing problems 'the normal way'.

In the same story, Graves records a curious anecdote about himself. One summer evening, as he was sitting behind the cricket pavilion (and presumably in a deeply relaxed state of mind, like T. E. Lawrence and Mark Bredin), he received a 'sudden celestial illumination'.

> It occurred to me that I knew everything.
>
> I remember letting my mind range rapidly over all the familiar subjects of knowledge; only to find that this was no foolish fancy. I did know everything. To be plain: though conscious of having come less than a third of the way along the path of formal education...I nevertheless held the key to truth in my hand, and could use it to open any lock of any door. Mine was no religious or philosophical theory, but a simple method of looking sideways at disorderly facts so as make perfect sense of them.

This, of course, is precisely what existentialism wants to do — and precisely what I am trying to do in this article: to 'look sideways' at the disorderly facts of human existence and try to find some way of making sense of them. Graves, apparently, did it when he was fifteen. He says that he tried out his insight 'on various obstinate locks' and found that they all opened smoothly. The insight was still intact when he woke up the next day. But when he tried to record it in the back of an exercise book 'my mind went too fast for my pen'. He had another try later, but the insight had vanished.

Nevertheless, together with Smilley's curious abilities, it convinced Graves that we possess a peculiar power which is not generally recognized by science, a 'supra-logic that cuts out all routine processes of thought and leaps straight from problem to answer'.

It is worth looking a little more closely into this mystery. There are certain numbers called 'primes', which cannot be divided by any other number without leaving a 'remainder' — numbers like 3, 5, 7 and 11. Nine is not a prime because it can be divided exactly. The actual number of primes is infinite, but if a number is very large, there is no way of telling whether it is a prime or not — except by the long and painful process of dividing every smaller number into it. Yet a Canadian 'calculating prodigy' named Zerah Colburn was asked whether a certain ten-digit number was a prime, and replied after a moment: 'No, it can be divided by 641.'

There is no *logical* way of doing this. The psychiatrist Oliver Sacks has described a pair of subnormal twins in a New York mental hospital who amuse themselves by swapping *twenty-four figure* primes. Obviously, the twins somehow rise into the air, like birds, over the whole number-field, and instantly see which number is a prime and which is not.

I would suggest that the ability that enabled Mark Bredin to 'know' that his taxi would be struck by another taxi is closely related to the ability of Zerah Colburn and Sacks's twins, and that both are related to T. E. Lawrence's feeling on the morning when 'the senses awoke before the intellect'.

Now, long before I became interested in 'the occult', I had been fascinated by another example of the powers that lie 'below the iceberg'. (I say 'below the iceberg' rather than 'below the visible part of the iceberg' because it has always seemed to me that man's hidden powers are located in the sea below the iceberg as much as in the iceberg itself.) As everyone knows, Proust's vast novel *A la recherche du temps perdu* sprang from a single incident in his childhood, just as Graves's theories in *The White Goddess* sprang from his experience behind the cricket pavilion. One day, feeling tired and depressed, Proust's hero is offered by his mother a small cake (called a madeleine) dipped in herb tea. As he tastes it he experiences an exquisite sensation of sheer happiness. 'I had now ceased to feel mediocre, accidental, mortal.' After eating another bite, he recalls what has caused this feeling of power and happiness: the madeleine has revived memories of his childhood in a small country town called Combray, where his Aunt Leonie used to give him a taste of her own madeleine dipped in the same herb tea.

Why should this make him feel so happy? Because it has reminded him of the depths *below the iceberg*. He had been feeling bored and depressed — in other words, *superficial*. Now he catches a glimpse of the depths of his own mind, and of its hidden powers. He also realizes that if only he could learn the 'trick' of bringing back this feeling, he would never be unhappy again. This is why he sets out to revive it by writing his enormous autobiographical novel. Yet this deliberate intellectual activity fails. When he catches other glimpses of this magical feeling of power and strength, it is always by accident, when he is thinking of something else.

In the tenth volume of his *Study of History*, Arnold Toynbee describes several occasions on which he also had these strange glimpses into the *reality* of the past — not his own past, but that of history. On each of these occasions, he actually seemed to see the past, as if he had been transported by a time machine. On one of these occasions, he seemed to see the battle of Pharsalus, which had taken place in 197 B.C., and saw some horsemen — of whose identity he was ignorant — galloping away from the massacre.

It seems clear from his descriptions that he felt this was not 'imagination', but some kind of glimpse of the past like Mark Bredin's glimpse of the future. (In *Beyond the Occult* I cite many other examples of more distant 'glimpses' of the future which proved to be accurate.)

On a snowy day in Washington in 1966, thinking about this curious ability to 'make real' other times and other places, I labelled it 'Faculty X'. But Faculty X should not be regarded as some 'paranormal' faculty. It is simply the *opposite* of that feeling which all of us feel when we are tired and depressed, and which Sartre calls contingency. And whenever Faculty X awakens, it tells us that we are *not* contingent, *not* mediocre, accidental, mortal. Our powers are far greater than we realize.

In *The Occult*, I had pointed out that animals seem to possess all kinds of 'paranormal' powers. The wife of the Scottish poet Hugh MacDiarmid told me that her dog knows when her husband will return from a long journey, and goes and sits at the end of their lane several days before he arrives. On one occasion, the dog knew he was going to return before *he* did — circumstances had caused him to make a sudden decision to return home.

In his book *Man Eaters of Kumaon*, the tiger hunter Jim Corbett describes how he came to develop a faculty which he called 'jungle sensitiveness', which told him when he was in danger. I argue that all our remote ancestors possessed such a faculty, and that we have gradually lost it because we do not need it. Yet many people have not lost it. The archaeologist Clarence Weiant described how the Montagnais Indians of eastern Canada are able to contact distant friends and relatives by telepathy. When they wish to make contact, the Indians go into a remote hut in the forest, and build up the necessary psychic energy ('mana') through meditation. Then the relative would *hear his voice* — distance made no difference.

Now it is obvious that it is simpler to pick up the telephone when we want to contact a distant relative. Yet this does not mean that picking up a telephone is 'just as good' as contacting him through clairaudience. The Indian who is able to call upon these faculties from the depths of his own mind has an understanding of nature, a sense of connection with the rest of the universe, and a *deeper knowledge of himself* that the rest of us have lost.

What has happened is obvious. Even towards the end of the nineteenth century, the English poet Matthew Arnold was mourning that Victorian man no longer had access to 'Wordsworth's healing power', while Tennyson was complaining that science had destroyed faith and left man in an empty universe, trapped in his own smallness. But the problem had started long before the nineteenth century — perhaps when Euclid systematized geometry and Archimedes rolled a weight down an inclined plane. This kind of knowledge — which Graves calls 'solar knowledge' —gradually eclipsed man's 'lunar knowledge', man's intuitive awareness of the hidden part of the iceberg.

This was the problem that I had discussed in the second volume of *The Outsider* (called *Religion and the Rebel*). Now, in *Beyond the Occult*, I attempted to bring together this philosophy of 'Outsiderism' and the insights I had gained from the study of 'the occult'.

Yet I began to write the book reluctantly, feeling that I was merely regurgitating something I had already expressed in previous books. But I soon realized that I was creating a new synthesis. The problem of human beings is that it is possible to 'know' something without really knowing it. The adult Proust thought he 'knew' he was a child in Combray, but the madeleine taught him that this 'adult' knowledge was superficial. I thought I knew the ideas I had expressed in books like *The Outsider* and *The Occult*. Writing about them again made me realize that my knowledge of them was superficial. In order to really know something we must meditate upon it until we have absorbed it into our being. (I have to confess that even writing this article has once again made me aware of this truth.)

Beyond the Occult is an attempt to draw together all the insights I have discussed in this article, and many more — particularly the insights of those who have had sudden 'mystical' experiences. They all teach us the same thing: that our 'ordinary' consciousness of ourselves is superficial and deceptive. We are all like Simone de Beauvoir, looking in the mirror and 'feeling that we can never grasp ourselves as an entire object'.

Here is a typical example of one of these experiences. A girl describes how, when she was sixteen, she set out to walk up a lane towards a wood. 'I was not feeling particularly happy or particularly sad, just ordinary.' As she stood in a cornfield, looking towards the wood, everything suddenly changed:

Everything surrounding me was this white, bright, sparkling light, like sun on frosty snow, like a million diamonds, and there was no cornfield, no trees, no sky, this *light* was everywhere…. The feeling was indescribable, but I have never experienced anything in the years that followed that I can compare with that glorious moment; it was blissful, uplifting, I felt open-mouthed wonder. Then the tops of the trees became visible once again, then a piece of sky, and gradually the *light* was no more, and the cornfield was spread before me. I stood there for a long time, trying in vain for *it* to come back, and have tried many times since, but I only saw it once; but I know in my heart it is still there — and here — around us.

The girl — who describes this in a book called *Seeing the Invisible* (which consists of letters about mysticism, written to the Alister Hardy Foundation) — obviously had an experience which, in some ways, resembled that of Proust. Something 'triggered' this marvellous perception of sparkling light. And she remains convinced that 'it is still there' — that our everyday consciousness somehow *filters it out*, just as if we were wearing a pair of dark glasses.

It is, of course, deeply frustrating that we cannot learn how to contact these depths 'below the iceberg' at will. Yet — as I have tried to show — it is not as difficult as it sounds.

The conclusions I have reached over the years are as follows. The romantics of the nineteenth century had many of these 'glimpses', because they knew how to 'relax'. (The girl in the anecdote above does not say so, but it is clear that she was deeply relaxed.) But because the romantics were inclined to weakness — like Samuel Beckett most of them could see no reason for getting out of bed — they failed to grasp the most important clue: that such experiences bring a feeling of *strength*, and that the best way to achieve them is certainly *not* to indulge in weakness and self-pity. Abraham Maslow, who called such moments 'peak experiences', discovered that his 'peakers' were usually strong and healthy people who coped well with their lives.

In *Beyond the Occult*, I describe an interesting example of how I succeeded in achieving 'higher consciousness' for most of an afternoon in 1979.

It was the New Year, and I had gone to a remote farmhouse in Devon to give a lecture to a group of extra-mural students. During that evening it began to snow, and by the following morning the snow was so thick that it would have been impossible to drive back home. I was forced to stay there another night. The following morning, the weather forecast announced more snow, and it was obvious that I might be unable to leave for a week. I determined to try to escape, and a group of us began to clear the snow in the farmyard with shovels. When the farmyard was clear, each of us tried to drive our cars up the slope that led to the gate; mine was the only car whose tyres would grip the slippery surface.

There was still half a mile of snow-covered farm track between the farmyard and the main road. I would drive a few yards, then get out and help to shovel snow. At one point, I even risked driving straight across a field to avoid a long bend in the road. And finally, after several hours of hard work, I walked back to the farmhouse to eat some lunch and collect my bags. Then I walked back to the main gate, and began the long drive back home.

Yet even now it was impossible to relax my vigilance, because the narrow country roads were covered in snow, and it was impossible to see the ditch on either side. It would have been easy to drive off the road and become stranded again perhaps all night. So I sat forward in my seat, peering out of the windscreen and focusing all my concentration.

Several hours later, I arrived at the main road, where heavy traffic had turned the snow into muddy slush, and it was possible to relax and drive normally again. And it was now that I realized that I was full of a sense of power and concentration. Everything I looked at was obviously fascinating, and I had a sense of *meanings* stretching around me into the distance. Everything I saw *reminded* me of something else — for example, of Christmases in my childhood. It was as if my normally narrow and limited consciousness had been widened and deepened by the concentration, until the whole world was seen to be fascinating. It taught me that 'higher consciousness', 'positive consciousness', can be achieved by an act of *focused concentration.*

In *Beyond the Occult* I also quote the experiences of a writer called R. H. Ward, whose book about psychedelic drugs, *A Drug Taker's Notes*, is a modern classic. Early in the book, Ward describes how he once had a remarkable experience under dental gas. He writes: 'I passed, after the first few inhalations of the gas, directly into a state of consciousness far more complete than the fullest degree of ordinary consciousness.' He had a sense of enormously extended vision, so that his mind was aware of all kinds of things that would normally have been beyond his natural range of awareness. Like Robert Graves behind the cricket pavilion, he seemed to understand everything. And as he continued 'rising', he seemed to pass through a 'region of ideas'. 'All was idea, and form did not exist.' And he adds, 'It seems to me very interesting that one should thus, in a dentist's chair and the twentieth century, receive practical confirmation of the theories of Plato.' In short, Ward had *seen* the truth of Plato's notion that the universe consists of two worlds: a world of becoming, and a world of true being. He had also seen the falseness of Heraclitus's belief that the only world is the world of becoming.

If we think once more of Dostoevsky in front of the firing squad, we can see that the expectation of death galvanized him to a new level of *attention*, in which he concentrated the mind as never before — and as I concentrated my mind as I drove through the snow. It is this act of concentration — like pulling back a spring-loaded piston, or the string of a crossbow — that gives the mind the ability to become aware of the immense depths that lie 'below the iceberg'.

POSTSCRIPT

After finishing this piece, I took my dog for a walk in the woods. I was tired — I had been working since early morning — yet in spite of my tiredness, I experienced a powerful sense of beauty and euphoria that filled me with optimism. This, I realized, was because the *contents* of this piece had penetrated to my unconscious mind, and made me clearly aware that the world of everyday consciousness is only the surface of the mind. For me, this underlines the certainty I have always felt: freedom does not have to come from some religious or yogic discipline. The most reliable way of achieving it is through *intellect*, through knowledge.

Chosen by Vaughan Rapatahana who is the author of *Wilson as Mystic* (Nottingham: Paupers' Press, 2001) and editor of Colin Wilson's *Introduction to 'The Faces of Evil': An Unpublished Book* (Paupers' Press, 2013) and *'Comments on Boredom' and 'Evolutionary Humanism and the New Psychology': Two Unpublished Essays* (Paupers' Press, 2013). He also wrote an introduction to Colin Wilson's *Lulu: An Unfinished Novel* (Paupers' Press, 2017). Rapatahana writes: '"Below the Iceberg" is an excellent summary of Colin Wilson's ideas…and is written in an especially relaxed fashion.'

THE SEVENTH DEGREE
OF CONCENTRATION

From *The Books in My Life*
Hampton Roads Publishing, 1998.

What should be clear by now is that, with rare exceptions, the books that have influenced me have been books that made me think. I have, of course, enjoyed many books that simply tell a 'good story' — as a child I devoured Rider Haggard and Edgar Rice Burroughs and R. L. Stevenson, but I am easily sated with mere narrative.

In an essay on Lindsay in *The Strange Genius of David Lindsay* I made a distinction between 'high fliers' and 'low fliers'. High fliers are writers like Dostoevsky, Tolstoy, Shaw and Wells, who want to know what we should do with our lives. Low fliers are writers like Jane Austen, Dickens and Thackeray, who may be intelligent, yet never ask the 'big question'. Lindsay is, of course, a high flier.

Now the basic problem of human existence seems to me quite clear. It is expressed with great clarity in Hermann Hesse's novel *Steppenwolf*. The hero of that novel has enough money to live comfortably, surrounded by books and gramophone records. Yet he finds his life oddly boring. A certain lukewarmness seems to pervade his everyday consciousness. Yet this can vanish quite abruptly, as when he drinks a glass of wine, and feels his spirit soar aloft like a golden bubble. In such a moment he is reminded 'of Mozart and the stars' — in other words, he achieves a kind of 'bird's-eye view' of his own existence.

Now it is true that our world is full of appalling tragedy — of mass starvation and injustice. Yet the problem for the average person is not deciding between misery and affirmation — what Carlyle called 'Everlasting Yes versus Everlasting No' — but rather, the bird's-eye view, which brings a sense of Everlasting Yes, versus that 'luke-warmness' — what Heidegger calls 'the triviality of everydayness'.

This is a fairly new problem for human beings. Our caveman ancestors found life so difficult that they had no time to be bored. But the human intellect has brought order and discovery to the world, and these have transformed civilization, so that a steadily increasing number of people are able to live lives of relative material comfort. But this comfort has brought the curse of 'lukewarm' consciousness, and we long for some simple method of being able to summon those moments 'of Mozart and the stars' at will.

It seems to me that all this implies is that mankind has a joint purpose, and that therefore no writer is justified in declaring that human existence is meaningless. This is why I have no patience whatsoever with a writer like Samuel Beckett, who seems to me totally worthless. He spent his life declaring that human existence is meaningless; yet if someone had pushed him into a river, he would have struggled to get out.

The problem with Beckett's work is that he does not think — he is an example of what the novelist Ayn Rand calls 'the anti-conceptual mentality'. His first novel, *Murphy*, begins, 'The sun shone, having no alternative, on the nothing new'. Beckett fails to see that he is not stating an objective truth — that the world is full of people who open their eyes in the morning and feel that the world is full of 'newness'. Beckett would dismiss them — as Artsybashev's Naumov dismisses them in *Breaking Point* — as unthinking optimists, who fail to grasp the sheer futility and repetitiveness of human existence. I could respect Beckett if he took the trouble to justify his views, in the manner of Schopenhauer; then we could point out where his arguments cease to be objective. But he will not stay to argue; he declares that existence is so meaningless that reason is a waste of time. Yet the sentence 'Reason is a waste of time' is a rational statement that reveals that Beckett has to make use of reason from the moment he wakes up in the morning until he goes to bed at night. Like all pessimists — as I have tried to show in the case of Huysmans, Andreyev and Artsybashev — his views are simply self-contradictory.

But the real objection to Beckett and his fellow pessimists is that they poison our cultural heritage, and in that sense are as culpable as someone who puts poison in a city's water supply. They actively impede the evolution of the human race. For they propagate the 'passive fallacy', the notion (fostered also by Cartesian philosophy) that we are merely passive observers looking at a world that we can do little to influence, just as we can do little to influence our own consciousness.

Now I have frequently cited the case of Graham Greene, who plunged into a state of depressive consciousness in his teens, until he decided to play Russian roulette with a revolver and live ammunition. He placed the revolver to his head and pulled the trigger; when the hammer clicked on an empty chamber, he experienced a surge of recognition that the world was full of 'infinite possibilities'. He also uses the significant phrase, 'It was as if a light had been turned on', clearly implying that he felt that he was seeing something, not merely 'feeling' it.

What had happened was that shock had blown away his boredom, like the wind blowing away clouds. But it was the sudden convulsion of his own mind that transformed his consciousness, not the revolver.

Abraham Maslow called this kind of convulsion of happiness the 'peak experience'. But he discovered that 'natural peakers' were people whose attitude to life was optimistic and purposive, and who were not inclined to surrender to their own laziness or self-pity. The human mind is like the human hand; it can clench into a fist, or simply hang slack. When Greene pulled the trigger, his mind suddenly 'clenched', and it was this clenching action that caused the surge of optimism. Our minds are not passive or paralyzed. Beckett's mind had fallen into a kind of paralysis due to laziness (he admitted that he was inclined to stay in bed all day because he could see no reason for getting up). So the muscles had atrophied until he found it difficult to clench or stretch them.

But the paralysis was due largely to the fact that his intellect had ratified his laziness, convincing him that there was no point in making any effort. And Beckett did his best to spread his paralysis to the rest of the human race. And such was the confusion and irrationality that prevailed in his time, and to a large extent still prevails, that he was awarded the Nobel Prize for his efforts to discourage us all. In Artsybashev's time, the instinct for health and meaning was stronger; no one suggested that Artsybashev deserved the Nobel Prize for *Breaking Point*.

For many years, I sought some method that might produce the same effect as Greene's Russian roulette, inducing an instant peak experience. More recently, I have come to recognize that we already know the basic method.

For example, during the writing of this book, I found that one of the files on my disk had corrupted — it was the one on Huysmans — and I had no copy. My son Rowan spent half a day trying to recover it on his computer (I use an old-fashioned word processor). Finally, he brought me the text on a new disk. But all its words had run together, all its commas had vanished, and meaningless symbols had inserted themselves into the text.

I proceeded to 'unscramble' it, and spent most of the day at this unrewarding activity. Yet I experienced no boredom, for I was too relieved to have recovered the chapter. I realized clearly that our boredom is a function of our assumption that something is not worth doing.

The next morning, I still had three pages to 'unscramble'. And this time, instead of merely working patiently at the text, I concentrated my full attention on it, as if my life depended on it, knitting my eyebrows and scowling like a madman. Almost immediately, I experienced a marvellous sense of control and meaning — I found myself regretting that I only had three pages to unscramble. Then it struck me that it made no difference what I was doing. If I chose to concentrate my attention on blowing my nose, it would have the same effect of creating a sense of control and of potentiality.

Such experiences make us suddenly aware that consciousness can achieve a far higher level of meaning-perception, and can maintain it by a small but continuous effort. The reason that no great effort is required is that once 'attention' has closed the usual leaks of mental energy, it is not difficult to maintain it.

The importance of sex lies in its ability to focus the mind, to give us a glimpse of the possibilities of consciousness.

It seems to me that its major possibility can be quite easily expressed. It will be remembered that William James began to recover from his nervous breakdown when he read Renouvier's remark that the proof of free will lies in the fact that we can think one thing rather than another. I can break off this chain of thought to think about my childhood, or what we are having for dinner tonight, or the implications of Gödel's theorem.

But although it is true that I can change the current of my thought, it is not so easy to change the current of my feeling. I can recall what I felt like on Christmas day as a child, or the first time I saw mountain scenery, or when my first book was accepted. But the glimpse lasts only a split second, then vanishes.

Yet there are moments when I seem to be able to control my feelings as well as my thoughts. If I am lying in bed on a cold winter morning, and I have to get up in ten minutes, I can somehow focus my mind on the warmth of the bed and wallow in contentment until the moment I have to climb out. I can remember the same sensation as a child, listening to the patter of rain on the windows, or sitting inside a 'house' made of cardboard boxes, broom handles and an old counterpane. In my teens,

I learned to control my moods by reading poetry or listening to music. And on rare occasions of happy relaxation, I seem to be able to control my feelings as easily as I can control a car with power steering. Yet under ordinary circumstances, my feelings respond to my attempt to 'steer' them as uncooperatively as one of those dodgem cars at a fairground.

In my childhood, I often lay awake at night, trying hard to get to sleep, feeling thoroughly bored with my thoughts, which insisted on pursuing their own course. In recent years, I have begun to learn the trick of lying awake and enjoying my thoughts, enjoying the warmth of the bed, enjoying the drift into dreams and out again.

It seems to me that this ability to 'steer' our feelings, and even our physical states (which closely echo our feelings), is a natural potentiality of consciousness, which human beings will one day take for granted as much as they now take their ability to 'steer' the body in any direction they wish to walk.

The simplest way of recognizing that consciousness can be 'steered' is to consider the implications of states of crisis.

When we experience any kind of relief from crisis, we catch a glimpse of the possibility of a totally affirmative consciousness. Yet once the relief has passed, we find it virtually impossible to understand what we saw.

The puzzle is this. It is not difficult to understand why Graham Greene experienced a tremendous sense of affirmation when the hammer clicked on an empty chamber, or why Dostoevsky felt that his reprieve was a kind of religious revelation. But then, as he stood in front of the firing squad, Dostoevsky had already recognized what he was about to lose; in other words, he had already achieved a 'bird's-eye view' of the world and his own life.

But we glimpse the same insight when the cause is relatively trivial. On my way back from a walk with my dogs, I grope in my pocket for the car keys and find they are missing. And just as I am reconciling myself to the thought of walking a mile to the nearest phone box and ringing my wife, I find that they have slipped through a hole in the lining. Such an 'emergency' is hardly life threatening, yet it brings, for a moment, exactly that same sense that life is infinitely valuable. Why?

The glimpse is akin to the 'holiday feeling' — that feeling of expansiveness and sheer joy we often experience when setting out on holiday. But that is easy to understand. The combination of relaxation and pleasant anticipation awakens our senses, and enables us to remove the kind of pressure we feel obliged to concentrate upon the present moment. This enables us to stand back and 'count our blessings'. But why should losing, and then finding, a car key produce the same effect?

The answer, I suspect, lies partly in the experience of Abraham Maslow. Maslow discovered that when his students began to talk to one another about their own peak experiences, they began to have peak experiences all the time. That is because the peak experience reminds us of what Graham Greene glimpsed when the hammer clicked on the chamber: that life is infinitely exciting.

But how is it possible for us to forget this? The answer lies in the nature of the evolution of human consciousness. In order to survive, we have had to learn to focus consciousness narrowly on the problems of the present. Most men spend their lives going back and forth to work; most women spend their lives in household chores. Now our state of cheerfulness depends upon how far we are succeeding with the present task. If it goes badly, we experience a certain depression, a 'sinking feeling'. This sinking feeling, of course, only applies to the present task; but since the present task occupies our whole internal horizon, then this horizon is darkened by thunderclouds from end to end. If you are staring at the sky through a telescope, then one single cloud can give the impression of an overcast day, although it may be the only cloud in an otherwise blue sky.

Emergency has the effect of causing us to remove the telescope from the eye and take a broader view. And peak experiences remind us that everyday consciousness is a kind of tunnel, and that we only have to remove the telescope to see how much we have to be grateful for.

In other words, we are 'trapped' in everyday consciousness. But this is not the fault of everyday consciousness; it is our own fault. Life has taught us to 'keep our noses to the grindstone', and we tend to do it from force of habit. If my wife calls me to say my dinner is ready when I am writing a letter, I abandon the letter reluctantly — even though I prefer eating my dinner. My desire to 'get things done' is so strong that I have to overcome a certain reluctance to abandon the letter.

As a child, I found it impossible to understand 'workaholics' like my father, who had an evening job in addition to his daytime work in a factory. But within a year or two, driven on by ambition, and a desire to escape the kind of life my father led, I spent all my time writing stories and essays that were invariably rejected. Wordsworth had remarked that 'shades of the prison house begin to close' around the growing youth; now I had to come to terms with the paradox that we encourage them to close around us.

What can be done about this? This analysis suggests the basic answer. The problem is that consciousness seems to have a compulsive tendency to contract into 'tunnel vision'. This hardly matters; we need tunnel vision to enable us to work with maximum efficiency. The problem is that when tunnel vision is combined with discouragement, the result is a lowering of inner pressure. And we can become so accustomed to living and working at reduced pressure that it becomes a permanent condition. We begin to live 'on the defensive', as it were, and all sense of pleasurable anticipation about the future evaporates. When this happens, trivial worries can plunge the mind into a permanent state of what Kierkegaard called angst. One step beyond that lies mental breakdown. (The novelist William Styron has provided a powerful description of such a breakdown in his book *Darkness Visible* — from which it also emerges that he has no insight whatsoever into the processes that led to the breakdown.)

We can be saved from tunnel vision by being shocked into wakefulness, as in the case of Greene or Dostoevsky. The problem lies in a combination of forgetfulness and laziness. Maslow's students reminded one another of the 'bird's-eye view', until perception of the bird's-eye view became a kind of habit. Sartre acquired the same habit during the war, when the threat of arrest and torture kept him in a state of high alertness.

But then Sartre, like Graham Greene, had made it virtually impossible to take any long-term advantage of this insight because his pessimistic philosophy negated it. I have laboured in this volume to make the point that long-term artistic development and negative philosophy are incompatible. I have also tried to show that the kind of negative philosophy indulged in by so many writers of the twentieth century is not in accordance with the facts. Pessimistic philosophy is an outcome of the combination of laziness and forgetfulness mentioned above. It has no objective justification. When 'the facts' are seen objectively, in a state of 'wakefulness', they justify Chesterton's sense of 'absurd good news', or Greene's recognition that life is full of infinite possibilities.

The basic answer, as Doctor Johnson recognized, lies in concentration of the mind. I have experienced it perhaps half a dozen times in the past twenty years, most notably as I drove through heavy snow returning from a lecture in Devon, and again on a train journey to Northampton to address a publisher's conference — both are described in a book called *Beyond the Occult*. On both occasions I recognized clearly the truth of Husserl's insight that consciousness is intentional. Our relationship to objects of perception is not passive, like a sponge absorbing water; it is active.

A better analogy might be a game of tennis. When we are lazy and mechanical, we play a purely defensive game; yet we are still forced to hit the ball, for all perception is intentional. But when consciousness achieves something like its proper level of vitality, we play a highly aggressive game, and can feel intentionality in action. In such moments we grasp the true nature of consciousness and the possibilities for human evolution, if we could truly understand this and escape from the fallacy of passive perception.

It seems to me that this leads to an insight which could transform our lives.

We think of consciousness as a mirror, and that what we see in that mirror is 'real'. This shows a total failure to grasp the nature of human consciousness.

It works by a process of attention and compression, and the faculty called imagination — or 'the reality function' — is central to its operation.

Consider Yeats' lines from *Lullaby*:

What were all the world's alarms
To mighty Paris when he found
Sleep upon a golden bed
That first dawn in Helen's arms.

The sheer ecstasy of finally possessing Helen must have transformed his consciousness, so that he felt that no problem could defeat him.

But look more closely at the phenomenology of sexual excitement, and you become aware that it operates through a series of movements of 'compression'. The first excitement causes us to focus the attention, and to achieve a still higher level of excitement and of focus. Shaw makes Captain Shotover say that what he wants to achieve is the 'seventh degree of concentration'. Imagine seven concentric circles, and that each new level of excitement causes the mind to contract within the next circle, bringing a still higher sense of control.

I am not now speaking simply about sexual excitement, but of every form of conscious intensity: the enjoyment of music, of art, of setting out on holiday, of physical achievement in sport, of the brilliant flash of insight that solves a problem.

When we throw a stone in a pond, concentric rings move outward. Imagine, instead, these same rings moving inward, and you have an image of the basic operation of consciousness.

When you are feeling tired and dull, consciousness is relaxed and passive, and you feel that the physical world is the only reality. As soon as something captures your interest, you move inside that 'first circle' of concentration. This is what happens, for example, when you read a newspaper or casually watch television.

If you suddenly see a story that deeply interests you, you focus your attention, and move inside the second circle.

If you become excited — for example, watching your favourite sport on television — you achieve the 'third degree of concentration'.

Sexual arousal also passes through these three phases — attention, focus, excitement.

Mystics and ascetics recognize the central importance of this process, and deliberately set out to strengthen the 'muscle' that aids concentration.

What they have achieved is a certain philosophical recognition. Things are not 'as they are'. Reality is not what it appears to be. Everyday reality is a mere reflection in a mirror before we achieve the first degree of concentration. It is like looking at a page of print and not 'taking it in'. This is the state Hemingway described when he said, 'You know that's all there is.' Sartre called it 'nausea'.

The first act of concentration brings the print into focus, and causes us to recognize that it has meaning.

The second degree of concentration makes us unaware of the print, as if it has become transparent. We are seeing through it to the events were are reading about.

We should now be able to grasp that, in a perfectly straightforward sense, 'everyday reality' is untrue.

Now our notion that everyday reality is 'true' is accompanied by another delusion. When you read a newspaper paragraph, you know that the 'meanings' have been put there by the journalist who wrote it. When you look at a tree, you feel it has no underlying meaning — apart from what your perception reveals — because no one 'wrote' it.

Yet when a poet looks at a tree, in the 'third degree of concentration', he is overwhelmed with a sense of its meaning.

When the mystic Jacob Boehme looked at a tree, he seemed to see inside it, to its inner life. He called this vision 'the signature of all things'. In other words, the tree had ceased to be 'merely itself', and was somehow related to everything else. Boehme had achieved the fourth degree of concentration.

We can see that a man who has achieved this fourth degree of concentration would always have a weapon against boredom and tiredness. He would know that everyday perception is partial, incomplete and that far deeper meanings lie below its surface. All he has to do is to begin that act of concentration.

Maslow's students had achieved this vital insight by discussing peak experiences; this is why they could achieve peak experiences at will.

At the present point in his evolution, man is still trapped in the animal stage. His attitude towards the world is essentially passive.

Yet man has evolved beyond the other animals because his attitude to his own existence is so much less passive than theirs. He is always trying to change things. And this desire to change things has created civilization, and made him the most evolved creature on the surface of the earth.

Yet his conscious attitude towards his perception of the world remains passive. He accepts that 'everyday perception' is the truth.

This could be compared to a short-sighted man believing that the blurred vision he experiences without his glasses is 'truer' than the clearer focus he achieves when he puts them on.

Man is taken in by a confidence trickster; but it is his own fault, because the confidence trickster is his naiveté. It is true that he makes instinctive attempts to control his consciousness — through such simple means as alcohol, sex, sport, holidays — but in a sense, these only make things worse, for he wrongly assumes that the means have changed his state of awareness, failing to realize that they have simply caused him to focus his attention.

Yet he merely has to recognize that the act of focusing attention causes a deeper perception of meaning to stand on the threshold of a new step in human evolution.

This is the purpose of literature — not just great literature, but of all literature: to become so absorbed in an imaginary world that we become suddenly aware that in the battle between the world and the mind, it is the mind that is destined to win.

Chosen by Geoff Ward, editor of the website *Colin Wilson World* and author of the chapter on *Super Consciousness* in the festschrift *Around the Outsider: essays presented to Colin Wilson on the occasion of his 80th birthday* edited by Colin Stanley (0-Books, 2011).
Ward writes: '…in this essay Colin Wilson leads up to an explanation of "the purpose of literature". Including this in the new edition ensures the presence of some of his indispensable writing about literature which was missing from the original *Essential Colin Wilson*.'

THE FIFTH WINDOW

From *The Misfits*, 1988

H. G. Wells points out in his autobiography that, since the beginning of time, all living creatures have been 'up against it', so life is a perpetual struggle. It is this struggle, as Darwin recognized, that has been the basic driving force behind the evolution of species.

Yet it would not be true to say that living creatures are merely slaves of their environment. We fight the environment, and often win the struggle. Life is an active, not a passive, force.

The real problem of living creatures is that for most of the time they are not aware that they are an active force. They become aware of it briefly — as the lion tracks its prey, as the warrior gallops into battle — but, for the most part, they feel as helpless as leaves carried on the wind. When we look back on our struggles, we often become aware of how much we have achieved. Meanwhile, as we plod along in the present moment, trying to anticipate the next problem, life seems a long uphill grind.

Yet man has always had these moments in which he sees that things are not as bad as they appear — those moments of exaltation or deep relaxation, when he suddenly becomes aware of the powers of his own mind. It is in these moments that he suddenly grasps the basic nature of his problem: that he is stifled and blinded by 'close-upness' — by the sheer pressure of the world against his senses. The moments of insight permit him a bird's-eye view of his own life, and make him aware that his everyday consciousness amounts to a worm's-eye view.

His problem is simple, yet oddly baffling. He achieves the bird's-eye view through excitement, determination, response to crisis; *then* he grasps the extent of his own hidden powers. If he could somehow *maintain* this sense of awareness, then his problem would be solved. But the moment life is 'back to normal' — the everyday struggle with trivialities — he sinks back into the worm's-eye view, with its tendency to exaggerate problems and waste energy on pointless worries.

Man finds himself caught in a particularly insidious trap because his basic aim is to overcome long-term problems and enjoy a relatively crisis-free existence. But it is mainly through crisis that he achieves the bird's-eye view that liberates him from boredom. Crises make him feel more alive. So, in a paradoxical sense, the greatest obstacle to his long-term happiness is this civilization that has cost him so much effort. He seems to be trapped in a kind of vicious circle.

Yet there is an obvious solution. A man appreciates a peaceful life for just as long as he can remember the inconveniences of a more unsettled existence. Another name for this memory of past inconveniences could be the 'sense of reality'. And human beings have a far more powerful sense of reality than any other living creature. We have more foresight than other creatures, more power to lay long-term plans and anticipate long-term problems. If a man knows that he must maintain a high level of vigilance to avoid disaster, then he will maintain it without any difficulty for as long as necessary.

He does this by somehow 'programming' his unconscious mind to a high level of vigilance. Surely, in that case, man could overcome the 'worm's-eye view' problem by the use of his imagination, his 'reality function'?

And this, in theory, is indeed the solution. But there is a purely practical problem. Man has reached his present stage of evolution after about fifteen million years of struggle. It is only during the past few thousand years that, with the aid of his imagination, he has succeeded in creating this remarkable civilization. It is hard to break the habit of fifteen million years and to recognize that he is not really the slave of his environment. And his habit of passivity is reinforced by the marvellous skill with which he has adapted to his environment. This has become so much a part of him that he is not even aware of it.

A simple mechanical analogy will clarify the point. If I drive a car with an automatic gearbox, the car appears to do most of the work for me. I approach a hill and the car slows down. I automatically depress the accelerator, and the engine goes into a lower gear, and sails up the hill without any difficulty. Once on the flat again, I ease my foot off the accelerator, and the engine slips into another gear.

If I drive a car with an ordinary four-speed gearbox, I am far more aware of my control over the vehicle. In fact, I may, like James Bond, prefer a car with an ordinary gearbox, because I enjoy this sense of control. An automatic gearbox *does too much for me*, and makes me feel as automatic as the car.

The human mind is like an automatic gearbox. When confronted by crisis, we slip into a more powerful gear without even noticing it. As a result, we tend to assume that *it is the crisis* that has galvanized us into effort; we fail to notice that we depressed the accelerator that caused us to change gear.

This may seem unimportant, but it has one immense disadvantage. When I am driving on the flat or downhill, the car slips automatically into fourth gear, and *I* drift into a state of bored indifference. And if I happen to detest boredom, my response is to *go and look for another hill*. In other words, when human beings find themselves slipping into the 'worm's-eye view', they do their best to create crises.

Now, as any driver knows, this is absurd; for even an automatic car has three manual gears in addition to its automatic mode. If I want to achieve a sense of greater control, I can use one of these.

Now we can begin to grasp the significance of the 'imaginative revolution' that has taken place over the past three thousand years. At the same time that man was building civilization, he was also trying — dimly and instinctively — to create a 'manual gearbox' that would prevent him from becoming the victim of his own success.

Chosen by Gary Lachman, author of *Beyond the Robot: The Life and Work of Colin Wilson* (TarcherPerigee, 2016).
Lachman comments: '[This provides] a neat summing up of the crisis/ civilization conundrum.'

THE PSYCHOLOGY
OF OPTIMISM

First published in *Adbusters: Journal of the Mental Environment*, vol. 14, no. 1 (Jan/Feb 2006).

During my teens, as an inveterate haunter of second-hand bookshops, I often saw copies of a book called *Sanine*, written in 1903 by a Russian writer named Mikhail Artsybashev. Very often it looked new, as if the former owner was glad to get rid of it. One day I bought it out of curiosity, and discovered that it was one of the most extraordinary novels I had ever read. The hero is a Russian student who shares the rebellious ideals of most of his generation. Vladimir Sanine is an attempt to create the ideal Russian hero — sane, balanced, intelligent, clear-sighted, totally unlike the neurotic heroes of Dostoyevsky.

In one typical scene he is in a boat with a girl who is attracted by him, and when she lets him kiss her, seizes his opportunity and, in spite of her resistance, takes her virginity.

The next day she is horrified at what has happened, and when he calls on her, tells him to go away. He begs her not to bear any ill will, and says that if she gives her fiancé as much happiness as she has given him, he will be a lucky man. Suddenly she decides to look on the bright side — after all, it is a beautiful day and they still find one another attractive. For a moment she sees the world as he sees it — as something simple and beautiful, which human beings spoil with their neurotic self-torments. They kiss 'like brother and sister', and when he has gone, she lies on the grass and reflects that some things are best forgotten.

Sanine exerted a tremendous influence on its generation, and although some of its ideas are simplistic, is still a delightful book to read.

I was reminded of *Sanine* when I came upon the ideas of one of the most remarkable of modern psychologists, Sydney Banks. He stumbled upon his central insight one day when he remarked to a friend: 'I'm so unhappy.' And the friend replied: 'You're not unhappy Syd — you just *think* you are.'

The idea hit him like a revelation: that most human beings cause their own problems by their *thoughts*.

Although an ordinary working man, without a formal education, Banks was so stunned by this insight that he began giving lectures about it. Soon, he was giving seminars that were crowded with professional men — doctors, business-men, psychiatrists.

A New York psychiatrist, George Pransky, who had begun to feel disillusioned about Freud, went along to a weekend seminar, and at first could not understand what Syd Banks meant when he said that all our problems are caused by our thoughts. But he observed that the people at the conference all seemed full of energy and optimism — that they were all 'copers' who were in charge of their lives. And when he grasped what Banks was saying, he suddenly began to share the feeling. He went on to apply these insights to his patients, and found that they worked. Pransky has created a psychology that is based on optimism about our capabilities.

The basic idea behind Pransky's 'psychology of mind' is simple. Our days are spent focusing on narrow horizons of awareness, a permanent state of 'close-upness', rather like going into a picture gallery and keeping your eyes two inches from the canvases. You would see the texture of the paint, but you would not see 'the picture'. Human beings are like this all the time. They are trapped in 'close-upness', in a worm's-eye view of reality. Their lives have an underpinning of boredom.

This vanishes the moment we are confronted by any kind of crisis. A man who was told he has an incurable disease would be rocketed out of the worm's-eye view into a bird's-eye-view, in which he is suddenly aware of the value of life. If, at that point, he learns that the doctors were mistaken and his life is in no danger, the relief would bring an interesting insight: that the bird's-eye view was true all along, and the worm's-eye view was a mistake caused by 'close-upness'. Now all he has to do is to tell himself beyond all possibility of doubt that the worm's-eye view is false and the bird's-eye view is true, and he has a means of transforming his life.

Hans Keller, former head of BBC music programmes, once described how, in the 1930s, he was living in Germany and became aware that fellow Jews were vanishing into concentration camps. He said that he prayed: 'O God, only let me get out of Germany, and I swear I'll never be unhappy again.' Of course, he didn't succeed in living up to his promise. But it is easy for all of us to identify with that feeling that it would be quite easy to live up to it. And he had grasped the essence of Syd Banks's insight.

Now just over fifty years ago, I suddenly woke up to the same insight, and settled down to try and capture it in a book called *The Outsider*. Its starting point was the high number of artists and writers in the 19th Century who committed suicide. I could see that the basic problem was that they found the world of everyday life boring and discouraging. Yet every now and then, they would experience moments of immense happiness and intensity, in which the whole world became self-evidently glorious. The trouble was that when they woke up the next morning, the vision had evaporated, and the world seemed once again dull and dreary.

Clearly, what they needed was simply to grasp *intellectually*, as Syd Banks did, that the worm's-eye view was false.

It seemed clear to me that it was this damned 19th century, with all its frustrated hopes, that was responsible for our neurotic civilization, with its underlying pessimism. It is the 19th Century underpinning we have to get rid of.

As to who to blame for it, the answer seemed clear: the philosophers.

For example, in November 1811, the dramatist and storywriter Heinrich von Kleist blew out his brains and those of his mistress because the philosophy of Kant had convinced him that life was meaningless and that the underlying reality is forever unattainable. Goethe's Faust had come to the same conclusion, and been on the point of suicide 'because we can nothing know' when the sound of the Easter bells caused his childhood to come flooding back and made him change his mind. But why should it matter if life is an illusion, so long as it is enjoyable? Because if it is an illusion, then free will is also an illusion, and we are merely machines. And that thought is enough to depress any sensitive soul. Descartes had argued that animals are machines, and in 1738 the French philosopher Julien de La Mettrie went one further in a book called *Man the Machine*, arguing that free will is an illusion. He was followed by a whole school of French thinkers like Condillac and Cabanis who argued that 'mental life' is merely a matter of physical sensations. Cabanis said the brain secretes thought as the liver secretes bile.

At which point, one of their school, Maine de Biran, had a revelation rather like Syd Banks's. He pointed out that whenever I make some real effort, I have a clear feeling that it is the 'I' who is doing this, and not a machine. But the French have always preferred pessimism to optimism, and Biran's insight was soon forgotten. And even now, two centuries later, psychology continues to insist that man is a machine, and that consciousness is a mere by-product of the brain.

But does it make any difference whether we are machines or not? Well yes, it does. If an intelligent person falls into depression, then the thought that he has no free will can push him over the edge, as it pushed Kleist.

An interesting new discovery in brain physiology underlines this. ECT, electroconvulsive therapy, was first used by Ugo Cerletti in the late 1930s. He discovered that if a current of about an amp is passed through the brain for half a minute, it is like a small version of an epileptic seizure, and it often cures depression. Johan Hellsten of Lund University now thinks he knows why. He tried giving rats ECT treatment, and found that it increased the number of epithelial cells — the cells that line blood vessels — in the part of the brain called the hippocampus. The vessels also increased their length by sixteen per cent. We know that long-term depressives have a smaller hippocampus than average, so curing it by ECT creates bigger and better cells.

Depression is a state in which we cease to use the will. And the muscles of the will suffer hypertrophy, just as the leg muscles of a bed-ridden patient will waste away. The shock of ECT seems to have the same effect as a sudden crisis, of stimulating us to effort. And willed effort causes something inside us to grow. So once George Pransky's patients have been taught to induce their own version of ECT by a combination of effort and optimism, they presumably begin to grow epithelial cells and turn into 'copers', suddenly finding they enjoy life.

All this is a striking justification for a theory of Nobel Prize winning brain physiologist, Roger Sperry, whose studies of the difference between our right and left cerebral hemispheres caused such a sensation in the 1960s.

Now, in traditional brain physiology, consciousness is regarded as a product of the brain, as heat is the product of a fire (or bile of the liver). As a traditional scientist, Sperry was willing to accept the proposition that consciousness is a product of the brain and cannot exist apart from it. But in a paper of 1980 called 'Mind-brain interaction: mentalism, yes; dualism, no', he shocked and upset his colleagues by announcing a view that struck them as pure heresy. He suggested that when we think and feel, consciousness operates on the brain as human fingers operate on a computer keyboard, or as an electric current operates on a television screen, making a picture out of 'dots'. Or, if you like, as the fingers of a pianist operate when he plays the piano. In other words, consciousness is not passive but active and 'creative'. Sperry had rediscovered Maine de Biran's free will.

Clearly there is one more step to take. And I suspect that if Sperry had not died in 1981 he would have taken it: to recognize that consciousness is not a mere product of the brain, but exists in its own right. A useful first move would be to persuade scientists like Johan Hellsten to begin experiments to try and show that brain cells can be created by a focused effort of will. That would lay the foundations for a new science, a new philosophy and a new civilization.

THE FUTURE OF MANKIND

Published as a Postscript to the new edition of *A Criminal History of Mankind* (Mercury Books, 2005).

At the age of seventy-two, it is inevitable that I often find myself thinking about the kind of world we are leaving to our grandchildren. With pollution, global warming and the population explosion, it certainly looks grimmer than at any time in history. But before I get depressed, I remind myself that things may be less bad than they look. The world began to look grim when I was a child, with the rise of Hitler and the brutal despotism of Stalin. And I can remember those newspaper photographs of piles of corpses in Belsen that made many of us feel that the twentieth century had achieved a new record in deliberately calculated evil. Yet Hitler was already dead by that time, and Stalin followed eight years later.

The truth, I suspect, is that human beings, as individuals, are now facing much the same problems they have faced throughout history. We all long for peace and security, yet human consciousness is so oddly limited that we are not particularly happy when we get it. The truth is that if some benevolent deity decided to give every human being the equivalent of a million pounds, he would not create very much more happiness in the world, for vast numbers of people would quickly find reasons to feel dissatisfied again.

Why should this be so? Quite obviously, because as a species, we lack the imagination to recognize when we are well off. The German philosopher Fichte made the point when he said: 'To *be* happy is nothing. To *become* happy is heavenly.'

Why? Because we only truly experience happiness when some crisis or problem disappears, and then we only feel happy for as long as it takes to get used to our relief. Within days, or hours, or even minutes, we are taking it for granted.

When I was at school, we had hosiery classes in which we knitted scarves on flat-bed machines. But you had to put a weight on the scarf to pull it towards the floor. And if you forgot, and let the weight touch the floor, the wool immediately climbed up over the needles and ruined the scarf. Human beings also need a 'weight on the needles'. That is why wealthy people are so often bored and dissatisfied. I recently saw again Fellini's film *La Dolce Vita*, which in this context means 'the soft life'; it is full of bored, well-off people who don't know what to do with their lives.

So there is a sense in which human beings are not yet ready for the civilization they have created.

Now all this sounds like Schopenhauer's indictment of human life in *The World as Will and Idea*. Men are incapable of being really happy or really unhappy because they are too vacillating and weak. Unhappiness makes them strive, but if their efforts are met with success, they are not happy for long because they quickly take it for granted…

This is undoubtedly true. Yet Schopenhauer was writing as if the human condition was fixed and immutable. And it is not. We *can* change, since we possess free will (although rather less than we habitually assume). The most amazing thing is that human beings have changed their condition so much since they were ice age hunters. And H. G. Wells pointed out that the world has evolved more in two centuries than in the past thousand years or so.

If an intelligent philosopher from the thirteenth century could study our present age, he would agree that some very interesting changes have taken place. The most important are in the realm of the human imagination. One of the most significant is the invention of the novel, which began its most influential period of evolution about 1750, with the works of Samuel Richardson. In effect, the novel taught people to leave their own lives behind, and to 'become someone else' for a few hours. It taught them not to be tied down to the mere world of events. I noted as a child that certain exciting books — for example, *King Solomon's Mines* — left me feeling as if I had just been for a swim or a long run: that is to say, the stimulated imagination produced a physical effect. And that is certainly an important step in escaping our slavery to the merely physical, to our tendency to yawn when nothing interesting is happening. It means we are learning to make interesting things happen in our heads.

That is obviously the direction in which the human race is evolving. H. G. Wells once said that the bird is a creature of the air, the fish is a creature of the water and man is a creature of the mind.

And here I need to state a personal conviction. Man's evolution is not simply a matter of natural selection and survival of the fittest. From the beginning, intelligent life has defied the laws of natural selection. The astronomer Fred Hoyle pointed out that life cannot have been created by chance; in order to evolve by random processes, life would have taken billions of times longer than the age of our universe. There is as little chance of life being created by accident, Hoyle says, than of rusty car parts in a junk yard being blown together to create a Rolls Royce.

In 1974, the astronomer Brandon Carter, of the Paris Observatory, formulated what he called the Anthropic Principle, which stated that not only did the universe create life, but that — the physics being what they are — it *had* to create life.

My own conviction is that life was not 'created' — I have always taken the view of Bergson and Shaw, that life was, so to speak, already there, but not in our universe of matter. It has spent fifteen billion years or so somehow 'inserting' itself into matter. Shaw expressed it by saying that the universe that began as a 'whirlpool of pure force' aims at becoming a 'whirlpool of pure intelligence'.

But then, Shaw did not believe, as I do, that certain invisible forces operate outside the arena of space and time. Its most obvious manifestation is in the form of what Jung called synchronicity, 'coincidences' so preposterous that we cannot believe they are mere chance. They create the impression that some cosmic joker, who normally keeps his face hidden behind the veil of matter, is trying to make us aware of his existence.

Here is an example. My friend Jacques Vallee, who is one of the most eminent historians of UFOs, has a most remarkable story of synchronicity.

Jacques had become interested in a Los Angeles religious cult called the Order of Melchizedek — the latter being one of the more obscure biblical prophets. He looked up Melchizedek in many encyclopaedias, without success. Then one day, he took a taxi in Los Angeles, and asked the lady driver for a receipt. She handed him one signed: 'M. Melchizedek'. Struck by the coincidence, Jacques wondered how many more Melchizedeks there were in Los Angeles. So he looked up the Los Angeles telephone directory. There was only one Melchizedek — his taxi driver.

Jacques said he felt as if he had stuck a notice on some universal noticeboard: 'Wanted — Melchizedeks', and fate had asked him 'How about this one?' 'No, no, that's a taxi driver!'

In 1990, I recounted this story in an article I was writing about synchronicity in an encyclopaedia of mysteries, and then broke off to take my afternoon walk. About to leave my study, I noticed a book lying on my untidy camp bed — one that I had no recollection of seeing before, although I had obviously purchased it, for it had my signature and the date on the flyleaf. It was called *You Are Sentenced to Life*, and was by a doctor called W. D. Chesney, on the subject of life after death. Evidently it had fallen off my bookshelf on to the camp bed. Since I had never read it, I tossed the book on to my armchair, to look at later.

When I came back from my walk I opened it casually, and found myself looking at a page headed ORDER OF MELCHIZEDEK. It was a letter from the founder of the order to the author of the book.

I have around thirty thousand books in my house, and I doubt whether another one of these contains a reference to Melchizedek. Yet I had managed to stumble on this one immediately after writing about Vallee's extraordinary coincidence. It was as if some fate was saying to me: 'If you really want me to show you what I can do, how about this?'

I could cite other personal experiences, but this one makes the point: that it is hard not to feel that some cosmic joker is digging you in the ribs and chuckling.

Again, writing about crime, I often have the strong feeling that particularly nasty criminals seem to be 'fated' to make some obvious mistake that will guarantee that they get caught. Of course, this is a far less striking phenomenon than the kind of synchronicity I have described above; all the same, it is something I have noted repeatedly.

Jung also cited many interesting examples of another 'absurd' phenomenon, precognition. In his student days, as a group of friends were sitting around a table drinking beer, one of them described a dream of the previous night. His father had promised to send him on a trip to Spain if he passed his finals, and he had dreamed that he was in a Spanish city, looking across a square at a Gothic cathedral. As he was about to cross the street, he had to wait while an elegant carriage with cream-coloured horses drove past.

Having passed his exams, he went to Spain, and found himself looking at the cathedral of his dream. About to cross the street, he had to wait while an elegant carriage with two cream-coloured horses went past.

This story, Jung realized, implies predestination. To dream of a Gothic cathedral could be explained in many ways — perhaps he had simply seen a picture of it. But when you get the detail of the carriage and horses, this explanation becomes implausible. The owner of the carriage may have decided to go for a drive on the spur of the moment, and certainly believed he was doing it of his own free will. But if Jung's friend dreamed of it months before it happened, then we might say that he was somehow 'fated' to do it. In short, his life was not as much subject to chance as he had thought.

When Jung's friend saw the carriage with the cream-coloured horses drive past, he must have felt something similar to Jacques Vallee's feeling when the taxi driver handed him a receipt signed Melchizedek, and that I felt when fate 'capped' that story by producing the book about the Order of Melchizedek: that life is not as meaningless as we tend to assume.

The disaster of the twin towers provides a piece of evidence that reinforces that view. According to a Princeton scientist, Roger Nelson, a machine called a Random Events Generator forecast the disaster three hours before the first plane struck.

A Random Events Generator monitors completely unpredictable processes, like the decay of a piece of radioactive material. You could describe it as an electronic coin-flipper. And in 1977, a Princeton scientist named Robert Jahn conducted experiments to see whether this coin-flipper could be influenced by human mental effort.

He brought in strangers off the street, and asked them to concentrate their minds on the coin-flipper. In effect, he was asking them to try and make it produce more heads than tails. And the results were amazing. Again and again, total strangers showed that their minds could influence the machine.

Jahn's friend and colleague Roger Nelson had an even more bizarre idea. When he heard that a group of yoga enthusiasts were organising a global 'meditation for peace', he decided to link together Random Events Generators all over the world, and see whether this burst of meditation, involving thousands of people, would influence the generators.

That, admittedly, sounds preposterous. Jahn's subjects had been trying to influence the coin-flipper by willing it to produce more heads than tails. What Nelson was asking was whether a worldwide burst of meditation would influence the machine non-deliberately — that is, unconsciously.

But again the results were startling. They demonstrated that not only were the generators influenced by the ten-minute burst of worldwide meditation, but the statistical results were seven times greater than Jahn had ever achieved. So now Nelson was unstoppable. He connected up forty Random Events Generators all over the world, linked them all to his laboratory computer in Princeton, and just kept the recorder going day and night.

Most of the time, the graph-pen made a wavy horizontal line across the paper, with a few minor variations, like a calm sea with the occasional small wave. But during the funeral of Princess Diana in September 1997 — which of course was televised all over the world — the graph shot up like a mountain.

Nelson admits that he was baffled. It seemed that great outbursts of emotion can influence electronic coin-flippers without intending to.

Nelson discovered that the graph responded to happy events as well as upsetting ones. Just before midnight on New Years Eve 1999, the graph peaked again, responding to lots of happy revellers singing *Auld Lang Syne*. This must have been the explanation, for it peaked several times, always just before midnight, at different time zones around the world. And to prove this was not some freak effect, the same thing happened on New Years Eve 2000, and again in 2001.

You can probably already guess what happened on September 11. Indeed, the graph peaked like the Eiffel Tower between 9 and 10 in the morning, New York time, just as Nelson expected. But it had started its rise soon after 6 a.m. This seems to demonstrate that hundreds of thousands of people began to feel a premonition of disaster nearly three hours before it happened.

In other words, we possess powers and abilities that we do not even begin to understand.

Such things explain why I do not take a gloomy view of the human future. I feel that some force has gone to an awful lot of trouble to get us to where we are at present, and that it does not intend to let us vanish off the face of the earth like the dinosaur.

Yet, contemplating problems like pollution and the population explosion, I cannot believe that we can simply carry on as we are. Something has to change. Something has to happen.

For the past forty-odd years I have believed that the 'something' is some fundamental change in human beings. I believe that man is on the point of an evolutionary change to a higher level.

The kind of challenges we face *demand* a new kind of effort, the kind of effort we have to make when we make a new year's resolution. Anyone who has ever made such a decision — perhaps simply to lose weight or give up smoking — knows that it takes an effort of concentrated determination to rise above old habit patterns.

This is the kind of determination we need to steer the human race on to a new course.

When a young Russian philosopher named Pyotr Demianovitch Ouspensky met his future guru, Georges Ivanovich Gurdjieff, in Moscow in 1915, he was deeply impressed by Gurdjieff's assertion that men are almost entirely mechanical. As they were walking along the street, a truck went past loaded with crutches destined for the front, and Ouspensky was struck by the thought that these crutches were intended for men whose limbs had not yet been blown off. Yet because men are so mechanical, nothing could be done to prevent it. We are asleep. And it was at this point that Ouspensky asked the question: 'Is it possible to wake up?' And Gurdjieff replied: 'It is possible, but it requires a tremendous effort'

This also applies to the present crisis in our world. It is possible to avert it, but it would require a kind of awakening. And this is the problem. Auden once remarked: 'Even war cannot frighten us enough'

Could the prospect of more events like September 11th have that effect? Even that is doubtful. One of the first things George W. Bush did when he became President was to declare that America would abandon its obligations to combat global warming.

And so, left to ourselves, the prospects for humanity seem dark. Of course, I do not believe that we are entirely left to ourselves. But neither do I believe that we can forget the problem and leave it to some 'anthropic principle' to steer us through to a solution. God helps those who help themselves. And helping ourselves is the necessary first step.

Chosen by Colin Stanley, author of *The Ultimate Colin Wilson Bibliography [1956–2015]* (Paupers' Press, 2015); *Colin Wilson's 'Occult Trilogy': A Guide for Students* (Axis Mundi Books, 2013); *An Evolutionary Leap: Colin Wilson on Psychology* (Karnac Books Ltd.).

Stanley writes: 'The Psychology of Optimism' adds-to and concludes Colin Wilson's writings on psychology. 'The Future of Mankind' anticipates his final book, *An End to Murder*, completed by his son Damon and published posthumously in 2015.

WATKINS
Sharing Wisdom Since 1893

The story of Watkins began in 1893, when scholar of esotericism John Watkins founded our bookshop, inspired by the lament of his friend and teacher Madame Blavatsky that there was nowhere in London to buy books on mysticism, occultism or metaphysics. That moment marked the birth of Watkins, soon to become the publisher of many of the leading lights of spiritual literature, including Carl Jung, Rudolf Steiner, Alice Bailey and Chögyam Trungpa.

Today, the passion at Watkins Publishing for vigorous questioning is still resolute. Our stimulating and groundbreaking list ranges from ancient traditions and complementary medicine to the latest ideas about personal development, holistic wellbeing and consciousness exploration. We remain at the cutting edge, committed to publishing books that change lives.

DISCOVER MORE AT:
www.watkinspublishing.com

Read our blog

Watch and listen to
our authors in action

Sign up to
our mailing list

We celebrate conscious, passionate, wise and happy living.
Be part of that community by visiting

 /watkinspublishing   @watkinswisdom

 /watkinsbooks   @watkinswisdom